Freedom, Authority, and Resistance

Lynchburg College Symposium Readings

Third Edition

2005

Volume II

Freedom, Authority, and Resistance

Edited by

Joseph F. Freeman III, Ph.D.

Library of Congress Number: 2004098814

ISBN:	Hardcover	1-4134-7624-4
	Softcover	1-4134-7623-6

This book was printed in the United States of America.

To order additional copies of this book, contact:
Xlibris Corporation
1-888-795-4274
www.Xlibris.com
Orders@Xlibris.com

23022

CONTENTS

III. RESISTANCE

Acknowledgements

The editors acknowledge with appreciation the permissions granted by these holders of the respective copyrights.

Documents on the Holocaust: Selected Sources on the Destruction of the Jews of Germany and Austria, Poland, and the Soviet Union. 1940-1945. Eds. Yitzhak Arad, Yisrael Gutman, and Abraham Margaliot. Jerusalem: Yad Vashem Publishing, 1981.

Havel, Vaclav. 1978. "Power of the Powerless." From *Open Letters: Selected Writings* 1965-1990 by Vaclav Havel, translated by Paul Wilson, copyright 1991 by A.G. Brain. Preface/translation copyright 1985, 1988, 1991 by Paul Wilson. Used by permission of Alfred A. Knopf, a division of Random House, Inc.

Hitler's Table Talk 1941-1944. 2000. with introduction by H.R. Trevor-Roper. New York: Enigma Books. Used by permission of Enigma Books.

Lenin, Vladimir. 1917. "Class Society and The State," *The State and Revolution.* In the *Collected Works 25.* 381-492. Marxist Internet Archive *www.marxists.org/archive/lenin/works/1917/staterev/index.htm.* Permission is granted by Marxist Archives to copy, distribute and/or modify this document under the terms of the GNU Free Documentation License. Version 1.2 or any later version published by Free Software Foundation.

King, Dr. Martin Luther, Jr. 1963. "I Have a Dream . . ." August 28. Washington, D.C. Reprinted by arrangement with the Estate of Martin Luther King, Jr., c/o Writers House (agent for the proprietor) New York, NY. *Copyright 1963 Martin Luther King, Jr., copyright renewed 1991 Coretta Scott King.*

King, Dr. Martin Luther, Jr. 1963. "Letter from a Birmingham Jail." April 16. Reprinted by arrangement with the Estate of Martin Luther King, Jr., c/o Writers House (agent for the proprietor) New York, NY. *Copyright 1963 Martin Luther King, Jr., copyright renewed 1991 Coretta Scott King.*

The editors further acknowledge with thanks the dedicated work of Elizabeth Giglio, English major, '05 and Rachel Moore, Communication Studies major, '08 for their dedicated work and editorial assistance.

Lynchburg College Symposium Readings, Senior Symposium, and the LCSR Program

The ten-volume series, Lynchburg College Symposium Readings, has been developed by Lynchburg College faculty for use in the Senior Symposium and the Lynchburg College Symposium Readings Program (SS/LCSR). Each volume presents primary source material organized around interdisciplinary, liberal arts themes.

In 1976, the College developed the Senior Symposium as a two-hour, interdisciplinary course, required of all graduating seniors. On Mondays students in all sections of the course come together for public lectures, given by invited guest speakers. On Wednesdays, Symposium students meet in their sections for student-led discussions and presentations on associated readings from the LCSR series. The course requires students, who have spent their later college years in narrowing the scope of their studies, to expand their fields of vision within a discussion group composed of and led by their peers. Students can apply analytical and problem-solving capabilities learned in their major fields of study to issues raised by guest speakers and classical readings.

This approach works against convention in higher education, which typically emphasizes the gradual exclusion of subject areas outside of a student's major field. But Senior Symposium leads students, poised for graduation, into their post-College intellectual responsibilities. They gain experience in taking their liberal education into real world problems, using it to address contemporary problems thoughtfully and critically. In order to do this successfully, students must abandon their habitual posture as docile receptors of authoritative information for a much more skeptical attitude toward opinion, proof, reasoning, and authoritative experience. The effort to think constructively through a variety of conflicting opinions—on a weekly basis—prepares them well for the mature, independent, well-reasoned points of view expected of educated adults.

The LCSR Program's primary goals are to foster an appreciation of the connection between basic skills and interdisciplinary knowledge, and to promote greater cross-disciplinary communication among faculty and students. General education core courses or courses that serve other program requirements may be classified as "LCSR," as long as they fulfill certain speaking and writing activities connected to LCSR readings. The effect of the program has been to help create the atmosphere of a residential academic community; shared learning creates a climate in which teaching and learning take root more forcefully.

Since its inception, the SS/LCSR Program has helped create opportunities for faculty interaction across the disciplines in "pre-service" and "in-service" workshops. Each May, the LCSR Program sponsors a four-day pre-service workshop to which all new full-time and part-time faculty members are invited. Participants receive individual sets of the Lynchburg College Symposium Readings, which they make their own by using them during the workshop in exercises designed to promote familiarity with a wide variety of the readings. The goals of the workshop are several: for those unfamiliar with the program, to begin planning an LCSR course; for new faculty, to become acquainted with those they have not met and get to know their acquaintances better; for other faculty of various experiential levels, to share their pedagogical successes; for new teachers, to ask questions about teaching, about the College, and about the students in an informal setting; for experienced teachers to re-visit some of their assumptions, pedagogies, and strategies; to inspire strong scholarship, creative teaching, risk-taking, and confidence among all participants.

Another opportunity comes with the "in-service" workshops, which occur each month during the school year. The LCSR Program sponsors luncheons and dinners at which faculty teaching in the program give informal presentations on their use of specific teaching strategies or reading selections. Attendance is voluntary, but many try to be present for every session. For those involved in the LCSR program, teaching has become what Lee Schulman, President of the Carnegie Foundation, calls "community property."

On the Lynchburg College campus, there is evidence of a systematic change in teaching effectiveness as well as sustained faculty commitment to the program. By the 2002-2003 academic year, nearly two-thirds of all full-time faculty members and more than half of all part-time faculty members had completed the workshop at some time during their time at Lynchburg College. In any given semester, roughly ten to fifteen percent of the total class enrollments are in LCSR courses, not counting the required Senior Symposium. An important feature of this program is that participation is voluntary on the part of the faculty and, except for the required Senior Symposium, on the part of students. The program's influence quietly pervades the campus community, improving teaching and scholarship. Many see the LCSR Program as the College's premier academic program.

The Senior Symposium/LCSR program publishes *The Agora,* an in-house journal that features the best of student writings responding to LCSR texts. The journal selections by students must integrate classical ideas and issues with contemporary ones. Faculty may also submit writings that address innovative teaching strategies. The journal takes its title from the marketplace at the heart of classical Athens, where much of Athenian public life was carried on: mercantile exchange, performance, political debate, athletic contests, and the public worship of deities?all took place within the hustle and bustle of the Athenian agora. Similarly, the journal seeks to be a marketplace for compelling ideas and issues. Faculty members and students serve together on the editorial committee.

Since 1976, the Senior Symposium and the LCSR Program have affected the academic community both on and beyond the Lynchburg College campus. In 1991, Professor Richard Marius from Harvard University's writing center in reviewing the program favorably said, "I have seldom in my life been so impressed by an innovation in college education. I suppose the highest compliment that I could pay to the program was that I wished I could teach in it." Also in 1991, Professor Donald Boileau of George Mason University's communication studies department wrote, "what I discovered was a sound program that not only enriches the education of students at Lynchburg College, but what I hope can be a model for many other colleges and universities throughout our country." In spring 2003, in an article titled, "Whither the Great Books," Dr. William Casement described the LCSR program as the "most fully organized version" of the recent growth of great-books programs that employ an "across-the-disciplines structure." According to him, this approach perhaps encourages the use of the great books across the curriculum, which can be less isolating than even interdisciplinary programs. The Senior Symposium and LCSR Programs have received national acclaim in such publications as Loren Popes's *Colleges That Change Lives* and Charles Sykes and Brad Miner's *The National Review of College Guide, America's 50 Top Liberal Arts Schools.*

Freedom, Authority, and Resistance is the second volume of the third edition of the Lynchburg College Symposium Readings series. The first edition, published in the early 1980s, included several selections also printed in the third edition. We gratefully acknowledge the work of Dr. James A. Huston, Dean of the College, Professor of History and International Relations, Emeritus (1972-1984), for his contributions to previous editions of this volume. The Senior Symposium was the creation of Dean Huston. Dr. Michael Santos, Professor of History, co-founded the LCSR program. Dean Huston served as the first series editor, and with Dr. Julius Sigler, Professor of Physics, as co-editor of the second series. They remain committed to the program today, and for this we are grateful.

Peggy A. Pittas, Ph.D.
Katherine Gray, Ph.D.
Series Co-Editors

Introduction

This volume presumes that citizens are more effective if, from time to time, they take a mental step back from the controversies of the day and develop their own sense of the deeper questions of political life. Propagandists and campaign managers do not care for this, because the practice of having second thoughts leads to independent thinking, and independent thinkers are not predictable. Those who have second thoughts may come to require good reasons for things and evidence to support the reasons. When thinking starts, slogans lose their force, and propaganda has to give way to evidence, arguments, and responsibility. The selections made here are intended to encourage such independent thinking, with the conviction that learning to think through and to make one's own decisions is the evidence of being liberally educated.

The mass media present democratic politics in terms of campaigning and elections. Elections are indeed the indispensable element of representative democracy, so it does make sense to cover how office seekers compete for the approval of the voters. But in our time, this is done in fast-breaking, up-to-date (and rapidly outdated) stories that follow each other in dizzying succession. Only alert and focused observers can keep up with them. Most of us are familiar with at least the broad order of presentation: the emergence of potential candidates, the nomination struggle, fund-raising efforts, polling to keep track of the course of the campaign, the personalities and statements of the candidates, and election results. Then, when the results are announced, the attention drains away, replaced by isolated speculation about the next round of elections. Concerns about politics are put away for a while.

Within its own frame of reference, this rubric appears coherent enough. However, it is not a complete view. It fails to connect elections to daily life or to create a sense that there are public things for which we are responsible. Though the practitioners of this style of democratic politics do not realize it, what they do undercuts key elements of democracy. Though year after year more and more money is spent on campaigning, fewer people vote. Politicians are held in low esteem. Short-term expediency outweighs longer-term considerations in the formation of even the most far-reaching public policy. Governmental decisions seem either hopelessly routine or idiosyncratic, if not corrupt. In these frantic contests for electoral success there is little place for the individual citizen and his or her reflective thought. Similarly, there is little time or place for informed deliberation among citizens about the possibilities and purposes of public life and how the preferences of the moment fit with them. The price we pay for being excited by up-to-the-minute campaign dramas is giving up a thoughtful, shared sense of the meaning of politics.

Paradoxically, without some such sense, democratic governance is even more difficult. Good leaders need followers who are responsible and capable of independent action. But to develop this, citizens need the capacity to put the anxieties of the moment into a broader context. They need to be invited to have second thoughts about public life and a chance to think about the choices before them and what is at stake in the long run. And because leaders are more likely to be fallible, citizens with second thoughts are essential to democracy.

Governance is always with us, whether in the form of a modern nation-state with representative democracy in a world with other such states or whether we live, like Antigone, in the city of Thebes in archaic Greece, ruled by a king like the other cities of that place and time. Most people take the arrangements under which they live for granted and live in obedience, submitting to power. But if we want to live in a democracy, where power is to be exercised by citizens, we must obey each other. How do we come to follow one apparently reasonable course of action and not another that is different, but also apparently reasonable? In dealing with our representatives, how do citizens establish a stopping point: the capacity to say, "this is too far," or "this is not enough," or "this is what we should accept," or "not accept"?

Asking and answering such questions is not only a matter of private values. Each of us deals with private matters every day. Public values are what we accept jointly. Most of the time, we accept these tacitly. What we expect of others and what they expect of us are not matters for discussion; we take them for granted so we can get on with things. But in times of crisis, public values may become explicit and subject to debate. The reader of this volume should note that the selections here are not academic exercises, undertaken to demonstrate a detached understanding of affairs. Quite the contrary, they were made to cut through the tangles of voices and arguments of turbulent times. They can be seen as efforts to constitute or re-constitute public values. The best of these seem to have the capacity to address times and circumstances far removed from those which compelled them to write in the first place.

For example, Hobbes and Locke wrote during the successive crises that were fought out in 17th century England. We can still understand why the killing of the king, the civil war, the takeover of government by militant Puritans, the imposition of military dictatorship, and the restoration of the monarchy were matters that cut deeply. The ultimate outcome of this was the establishment of a representative democracy with a constitutional monarch and enormous economic and military power for the United Kingdom in the century that followed. Those controversies and their resolutions lie at the foundation of the English-speaking approach to politics. The arguments that Hobbes and Locke worked out still contain relevance for our circumstances. More important, their reflections provide food for thought, prisms through which we can try to see political life a little differently, to see how things look in their view, and enrich our own perspective by being better able to understand what distinguishes it from others.

Classical Greece is even farther from us than seventeenth century England, but the writings of Plato and Aristotle have an uncannily modern feel to them. Plato's account of Socrates's defense of his questioning of the Athenian political leadership is essential reading. Aristotle was the director of a research institute that gathered extensive information on the democracies and oligarchies (and tyrannies) that governed the Greek city-states, without removing politics from its broader context. Like Hobbes and Locke, Plato and Aristotle wrote about politics in a time of crisis—the aftermath of the Peloponnesian War and the rise of Alexander the Great. Diderot and Rousseau are regarded as contributors to the French Revolution, which developed its own understanding, different from Locke and Jefferson, of what democracy is and how one makes it work. Havel describes the moral and existential bankruptcy of the Communist regimes in Central and Eastern Europe shortly before they collapsed under the weight of their own cynicism and incompetence.

America's best political writing came at the time of the War of Independence and the consequent struggle to establish a government strong enough to do its job, but limited enough to not endanger basic rights. The extension of those rights, and the failure to extend them, are the subjects of the selections from Martin Luther King and Chief Joseph. Thoreau was concerned about how to give substance to freedom in daily living.

Not all of the selections are from authors now regarded as philosophers, or at least political thinkers. Hitler and Lenin are included as bad, though instructive, examples. The personal account from the writings of Frederick Douglass is a good story with a powerful moral. The Holocaust documents are similarly personal accounts that speak for themselves. Sophocles's play *Antigone* was, in its day, an entertainment. Nearly all of the selections are from readily available literature. The reader who may wish to consider more than these short selections can easily do so.

This replacement volume for the Lynchburg College Senior Symposium volume *Tyranny and Freedom* expands the themes of the volume to freedom, authority, and resistance. Of the political ideals that have caught the human imagination, few are more powerful than freedom, the idea that command and obedience can somehow be transcended, so that people might live as they wish and do what they want. The excerpts here are not a survey of the topic. They are only a few indications of the historical range of the idea, its variation over time and circumstance, and a reminder that there have always been careful and humane opponents of the claim that self-realization can be achieved through complete freedom.

Similarly, the selections on authority demonstrate the range of thinking on public power and its use. The continuing gift of the American founders is the explicit attention they gave to the question of how the desire for freedom can be balanced with the need for government that has enough power to accomplish its purposes. They are heavily represented in this section. But there have always been those who have seen the question differently, as well as those who seek power merely to abuse it.

Authority can go wrong and turn into oppression. When should one resist authority? The question has both moral and practical dimensions, and this necessarily limited number of selections cannot be taken as anything more than an introduction to the issue. The selections on resistance were chosen to give a sense of how broad a question this is in practice. The selections from Frederick Douglass and Martin Luther King will strike familiar chords in the American reader, but the fundamental question is both deeper in time and broader in reach. Along with freedom and authority, resistance has become a universal question.

Joseph F. Freeman III, Ph. D.

Freedom

Introduction

Some may think of freedom as a distinctively modern desire, but we should remember that some of the oldest literature available to us contains vivid expressions of it. The Hebrew yearning for a lost Garden of Eden and Greek nostalgia for a long-lost Golden Age remind us not to think of freedom too narrowly. The claim in Diderot's "Supplement" that freedom has been discovered in the contemporary "primitive" seems to look both to the past as well as a future free from authority. King places his dream in a future that is our responsibility.

However, cautions about freedom are as old as the zeal for it. Nor is the modern course of the idea direct. Both Hobbes and Locke portray freedom not as a way of life, but as a reference point from which we can measure civil society. Locke argues that freedom is the necessary foundation for society and for understanding rights, but as a condition of existence is inconvenient and risky. Hobbes is less equivocal; any benefits freedom may appear to have are illusory. Real freedom is chaos and must be shunned.

For Jefferson, freedom is a political matter. National freedom is the key to personal freedom, and the other way around, as well. We are naturally free as persons and the right to that freedom gives us a corresponding right to frame government to protect it.

Genesis

_ca._ 1000-500 B.C.E.

The story of Adam and Eve in the Garden of Eden is the best known account of Creation in Western literature. Living in peace and freedom, Adam and Eve had no human laws or government to restrict them, just one divine prohibition they were required to observe. But it was still too much for them to do. Yielding to temptation brought about a world of hard work, conflict, and struggle for domination. The vision of Eden remains a picture of what life might have been had we proven ourselves worthy of it.

Selections from: "Genesis." *ca.* 1000-550 B.C.E. *The Holy Bible.* New York: Oxford University Press. 1898.

1:26-31
2:1-25
3:1-24

Genesis 1:26-31

26 And God said, Let us make man in our image, after
our likeness: and let them have dominion over the fish of
the sea, and over the fowl of the air, and over the cattle, and
over all the earth, and over every creeping thing that
creepeth upon the earth. *27* And God created man in his
own image, in the image of God created he him; male and

female created he them. *28* And God blessed them: and
God said unto them, Be fruitful, and multiply, and replenish
the earth, and subdue it; and have dominion over the fish
of the sea, and over the fowl of the air, and over every living
thing that moveth upon the earth.

29 And God said, Behold, I have given you every herb
yielding seed, which is upon the face of all the earth, and
every tree, in the which is the fruit of a tree yielding seed; to
you it shall be for meat: *30* and to every beast of the earth,
and to every fowl of the air, and to every thing that creepeth
upon the earth, wherein there is life, I have given every
green herb for meat: and it was so. *31* And God saw every
thing that he had made, and, behold, it was very good. And
there was evening and there was morning, the sixth day.

Genesis 2:1-25

1 And the heavens and the earth were finished, and all
the host of them. *2* And on the seventh day God finished his
work which he had made; and he rested on the seventh day
from all his work which he had made. *3* And God blessed the
seventh day, and hallowed it: because that in it he rested from
all his work which God created and made.

4 These are the generations of the heavens and of the
earth when they were created, in the day that the Lord God
made the earth and the heaven. *5* And no plant of the field
was yet in the earth, and no herb of the field had yet sprung
up: for the Lord God had not caused it to rain upon the
earth, and there was not a man to till the ground, *6* but
there went up a mist from the earth, and watered the whole
face of the ground. *7* And the Lord God formed man of the
dust of the ground, and breathed into his nostrils the breath
of life; and man became a living soul. *8* And the Lord God
planted a garden eastward in Eden; and there he put the
man whom he had formed. *9* And out of the ground made
the Lord God to grow every tree that is pleasant to the sight,

and good for food; the tree of life also in the midst of the
garden, and the tree of knowledge of good and evil. ***10*** And
a river went out of Eden to water the garden; and from
thence it was parted, and became four heads. ***11*** The name
of the first is Pishon: that is it which compasseth the whole
land of Havilah, where there is gold; ***12*** and the gold of that
land is good: there is bdellium and the onyx stone. ***13*** And
the name of the second river is Gihon: the same is it that
compasseth the whole land of Cush. ***14*** And the name of
the third river is Hiddekel: that is it which goeth in front of
Assyria. And the fourth river is Euphrates. ***15*** And the LORD
GOD took the man, and put him into the garden of Eden to
dress it and to keep it. ***16*** And the LORD GOD commanded
the man, saying, Of every tree of the garden thou mayest
freely eat: ***17*** but of the tree of the knowledge of good and
evil, thou shalt not eat of it: for in the day that thou eatest
thereof thou shalt surely die.

18 And the LORD GOD said, It is not good that the man
should be alone; I will make him an help meet for him. ***19***
And out of the ground the LORD GOD formed every beast of
the field, and every fowl of the air; and brought them unto
the man to see what he would call them: and whatsoever the
man called every living creature, that was the name thereof.
20 And the man gave names to all cattle, and to the fowl of
the air, and to every beast of the field; but for the man there
was not found an help meet for him. ***21*** And the LORD GOD
caused a deep sleep to fall upon the man and he slept: and
he took one of his ribs, and closed up the flesh instead thereof;
22 And the rib, which the LORD GOD had taken from man,
made he a woman, and brought her unto the man. ***23*** And
the man said, This is now bone of my bones, and flesh of my
flesh: she shall be called Woman, because she was taken out
of Man. ***24*** Therefore shall a man leave his father and his
mother, and shall cleave unto his wife: and they shall be one
flesh. ***25*** And they were both naked, the man and his wife,
and were not ashamed.

Genesis 3:1-24

1 Now the serpent was more subtil than any beast of the
field which the LORD GOD had made. And he said unto the
woman, Yea, hath God said, Ye shall not eat of every tree of
the garden? ***2*** And the woman said unto the serpent, of the
fruit of the trees of the garden we may eat: ***3*** but of the fruit
of the tree which is in the midst of the garden, God hath
said, Ye shall not eat of it, neither shall ye touch it, lest ye
die. ***4*** And the serpent said unto the woman, Ye shall not
surely die: ***5*** for God doth know that in the day ye eat thereof,
then your eyes shall be opened, and ye shall be as God,
knowing good and evil. ***6*** And when the woman saw that the
tree was good for food, and that it was a delight to the eyes,
and that the tree was to be desired to make one wise, she
took of the fruit thereof, and did eat; and she gave also unto
her husband with her; and he did eat.

7 And the eyes of them both were opened, and they knew
that they were naked; and they sewed fig leaves together,
and made themselves aprons. ***8*** And they heard the voice of
the LORD GOD walking in the garden in the cool of the day:
and the man and his wife hid themselves from the presence
of the LORD GOD amongst the trees of the garden. ***9*** And the
LORD GOD called unto the man, and said unto him, Where
art thou? ***10*** And he said, I heard thy voice in the garden,
and I was afraid, because I was naked; and I hid myself.

11 And he said, Who told thee that thou wast naked?
Hast thou eaten of the tree, whereof I commanded thee
that thou shouldest not eat? ***12*** And the man said, The woman
whom thou gavest to be with me, she gave me of the tree,
and I did eat. ***13*** And the LORD GOD said unto the woman,
What is this that thou hast done? And the woman said, The
serpent beguiled me, and I did eat. ***14*** And the LORD GOD
said unto the serpent, Because thou hast done this, thou art
cursed above all cattle, and above every beast of the field;
upon thy belly shalt thou go, and dust shalt thou eat all the

days of thy life: *15* and I will put enmity between thee and
the woman, and between thy seed and her seed; it shall
bruise thy head, and thou shalt bruise his heel. *16* Unto the
woman he said, I will greatly multiply thy sorrow and thy
conception; in sorrow thou shalt bring forth children; and
thy desire shall be to thy husband, and he shall rule over
thee. *17* And unto Adam he said, Because thou hast
hearkened unto the voice of thy wife, and hast eaten of the
tree, of which I commanded thee, saying, Thou shalt not
eat of it: cursed is the ground for thy sake; in toil thou eat of
it all the days of thy life; *18* Thorns also and thistles shall it
bring forth to thee; and thou shalt eat the herb of the field;
19 in the sweat of thy face shalt thou eat bread, till thou
return unto the ground; for out of it wast thou taken: for
dust thou art, and unto dust shalt thou return. *20* And the
man called his wife's name Eve; because she was the mother
of all living. *21* And the Lord God made for Adam and for
his wife coats of skins, and clothed them.

22 And the Lord God said, Behold, the man is become as
one of us, to know good and evil: and now, lest he put forth
his hand, and take also of the tree of life, and eat, and live
for ever: *23* therefore the Lord God sent him forth from the
garden of Eden, to till the ground from whence he was taken.
24 So he drove out the man; and he placed at the east of
the garden of Eden the Cherubim, and the flame of a sword
which turned every way, to keep the way of the tree of life.

Hesiod

***ca.* 700 B.C.E.**

WORKS AND DAYS

***ca.* 700 B.C.E.**

Little is known about Hesiod, though his works were popular with Greeks for centuries. What is accepted about him derives from internal evidence in his writings. It seems clear that he wrote *Works and Days* (a collection of folk wisdom, advice, and tales) and *Theogony* (a collection of the legends of the gods of Olympus). Other writing has been attributed to him, but not with certainty. His comfortable retelling of old tales makes his writing quite different from the rigorous and intellectually precise work of Plato and Aristotle. In this short selection, note how he accounts for the troubles of the world in comparing the present "Age of Iron" to an earlier "Golden Age" of freedom, prosperity, and virtue. No doubt his Greek audiences of 2,700 years ago found themselves nostalgic about "the good old days."

Selection from: Hesiod. *ca.* 700 B.C.E. *Hesiod: The Homeric Hymns and Homerica.* London: William Heinemann, New York: The Macmillan Co. Trans. Hugh G. Evelyn-White. 1914. 11-17.

. . . Or if you will, I will sum you up another tale well and skillfully—and do you lay it up in your heart,—how the gods and mortal men sprang from one source.

First of all the deathless gods who dwell on Olympus made a golden race of mortal men who lived in the time of Cronos when he was reigning in heaven. And they lived like gods without sorrow of heart, remote and free from toil and grief: miserable age rested not on them; but with legs and arms never failing they made merry with feasting beyond the reach of all evils. When they died, it was as though they were overcome with sleep, and they had all good things; for the fruitful earth unforced bare them fruit abundantly and without stint. They dwelt in ease and peace upon their lands with many good things, rich in flocks and loved by the blessed gods.

But after earth had covered this generation—they are called pure spirits dwelling on the earth, and are kindly, delivering from harm, and guardians of mortal men; for they roam everywhere over the earth, clothed in mist and keep watch on judgements and cruel deeds, givers of wealth; for this royal right also they received;—then they who dwell on Olympus made a second generation which was of silver and less noble by far. It was like the golden race neither in body nor in spirit. A child was brought up at his good mother's side an hundred years, an utter simpleton, playing childishly in his own home. But when they were full grown and were come to the full measure of their prime, they lived only a little time in sorrow because of their foolishness, for they could not keep from sinning and from wronging one another, nor would they serve the immortals, nor sacrifice on the holy altars of the blessed ones as it is right for men to do wherever they dwell. Then Zeus the son of Cronos was angry and put them away, because they would not give honour to the blessed gods who live on Olympus.

But when earth had covered this generation also—they are called blessed spirits of the underworld by men, and, though they are of second order, yet honour attends them also—Zeus the Father made a third generation of mortal men, a brazen race, sprung from ash-trees;[1] and it was in no way equal to the silver age, but was terrible and strong. They loved the lamentable works of Ares and deeds of violence; they ate no bread, but were hard of heart like adamant, fearful men. Great was their strength and unconquerable the arms which grew from their shoulders on their strong limbs. Their armour was of bronze, and their houses of bronze, and of bronze were their implements: there was no black iron. These were destroyed by their own hands and passed to the dank house of chill Hades, and left no name: terrible though they were, black Death seized them, and they left the bright light of the sun.

But when earth had covered this generation also, Zeus the son of Cronos made yet another, the fourth, upon the fruitful earth, which was nobler and more righteous, a god-like race of hero-men who are called demi-gods, the race before our own, throughout the boundless earth. Grim war and dread battle destroyed a part of them, some in the land of Cadmus at seven-gated Thebe when they fought for the flocks of Oedipus, and some, when it had brought them in ships over the great sea gulf to Troy for rich-haired Helen's sake: there death's end enshrouded a part of them. But to the others father Zeus the son of Cronos gave a living and an abode apart from men, and made them dwell at the ends of earth. And they live untouched by sorrow in the islands of the blessed along the shore of deep swirling Ocean, happy heroes for whom the grain-giving earth bears honey-sweet fruit flourishing thrice a year, far from the deathless gods, and Cronos rules over them for the father of men and gods released him from his bonds. And these last equally have honour and glory.

---

1 Eustathius refers to Hesiod as stating that men sprung "from oaks and stones and ashtrees." Proclus believed that the Nymths called Meliae (*Theogony,* 187) are intended. Goettling would render: "A race terrible because of their (ashen) spears." (H. G. E-W)

And again far-seeing Zeus made yet another generation, the fifth, of men who are upon the bounteous earth.

Thereafter, would that I were not among the men of the fifth generation, but either had died before or been born afterwards. For now truly is a race of iron, and men never rest from labour and sorrow by day, and from perishing by night; and the gods shall lay sore trouble upon them. But, notwithstanding, even these shall have some good mingled with their evils. And Zeus will destroy this race of mortal men also when they come to have grey hair on the temples at their birth.[2] The father will not agree with his children, nor the children with their father, nor guest with his host, nor comrade with comrade; nor will brother be dear to brother as aforetime. Men will dishonour their parents as they grow quickly old, and will carp at them, chiding them with bitter words, hard-hearted they, not knowing the fear of the gods. They will not repay their aged parents the cost of their nurture, for might shall be their right: and one man will sack another's city. There will be no favour for the man who keeps his oath or for the just or for the good; but rather men will praise the evil-doer and his violent dealing. Strength will be right and reverence will cease to be; and the wicked will hurt the worthy man, speaking false words against him, and will swear an oath upon them. Envy, foul-mouthed, delighting in evil, with scowling face, will go along with wretched men one and all. And then Aidôs and Nemesis,[3] with their sweet forms wrapped in white robes, will go from the wide-pathed earth and forsake mankind to join the company of the deathless gods: and bitter sorrows will be left for mortal men, and there will be no help against evil.

---

2 i.e., the race will so degenerate that at the last even a new-born child will show the marks of old age. (H.G.E-W)

3 Adidôs, as a quality, is that feeling of reverence or shame which restrains men from wrong: Nemesis is the feeling of righteous indignation aroused especially by the sight of the wicked in undeserved prosperity (*cf. Psalms*, lxxii.1-19). (H. G. E-W)

John Locke

1632-1704

TWO TREATISES OF GOVERNMENT

1689

Locke wrote during the ongoing crisis of seventeenth century England but was a generation younger than Hobbes. Like Hobbes, he rebelled against the classical curriculum at Oxford and championed rational, scientific methods of analysis. He studied medicine, and on the strength of his medical skill became close to the first Earl of Shaftesbury. He became a political advisor to Shaftsbury, a leading figure in the government of Charles II during the political turmoil of the Restoration. When Shaftsbury fell from power and charged with high treason, Locke fled to Holland. He returned to England only after the Glorious Revolution of 1689 put Parliament firmly in control of the government. His two major works, *Two Treatises of Government* and *An Essay Concerning Human Understanding*, were published the year of his return. Compare his depiction of the state of nature with that of Hobbes.

Selections from: Locke, John. 1689. *Two Treatises of Government.* In *Two Treatises on Civil Government by John Locke.* Ed. Henry Morley. Second Edition. London: George Routledge and Sons. 1887.

Book II, Chapter II: Of the State of Nature (192-199)

Book II
Chapter II

OF THE STATE OF NATURE

4. To understand political power aright, and derive it from its original, we must consider what estate all men are naturally in, and that is, a state of perfect freedom to order their actions, and dispose of their possessions and persons as they think fit, within the bounds of the law of Nature, without asking leave or depending upon the will of any other man.

A state also of equality, wherein all the power and jurisdiction is reciprocal, no one having more than another, there being nothing more evident than that creatures of the same species and rank, promiscuously born to all the same advantages of Nature, and the use of the same faculties, should also be equal one amongst another, without subordination or subjection, unless the lord and master of them all should, by any manifest declaration of his will, set one above another, and confer on him, by an evident and clear appointment, an undoubted right to dominion and sovereignty.

5. This equality of men by Nature, the judicious Hooker looks upon as so evident in itself, and beyond all question, that he makes it the foundation of that obligation to mutual love amongst men on which he builds the duties we owe one another, and from whence he derives the great maxims of justice and charity. His words are:—

The like natural inducement hath brought men to know that it is no less their duty to love others than themselves, for seeing those things which are equal, must needs all have one measure; if I cannot but wish to receive good, even as much at every man's hands as any man can wish unto his own soul, how should I look to have any part of my desire herein satisfied, unless myself be careful to satisfy the like desire, which is undoubtedly in other men weak, being of one and the same nature: to have anything offered them repugnant to this desire must needs, in all respects, grieve them as much as me; so that if I do harm, I must look to suffer, there being no reason that others should show greater measure of love to me than they have by me showed unto them; my desire, therefore, to be loved of my equals in Nature, as much as possible may be, imposeth upon me a natural duty of bearing to themward fully the like affection. From which relation of equality between ourselves and them that are as ourselves, what several rules and canons natural reason hath drawn for direction of life, no man is ignorant. (Eccl. Pol. lib. i.)

6. But though this be a state of liberty, yet it is not a state of license; though man in that state have an uncontrollable liberty to dispose of his person or possessions, yet he has not liberty to destroy himself, or so much as any creature in his possession, but where some nobler use than its bare preservation calls for it. The state of Nature has a law of Nature to govern it, which obliges every one, and reason, which is that law, teaches all mankind who will but consult it, that being all equal and independent, no one ought to harm another in his life, health, liberty or possessions; for men being all the workmanship of one omnipotent and infinitely wise Maker; all the servants of one sovereign Master, sent into the world by His order and about His business; they are His property, whose workmanship they are made to last during His, not one another's

pleasure. And, being furnished with like faculties, sharing all in one community of Nature, there cannot be supposed any such subordination among us that may authorize us to destroy one another, as if we were made for one another's uses, as the inferior ranks of creatures are for ours. Every one as he is bound to preserve himself, and not to quit his station wilfully, so by the like reason, when his own preservation comes not in competition, ought he as much as he can, to preserve the rest of mankind, and not unless it be to do justice on an offender, take away, or impair the life, or what tends to the preservation of the life, the liberty, health, limb, or goods of another.

7. And that all men may be restrained from invading others' rights, and from doing hurt to one another, and the law of Nature be observed, which willeth the peace and preservation of all mankind, the execution of the law of Nature is in that state put into every man's hands, whereby every one has a right to punish the transgressors of that law to such a degree, as may hinder its violation. For the law of Nature would, as all other laws that concern men in this world, be in vain if there were nobody that in that state of Nature had a power to execute that law, and thereby preserve the innocent and restrain offenders; and if any one in the state of Nature may punish another for any evil he has done, everyone may do so. For in that state of perfect equality, where naturally there is no superiority or jurisdiction of one over another, what any may do in prosecution of that law, every one must needs have a right to do.

8. And thus, in the state of Nature, one man comes by a power over another, but yet no absolute or arbitrary power to use a criminal, when he has got him in his hands, according to the passionate heats, or boundless extravagance of his own will, but only to retribute to him, so far as calm reason and conscience dictate, what

is proportionate to his transgression, which is so much as may serve for reparation and restraint. For these two are the only reasons why one man may lawfully do harm to another, which is that we call punishment. In transgressing the law of Nature, the offender declares himself to live by another rule than that of reason and common equity, which is that measure God has set to the actions of men for their mutual security, and so he becomes dangerous to mankind; the tie which is to secure them from injury and violence being slighted and broken by him, which being a trespass against the whole species, and the peace and safety of it, provided for by the law of Nature, every man upon this score, by the right he hath to preserve mankind in general, may restrain, or where it is necessary, destroy things noxious to them, and so may bring such evil on any one who has transgressed that law, as may make him repent the doing of it, and thereby deter him, and, by his example, others from doing the like mischief. And in the case, and upon this ground, every man has a right to punish the offender, and be executioner of the law of Nature.

9. I doubt not but this will seem a very strange doctrine to some men; but before they condemn it, I desire them to resolve me by what right any prince or state can put to death or punish an alien for any crime he commits in their country? It is certain their laws, by virtue of any sanction they receive from the promulgated will of the legislature, reach not a stranger. They speak not to him, nor, if they did, is he bound to hearken to them. The legislative authority by which they are in force over the subjects of that commonwealth hath no power over him. Those who have the supreme power of making laws in England, France, or Holland are, to an Indian, but like the rest of the world—men without authority. And therefore, if by the law of Nature every man hath not a power to punish offenses against it, as he soberly judges

the case to require, I see not how the magistrates of any community can punish an alien of another country, since, in reference to him, they can have no more power than what every man naturally may have over another.

10. Besides the crime which consists in violating the laws, and varying from the right rule of reason, whereby a man so far becomes degenerate, and declares himself to quit the principles of human nature and to be a noxious creature, there is commonly injury done, and some person or other, some other man, receives damage by his transgression; in which case, he who hath received any damage has (besides the right of punishment common to him, with other men) a particular right to seek reparation from him that hath done it. And any other person who finds it just may also join with him that is injured, and assist him in recovering from the offender so much as may make satisfaction for the harm he hath suffered. . . .

Denis Diderot

1713-1784

SUPPLEMENT TO THE VOYAGE OF BOUGAINVILLE

1772

One of the intellectual founders of the French Revolution, Diderot is best known for his work on the *Encyclopedia*, a thirty-three volume work that took him and his collaborators twenty-six years to complete. The *Encyclopedia* sought to summarize knowledge of the arts and sciences in a form that would make them accessible to anyone, a revolutionary ambition at that time. The depth of Diderot's revolutionary political sentiments is indicated by the vehemence of his famous statement: "Man will never be free until the last king is strangled with the entrails of the last priest." In this extract from his "Supplement to the Voyage of Bougainville" he condemns modern society through an imaginary conversation with a "primitive" Tahitian who is gentler and more civilized and freer than the Europeans he encounters. Like much of Diderot's work, it was published after his death.

Selections from: Diderot, Denis. 1772. "Supplement to the Voyage of Bougainville." In *Dialogues.* Trans. Francis Birrell. New York: Brentano's, 1927.

I.
JUDGMENT ON THE VOYAGE OF BOUGAINVILLE

A.: . . . Have you seen the Tahitien whom Bougainville took on board and brought back here?

B.: Yes. He was called Aotourou. He took the first piece of land he saw for the home of the travellers. Either they had lied to him about the length of the journey, or else he was deceived quite naturally by the apparently small distance between the shores of the sea, by which he dwelt, to the spot where the sky seemed to merge in the horizon, and knew nothing about the real measurement of the earth. The holding of women in common was a custom so well established in his mind that he threw himself on the first European woman he met, and very seriously intended to show her the courtesy of Tahiti. He grew bored with us. As the Tahitien alphabet has neither b, c, d, f, g, x, y nor z he could never learn to speak our language. It offered his rigid organs too many strange articulations and new sounds. He never stopped sighing after his own country, and I am not surprised at it. The voyage of Bougainville is the only one to give me the taste for a country other than my own. Till I had read it, I had always thought that one was nowhere so contented as at home; a state of mind which held good, I thought, for each inhabitant of the globe; and which sprang quite naturally from the charm of the soil, and the comforts which gather round the conveniences one enjoys and is not equally sure of finding elsewhere.

A.: What! Do you not think that the inhabitants of Paris are as sure that corn grows in the Roman Campagna as in the fields of the Beauce?[1]

B.: No, I do not. Bougainville sent back Aotourou, after providing for his expenses and the safety of his journey.

A.: O Aotourou! How happy wilt thou be to see once more thy father, thy mother, thy brothers, thy sisters, thy mistresses, thy compatriots! What wilt thou tell them of us?

B.: Very little, and that they will not believe.

A.: Why very little?

B.: Because he has taken in very little, and because he will find in his own language no terms corresponding to that little of which he has gathered some notion.

A.: And why will they not believe him?

B.: Because after comparing their own customs to ours, they will rather think Aotourou a liar than believe we are so mad.

A.: Really?

B.: No doubt of it. Savage life is so simple and our societies are such complicated mechanisms. The Tahitien is near the origin of the world, the European near its old age. The interval which separates him and us is greater than that between the child at birth and the tottering old man. He understands nothing of our laws and customs or only sees in them impediments disguised in a hundred forms, impediments which can excite only the indignation and contempt of a being in whom the sentiment of liberty is the deepest of all. . . .

II.
THE OLD MAN'S FAREWELL

He was the father of a large family. On the arrival of the Europeans, he cast looks of disdain at them, showing neither

[1] Pronounced bOs; a region, in Northern France noted for growing corn, wheat, beets, potatoes, barley, and oats.

astonishment, fright, nor curiosity.[2] They came up to him: he turned his back on them and retired into his cabin. His silence and his anxiety revealed his thoughts too well. He groaned within himself over the happy days of his country, now for ever eclipsed. On the departure of Bougainville, as the inhabitants rushed in a crowd on to the beach, attached themselves to his clothing, hugged his comrades in their arms and wept, this old man advanced, severe in mien, and said: "Weep, luckless Tahitiens, weep, but for the arrival not for the departure of these ambitious and wicked men. One day you will know them better. One day they will return, holding in one hand the morsel of wood you see attached to this man's belt, in the other, the iron which hangs from that man's side: they will return to throw you into chains, to cut your throats, or to subject you to their extravagance and vices: one day you will serve under them, as corrupted, as vile, as luckless as they. One consolation I have. My life is drawing to its close. And the calamity I announce to you, I shall not see. O Tahitiens, my friends, there is one method which might save you from your tragic future. But I would rather die than advise it. Let them withdraw and live."

Then addressing Bougainville, he added:

"And thou, chief of the brigands who obey thee, quickly push off thy vessel from our shore. We are innocent; we are happy: and thou canst not but spoil our happiness. We follow the pure instinct of nature: thou hast sought to efface its character from our souls. Here all things belong to all men. Thou hast preached some strange distinction between 'thine' and 'mine.' Our daughters and our wives were held in common by us all: thou hast shared this privilege with us, and thou hast come and inflamed them with frenzies unknown before. They have lost their reason in thy arms. Thou hast become ferocious in theirs. They have come to hate each other. You have slaughtered each other for them: they have come back stained

2 The presence of this old man and his attitude to the Europeans are mentioned by Bougainville.

with your blood. We are free: and see thou hast planted in our earth the title of our future slavery. Thou art neither god nor demon. Who art thou then to make slaves? Orou! thou who understandest the language of these men, tell us all as thou hast told me, what they have written on this metal blade! *This country is ours.* This country is thine! And why? Because thou hast set foot there? If a Tahitien disembarked one day upon your shores, and graved upon one of your stones or on the bark of one of your trees: *This country belongs to the inhabitants of Tahiti,* what wouldst thou think of such a proceeding? Thou art the stronger! But what of that? When someone took from you one of those rubbishy trifles with which your hut is filled, thou didst cry out and take thy revenge. Yet at that moment thou wast projecting in the depth of thy heart the theft of a whole country. Thou art not a slave. Thou wouldst suffer death rather than become one, yet us thou wouldst enslave. Thinkest thou then that the Tahitien cannot defend his liberty and die? He, whom thou wishest to seize like an animal, the Tahitien, is thy brother. You are both children of nature. What right hast thou over him that he has not over thee? Thou art come. Did we fall upon thee? Did we pillage thy ship? Did we seize thee and expose thee to the arrows of our enemies? Did we yoke thee to our animals toiling in the fields? No. We have respected our image in thee. Leave us our customs. They are wiser and more honourable than thine. We have no wish to barter what thou callest our ignorance against thy useless knowledge. We possess all that is necessary and good for us. Do we deserve contempt because we have not known how to fabricate for ourselves wants in superfluity? When we are hungry we have enough to eat; when we are cold, the means to clothe ourselves. Thou hast entered our cabins. What, in thy opinion, is lacking? Pursue as long as thou wilt what thou callest the commodities of life. But permit sensible beings to stop, when by continuing their painful labour they will gain but imaginary good. If thou persuadest us to cross the narrow limit of necessity, when shall we stop working? What time will be left over for enjoying ourselves? We have reduced to the smallest possible the sum of our annual and daily toil, because to us nothing seems better than repose. Go back to thine own country to trouble and torment thyself as much as thou wilt. Trouble us neither with thy artificial needs, nor thy imaginary virtues. Look at these men: how straight, healthy, and robust they are! Look at these women! How straight, healthy, fresh and fair they are. Take this bow. It is mine. Call to help thee, one, two, three, four of thy comrades and try to bend it. I bend it myself alone. I plough the earth. I climb the mountain. I pierce the forest. I cover a league of the plain in less than an hour. Thy young companions can scarcely follow me, and I am ninety years old and more. Woe to this island! Woe to all Tahitiens present and to come for the day of this thy visit! . . .

III.
CONVERSATION BETWEEN THE CHAPLAIN AND OROU

[The Chaplain argues that Tahatiens should adopt the Christian religion and the European way of life, and Orou makes the following speech rejecting him.]

. . . Believe me, you have made the condition of men worse than that of animals. I know not who thy great workman is. But I am glad he has never spoken to our fathers and I hope he never speaks to our children. For he might say the same silly things to them and they might be silly enough to believe him. Yesterday at supper thou toldest of *magistrates* and *priests*, whose authority rules your conduct. But tell me, are they lords of good and evil? Can they make what is just unjust, and what is unjust just? Does it rest with them to label good actions harmful and harmful actions innocent or useful? Thou canst not well admit it, for then there would be neither true nor false, good nor bad, beautiful nor ugly, except in so far as thy great workman, thy magistrates and priests thought good to say so. Then from one moment to another thou wouldst be compelled to change thy opinion and thy conduct. One day one of thy three masters would give the order *kill* and thou wouldst be obliged, in conscience, to kill. Another day *steal* and thou wouldst have to steal; or, *Do not eat this fruit* and thou wouldst not dare eat it; or, *I forbid thee this fruit or animal* and thou couldst not touch it. There is no goodness they could not forbid thee: no wickedness they could not order. And where wouldst thou be, if thy three masters, falling out among themselves, took it into their heads to permit, enjoin and forbid the same thing as I am sure often happens? Then to please the priest, thou must needs quarrel with the magistrate: to satisfy the magistrate, thou must anger the great workman; and to be agreeable to the great workman, turn thy back on nature. . . .

IV.
CONTINUATION OF THE DIALOGUE

A.: I respect this polite chaplain.

B.: And I rather the morals of the Tahitiens and the speech of Orou.

A.: Though a trifle European in style.

B.: Undoubtedly.

At this point the worthy chaplain regrets the shortness of his stay in Tahiti, and the difficulty of getting to know better the customs of a people sufficiently wise to stop of their own accord at mediocrity or lucky enough to enjoy a climate whose fertility guaranteed them a prolonged laziness, active enough to be beyond the absolute needs of life and indolent enough for their innocence, repose and felicity to have nothing to fear from a too rapid advance in knowledge. There nothing was condemned by public opinion or law, save what was condemned by nature. Village work and harvesting were done in common. The meaning attached to the word *property* was very restricted: the passion of love, by its reduction to a simple physical appetite, produced none of the disorders it does with us. The whole island presented the picture of a single large family and each cabin seemed more like different rooms in one of our big houses. He ended up by protesting that the Tahitiens will always be present in his memory, that he had been tempted to throw his clothes into the ship and pass the rest of his life among them; and that he is afraid of repenting more than once of not having done so.

A.: For all his eulogium, what conclusions can be usefully drawn from the morals and strange customs of an uncivilized people?

B.: I see that as soon as certain physical causes, as, for instance, the necessity of defeating an ungrateful soil, have brought out the intellectuality in man, this impulse carries him far beyond his goal, and once the limits of need passed, he is carried out into the boundless ocean of his phantasies from which he is never pulled back. May the lucky Tahitien stop where he is! For except in this distant nook of the globe, I perceive there never have been any morals and perhaps never will be anywhere.

A.: What do you mean, then, by morals?

B.: I mean general submission to, and conduct consequent on, laws good or bad. If the laws are good, morals are good. If the laws are bad, morals are bad. And if the laws, be they good or bad, are not observed, which is the worst of all social conditions, there are no morals at all. Then how do you wish laws to be observed when they are contradictory? Run through the history of the centuries, of nations both ancient and modern, and you will find man in subjection to three codes, the natural code, the civil code, the religious code, and bound to infringe these three codes in turn, as they never agree. So it happens, as Orou guessed about ours, that in no country is there a natural man, a citizen or a pious person.

A.: From which you will doubtless conclude that if we base morals on the eternal relations subsisting between men, perhaps the religious law becomes unnecessary and the civil need only be the enunciation of the natural law.

B.: Certainly, unless we would multiply wicked men instead of making good ones.

A.: Or, if we must keep all three, the two last should be strict copies of the first, which we carry graved on the bottom of our hearts, and which will always be the stronger.

B.: That is not accurate. All we bring with us at birth is an organism like that of others, the same needs, a delight in the same pleasures, and a common aversion from the same pains. This is what makes up man as he is and should be the basis of a morality suited to him.

A.: That is far from easy.

B.: It is, in fact, so difficult that I would gladly believe the most savage nation in the world, the Tahitien, who has observed most strictly the natural law, to be nearer a satisfactory system of law than any civilized people. . . .

[The parties to the conversation then go on to discuss the relative merits of living by the vast and complicated network of human law, constructed and enforced by judges and lawyers who frequently become corrupt, or living according to reason and obeying the natural law that is inherent in all human beings.]

A.: How short the code of nations would be if it conformed rigidly to the law of nature. How many errors and vices man would be spared!

B.: Would you like an abridged account of almost all our wretchedness? Here it is. There existed a natural man. There was introduced into this man an artificial man: and a civil war, enduring the whole of life, arose in the cavern. Sometimes the natural man is the stronger, sometimes he is struck down by the moral and artificial man. In either case the poor monster is pulled about, pinched with tweezers, tortured, stretched on the wheel, ceaselessly groaning, ceaselessly unhappy, either because a false enthusiasm for glory transports and intoxicates him or because a false humiliation curbs and depresses him. But still there are some exceptional circumstances which restore man to his first simplicity.

A.: Wretchedness and sickness, two great exorcisers.

B.: You have named them right. And then what happens to all our conventional virtues! In wretchedness a man has no remorse, in sickness no woman is modest.

A.: I have observed it.

B.: There is another phenomenon which will not have escaped you either. The return of the moral, artificial man follows step by step the progress from the state of sickness to that of convalescence and from the state of convalescence to that of health. The moment the illness is over, the internal struggles begin again and the intruder is nearly always vanquished.

A.: That is true. I have myself experienced that the natural man, when convalescent, enjoys a vigour fatal to the artificial moral man. But finally tell me, ought we to civilize man or abandon him to instinct?

B.: Must I answer you straight?

A.: Yes.

B.: If you aspire to be a tyrant, civilize him. Poison him as best you can with a morality contrary to nature. Put every kind of hindrance in his path. Embarrass his movements with a thousand obstacles. Attach terrifying spectres to him. Perpetuate the war in the cavern and see to it that the natural man is always enchained there under the foot of the moral artificial man. Do you wish him to be happy and free? Then do not meddle in his affairs. There will be quite enough unforeseen accidents to lead him to knowledge and depravity. One thing you may always be sure of. These wise law-givers have moulded and fashioned you to what you are not in your interests but in their own. I appeal to all political, civil, and religious institutions. Look below the surface. And unless I am very much mistaken you will find the human race from century to century bent beneath the yoke it pleased a handful of rascals to impose on it. Mistrust the man who comes to bring order. Order is always a means of getting control of other people by embarrassing them: and the Calabrians are almost the only people who have not been tricked by the flattery of law-givers.

A.: And you like this anarchy in Calabria?

B.: I appeal to experience, and dare swear their barbarism is less vicious than our urbanity. How many small meannesses go to equal the atrocity of a few great crimes about which so much pother is made? I regard uncivilized men as a multitude of scattered and isolated springs. Naturally if two of these springs crashed together, one or other or both would break. To obviate their inconvenience, an individual of profound wisdom and sublime genius collected these springs and made a machine with them. And in this machine called Society all the springs were made to act and react on each other and wear themselves out unceasingly. And more were smashed in a day in a state of legislation than in a year in the anarchy of nature. But what a noise! What ruin! What an enormous destruction of small springs when two, three or four of these huge machines crashed violently into each other.

A.: So you would prefer a state of brutal savage nature?

B.: Really I cannot say. But this I know. Townsmen have several times been seen to strip themselves and return to the forest. The woods-man has never put on clothes and come to the town.

A.: It has often occurred to me that the total of good and bad was variable for each individual, but that the happiness or unhappiness of any animal species had its limit which could not be crossed, and that our efforts perhaps finally resulted in an equal quantity of drawbacks and advantages, as if we were harassing ourselves to increase the two sides of an equation, between which an eternal and necessary equality subsisted. However, I have no doubt that the average life of the civilized man is longer that of the savage.

B.: But supposing the duration of a machine is no true measure of the exhaustion it endures, what then?

A.: I see that on the whole you would be inclined to believe men get more wicked and miserable the more they are civilized.

B.: I shall not visit all the countries of the universe. I merely warn you that you will find the lot of man happy only in Tahiti, and tolerable in but one corner of Europe. In the second case the governors, being suspicious and jealous of their security, are busy keeping man in what you call brutishness. . . .

DR. MARTIN LUTHER KING JR.

1929-1968

"I HAVE A DREAM"[1]

AUGUST 28, 1963

Martin Luther King's international reputation was confirmed when he was given the Nobel Peace Prize in 1964 for his leadership of the non-violent civil rights movement to end racial segregation in the American South. He was educated at Morehouse College in his native Atlanta and at Crozer Theological Seminary in Chester, Pennsylvania. He earned his Ph.D. degree at Boston University in 1955. The civil rights movement reached its zenith with the March on Washington in 1963, where, on August 28, King delivered this speech to the 250,000 marchers who had assembled on the Mall. A few months later, President John F. Kennedy, who had supported the marchers, was assassinated. President Lyndon Johnson succeeded Kennedy and even more strongly supported civil rights legislation that had been blocked for years in Congress. Racial segregation in public places was ended by the Civil Rights Act of 1964 and access to the ballot for African Americans was enforced by the federal government by the Voting Rights Act of 1965. King saw the end of racial segregation but did not live to see what it would bring. He was assassinated in Memphis, Tennessee, in 1968.

I Have A Dream

DR. MARTIN LUTHER KING, JR.
AUGUST 28, 1963. WASHINGTON, D.C.

I am happy to join with you today in what will go down in history as the greatest demonstration for freedom in the history of our nation.

Fivescore years ago, a great American, in whose symbolic shadow we stand today, signed the Emancipation Proclamation. This momentous decree came as a great beacon light of hope to millions of Negro slaves who had been seared in the flames of withering injustice. It came as a joyous daybreak to end the long night of their captivity.

But one hundred years later, the Negro is still not free. One hundred years later, the life of the Negro is still sadly crippled by the manacles of segregation and the chains of discrimination. One hundred years later, the Negro lives on a lonely island of poverty in the midst of a vast ocean of material prosperity. One hundred years later, the Negro is still languished in the corners of American society and finds himself in exile in his own land. And so we've come here today to dramatize a shameful condition.

In a sense we've come to our nation's capital to cash a check. When the architects of our republic wrote the magnificent words of the Constitution and the Declaration of Independence, they were signing a promissory note to which every American was to fall heir. This not was a promise that all men, yes, black men as well as white men, would be guaranteed the "unalienable Rights of Life, Liberty, and the pursuit of Happiness." It is obvious today that America has defaulted on this promissory note insofar as her citizens of color are concerned. Instead of honoring this sacred obligation, America has given the Negro people a bad check, a check which has come back marked "insufficient funds."

But we refuse to believe that the bank of justice is bankrupt. We refuse to believe that there are insufficient funds in the great vaults of opportunity of this nation. And so we've come to cash this check, a check that will give us upon demand the riches of freedom and the security of justice.

We have also come to this hallowed spot to remind America of the fierce urgency of now. This is no time to engage in the luxury of cooling off or to take the tranquilizing drug of gradualism. Now is the time to make real the promises of democracy. Now is the time to rise from the dark and desolate valley of segregation to the sunlit path of racial justice. Now is the time to lift our nation from the quicksands of racial injustice. Now is the time to make justice a reality for all of God's children.

It would be fatal for the nation to overlook the urgency of the moment. This sweltering summer of the Negro's legitimate discontent will not pass until there is an invigorating autumn of freedom and equality. Nineteen sixty-three is not an end, but a beginning. And those who hope that the Negro needed to blow off steam and will now be content will have a rude awakening if the nation returns to business as usual. There will be neither rest nor tranquility in America until the Negro is granted his citizenship rights. The whirlwinds of revolt will continue to shake the foundations of our nation until the bright day of justice emerges.

But there is something I must say to my people, who stand on the warm threshold which leads into the palace of justice: In the process of gaining our rightful place, we must not be guilty of wrongful deeds. Let us not seek to satisfy our thirst for freedom by drinking from the cup of bitterness and hatred. We must forever conduct our struggle on the high plane of dignity and discipline. We must not allow our creative protest to degenerate into physical violence. Again and again, we must rise to the majestic heights of meeting physical force with soul force. The marvelous new militancy which has engulfed the Negro community must not lead us to a distrust of all white people, for many of our white brothers, as evidenced by their presence here today, have come to realize that their destiny is tied up with our destiny. And they have come to realize that their freedom is inextricably bound to our freedom. We cannot walk alone.

And as we walk, we must make the pledge that we shall always march ahead. We cannot turn back. There are those who are asking the devotes of civil rights, "When will you be satisfied?"

We can never be satisfied as long as the Negro is the victim of the unspeakable horrors of police brutality. We can never be satisfied as long as our bodies, heavy with fatigue of travel, cannot gain lodging in the motels of the highways and the hotels of the cities. We cannot be satisfied as long the Negro's basic mobility is from a smaller ghetto to a larger one. We can never be satisfied as long as our children are stripped of their selfhood and robbed of their dignity by signs stating, "for whites only." We cannot be satisfied as long as a Negro in Mississippi cannot vote and a Negro in New York believes he has nothing for which to vote. No, no, we are not satisfied and we will not be satisfied until "justice rolls down like waters and righteousness like a mighty stream."

I am not unmindful that some of you have come here out of great trials and tribulations. Some of you have come fresh from narrow jail cells. Some of you have come from areas where quest for freedom left you battered by the storms of persecution and staggered by the winds of police brutality. You have been the veterans of creative suffering. Continue to work with the faith that unearned suffering is redemptive. Go back to Mississippi, go back to Alabama, go back to South Carolina, go back to Georgia, go back to Louisiana, go back to the slums and ghettos of our northern cities, knowing that somehow this situation can and will be changed. Let us not wallow in the valley of despair.

I say to you today, my friends, so even though we face the difficulties of today and tomorrow, I still have a dream. It is a dream deeply rooted in the American dream.

I have a dream that one day this nation will rise up and live out the true meaning of its creed: "We hold these truths to be self-evident, that all men are created equal."

I have a dream that one day on the red hills of Georgia, the sons of former slaves and the sons of former slave owners will be able to sit down together at the table of brotherhood.

I have a dream that one day even the state of Mississippi, a state sweltering with the heat of injustice, sweltering with the heat of oppression, will be transformed into an oasis of freedom and justice.

I have a dream that my four little children will one day live in a nation where they will not be judged by the color of their skin but by the content of their character. I have a dream today.

I have a dream that one day down in Alabama, with its vicious racists, with its governor having his lips dripping with the words of "interposition" and "nullification," one day right there in Alabama little black boys and black girls will be to join hands with little white boys and white girls as sisters and brothers. I have a dream today.

I have a dream that one day "every valley shall be exalted, and every hill and mountain shall be made low; the rough places will be made plain, and the crooked places will be made straight; and the glory of the Lord shall be revealed, and all flesh shall see it together."

This is our hope. This is the faith that I go back to the South with. With this faith we will be able to hew out of the mountain of despair a stone of hope. With this faith we will be able to transform the jangling discords of our nation into a beautiful symphony of brotherhood. With this faith we will be able to work together, to pray together, to struggle together, to go to jail together, to stand up for freedom together, knowing that we will be free one day. This will be the day, this will be the day when all God's children will be able to sing with new meaning:

> My country, 'tis of thee, sweet land of liberty,
> of thee I sing.
> Land where my fathers died, land of the
> pilgrim's pride,
> From every mountainside, let freedom
> ring!

And if America is to be a great nation, this must become true.

And so let freedom ring from the prodigious hilltops of New Hampshire.

Let freedom ring from the mighty mountains of New York.

Let freedom ring from the heightening Alleghenies of Pennsylvania.

Let freedom ring from the snowcapped Rockies of Colorado.

Let freedom ring from the curvaceous slopes of California.

But not on that: Let freedom ring from Stone Mountain of Georgia.

Let freedom ring from Lookout Mountain of Tennessee.

Let freedom ring from ever hill and molehill of Mississippi.

From every mountainside, let freedom ring.

And when this happens, when we allow freedom ring, when we let it ring from every village and every hamlet, form every state and every city, we will be able to speed up that day when all of God's children, black men and white men, Jews and Gentiles, Protestants and Catholics, will be able to join hands and sing in the words of the old Negro spiritual:

> Free at last! Free at last!
> Thank God Almighty, we are free at last!

Thomas Hobbes

1588-1679

LEVIATHAN

1651

The crisis of seventeenth century England is the backdrop for Hobbes's concern about claims for freedom that went too far. As a royalist sympathizer, this scholar, teacher, and writer fled to France in 1640 at the outbreak of the English Civil War, not returning until after Oliver Cromwell has installed himself as Lord Protector and brought a measure of peace. His masterpiece, *Leviathan,* was published in 1651, the year of his return. He was convinced that a new approach to the question of the proper relation between freedom and authority required discarding the old arguments for obedience that were based on religious sanctions. After all, these had failed to resolve the destructive wars of religion that plagued Europe. Like the other "social contract" theorists excerpted here (Locke and Rousseau), Hobbes started with a consideration of the "natural" state of humankind—the conditions that would exist if there were no government at all. His expression of this was passionate and is still often quoted.

Selection from: Hobbes, Thomas. 1651. *Leviathan.* Oxford: Oxford UP, 1909.

Chapter XIII: Of the Natural Condition of Mankind as Concerning Their Felicity and Misery (94-97)

CHAPTER XIII

OF THE NATURAL CONDITION OF MANKIND, AS CONCERNING THEIR FELICITY, AND MISERY.

Nature hath made men so equall, in the faculties of body, and mind; as that though there bee found one man sometimes manifestly stronger in body, or of quicker mind then [sic] another; yet when all is reckoned together, the difference between man, and man, is not so considerable, as that one man can thereupon claim to himselfe any benefit, to which another may not pretend, as well as he. For as to the strength of body, the weakest has strength enough to kill the strongest, either by secret machination, or by confederacy with others, that are in the same danger with himselfe.

And as to the faculties of the mind, (setting aside the arts grounded upon words, and especially that skill of proceeding upon generall, and infallible rules, called Science; which very few have, and but in few things; as being not a native faculty, born with us; nor attained, (as Prudence,) while we look after somewhat els,) I find yet a greater equality amongst men, than that of strength. For Prudence, is but Experience; which equall time, equally bestowes on all men, in those things they equally apply themselves unto. That which may perhaps make such equality incredible, is but a vain conceipt of ones owne wisdome, which almost all men think they have in a greater degree, than the Vulgar; that is, than all men but themselves, and a few others, whom by Fame, or for concurring with themselves, they approve. For such is the nature of men, that howsoever they may acknowledge many others to be more witty, or more eloquent, or more learned; Yet they will hardly believe there be many so wise as themselves: For they see their own wit at hand, and other mens at a distance. But this proveth rather that men are in that point equall, than unequall. For there is not ordinarily a greater signe of the equall distribution of any thing, than that every man is contented with his share.

From this equality of ability, ariseth equality of hope in the attaining of our Ends. And therefore if any two men desire the same thing, which neverthelesse they cannot both enjoy, they become enemies; and in the way to their End, (which is principally their owne conservation, and sometimes their delectation only,) endeavour to destroy, or subdue one an other. And from hence it comes to passe, that where an Invader hath no more to feare, than an other mans single power; if one plant, sow, build, or possesse a convenient Seat, others may probably be expected to come prepared with forces united, to dispossesse, and deprive him, not only of the fruit of his labour, but also of his life, or liberty. And the Invader again is in the like danger of another.

And from this diffidence of one another, there is no way for any man to secure himselfe, so reasonable, as Anticipation; that is, by force, or wiles, to master the persons of all men he can, so long, till he see no other power great enough to endanger him: And this is no more than his own conservation requireth, and is generally allowed. Also because there be some, that taking pleasure in contemplating their own power in the acts of conquest, which they pursue farther than their security requires; if others, that otherwise would be glad to be at ease within modest bounds, should not by invasion increase their power, they would not be able, long time, by standing only on their defence, to subsist. And by consequence, such augmentation of dominion over men, being necessary to a mans conservation, it ought to be allowed him.

Againe, men have no pleasure, (but on the contrary a great deale of griefe) in keeping company, where there is no power able to over-awe them all. For every man looketh that his companion should value him, at the same rate he sets upon himselfe: And upon all signes of contempt, or undervaluing, naturally endeavours, as far as he dares (which amongst them that have no common power to keep them in quiet, is far enough to make them destroy each other,) to extort a greater value from his contemners, by dommage; and from others, by the example.

So that in the nature of man, we find three principall causes of quarrell. First, Competition; Secondly, Diffidence; Thirdly, Glory.

The first, maketh men invade for Gain; the second, for Safety; and the third, for Reputation. The first use Violence, to make themselves Masters of other mens persons, wives, children, and cattell; the second, to defend them; the third, for trifles, as a word, a smile, a different opinion, and any other signe of undervalue, either direct in their Persons, or by reflexion in their Kindred, their Friends, their Nation, their Profession, or their Name.

Hereby it is manifest, that during the time men live without a common Power to keep them all in awe, they are in that condition which is called Warre; and such a warre, as is of every man, against every man. For Warre consisteth not in Battell onely, or the act of fighting; but in a tract of time, wherein the Will to contend by Battell is sufficiently known: and therefore the notion of *Time*, is to be considered in the nature of Warre; as it is in the nature of Weather. For as the nature of Foule weather, lyeth not in a showre or two of rain; but in an inclination thereto of many dayes together: So the nature of War, consisteth not in actuall fighting; but in the known disposition thereto, during all the time there is no assurance to the contrary. All other time is PEACE.

Whatsoever therefore is consequent to a time of Warre, where every man is Enemy to every man; the same consequent to the time, wherein men live without other security, than what their own strength, and their own invention shall furnish them withall. In such condition, there is no place for Industry; because the fruit thereof is uncertain: and consequently no Culture of the Earth; no Navigation, nor use of the commodities that may be imported by Sea; no commodious Building; no Instruments of moving, and removing such things as require much force; no Knowledge of the face of the Earth; no account of Time; no Arts; no Letters; no Society; and which is worst of all, continuall feare, and danger of violent death; And the life of man, solitary, poore, nasty, brutish, and short.

It may seem strange to some man, that has not well weighed these things; that Nature should thus dissociate, and render men apt to invade, and destroy one another: and he may therefore, not trusting to this Inference, made from the Passions, desire perhaps to have the same confirmed by Experience. Let him therefore consider with himselfe, when taking a journey, he armes himselfe, and seeks to go well accompanied; when going to sleep, he locks his dores; when even in his house he locks his chests; and this when he knowes there bee Laws, and publike Officers, armed, to revenge all injuries shall bee done him; what opinion he has of his fellow subjects, when he rides armed; of his fellow Citizens, when he locks his dores; and of his children, and servants, when he locks his chests. Does he not there as much accuse mankind by his actions, as I do by my words? But neither of us accuse mans nature in it. The Desires, and other Passions of man, are in themselves no Sin. No more are the Actions, that proceed from those Passions, till they know a Law that forbids them: which till Lawes be made they cannot know: nor can any Law be made, till they have agreed upon the Person that shall make it.

AUTHORITY

Introduction

The conclusion of most of humanity has been that, likeable or not, authority is a necessary part of life as we know it. In Aristotle's view, it is a positive good. Though when used wrongly it ranks among the worst of human possibilities, he asserts that when used rightly, it can be among the greatest human achievements. Hobbes is less demanding. Authority must protect lives by preventing conflict, and we should welcome strong leadership. Locke is, in this as in other things, more relaxed than Hobbes. However, he makes more complex institutional demands. Authority should rest not with a single leader but with the majority, as represented in an elected legislature. The American founders had to wrestle with exactly this problem as well. How can governing institutions be organized and given power without taking away the freedoms that were the aim of independence? Their solution revolved around law, especially the law of the *Constitution.*

For Rousseau, legal and institutional frameworks, or, for that matter, mathematically calculated majorities, are not as compelling a source of authority as the general will, what people would want if they thought without bias. Unhappily, claiming to represent the people's will has been the standard practice of tyrants. For Lenin, this meant the need to establish a "dictatorship of the proletariat." Dictators and tyrants act without limits, as the short example of Hitler's zeal to manipulate the press illustrates. And the Holocaust documents and Chief Joseph's famous speech remind us that the abuse of authority can be final.

ARISTOTLE

384-324 B.C.E.

POLITICS

350 B.C.E.

Aristotle was born in northern Greece, son of a physician who had ties to the court of the kingdom of Macedonia. He went to Athens to study at the Academy with Plato and stayed in Athens for twenty years. He subsequently went to Macedonia to become tutor to the prince, Alexander, who was to become Alexander the Great. He then returned to Athens and started the Lyceum, which was both a school and a research institute. The empirical foundation of the *Politics* is based on the collection of Greek city-state constitutions housed there, in what we now know was the twilight of the city-state as a form of government. Unlike modern social scientists, Aristotle considered the purposes of politics as much a part of political studies as the gathering of specifically political information. It is often said that the *Nichomachean Ethics* should be read as a companion volume to the *Politics*.

Selections from: Aristotle. 350 B.C.E. *Aristotle's Politics.* Ed. H.W.C. Davis, M.A. Trans. Benjamin Jowett. Oxford: Oxford UP, 1905.

Book I: (excerpted 25-30)

Book III: (excerpted 105-109, 114-115)

Book IV: (excerpted 145-148, 162-171)
Book VII: (excerpted 257-260)

THE POLITICS

Book I

I. (1) EVERY state is a community of some kind, and every community is established with a view to some good; for mankind always act in order to obtain that which they think good. But, if all communities aim at some good, the state or political community, which is the highest of all, and which embraces all the rest, aims, in a greater degree than any other, at the highest good.

Now there is an erroneous opinion[1] that a statesman, king, householder, and master are the same, and that they differ, not in kind, but only in the number of their subjects. For example, the ruler over a few is called a master; over more, the manager of a household; over a still larger number, a statesman or king, as if there were no difference between a great household and a small state. The distinction which is made between the king and the statesman is as follows: When the government is personal, the ruler is a king; when, according to the principles of the political science, the citizens rule and are ruled in turn, then he is called a statesman.

But all this is a mistake; for governments differ in kind, as will be evident to any one who considers the matter according to the method[2] which has hitherto guided us. As in other departments of science, so in politics, the compound should always be resolved into the simple elements or least parts of the whole. We must therefore look at the elements of which the state is composed, in

---

1 Cp. Plato, *Politicus*, 258 E foll.

2 Cp. c.8. § I.

order that we may see[1] in what they differ from one another, and whether any scientific distinction can be drawn between the different kinds of rule.

2. He who thus considers things in their first growth and origin, whether a state or anything else, will obtain the clearest view of them. In the first place (1) there must be a union of those who cannot exist without each other; for example, of male and female, that the race may continue; and this is a union which is formed, not of deliberate purpose, but because, in common with other animals and with plants, mankind have a natural desire to leave behind them an image of themselves. And (2) there must be a union of natural ruler and subject, that both may be preserved. For he who can foresee with his mind is by nature intended to be lord and master, and he who can work with his body is a subject, and by nature a slave; hence master and slave have the same interest. Nature, however, has distinguished between the female and the slave. For . . . she makes each thing for a single use, and every instrument is best made when intended for one and not for many uses. But among barbarians no distinction is made between women and slaves, because there is no natural ruler among them: they are a community of slaves, male and female. Wherefore the poets say,—

> 'It is meet that Hellenes should rule over barbarians;'[2]

as if they thought that the barbarian and the slave were by nature one.

Out of these two relationships between man and woman,

---

1 Or, with Bernays, 'how the different kinds of rule differ from one another, and generally whether any scientific result can be attained about each one of them.'

2 Eurip. Iphig, in Aulid. 1400.

master and slave, the family first arises, and Hesiod is right when he says,—

> 'First house and wife and an ox for the plough,'[1]

for the ox is the poor man's slave. The family is the association established by nature for the supply of men's every-day wants, and the members of it are called by Charondas 'companions of the cupboard' [ὁμοσιπύους], and by Epimenides the Cretan, 'companions of the manger'[2] [Ὁμοκάπνους]. But when several families are united, and the association aims at something more than the supply of daily needs, then comes into existence the village. . . .

When several villages are united in a single community, perfect and large enough to be nearly or quite self-sufficing, the state comes into existence, originating in the bare needs of life, and continuing in existence for the sake of a good life. And therefore, if the earlier forms of society are natural, so is the state, for it is the end of them, and the [completed] nature is the end. For what each thing is when fully developed, we call its nature, whether we are speaking of a man, a horse, or a family. Besides, the final cause and end of a thing is the best, and to be self-sufficing is the end and the best.

Hence it is evident that the state is a creation of nature, and that man is by nature a political animal. And he who by nature and not by mere accident is without a state, is either above humanity, or below it; he is the

> 'Tribeless, lawless, hearthless one,'

---

1 Op. et Di. 405.

2 Or, reading with the old translator (William of Moerbek), Ὁμοκάπνους, 'companions of the hearth.'

whom Homer[1] denounces—the outcast who is a lover of war; he may be compared to an unprotected piece in the game of draughts [checkers].

Now the reason why man is more of a political animal than bees or any other gregarious animals is evident. Nature, as we often say, makes nothing in vain,[2] and man is the only animal whom she has endowed with the gift of speech.[3] And whereas mere sound is but an indication of pleasure or pain, and is therefore found in other animals (for their nature attains to the perception of pleasure and pain and the intimation of them to one another, and no further), the power of speech is intended to set forth the expedient and inexpedient, and likewise the just and the unjust. And it is a characteristic of man that he alone has any sense of good and evil, of just and unjust, and the association of living beings who have this sense makes a family and a state.

Thus the state is by nature clearly prior to the family and to the individual, since the whole is of necessity prior to the part; for example, if the whole body be destroyed, there will be no foot or hand, except in an equivocal sense, as we might speak of a stone hand; for when destroyed the hand will be no better. But things are defined by their working and power; and we ought not to say that they are the same when they are no longer the same, but only that they have the same name. The proof that the state is a creation of nature and prior to the individual is that the individual, when isolated, is not self-sufficing; and therefore he is like a part in relation to the whole. But he who is unable to live in society, or who has no need because he is sufficient for himself, must be either a beast or a god: he is no part of a state. A social instinct is implanted in all men by nature, and yet he who first founded the state was the greatest of benefactors. For man, when perfected, is the best of animals,

1 Il. ix. 63

2 Cp.c. 8. § 12.

3 Cp. c. 13. § 12.

but, when separated from law and justice, he is the worst of all; since armed injustice is the more dangerous, and he is equipped at birth with the arms of intelligence and with moral qualities which he may use for the worst ends. Wherefore, if he have not virtue, he is the most unholy and the most savage of animals, and the most full of lust and gluttony. But justice is the bond of men in states, and the administration of justice, which is the determination of what is just,[1] is the principle of order in political society. . . .

Book III

III (4) . . . It is quite another question, whether a state ought or ought not to fulfil engagements when the form of government changes.

There is a point nearly allied to the preceding: Whether the virtue of a good man and a good citizen is the same or not.[2] But, before entering on this discussion, we must first obtain some general notion of the virtue of the citizen. Like the sailor, the citizen is a member of a community. Now, sailors have different functions, for one of them is a rower, another a pilot, and a third a look-out man, and a fourth is described by some similar term; and while the precise definition of each individual's virtue applies exclusively to him, there is, at the same time, a common definition applicable to them all. For they have all of them a common object, which is safety in navigation. Similarly, one citizen differs from another, but the salvation of the community is the common business of them all. This community is the state; the virtue of the citizen must therefore be relative to the constitution of which he is a member. If, then, there are many forms of government, it is evident that the virtue of the good citizen cannot be the one perfect virtue. But we

1 Cp. N. Eth. v.6. § 4.

2 Cp. N. Eth. v. 2. § 11.

say that the good man is he who has perfect virtue. Hence it is evident that the good citizen need not of necessity possess the virtue which makes a good man.

The same question may also be approached by another road, from a consideration of the perfect state. If the state cannot be entirely composed of good men, and each citizen is expected to do his own business well, and must therefore have virtue, inasmuch as all the citizens cannot be alike, the virtue of the citizen and of the good man cannot coincide. All must have the virtue of the good citizen—thus, and thus only, can the state be perfect; but they will not have the virtue of a good man, unless we assume that in the good state all the citizens must be good.

Again, the state may be compared to the living being: as the first elements into which a living being is resolved are soul and body, as the soul is made up of reason and appetite, the family of husband and wife, property of master and slave, so out of all these, as well as other dissimilar elements, the state is composed; and, therefore, the virtue of all the citizens cannot possibly be the same, any more than the excellence of the leader of a chorus is the same as that of the performer who stands by his side. I have said enough to show why the two kinds of virtue cannot be absolutely and always the same.

But will there then be no case in which the virtue of the good citizen and the virtue of the good man coincide? To this we answer [not that the good citizen, but] that the good ruler is a good and wise man, and that he who would be a statesman must be a wise man. And some persons say that even the education of the ruler should be of a special kind; for are not the children of kings instructed in riding and military exercises? As Euripides says:

> "No subtle arts for me, but what the state requires."[1]

1 Fragment from the Aeolus, quoted in Stobaeus, 45. 13.

As though there were a special education needed by a ruler. If then the virtue of a good ruler is the same as that of a good man, and we assume further that the subject is a citizen as well as the ruler, the virtue of the good citizen and the virtue of the good man cannot be always the same, although in some cases [i.e. in the perfect state] they may; for the virtue of a ruler differs from that of a citizen. It was the sense of this difference which made Jason say that 'he felt hungry when he was not a tyrant,' meaning that he could not endure to live in a private station. But, on the other hand, it may be argued that men are praised for knowing both how to rule and how to obey, and he is said to be a citizen of approved virtue who is able to do both. Now if we suppose the virtue of a good man to be that which rules, and the virtue of the citizen to include ruling and obeying, it cannot be said that they are equally worthy of praise. Since, then, it is occasionally held that the ruler and the ruled learn different things and not the same things, and that the citizen must know and share in both; the inference is obvious.[1] There is, indeed, the rule of a master, which is concerned with menial offices,[2]—the master need not know how to perform these, but may employ others in the execution of them: anything else would be degrading; and by anything else I mean the menial duties, which vary much in character and are executed by various classes of slaves, such, for example, as handicraftsmen, who, as their name signifies, live by the labor of their hands:—under these the mechanic is included. Hence in ancient times, and among some nations, the working classes had no share in the government—a privilege which they only acquired under the extreme democracy. Certainly the good man and the statesman and the good citizen ought not to learn the crafts

1 Viz. that some kind of previous subjection is an advantage to the ruler. Cp. Infra, § 14.

2 Cp. i. 7. §§ 2-5.

of inferiors except for their own occasional use;[1] if they habitually practise them, there will cease to be a distinction between master and slave.

This is not the rule of which we are speaking; but there is a rule of another kind, which is exercised over freemen and equals by birth—a constitutional rule, which the ruler must learn by obeying, as he would learn the duties of a general of cavalry or by being under the orders of a general of cavalry, or the duties of a general of infantry by being under the orders of a general of infantry, and by having had the command of a company or brigade. It has been well said that 'he who has never learned to obey cannot be a good commander.' The two are not the same, but the good citizen ought to be capable of both; he should know how to govern like a freeman, and how to obey like a freeman—these are the virtues of a citizen. And, although the temperance and justice of a ruler are distinct from those of a subject, the virtue of a good man will include both; for the good man, who is free and also a subject, will not have one virtue only, say justice, but he will have distinct kinds of virtue, the one qualifying him to rule, the other to obey, and differing as the temperance and courage of men and women differ.[2] For a man would be thought a coward if he had no more courage than a courageous woman, and a woman would be thought loquacious if she imposed no more restraint on her conversation than the good man; and indeed their part in the management of the household is different, for the duty of the one is to acquire, and of the other to preserve. Practical wisdom only is characteristic of the ruler:[3] it would seem that all other virtues must equally belong to ruler and subject. The virtue of the subject is certainly not wisdom, but only true opinion; he may be compared to the maker of the flute, while his master is like the flute-player or user of the flute.... [4]

---

1 Cp. viii. 2. §5.

2 Cp. ii 13. § 9.

3 Cp. Rep. Iv. 428.

4 Cp. Rep. X. 601. D, E.

III (7) . . . . Having determined these points, we have next to consider how many forms of government there are, and what they are; and in the first place what are the true forms, for when they are determined the perversions[1] of them will at once be apparent. The words constitution and government have the same meaning, and the government, which is the supreme authority in states, must be in the hands of one, or of a few, or of many. The true forms of government, therefore, are those in which the one, or the few, or the many, govern with a view to the common interest; but governments which rule with a view to the private interest, whether of the one, or of the few, or of the many, are perversions. For citizens, if they are truly citizens, ought to participate in the advantages of a state. Of forms of government in which one rules, we call that which regards the common interests, kingship or royalty; that in which more than one, but not many, rule, aristocracy [the rule of the best]; and it is so called, either because the rulers are the best men, or because they have at heart the best interests of the state and of the citizens. But when the citizens at large administer the state for the common interest, the government is called by the generic name—a constitution [Πολιτεία]. And there is a reason for this use of language. One man or a few may excel in virtue; but of virtue there are many kinds: and as the number increases it becomes more difficult for them to attain perfection in every kind, though they may in military virtue, for this is found in the masses. Hence, in a constitutional government the fighting-men have the supreme power, and those who possess arms are the citizens.

Of the above-mentioned forms, the perversions are as follows:—of royalty, tyranny; of aristocracy, oligarchy; of constitutional government, democracy. For tyranny is a kind of monarchy which has in view the interest of the monarch only; oligarchy has in view the interest of the wealthy; democracy, of the needy: none of them the common good of all. . . .

---

1 Cp. Eth. viii.10.

Book IV

IV (1). In all arts and sciences which embrace the whole of any subject, and are not restricted to a part only, it is the province of a single art or science to consider all that appertains to a single subject. For example, the art of gymnastic considers not only the suitableness of different modes of training to different bodies (2), but what sort is absolutely the best (1) (for the absolutely best must suit that which is by nature best and best furnished with the means of life), and also what common form of training is adapted to the great majority of men (4). And if a man does not desire the best habit of body or the greatest skill in gymnastics, which might be attained by him, still the trainer or the teacher of gymnastic should be able to impart any lower degree of either.[1] The same principle equally holds in medicine and ship-building, and the making of clothes, and in the arts generally.[2]

Hence it is obvious that government too is the subject of a single science, which has to consider what kind of government would be best and most in accordance with our aspirations, if there were no external impediment, and also what kind of government is adapted to particular states. For the best is often unattainable, and therefore the true legislator and statesman ought to be acquainted, not only with (1) that which is best in the abstract, but also with (2) that which is best relatively to circumstance. We should be able further to say how a state may be constituted under any given conditions (3); both how it is originally formed and, when formed, how it may be longest preserved; the supposed state being so far from the very best that it is unprovided even with the conditions necessary for the very best; neither is it the best under the circumstances, but of an inferior type.

---

1 Cp. ii. 6. § 16.

2 The numbers in this paragraph are made to correspond with the numbers in the next. (Davis)

He ought, moreover, to know (4) the form of government which is best suited to states in general; for political writers, although they have excellent ideas, are often unpractical. We should consider, not only what form of government is best, but also what is possible and what is easily attainable by all. There are some who would have none but the most perfect; for this many natural advantages are required. Others, again speak of a more attainable form, and, although they reject the constitution under which they are living, they extol some one in particular, for example the Lacedaemonian.[1] Any change of government which has to be introduced should be one which men will be both willing and able to adopt, since there is quite as much trouble in the reformation of an old constitution as in the establishment of a new one, just as to unlearn is as hard as to learn. And therefore, in addition to the qualifications of the statesman already mentioned, he should be able to find remedies for the defects of existing constitutions.[2] This he cannot do unless he knows how many forms of government there are. It is often supposed that there is only one kind of democracy and one of oligarchy. But this is a mistake; and, in order to avoid such mistakes, we must ascertain what differences there are in the constitutions of states, and in how many ways they are combined. The same political insight will enable a man to know which laws are the best, and which are suited to different constitutions; for the laws are, and ought to be, relative to the constitution, and not the constitution to the laws. A constitution is the organization of offices in a state, and determines what is to be the governing body, and what is the end of each community. But laws are not to be confounded with the principles of the constitution:[3] they

---

1 Cp. ii. 6. § 16.

2 Cp. § 4.

3 Or, 'laws, though in themselves distinct, show the character of the constitution.'

are the rules according to which the magistrates should administer the state, and proceed against offenders. So that we must know the number and varieties of the several forms of government, if only with a view to making laws. For the same laws cannot be equally suited to all oligarchies and to all democracies, and there is certainly more than one form both of democracy and of oligarchy.

IV (2). In our original discussion[1] about governments we divided them into three true forms: kingly rule, aristocracy, and constitutional government, and three corresponding perversions—tyranny, oligarchy, and democracy. Of kingly rule and of aristocracy we have already spoken, for the enquiry into the perfect state is the same thing with the discussion of the two forms thus named, since both imply a principle of virtue provided with external means. We have already determined in what aristocracy and kingly rule differ from one another, and when the latter should be established.[2] In what follows we have to describe the so-called constitutional government, which bears the common name of all constitutions, and the other forms, tyranny, oligarchy, and democracy.

It is obvious which of the three perversions is the worst, and which is the next in badness. That which is the perversion of the first and most divine is necessarily the worst. And just as a royal rule, if not a mere name, must exist by virtue of some great personal superiority in the king, so tyranny, which is the worst of governments, is necessarily the farthest removed from a well-constituted form; oligarchy is little better, but a long way from aristocracy, and democracy is the most tolerable of the three.

A writer[3] who preceded me has already made these distinctions, but his point of view is not the same as mine. For

---

1 Book iii. 7; N. Eth. viii 10.

2 Cp. iii. 17. § 8.

3 Plato, Polit. 303 A.

he lays down the principle that when all good constitutions (under which he would include a virtuous oligarchy and the like) democracy is the worst, but the best of bad ones. Whereas we maintain that they are all defective, and that one oligarchy is not to be accounted better than another, but only less bad. . . .

VI (8) . . . . I have yet to speak of the so-called polity and of tyranny. I put them in this order, not because a polity or constitutional government is to be regarded as a perversion any more than the above-mentioned aristocracies. The truth is, that they all fall short of the most perfect form of government, and so they are reckoned among perversions, and other forms (*sc.* the really perverted forms) are perversions of these, as I said before.[1] Last of all I will speak of tyranny, which I place last in the series because I am inquiring into the constitutions of states, and this is the very reverse of a constitution.

Having explained why I have adopted this order, I will proceed to consider constitutional government; of which the nature will be clearer now that oligarchy and democracy have been defined. For polity or constitutional government may be described generally as a fusion of oligarchy and democracy; but the term is usually applied to those forms of government which incline towards democracy, and the term aristocracy to those which incline towards oligarchy, because birth and education are commonly the accompaniments of wealth. Moreover, the rich already possess the external advantages the want of which is a temptation to crime, and hence they are called noblemen and gentlemen. And inasmuch as aristocracy seeks to give predominance to the best of the citizens, people say also of oligarchies that they are composed of noblemen and gentlemen. Now it appears to be an impossible thing that the state which is governed by the best citizens should be ill-governed,[2] and equally impossible that the state which is ill-

1 Cp. iii. 7.

2 Omitting *ἀλλὰ πονηροκρατομένην.*

governed should be governed by the best. But we must remember that good laws, if they are not obeyed, do not constitute good government. For there are two parts of good government; one is the actual obedience of citizens to the laws, the other part is the goodness of the laws which they obey; they may obey bad laws as well as good. And there may be a further subdivision; they may obey either the best laws which are attainable to them, or the best absolutely.

The distribution of offices according to merit is a special characteristic of aristocracy, for the principle of an aristocracy is virtue, as wealth is of an oligarchy, and freedom of a democracy. In all of them there of course exists the right of the majority, and whatever seems good to the majority of those who share in the government has authority. Generally, however, a state of this kind is called a constitutional government [not an aristocracy], for the fusion goes no further than the attempt to unite the freedom of the poor and the wealth of the rich, who commonly take the place of the noble. And as there are three grounds on which men claim an equal share in the government—freedom, wealth, and virtue (for the fourth or good birth is the result of the two last, being only ancient wealth and virtue)—it is clear that the admixture of the two elements, that is to say, of the rich and poor, is to be called a polity or constitutional government; and the union of the three is to be called aristocracy or the government of the best, and more than any other form of government, except the true and ideal, has a right to this name.

Thus far I have shown the different forms of states which exist besides monarchy, democracy, and oligarchy, and what they are, and in what aristocracies differ from one another, and polities from aristocracies—that the two latter are not very unlike is obvious.

IV (9). Next we have to consider how by the side of oligarchy and democracy the so-called polity or constitutional government springs up, and how it should be organized. The nature of it will be at once understood from a comparison of oligarchy and democracy; we must ascertain their different characteristics, and taking a portion from each, put the two together, like the parts of an indenture. Now there are three modes in which fusions of government may be effected. The nature of the fusion will be made intelligible by an example of the manner in which different governments legislate, say concerning the administration of justice. In oligarchies they impose a fine on the rich if they do not serve as judges, and to the poor they give no pay; but in democracies they give pay to the poor and do not fine the rich. Now (1) the union of these two modes[1] is a common or middle term between them, and is therefore characteristic of a constitutional government, for it is a combination of both. This is one mode of uniting the two elements. Or (2) a mean may be taken between the enactments of the two: thus democracies require no property qualification, or only a small one, from members of the assembly, oligarchies a high one; here neither of these is the common term, but a mean between them. (3) There is a third mode, in which something is borrowed from the oligarchical and something from the democratical principle. For example, the appointment of magistrates by lot is democratical, and the election of them oligarchical; democratical again when there is no property qualification, oligarchical when there is. In the aristocratical or constitutional state, one element will be taken from each—from oligarchy the mode of electing to offices, from democracy the disregard of qualification. Such are the various modes of combination. . . .

IV (10). Of the nature of tyranny I have still to speak, in order that it may have its place in our enquiry, since even tyranny is reckoned by us to be a form of government, although

[1] Cp. c. 13. § 6.

there is not much to be said about it. I have already in the former part of this treatise[1] discussed royalty or kingship according to the most usual meaning of the term, and considered whether it is or is not advantageous to states, and what kind of royalty should be established, and whence, and how it arises.

When speaking of royalty we also spoke of two forms of tyranny, which are both according to law, and therefore easily pass into royalty. Among Barbarians there are elected monarchs who exercise a despotic power; despotic rulers were also elected in ancient Hellas, called Aesymnetes or dictators. These monarchies, when compared with one another, exhibit certain differences. And they are, as I said before, royal, in so far as the monarch rules according to law and over willing subjects; but they are tyrannical in so far as he is despotic and rules according to his own fancy. There is also a third kind of tyranny, which is the most typical form, and is the counterpart of the perfect monarchy. This tyranny is just that arbitrary power of an individual which is responsible to no one, and governs all alike, whether equals or betters, with a view to its own advantage, not to that of its subjects, and therefore against their will. No freeman, if he can escape from it, will endure such a government.

The kinds of tyranny are such and so many, and for the reasons which I have given.

IV (11). We have now to inquire what is the best constitution for most states, and the best life for most men, neither assuming a standard of virtue which is above ordinary persons, nor an education which is exceptionally favoured by nature and circumstances, nor yet an ideal state which is an aspiration only, but having regard to the life in which the majority are able to share, and to the form of government which states in general can attain. As to those aristocracies,

---

1 iii. 14-17.

as they are called, of which we were just now speaking, they either lie beyond the possibilities of the greater number of states, or they approximate to the so-called constitutional government, and therefore need no separate discussion. And in fact the conclusion at which we arrive respecting all these forms rests upon the same grounds. For if it has been truly said in the *Ethics*[1] that the happy life is the life according to unimpeded virtue, and that virtue is a mean, then the life which is in a mean, and in a mean attainable by every one, must be the best. And the same criteria of virtue and vice apply both to cities and to constitutions; for the constitution is in a figure the life of the city.[2]

Now in all states there are three elements; one class is very rich, another very poor, and a third in a mean. It is admitted that moderation and the mean are best, and therefore it will clearly be best to possess the gifts of fortune in moderation; for in that condition of life men are most ready to listen to reason. But he who greatly excels in beauty, strength, birth or wealth, or on the other hand who is very poor, or very weak, or very much disgraced, finds it difficult to follow reason.[3] Of these two the one sort grow into violent and great criminals, the others into rogues and petty rascals. And two sorts of offences correspond to them,[4] the one committed from violence, the other from roguery. The petty rogues are disinclined to hold office, whether military or civil, and their aversion to these two duties is as great an injury to the state as the tendency to crime. Again, those who have too much of the goods of fortune, strength, wealth, friends, and the like, are neither willing nor able to submit to authority. The evil begins at home: for when they are boys, by reason of the luxury in which they are brought up,

---

1 N. Eth. vii 13.§ 2.

2 Cp. iii. 3. §§ 7,8.

3 Cp. Pl. Rep. Iv. 421 C, D ff.

4 Laws, viii. 831 E.

they never learn, even at school, the habit of obedience. On the other hand, the very poor, who are in the opposite extreme, are too degraded. So that the one class cannot obey, and can only rule despotically; the other knows not how to command and must be ruled like slaves. Thus arises a city, not of freemen, but of masters and slaves, the one despising, the other envying; and nothing can be more fatal to friendship and good fellowship in states than this: for good fellowship tends to friendship; when men are at enmity with one another, they would rather not even share the same path. But a city ought to be composed, as far as possible, of equals and similars; and these are generally the middle classes. Wherefore the city which is composed of middle-class citizens is necessarily best governed; they are, as we say, the natural elements of a state. And this is the class of citizens which is most secure in a state, for they do not, like the poor, covet their neighbours' goods; nor do others covet theirs, as the poor covet the goods of the rich; and as they neither plot against others, nor are themselves plotted against, they pass through life safely. Wisely then did Phocylides pray—

> 'Many things are best in the mean; I desire
> to be of a middle condition in my city.'

Thus it is manifest that the best political community is formed by citizens of the middle class, and that those states are likely to be well-administered, in which the middle class is large, and larger if possible than both the other classes, or at any rate than either singly; for the addition of the middle class turns the scale, and prevents either of the extremes from being dominant. Great then is the good fortune of a state in which the citizens have a moderate and sufficient property; for where some possess much, and the others nothing, there may arise an extreme democracy, or a pure oligarchy; or a tyranny may grow out of either extreme—either out of the most rampant democracy, or out of an oligarchy; but it is not so likely to arise out of the middle and nearly equal condition. I will explain the reason of this hereafter, when I speak of the revolutions of states.[1] The mean condition of states is clearly best, for no other is free from faction; and where the middle class is large, there are least likely to be factions and dissensions. For a similar reason large states are less liable to faction than small ones, because in them the middle class is large; whereas in small states it is easy to divide all the citizens into two classes who are either rich or poor, and to leave nothing in the middle. And democracies are safer[2] and more permanent than oligarchies, because they have a middle class which is more numerous and has a greater share in the government; for when there is no middle class, and the poor greatly exceed in number, troubles arise, and the state soon comes to an end. A proof of the superiority of the middle class is that the best legislators have been of a middle condition; for example, Solon, as his own verses testify; and Lycurgus, for he was not a king; and Charondas, and almost all legislators.

These considerations will help us to understand why most governments are either democratical or oligarchical. The reason is that the middle class is seldom numerous in them, and whichever party, whether the rich or the common people, transgresses the mean and predominates, draws the government to itself, and thus arises either oligarchy or democracy. There is another reason—the poor and the rich quarrel with another, and whichever side gets the better, instead of establishing a just or popular government, regards political supremacy as the prize of victory, and the one party sets up a democracy and the other an oligarchy. Both the parties which had the supremacy in Hellas looked only to the interest of their own form of government, and established in states, the one, democracies, and the other, oligarchies; they thought

1 Cp. Bk. v.

2 Cp. v. I. § 15; 7. § 6.

of their own advantage, of the public not at all. For these reasons the middle form of government has rarely if ever, existed, and among a very few only. One man alone of all who ever ruled in Hellas was induced to give this middle constitution to states. But it has now become a habit among the citizens of the states, not even to care about equality; all men are seeking for dominion, or, if conquered, are willing to submit.

What then is the best form of government, and what makes it the best, is evident; and of other states, since we say that there are many kinds of democracy and many of oligarchy, it is not difficult to see which has the first and which the second or any other place in the order of excellence, now that we have determined which is the best. For that which is nearest to the best must of necessity be better, and that which is furthest from it worse, if we are judging absolutely and not relatively to given conditions: I say 'relatively to given conditions,' since a particular government may be preferable for some, but another form may be better for others. . . .

Book VII

VII (1). He who would duly inquire about the best form of a state ought first to determine which is the most eligible life; while this remains uncertain the best form of the state must also be uncertain; for, in the natural order of things, those may be expected to lead the best life who are governed in the best manner of which their circumstances admit. We ought therefore to ascertain, first of all, which is the most generally eligible life, and then whether the same life is or is not best for the state and for individuals.

Assuming that enough has been already said in exoteric discourses outside the school concerning the best life, we will now only repeat the statements contained in them. Certainly no one will dispute the propriety of that partition of goods which separates them into three classes,[1] viz.,

[1] Cp. N. Eth. i. 8. § 2.

external goods, goods of the body, and goods of the soul, or deny that the happy man must have all three. For no one would maintain that he is happy who has not in him a particle of courage or temperance or justice or prudence, who is afraid of every insect which flutters past him, and will commit any crime, however great, in order to gratify his lust of meat or drink, who will sacrifice his dearest friend for the sake of half a farthing, and is as feeble and false in mind as a child or a madman. These propositions are almost universally acknowledged as soon as they are uttered,[1] but men differ about the quality which is desirable or the relative superiority of this or that good. Some think that a very moderate amount of virtue is enough, but set no limit to their desires of wealth, property, power, reputation, and the like. To whom we reply by an appeal to facts, which easily prove that mankind do not acquire or preserve virtue by the help of external goods, but external goods by the help of virtue, and that happiness, whether consisting in pleasure or virtue, or both, is more often found with those who are most highly cultivated in their mind and in their character, and have only a moderate share of external goods, than among those who possess external goods to a useless extent but are deficient in higher qualities; and this is not only matter of experience, but, if reflected upon, will easily appear to be in accordance with reason. For, whereas external goods have a limit, like any other instrument,[2] and all things useful are of such a nature that where there is too much of them they must either do harm, or at any rate be of no use, to their possessors, every good of the soul, the greater it is, is also of greater use, if the epithet 'useful' as well as 'noble' is appropriate to such subjects. No proof is required to show that the best state of one thing in relation to another is proportioned to the degree of excellence by which the natures corresponding to these states

---

1 Omitting ὥσπερ, which is bracketed by Bekker in his second edition. (Davis)

2 Cp. i. 8. § 15.

are separated from each other: so that, if the soul is more noble than our possessions or our bodies, both absolutely and in relation to us, it must be admitted that the best state of either has a similar ratio to the other. Again, it is for the sake of the soul that goods external and goods of the body are eligible at all, and all wise men ought to choose them for the sake of the soul, and not the soul for the sake of them.

Let us acknowledge then that each one has just so much of happiness as he has of virtue and wisdom, and of virtuous and wise action. God is a witness to us of this truth;[1] for he is happy and blessed, not by reason of any external good, but in himself and by reason of his own nature. And herein of necessity lies the difference between good fortune and happiness; for external goods come of themselves, and chance is the author of them, but no one is just or temperate by or through chance.[2] In like manner, and by a similar train of argument, the happy state may be shown to be that which is [morally] best and which acts rightly; and rightly it cannot act without doing right actions, and neither individual nor state can do right actions without virtue and wisdom. Thus the courage, justice, and wisdom of a state have the same form and nature as the qualities which give the individual who possesses them the name of just, wise, or temperate.

Thus much may suffice by way of preface: for I could not avoid touching upon these questions, neither could I go through all the arguments affecting them; these must be reserved for another discussion.

Let us assume then that the best life, both for individuals and states, is the life of virtue, when virtue has external goods enough for the performance of good actions. If there are any who controvert our assertion, we will in this treatise pass them over, and consider their objections hereafter.

---

1 Cp. c. 3. §. 10; N. Eth. x. 8. § 7; Met. xii. 7.

2 Ethics i. 9. § 6.

VII (2). There remains to be discussed the question, Whether the happiness of the individual is the same as that of the state, or different? Here again there can be no doubt—no one denies that they are the same. For those who hold that the well-being of the individual consists in his wealth, also think that riches make the happiness of the whole state, and those who value most highly the life of a tyrant deem that city the happiest which rules over the greatest number; while they who approve an individual for his virtue say that the more virtuous a city is, the happier it is. Two points here present themselves for consideration: first (1), which is the more eligible life, that of a citizen who is a member of a state, or that of an alien who has no political ties; and again (2), which is the best form of constitution or the best condition of a state, either on the supposition that political privileges are given to all, or that they are given to a majority only? Since the good of the state and not of the individual is the proper subject of political thought and speculation, and we are engaged in a political discussion, while the first of these two points has a secondary interest for us, the latter will be the main subject of our inquiry.

Now it is evident that the form of government is best in which every man, whoever he is, can act best and live happily. . . .

John Locke

1632-1704

TWO TREATISES OF GOVERNMENT

1689

Locke argued that majority rule, exercised through an elected legislature, was the only legitimate government. If, as is presented in this volume's earlier excerpt from Locke, people in the state of nature are free, equal, and want to protect their rights, then no government can legitimately be based on any presumption that some people have to obey others, such as kings and nobles, who claim (falsely) to possess legitimate inherited power. Government must be understood to be based on the agreement that we submit to being governed only to protect our rights.

Selections from: Locke, John. 1689. *Two Treatises of Government.* In *Two Treatises on Civil Government by John Locke.* Ed. Henry Morley. Second Edition. London: George Routledge and Sons. 1887.

Book II

Chapter VIII: Of the Beginning of Political Societies (excerpted 240-242)

Chapter X: Of the Forms of a Commonwealth (excerpted 259-260)

Chapter XI: Of the Extent of the Legislative Power (excerpted 263-267)

Book II

Chapter VIII

OF THE BEGINNING OF POLITICAL SOCIETIES

95. MEN being, as has been said, by nature all free, equal, and independent, no one can be put out of this estate and subjected to the political power of another without his own consent, which is done by agreeing with other men, to join and unite into a community for their comfortable, safe, and peaceable living, one amongst another, in a secure enjoyment of their properties, and a greater security against any that are not of it. This any number of men may do, because it injures not the freedom of the rest; they are left, as they were, in the liberty of the state of Nature. When any number of men have so consented to make one community or government, they are thereby presently incorporated, and make one body politic, wherein the majority have a right to act and conclude the rest.

96. For, when any number of men have, by the consent of every individual, made a community, they have thereby made that community one body, with a power to act as one body, which is only by the will and determination of the majority. For that which acts any community, being only the consent of the individuals of it, and it being one body, must move one way, it is necessary the body should move that way whither the greater force carries it, which is the consent of the majority, or else it is impossible it should act or continue one body, one community, which the consent of every individual that united into it agreed that it should; and so every one is

bound by that consent to be concluded by the majority. And therefore we see that in assemblies empowered to act by positive laws where no number is set by that positive law which empowers them, the act of the majority passes for the act of the whole, and of course determines as having, by the law of Nature and reason, the power of the whole.

97. And thus every man, by consenting with others to make one body politic under one government, puts himself under an obligation to every one of that society to submit to the determination of the majority, and to be concluded by it; or else this original compact, whereby he with others incorporates into one society, would signify nothing, and be no compact if he be left free and under no other ties than he was in before in the state of Nature. For what appearance would there be of any compact? What new engagement if he were no further tied by any decrees of the society than he himself thought fit and did actually consent to? This would be still as great a liberty as he himself had before his compact, or any one else in the state of Nature, who may submit himself and consent to any acts of it if he thinks fit.

98. For if the consent of the majority shall not in reason be received as the act of the whole, and conclude every individual; nothing but the consent of every individual can make anything to be the act of the whole, which, considering the infirmities of health and avocations of business, which in a number though much less than that of a commonwealth, will necessarily keep many away from the public assembly; and the variety of opinions and contrariety of interests which unavoidably happen in all collections of men, it is next to impossible ever to be had. And, therefore, if coming into society be upon such terms, it will be only like Cato's coming into the theatre, *tantum ut exiret*. Such a constitution as

this would make the mighty leviathan of a shorter duration than the feeblest creatures, and not let it outlast the day it was born in, which cannot be supposed till we can think that rational creatures should desire and constitute societies only to be dissolved. For where the majority cannot conclude the rest, there they cannot act as one body, and consequently will be immediately dissolved again.

99. Whosoever, therefore, out of a state of Nature unite into a community, must be understood to give up all the power necessary to the ends for which they unite into society to the majority of the community, unless they expressly agreed in any number greater than the majority. And this is done by barely agreeing to unite into one political society, which is all the compact that is, or needs be, between the individuals that enter into or make up a commonwealth. And thus, that which begins and actually constitutes any political society is nothing but the consent of any number of freemen capable of a majority, to unite and incorporate into such a society. And this is that, and that only, which did or could give beginning to any lawful government in the world.

Chapter X

OF THE FORMS OF A COMMONWEALTH.

132. The majority having, as has been showed, upon men's first uniting into society, the whole power of the community naturally in them, may employ all that power in making laws for the community from time to time, and executing those laws by officers of their own appointing, and then the form of the government is a perfect democracy; or else may put the power of

making laws into the hands of a few select men, and their heirs or successors, and then it is an oligarchy; or else into the hands of one man, and then it is a monarchy; if to him and his heirs, it is a hereditary monarchy; if to him only for life, but upon his death the power only of nominating a successor, to return to them, an elective monarchy. And so accordingly of these make compounded and mixed forms of government, as they think good. And if the legislative power be at first given by the majority to one or more persons only for their lives, or any limited time, and then the supreme power to revert to them again, when it is so reverted the community may dispose of it again anew into what hands they please, and so constitute a new form of government; for the form of government depending upon the placing the supreme power, which is the legislative, it being impossible to conceive that an inferior power should prescribe to a superior, or any but the supreme make laws, according as the power of making laws is placed, such is the form of the commonwealth.

133. By "commonwealth" I must be understood all along to mean not a democracy, or any form of government, but any independent community which the Latins signified by the word *civitas,* to which the word which best answers in our language is "commonwealth," and most properly expresses such a society of men which "community" does not (for there may be subordinate communities in a government), and "city" much less. And therefore, to avoid ambiguity, I crave leave to use the word "commonwealth" in that sense, in which sense I find the word used by King James himself, which I think to be its genuine signification, which, if anybody dislike, I consent with him to change it for a better.

Chapter XI

OF THE EXTENT OF THE LEGISLATIVE POWER.

137. Absolute arbitrary power, or governing without settled standing laws, can neither of them consist with the ends of society and government, which men would not quit the freedom of the state of Nature for, and tie themselves up under were it not to preserve their lives, liberties, and fortunes; and by stated rules of right and property to secure their peace and quiet. It cannot be supposed that they should intend, had they a power so to do, to give to any one or more an absolute arbitrary power over their persons and estates, and put a force into the magistrate's hand to execute his unlimited will arbitrarily upon them; this were to put themselves into a worse condition than the state of Nature, wherein they had a liberty to defend their right against the injuries of others, and were upon equal terms of force to maintain it, whether invaded by a single man or many in combination. Whereas by supposing they have given up themselves to the absolute arbitrary power and will of a legislator, they have disarmed themselves, and armed him to make prey of them when he pleases; he being in a much worse condition that is exposed to the arbitrary power of one man who has the command of one hundred thousand than he that is exposed to the arbitrary power of one hundred thousand single men, nobody being secure, that his will who has such a command is better than that of other men, though his force be a hundred thousand times stronger. And, therefore, whatever form the commonwealth is under, the ruling power ought to govern by declared and received laws, and not by extemporary dictates and undetermined resolutions; for then mankind will be

in a far worse condition than in the state of Nature if they shall have armed one or a few men with the joint power of a multitude, to force them to obey at pleasure the exorbitant and unlimited decrees of their sudden thoughts, or unrestrained, and till that moment, unknown wills, without having any measures set down which may guide and justify their actions. For all the power the government has, being only for the good of the society, as it ought not to be arbitrary and at pleasure, so it ought to be exercised by established and promulgated laws, that both the people may know their duty, and be safe and secure within the limits of the law, and the rulers, too, kept within their due bounds, and not be tempted by the power they have in their hands to employ it to purposes, and by such measures as they would not have known, and own not willingly.

138. Thirdly, the supreme power cannot take from any man any part of his property without his own consent. For the preservation of property being the end of government, and that for which men enter into society, it necessarily supposes and requires that the people should have property, without which they must be supposed to lose that by entering into society, which was the end for which they entered into it; too gross an absurdity for any man to own. Men, therefore, in society having property, they have such a right to the goods, which by the law of the community are theirs, that nobody hath a right to take them, or any part of them, from them without their own consent; without this they have no property at all. For I have truly no property in that which another can by right take from me when he pleases against my consent. Hence it is a mistake to think that the supreme or legislative power of any commonwealth can do what it will, and dispose of the estates of the subjects arbitrarily, or take any part of

them at pleasure. This is not much to be feared in governments where the legislative consists, wholly or in part in assemblies which are variable, whose members upon the dissolution of the assembly are subjects under the common laws of their country, equally with the rest. But in governments where the legislative is in one lasting assembly, always in being or in one man as in absolute monarchies, there is danger still, that they will think themselves to have a distinct interest from the rest of the community, and so will be apt to increase their own riches and power by taking what they think fit from the people. For a man's property is not at all secure, though there be good and equitable laws to set the bounds of it between him and his fellow-subjects, if he who commands those subjects have power to take from any private man what part he pleases of his property, and use and dispose of it as he thinks good.

139. But government into whosesoever hands it is put, being as I have before showed, entrusted with this condition, and for this end, that men might have and secure their properties, the prince or senate, however it may have power to make laws for the regulating of property between the subjects one amongst another, yet can never have a power to take to themselves the whole, or any part of the subjects' property, without their own consent; for this would be in effect to leave them no property at all. And to let us see that even absolute power, where it is necessary, is not arbitrary by being absolute, but is still limited by that reason, and confined to those ends which required it in some cases to be absolute, we need look no farther than the common practice of martial discipline. For the preservation of the army, and in it the whole commonwealth, requires an absolute obedience to the command of every superior officer, and it is justly death to disobey or

dispute the most dangerous or unreasonable of them; but yet we see that neither the serjeant that could command a soldier to march up to the mouth of a cannon, or stand in a breach where he is almost sure to perish, can command that soldier to give him one penny of his money; nor the general that can condemn him to death for deserting his post, or not obeying the most desperate orders, cannot yet with all his absolute power of life and death dispose of one farthing of that soldier's estate, or seize one jot of his goods; whom yet he can command anything, and hang for the least disobedience. Because such a blind obedience is necessary to that end for which the commander has his power—viz., the preservation of the rest, but the disposing of his goods has nothing to do with it.

140. It is true governments cannot be supported without great charge, and it is fit every one who enjoys a share of the protection should pay out of his estate his proportion for the maintenance of it. But still it must be with his own consent—*i.e.*, the consent of the majority, giving it either by themselves or their representatives chosen by them; for if any one shall claim a power to lay and levy taxes on the people by his own authority, and without such consent of the people, he thereby invades the fundamental law of property, and subverts the end of government. For what property have I in that which another may by right take when he pleases to himself?

141. Fourthly. The legislative cannot transfer the power of making laws to any other hands, for it being but a delegated power from the people, they who have it cannot pass it over to others. The people alone can appoint the form of the commonwealth, which is by constituting the legislative, and appointing in whose hands that shall be. And when the people have said,

"We will submit, and be governed by laws made by such men, and in such forms," nobody else can say other men shall make laws for them; nor can they be bound by any laws but such as are enacted by those whom they have chosen and authorized to make laws for them.

142. These are the bounds which the trust that is put in them by the society and the law of God and Nature have set to the legislative power of every commonwealth, in all forms of government. First: They are to govern by promulgated established laws, not to be varied in particular cases, but to have one rule for rich and poor, for the favourite at Court, and the countryman at plough. Secondly: These laws also ought to be designed for no other end ultimately but the good of the people. Thirdly: They must not raise taxes on the property of the people without the consent of the people given by themselves or their deputies. And this properly concerns only such governments where the legislative is always in being, or at least where the people have not reserved any part of the legislative to deputies, to be from time to time chosen by themselves. Fourthly: Legislative neither must nor can transfer the power of making laws to anybody else, or place it anywhere but where the people have.

JAMES MADISON

1751-1836

THE FEDERALIST PAPERS

1787-1788

After the Constitutional Convention of 1787 completed its work by proposing a constitution, the next step required ratification by the states for the proposal to become the legally enforceable *Constitution of the United States.* As a practical matter, this required the states to agree to something that would diminish their powers. Some states agreed readily, but the larger states were slower to ratify. New York, Virginia, and Massachusetts had powerful political factions that did not want the federal government to be so powerful. New York was the most reluctant. A letters-to-the-editor campaign conducted in New York city newspapers have given us a contemporary, authoritative account of the arguments in favor of the *Constitution.* They are now commonly referred to as *The Federalist Papers.* Following the practice of that time of allowing prominent people to use pen names, the letters were all signed "Publius" when they first appeared. It was no secret that the authors were James Madison (1751-1836), Alexander Hamilton (1755-1804), and John Jay (1745-1829). The numbers presented here were written principally by Madison and explain how the proposed system of divided and dispersed authority could both provide for effective rule and still not encroach on the freedoms of American citizens. Note the political realism of Madison. He does not appeal to idealism. Instead, he makes constant reference to the tendency of politics to be driven by self-interest and political ambition and the need for any constitution to be based on human nature as it is, not as we might wish it to be

Selections from: Madison, James. 1787-88. *The Federalist.* Papers 10, 47, 51. In Sherman F. Mittell, Ed. *The Federalist.* From the Original Text of Alexander Hamilton, John Jay, and James Madison, Sesquicentennial Edition. Washington DC: National Home Library Foundation. 1988.

The Federalist no. 10 (53-62)
The Federalist no. 47 (312-320)
The Federalist no. 51 (335-341)

From the New York Packet, Friday, November 23, 1787

THE FEDERALIST NO. 10

TO THE PEOPLE OF THE STATE OF NEW YORK:

Among the numerous advantages promised by a well-constructed Union, none deserves to be more accurately developed than its tendency to break and control the violence of faction. The friend of popular governments never finds himself so much alarmed for their character and fate, as when he contemplates their propensity to this dangerous vice. He will not fail, therefore, to set a due value on any plan which, without violating the principles to which he is attached, provides a proper cure for it. The instability, injustice, and confusion introduced into the public councils, have, in truth, been the mortal diseases under which popular governments have everywhere perished; as they continue to be the favorite and fruitful topics from which the adversaries to liberty derive their most specious declamations. The valuable improvements made by the American constitutions on the popular models, both ancient and modern, cannot certainly be too much admired; but it would be an unwarrantable partiality, to contend that they have as effectually obviated the danger on this side, as was wished and expected. Complaints are everywhere heard from our most considerate and virtuous citizens, equally the friends of public and private faith, and of public and personal liberty, that our governments are too unstable, that the public good is disregarded in the conflicts of rival parties, and that measures are too often decided, not according to the rules of justice and the rights of the minor party, but by the superior force of an interested and overbearing majority. However anxiously we may wish that these complaints had no foundation, the evidence of known facts will not permit us to deny that they are in some degree true. It will be found, indeed, on a candid review of our situation, that some of the distresses under which we labor have been erroneously charged on the operation of our governments; but it will be found, at the same time, that other causes will not alone account for many of our heaviest misfortunes; and, particularly, for that prevailing and increasing distrust of public engagements, and alarm for private rights, which are echoed from one end of the continent to the other. These must be chiefly, if not wholly, effects of the unsteadiness and injustice with which a factious spirit has tainted our public administrations.

By a faction, I understand a number of citizens, whether amounting to a majority or minority of the whole, who are united and actuated by some common impulse of passion, or of interest, adverse to the rights of other citizens, or to the permanent and aggregate interests of the community.

There are two methods of curing the mischiefs of faction: the one, by removing its causes; the other, by controlling its effects.

There are again two methods of removing the causes of faction: the one, by destroying the liberty which is essential to its existence; the other, by giving to every citizen the same opinions, the same passions, and the same interests.

It could never be more truly said than of the first remedy, that it was worse than the disease. Liberty is to faction what air is to fire, an aliment without which it instantly expires. But it could not be less folly to abolish liberty, which is essential to political life, because it nourishes faction, than it would be to wish the annihilation of air, which is essential to animal life, because it imparts to fire its destructive agency.

The second expedient is as impracticable as the first would be unwise. As long as the reason of man continues fallible, and he is at liberty to exercise it, different opinions will be formed. As long as the connection subsists between his reason and his self-love, his opinions and his passions will have a reciprocal influence on each other; and the former will be objects to which the latter will attach themselves. The diversity in the faculties of men, from which the rights of property originate, is not less an insuperable obstacle to a uniformity of interests. The protection of these faculties is the first object of government. From the protection of different and unequal faculties of acquiring property, the possession of different degrees and kinds of property immediately results; and from the influence of these on the sentiments and views of the respective proprietors, ensues a division of the society into different interests and parties.

The latent causes of faction are thus sown in the nature of man; and we see them everywhere brought into different degrees of activity, according to the different circumstances of civil society. A zeal for different opinions concerning religion, concerning government, and many other points, as well of speculation as of practice; an attachment to different leaders ambitiously contending for pre-eminence and power; or to persons of other descriptions whose fortunes have been interesting to the human passions, have, in turn, divided mankind into parties, inflamed them with mutual animosity, and rendered them much more disposed to vex and oppress each other than to co-operate for their common good. So strong is this propensity of mankind to fall into mutual animosities, that where no substantial occasion presents itself, the most frivolous and fanciful distinctions have been sufficient to kindle their unfriendly passions and excite their most violent conflicts. But the most common and durable source of factions has been the various and unequal distribution of property. Those who hold and those who are without property have ever formed distinct interests in society. Those who are creditors, and those who are debtors, fall under a like discrimination. A landed interest, a manufacturing interest, a mercantile interest, a moneyed interest, with many lesser interests, grow up of necessity in civilized nations, and divide them into different classes actuated by different sentiments and views. The regulation of these various and interfering interests forms the principal task of modern legislation, and involves the spirit of party and faction in the necessary and ordinary operations of the government.

No man is allowed to be a judge in his own cause, because his interest would certainly bias his judgment, and, not improbably, corrupt his integrity. With equal, nay with greater reason, a body of men are unfit to be both judges and parties at the same time; yet what are many of thc most important acts of legislation, but so many judicial determinations, not indeed concerning the rights of single persons, but concerning the rights of large bodies of citizens? And what are the different classes of legislators but advocates and parties to the causes which they determine? Is a law proposed concerning private debts? It is a question to which the creditors are parties on one side and the debtors on the other. Justice ought to hold the balance between them. Yet the parties are, and must be, themselves the judges; and the most numerous party, or, in other words, the most powerful faction must be expected to prevail. Shall domestic manufactures be encouraged, and in what degree, by restrictions on foreign manufactures? are questions which would be differently decided by the landed and the manufacturing classes, and probably by neither with a sole regard to justice and the public good. The apportionment of taxes on the various descriptions of property is an act which seems to require the most exact impartiality; yet there is, perhaps, no legislative act in which greater opportunity and temptation are given to a predominant party to trample on the rules of justice. Every shilling with which they overburden the inferior number, is a shilling saved to their own pockets.

It is in vain to say that enlightened statesmen will be able to adjust these clashing interests, and render them all subservient to the public good. Enlightened statesmen will not always be at the helm. Nor, in many cases, can such an adjustment be made at all without taking into view indirect and remote considerations, which will rarely prevail over the immediate interest which one party may find in disregarding the rights of another or the good of the whole.

The inference to which we are brought is, that the *causes* of faction cannot be removed, and that relief is only to be sought in the means of controlling its *effects.*

If a faction consists of less than a majority, relief is supplied by the republican principle, which enables the majority to defeat its sinister views by regular vote. It may clog the administration, it may convulse the society; but it will be unable to execute and mask its violence under the forms of the Constitution. When a majority is included in a faction, the form of popular government, on the other hand, enables it to sacrifice to its ruling passion or interest both the public good and the rights of other citizens. To secure the public good and private rights against the danger of such a faction, and at the same time to preserve the spirit and the form of popular government, is then the great object to which our inquiries are directed. Let me add that it is the great desideratum by which this form of government can be rescued from the opprobrium under which it has so long labored, and be recommended to the esteem and adoption of mankind.

By what means is this object attainable? Evidently by one of two only. Either the existence of the same passion or interest in a majority at the same time must be prevented, or the majority, having such coexistent passion or interest, must be rendered, by their number and local situation, unable to concert and carry into effect schemes of oppression. If the impulse and the opportunity be suffered to coincide, we well know that neither moral nor religious motives can be relied on as an adequate control. They are not found to be such on the injustice and violence of individuals, and lose their efficacy in proportion to the number combined together, that is, in proportion as their efficacy becomes needful.

From this view of the subject it may be concluded that a pure democracy, by which I mean a society consisting of a small number of citizens, who assemble and administer the government in person, can admit of no cure for the mischiefs of faction. A common passion or interest will, in almost every case, be felt by a majority of the whole; a communication and concert result from the form of government itself; and there is nothing to check the inducements to sacrifice the weaker party or an obnoxious individual. Hence it is that such democracies have ever been spectacles of turbulence and contention; have ever been found incompatible with personal security or the rights of property; and have in general been as short in their lives as they have been violent in their deaths. Theoretic politicians, who have patronized this species of government, have erroneously supposed that by reducing mankind to a perfect equality in their political rights, they would, at the same time, be perfectly equalized and assimilated in their possessions, their opinions, and their passions.

A republic, by which I mean a government in which the scheme of representation takes place, opens a different prospect, and promises the cure for which we are seeking. Let us examine the points in which it varies from pure democracy, and we shall comprehend both the nature of the cure and the efficacy which it must derive from the Union.

The two great points of difference between a democracy and a republic are: first, the delegation of the government, in the latter, to a small number of citizens elected by the rest; secondly, the greater number of citizens, and greater sphere of country, over which the latter may be extended.

The effect of the first difference is, on the one hand, to refine and enlarge the public views, by passing them through the medium of a chosen body of citizens, whose wisdom may best discern the true interest of their country, and whose patriotism and love of justice will be least likely to sacrifice it to temporary or partial considerations. Under such a regulation, it may well happen that the public voice, pronounced by the representatives of the people, will be more consonant to the public good than if pronounced by the people themselves, convened for the purpose. On the other hand, the effect may be inverted. Men of factious tempers, of local prejudices, or of sinister designs, may, by intrigue, by corruption, or by other means, first obtain the suffrages, and then betray the interests, of the people. The question resulting is, whether small or extensive republics are more favorable to the election of proper guardians of the public weal; and it is clearly decided in favor of the latter by two obvious considerations:

In the first place, it is to be remarked that, however small the republic may be, the representatives must be raised to a certain number, in order to guard against the cabals of a few; and that, however large it may be, they must be limited to a certain number, in order to guard against the confusion of a multitude. Hence, the number of representatives in the two cases not being in proportion to that of the two constituents, and being proportionally greater in the small republic, it follows that, if the proportion of fit characters be not less in the large than in the small republic, the former will present a greater option, and consequently a greater probability of a fit choice.

In the next place, as each representative will be chosen by a greater number of citizens in the large than in the small republic, it will be more difficult for unworthy candidates to practise with success the vicious arts by which elections are too often carried; and the suffrages of the people being more free, will be more likely to centre in men who possess the most attractive merit and the most diffusive and established characters.

It must be confessed that in this, as in most other cases, there is a mean, on both sides of which inconveniences will be found to lie. By enlarging too much the number of electors, you render the representative too little acquainted with all their local circumstances and lesser interests; as by reducing it too much, you render him unduly attached to these, and too little fit to comprehend and pursue great and national objects. The federal Constitution forms a happy combination in this respect; the great and aggregate interests being referred to the national, the local and particular to the State legislatures.

The other point of difference is, the greater number of citizens and extent of territory which may be brought within the compass of republican than of democratic government; and it is this circumstance principally which renders factious combinations less to be dreaded in the former than in the latter. The smaller the society, the fewer probably will be the distinct parties and interests composing it; the fewer the distinct parties and interests, the more frequently will a majority be found of the same party; and the smaller the number of individuals composing a majority, and the smaller the compass within which they are placed, the more easily will they concert and execute their plans of oppression. Extend the sphere and you take in a greater variety of parties and interests; you make it less probable that a majority of the whole will have a common motive to invade the rights of other citizens; or if such a common motive exists, it will be more difficult for all who feel it to discover their own strength, and to act in unison with each other. Besides other impediments, it may be remarked that, where there is a consciousness of unjust or dishonorable purposes, communication is always checked by distrust in proportion to the number whose concurrence is necessary.

Hence, it clearly appears, that the same advantage which a republic has over a democracy, in controlling the effects of faction, is enjoyed by a large over a small republic,—is enjoyed by the Union over the States composing it. Does the advantage consist in the substitution of representatives whose enlightened views and virtuous sentiments render them superior to local prejudices and to schemes of injustice? It will not be denied that the representation of the Union will be most likely to possess these requisite endowments. Does it consist in the greater security afforded by a greater variety of parties, against the event of any one party being able to outnumber and oppress the rest? In an equal degree does the increased variety of parties comprised within the Union, increase this security. Does it, in fine, consist in the greater obstacles opposed to the concert and accomplishment of the secret wishes of an unjust and interested majority? Here, again, the extent of the Union gives it the most palpable advantage.

The influence of factious leaders may kindle a flame within their particular States, but will be unable to spread a general conflagration through the other States. A religious sect may degenerate into a political faction in a part of the Confederacy; but the variety of sects dispersed over the entire face of it must secure the national councils against any danger from that source. A rage for paper money, for an abolition of debts, for an equal division of property, or for any other improper or wicked project, will be less apt to pervade the whole body of the Union than a particular member of it; in the same proportion as such a malady is more likely to taint a particular county or district, than an entire State.

In the extent and proper structure of the Union, therefore, we behold a republican remedy for the diseases most incident to republican government. And according to the degree of pleasure and pride we feel in being republicans, ought to be our zeal in cherishing the spirit and supporting the character of Federalists. PUBLIUS.

From the New York Packet, Friday, February 1, 1788

THE FEDERALIST NO. 47

TO THE PEOPLE OF THE STATE OF NEW YORK:

Having reviewed the general form of the proposed government and the general mass of power allotted to it, I proceed to examine the particular structure of this government, and the distribution of this mass of power among its constituent parts.

One of the principal objections inculcated by the more respectable adversaries to the Constitution, is its supposed violation of the political maxim, that the legislative, executive, and judiciary departments ought to be separate and distinct. In the structure of the federal government, no regard, it is said, seems to have been paid to this essential precaution in favor of liberty. The several departments of power are distributed and blended in such a manner as at once to destroy all symmetry and beauty of form, and to expose some of the essential parts of the edifice to the danger of being crushed by the disproportionate weight of other parts.

No political truth is certainly of greater intrinsic value, or is stamped with the authority of more enlightened patrons of liberty, than that on which the objection is founded. The accumulation of all powers, legislative, executive, and judiciary, in the same hands, whether of one, a few, or many, and whether hereditary, self-appointed, or elective, may justly be pronounced the very definition of tyranny. Were the federal Constitution, therefore, really chargeable with the accumulation of power, or with a mixture of powers, having a dangerous tendency to such an accumulation, no further arguments would be necessary to inspire a universal reprobation of the system. I persuade myself, however, that it will be made apparent to every one, that the charge cannot be supported, and that the maxim on which it relies has been totally misconceived and misapplied. In order to form correct ideas on this important subject, it will be proper to investigate the sense in which the preservation of liberty requires that the three great departments of power should be separate and distinct.

The oracle who is always consulted and cited on this subject is the celebrated Montesquieu. If he be not the author of this invaluable precept in the science of politics, he has the merit at least of displaying and recommending it most effectually to the attention of mankind. Let us endeavor, in the first place, to ascertain his meaning on this point.

The British Constitution was to Montesquieu what Homer has been to the didactic writers on epic poetry. As the latter have considered the work of the immortal bard as the perfect model from which the principles and rules of the epic art were to be drawn, and by which all similar works were to be judged, so this great political critic appears to have viewed the Constitution of England as the standard, or to use his own expression, as the mirror of political liberty; and to have delivered, in the form of elementary truths, the several characteristic principles of that particular system. That we may be sure, then, not to mistake his meaning in this case, let us recur to the source from which the maxim was drawn.

On the slightest view of the British Constitution, we must perceive that the legislative, executive, and judiciary departments are by no means totally separate and distinct from each other. The executive magistrate forms an integral part of the legislative authority. He alone has the prerogative of making treaties with foreign sovereigns, which, when made, have, under certain limitations, the force of legislative acts. All the members of the judiciary department are appointed by him, can be removed by him on the address of the two Houses of Parliament, and form, when he pleases to consult them, one of his constitutional councils. One branch of the legislative department forms also a great constitutional council to the executive chief, as, on another hand, it is the sole depositary of judicial power in cases of impeachment, and is invested with the supreme appellate jurisdiction in all other cases. The judges, again, are so far connected with the legislative department as often to attend and participate in its deliberations, though not admitted to a legislative vote.

From these facts, by which Montesquieu was guided, it may clearly be inferred that, in saying "There can be no liberty where the legislative and executive powers are united in the same person, or body of magistrates," or, "if the power of judging be not separated from the legislative and executive powers," he did not mean that these departments ought to have no *partial agency* in, or no *control* over, the acts of each other. His meaning, as his own words import, and still more conclusively as illustrated by the example in his eye, can amount to no more than this, that where the *whole* power of one department is exercised by the same hands which possess the *whole* power of another department, the fundamental principles of a free constitution are subverted. This would have been the case in the constitution examined by him, if the king, who is the sole executive magistrate, had possessed also the complete legislative power, or the supreme administration of justice; or if the entire legislative body had possessed the supreme judiciary, or the supreme executive authority. This, however is not among the vices of that constitution. The magistrate in whom the whole executive power resides cannot of himself make a law, though he can put a negative on every law; nor administer justice in person, though he has the appointment of those who do administer it. The judges can exercise no executive prerogative, though they are shoots from the executive stock; nor any legislative function, though they may be advised with by the legislative councils. The entire legislature can perform no judiciary act, though by the joint act of two of its branches the judges may be removed from their offices, and though one of its branches is possessed of the judicial power in the last resort. The entire legislature, again, can exercise no executive prerogative, though one of its branches constitutes the supreme executive magistracy, and another, on the impeachment of a third, can try and condemn all the subordinate officers in the executive department.

The reasons on which Montesquieu grounds his maxim are a further demonstration of his meaning. "When the legislative and executive powers are united in the same person or body," says he, "there can be no liberty, because apprehensions may arise lest *the same* monarch or senate should *enact* tyrannical laws to *execute* them in a tyrannical manner." Again: "Were the power of judging joined with the legislative, the life and liberty of the subject would be exposed to arbitrary control, for *the judge* would then be *the legislator.* Were it joined to the executive power, *the judge* might behave with all the violence of *an oppressor.*" Some of these reasons are more fully explained in other passages; but briefly stated as they are here, they sufficiently establish the meaning which we have put on this celebrated maxim of this celebrated author.

If we look into the constitutions of the several States, we find that, notwithstanding the emphatical and, in some instances, the unqualified terms in which this axiom has been laid down, there is not a single instance in which the several departments of power have been kept absolutely separate and distinct. New Hampshire, whose constitution was the last formed, seems to have been fully aware of the impossibility and inexpediency of avoiding any mixture whatever of these departments, and has qualified the doctrine by declaring "that the legislative, executive, and judiciary powers ought to be kept as separate from, and independent of, each other *as the nature of a free government will admit; or as is consistent with that chain of connection that binds the whole fabric of the constitution in one indissoluble bond of unity and amity.*" Her constitution accordingly mixes these departments in several respects. The Senate, which is a branch of the legislative department, is also a judicial tribunal for the trial of impeachments. The President, who is the head of the executive department, is the presiding member also of the Senate; and, besides an equal vote in all cases, has a casting vote in case of a tie. The executive head is himself eventually elective every year by the legislative department, and his council is every year chosen by and from the members of the same department. Several of the officers of state are also appointed by the legislature. And the members of the judiciary department are appointed by the executive department.

The constitution of Massachusetts has observed a sufficient though less pointed caution, in expressing this fundamental article of liberty. It declares "that the legislative departments shall never exercise the executive and judicial powers, or either of them; the executive shall never exercise the legislative and judicial powers, or either of them; the judicial shall never exercise the legislative and executive powers, or either of them." This declaration corresponds precisely with the doctrine of Montesquieu, as it has been explained, and is not in a single point violated by the plan of the convention. It goes no farther than to prohibit any one of the entire departments from exercising the powers of another department. In the very Constitution to which it is prefixed, a partial mixture of powers has been admitted. The executive magistrate has a qualified negative on the legislative body, and the Senate, which is a part of the legislature, is a court of impeachment for members both of the executive and judiciary departments. The members of the judiciary department, again, are appointable by the executive department, and removable by the same authority on the address of the two legislative branches. Lastly, a number of the officers of government are annually appointed by the legislative department. As the appointment to offices, particularly executive offices, is in its nature an executive function, the compilers of the Constitution have, in this last point at least, violated the rule established by themselves.

I pass over the constitutions of Rhode Island and Connecticut, because they were formed prior to the Revolution, and even before the principle under examination had become an object of political attention.

The constitution of New York contains no declaration on this subject; but appears very clearly to have been framed with an eye to the danger of improperly blending the different departments. It gives, nevertheless, to the executive magistrate, a partial control over the legislative department; and, what is more, gives a like control to the judiciary department; and even blends the executive and judiciary departments in the exercise of this control. In its council of appointment members of the legislative are associated with the executive authority, in the appointment of officers, both executive and judiciary. And its court for the trial of impeachments and correction of errors is to consist of one branch of the legislature and the principal members of the judiciary department.

The constitution of New Jersey has blended the different powers of government more than any of the preceding. The governor, who is the executive magistrate, is appointed by the legislature; is chancellor and ordinary, or surrogate of the State; is a member of the Supreme Court of Appeals, and president, with a casting vote, of one of the legislative branches. The same legislative branch acts again as executive council of the governor, and with him constitutes the Court of Appeals. The members of the judiciary department are appointed by the legislative department, and removable by one branch of it, on the impeachment of the other.

According to the constitution of Pennsylvania, the president, who is the head of the executive department, is annually elected by a vote in which the legislative department predominates. In conjunction with an executive council, he appoints the members of the judiciary department, and forms a court of impeachment for trial of all officers, judiciary as well as executive. The judges of the Supreme Court and justices of the peace seem also to be removable by the legislature; and the executive power of pardoning in certain cases, to be referred to the same department. The members of the executive council are made EX-OFFICIO justices of peace throughout the State.

In Delaware, the chief executive magistrate is annually elected by the legislative department. The speakers of the two legislative branches are vice-presidents in the executive department. The executive chief, with six others, appointed, three by each of the legislative branches, constitutes the Supreme Court of Appeals; he is joined with the legislative department in the appointment of the other judges. Throughout the States, it appears that the members of the legislature may at the same time be justices of the peace; in this State, the members of one branch of it are EX-OFFICIO justices of the peace; as are also the members of the executive council. The principal officers of the executive department are appointed by the legislative; and one branch of the latter forms a court of impeachments. All officers may be removed on address of the legislature.

Maryland has adopted the maxim in the most unqualified terms; declaring that the legislative, executive, and judicial powers of government ought to be forever separate and distinct from each other. Her constitution, notwithstanding, makes the executive magistrate appointable by the legislative department; and the members of the judiciary by the executive department.

The language of Virginia is still more pointed on this subject. Her constitution declares, "that the legislative, executive, and judiciary departments shall be separate and distinct; so that neither exercise the powers properly belonging to the other; nor shall any person exercise the powers of more than one of them at the same time, except that the justices of county courts shall be eligible to either House of Assembly." Yet we find not only this express exception, with respect to the members of the inferior courts, but that the chief magistrate, with his executive council, are appointable by the legislature; that two members of the latter are triennially displaced at the pleasure of the legislature; and that all the principal offices, both executive and judiciary, are filled by the same department. The executive prerogative of pardon, also, is in one case vested in the legislative department.

The constitution of North Carolina, which declares "that the legislative, executive, and supreme judicial powers of government ought to be forever separate and distinct from each other," refers, at the same time, to the legislative department, the appointment not only of the executive chief, but all the principal officers within both that and the judiciary department.

In South Carolina, the constitution makes the executive magistracy eligible by the legislative department. It gives to the latter, also, the appointment of the members of the judiciary department, including even justices of the peace and sheriffs; and the appointment of officers in the executive department, down to captains in the army and navy of the State.

In the constitution of Georgia, where it is declared "that the legislative, executive, and judiciary departments shall be separate and distinct, so that neither exercise the powers properly belonging to the other," we find that the executive department is to be filled by appointments of the legislature; and the executive prerogative of pardon to be finally exercised by the same authority. Even justices of the peace are to be appointed by the legislature.

In citing these cases, in which the legislative, executive, and judiciary departments have not been kept totally separate and distinct, I wish not to be regarded as an advocate for the particular organizations of the several State governments. I am fully aware that among the many excellent principles which they exemplify, they carry strong marks of the haste, and still stronger of the inexperience, under which they were framed. It is but too obvious that in some instances the fundamental principle under consideration has been violated by too great a mixture, and even an actual consolidation, of the different powers; and that in no instance has a competent provision been made for maintaining in practice the separation delineated on paper. What I have wished to evince is, that the charge brought against the proposed Constitution, of violating the sacred maxim of free government, is warranted neither by the real meaning annexed to that maxim by its author, nor by the sense in which it has hitherto been understood in America. This interesting subject will be resumed in the ensuing paper. PUBLIUS.

From the New York Packet, Friday, February 8, 1788

THE FEDERALIST NO. 51

TO THE PEOPLE OF THE STATE OF NEW YORK:

To what expedient, then, shall we finally resort, for maintaining in practice the necessary partition of power among the several departments, as laid down in the Constitution? The only answer that can be given is, that as all these exterior provisions are found to be inadequate, the defect must be supplied, by so contriving the interior structure of the government as that its several constituent parts may, by their mutual relations, be the means of keeping each other in their proper places. Without presuming to undertake a full development of this important idea, I will hazard a few general observations, which may perhaps place it in a clearer light, and enable us to form a more correct judgment of the principles and structure of the government planned by the convention.

In order to lay a due foundation for that separate and distinct exercise of the different powers of government, which to a certain extent is admitted on all hands to be essential to the preservation of liberty, it is evident that each department should have a will of its own; and consequently should be so constituted that the members of each should have as little agency as possible in the appointment of the members of the others. Were this principle rigorously adhered to, it would require that all the appointments for the supreme executive, legislative, and judiciary magistracies should be drawn from the same fountain of authority, the people, through channels having no communication whatever with one another. Perhaps such a plan of constructing the several departments would be less difficult in practice than it may in contemplation appear. Some difficulties, however, and some additional expense would attend the execution of it. Some deviations, therefore, from the principle must be admitted. In the constitution of the judiciary department in particular, it might be inexpedient to insist rigorously on the principle: first, because peculiar qualifications being essential in the members, the primary consideration ought to be to select that mode of choice which best secures these qualifications; secondly, because the permanent tenure by which the appointments are held in that department, must soon destroy all sense of dependence on the authority conferring them.

It is equally evident, that the members of each department should be as little dependent as possible on those of the others, for the emoluments annexed to their offices. Were the executive magistrate, or the judges, not independent of the legislature in this particular, their independence in every other would be merely nominal.

But the great security against a gradual concentration of the several powers in the same department, consists in giving to those who administer each department the necessary constitutional means and personal motives to resist encroachments of the others. The provision for defence must in this, as in all other cases, be made commensurate to the danger of attack. Ambition must be made to counteract ambition. The interest of the man must be connected with the constitutional rights of the place. It may be a reflection on human nature, that such devices should be necessary to control the abuses of government. But what is government itself, but the greatest of all reflections on human nature? If men were angels, no government would be necessary. If angels were to govern men, neither external nor internal controls on government would he necessary. In framing a government which is to be administered by men over men, the great difficulty lies in this: you must first enable the government to control the governed; and in the next place oblige it to control itself. A dependence on the people is, no doubt, the primary control on the government; but experience has taught mankind the necessity of auxiliary precautions.

This policy of supplying, by opposite and rival interests, the defect of better motives, might be traced through the whole system of human affairs, private as well as public. We see it particularly displayed in all the subordinate distributions of power, where the constant aim is to divide and arrange the several offices in such a manner as that each may be a check on the other—that the private interest of every individual may be a sentinel over the public rights.

These inventions of prudence cannot be less requisite in the distribution of the supreme powers of the State.

But it is not possible to give to each department an equal power of self-defence. In republican government, the legislative authority necessarily predominates. The remedy for this inconveniency is to divide the legislature into different branches; and to render them, by different modes of election and different principles of action, as little connected with each other as the nature of their common functions and their common dependence on the society will admit. It may even be necessary to guard against dangerous encroachments by still further precautions. As the weight of the legislative authority requires that it should be thus divided, the weakness of the executive may require, on the other hand, that it should he fortified. An absolute negative on the legislature appears, at first view, to be the natural defence with which the executive magistrate should be armed. But perhaps it would be neither altogether safe nor alone sufficient. On ordinary occasions it might not be exerted with the requisite firmness, and on extraordinary occasions it might be perfidiously abused. May not this defect of an absolute negative be supplied by some qualified connection between this weaker department and the weaker branch of the stronger department, by which the latter may be led to support the constitutional rights of the former, without being too much detached from the rights of its own department?

If the principles on which these observations are founded be just, as I persuade myself they are, and they be applied as a criterion to the several State constitutions, and to the federal Constitutions, it will be found that if the latter does not perfectly correspond with them, the former are infinitely less able to bear such a test.

There are, moreover, two considerations particularly applicable to the federal system of America, which place that system in a very interesting point of view.

First. In a single republic, all the power surrendered by the people is submitted to the administrations of a single government; and the usurpations are guarded against by a division of the government into distinct and separate departments. In the compound republic of America, the power surrendered by the people is first divided between two distinct governments, and then the portion allotted to each subdivided among distinct and separate departments. Hence a double security arises to the rights of the people. The different governments will control each other, at the same time that each will be controlled by itself.

Second. It is of great importance in a republic not only to guard the society against the oppression of its rulers, but to guard one part of the society against the injustice of the other part. Different interests necessarily exist in different classes of citizens. If a majority be united by a common interest, the rights of the minority will be insecure. There are but two methods of providing against this evil: the one by creating a will in the community independent of the majority—that is, of the society itself; the other, by comprehending in the society so many separate descriptions of citizens as will render an unjust combination of a majority of the whole very improbable, if not impracticable. The first method prevails in all governments possessing an hereditary or self-appointed authority. This, at best, is but a precarious security; because a power independent of the society may as well espouse the unjust views of the major, as the rightful interests of the minor party, and may possibly be turned against both parties. The second method will be exemplified in the federal republic of the United States. Whilst all authority in it will be derived from and dependent on the society, the society itself will be broken into so many parts, interests and classes of citizens, that the rights of individuals, or of the minority, will be in little danger from interested combinations of the majority. In a free government the security for civil rights must be the same as that for religious rights. It consists in the one case in the multiplicity of interests, and in the other in the multiplicity of sects. The degree of security in both cases will depend on the number of interests and sects; and this may be presumed to depend on the extent of country and number of people comprehended under the same government. This view of the subject must particularly recommend a proper federal system to all the sincere and considerate friends of republican government, since it shows that in exact proportion as the territory of the Union may be formed into more circumscribed Confederacies, or States, oppressive combinations of a majority will be facilitated; the best security, under the republican forms, for the rights of every class of citizens, will be diminished; and consequently the stability and independence of some member of the government, the only other security, must be proportionally increased. Justice is the end of government. It is the end of civil society. It ever has been and ever will be pursued until it be obtained, or until liberty be lost in the pursuit. In a society under the forms of which the stronger faction can readily unite and oppress the weaker, anarchy may as truly be said to reign as in a state of nature, where the weaker individual is not secured against the violence of the stronger; and as, in the latter state, even the stronger individuals are prompted, by the uncertainty of their condition, to submit to a government which may protect the weak as well as themselves; so, in the former state, will the more powerful factions or parties be gradually induced, by a like motive, to wish for a government which will protect all parties, the weaker as well as the more powerful. It can be little doubted that if the State of Rhode Island was separated from the Confederacy and left to itself, the insecurity of rights under the popular form of government within such narrow limits would be displayed by such reiterated oppressions of factious majorities that some power altogether independent of the people would soon be called for by the voice of the very factions whose misrule had proved the necessity of it. In the extended republic of the United States, and among the great variety of interests, parties, and sects which it embraces, a coalition of a majority of the whole society could seldom take place on any other principles than those of justice and the general good; whilst there being thus less danger to a minor from the will of a major party, there must be less pretext, also, to provide for the security, of the former, by introducing into the government a will not dependent on the latter, or, in other words, a will independent of the society itself. It is no less certain than it is important, notwithstanding the contrary opinions which have been entertained, that the larger the society, provided it lie within a practical sphere, the more duly capable it will be of self-government. And happily for the *republican cause*, the practicable sphere may be carried to a very great extent, by a judicious modification and mixture of the *federal principle.* PUBLIUS

CHARLES COTESWORTH PINCKNEY

1740-1825

The Brief Submitted by Charles Cotesworth Pinckney in *McCulloch vs. Maryland*

FEBRUARY TERM 1819

The distinctively American solution to the problem of reconciling freedom and authority has been to rely on the *Constitution* and the law that flows from it. No other country so reveres its basic law. In this selection, written by one of the participants in the Constitutional Convention, we see the idea that the *Constitution* can be broadly construed because it contains within its brief pages a basic set of legal principles that offers guidance for the continued construction of a full system of laws, performing all the functions expected of law in a civilized society, and still maintaining a balance between freedom and authority. The occasion for Pinckney's writing this was the famous case *McCulloch vs. Maryland* (1819). Pinckney submitted this brief in support of the position taken by the government of the United States against the State of Maryland.

The case itself grew out of Congress's creation of a corporation, the Bank of the United States, even though no power to create corporations is listed in the *Constitution*, and out of Maryland's effort to tax that bank. The case was controversial at the time, and it attracted much attention. The formal legal decision rendered by the Supreme Court was written by Chief Justice John Marshall and is still frequently reprinted and read. The Court ruled that the power to create corporations did not need to be listed explicitly because it was already "implied" in the *Constitution*. Further, Maryland did not have the authority to tax the Bank because the *Constitution* was the supreme law of the land, beyond the reach of state powers. The case was a twin victory for broad construction of the *Constitution* and federal supremacy. But Marshall's decision deals with the particulars of the dispute—Congress's authorization of the Bank of the United States and Maryland's effort to tax it. Pinckney's brief describes in more general terms than Marshall's decision the network of law and authority that was created by the *Constitution*.

Pinckney had been educated at Oxford and had pursued an English legal education, opportunities available to few of the other founders. The South Carolinian was a veteran of the American Revolution, had served as Minister to France, and had been an active member of the Constitutional Convention. He was uniquely suited to present this overview of the law of the *Constitution* at a time when the young United States was struggling to define what it would be.

Selected from: "M'Culloch v. State of Maryland." 1819. (*7 U.S. 316*) 'Lectric Law Library. <http://www.lectlaw.com/files/case15.htm>.

McCulloch vs. Maryland (1819)

... Pinckney, for the plaintiff in error,[1] in reply, stated: 1. That the cause must first be cleared of a question which ought

---

1 The plaintiff in error is the party who appeals a decision of a lower court, or the appellant.

not to have been forced into the argument—whether the act of congress establishing the bank was consistent with the constitution? This question depended both on authority and on principle. No topics to illustrate it could be drawn from the confederation, since the present constitution was as different from that, as light from darkness. The former was a mere federative league; an alliance offensive and defensive between the states, such as there had been many examples of in the history of the world. It had no power of coercion but by arms. Its radical vice, and that which the new constitution was intended to reform, was legislation upon sovereign states in their corporate capacity. But the constitution acts directly on the people, by means of powers communicated directly from the people. No state, in its corporate capacity, ratified it; but it was proposed for adoption to popular conventions. It springs from the people, precisely as the state constitution springs from the people, and acts on them in a similar manner. It was adopted by them in the geographical sections into which the country is divided. The federal powers are just as sovereign as those of the states. The state sovereignties are not the authors of the constitution of the United States. They are preceding in point of time, to the national sovereignty, but they are postponed to it, in point of supremacy, by the will of the people. The means of giving efficacy to the sovereign authorities vested by the people in the national government, are those adapted to the end; fitted to promote, and having a natural relation and connection with, the objects of that government. The constitution, by which these authorities, and the means of executing them, are given, and the laws made in pursuance of it, are declared to be the supreme law of the land; and they would have been such, without the insertion of this declaratory clause; they must be supreme, or they would be nothing. The constitutionality of the establishment of the bank, as one of the means necessary to carry into effect the authorities vested in the national government, is no longer an open question. It has been long since settled by decisions of the most revered authority, legislative, executive and judicial. A legislative construction, in a doubtful case, persevered in for a course of years, ought to be binding upon the court. This, however, is not a question of construction merely, but of political necessity, on which congress must decide. It is conceded, that a manifest usurpation cannot be maintained in this mode; but, we contend, that this is such a doubtful case, that congress may expound the nature and extent of the authority under which it acts, and that this practical interpretation had become incorporated into the constitution. There are two distinguishing points which entitle it to great respect. The first is, that it was a contemporaneous construction; the second is, that it was made by the authors of the constitution themselves. The members of the convention who framed the constitution, passed into the first congress, by which the new government was organized; they must have understood their own work. They determined that the constitution gave to congress the power of incorporating a banking company. It was not required, that this power should be expressed in the text of the constitution; it might safely be left to implication. An express authority to erect corporations generally, would have been perilous; since it might have been constructively extended to the creation of corporations entirely unnecessary to carry into effect the other powers granted; we do not claim an authority in this respect, beyond the sphere of the specific powers. The grant of an authority to erect certain corporations, might have been equally dangerous, by omitting to provide for others, which time and experience might show to be equally, and even more necessary. It is a historical fact, of great importance in this discussion, that amendments to the constitution were actually proposed, in order to guard against the establishment of commercial monopolies. But if the general power of incorporating did not exist, why seek to qualify it, or to guard against its abuse? The legislative precedent, established in 1791, has been followed up by a series of acts of congress, all confirming the authority. Political considerations alone might have produced the refusal to renew the charter in 1811; at any rate, we know that they mingled themselves in the debate, and the determination.

*380 In 1815, a bill was passed by the two houses of congress, incorporating a national bank; to which the president refused his assent, upon political considerations only, waiving the question of constitutionality, as being settled by contemporaneous exposition, and repeated subsequent recognitions. In 1816, all branches of the legislature concurred in establishing the corporation, whose chartered rights are now in judgment before the court. None of these measures ever passed sub silentio;[1] the proposed incorporation was always discussed, and opposed, and supported, on constitutional grounds, as well as on considerations of political expediency.

Congress is prima facie[2] a competent judge of its own constitutional powers. It is not, as in questions of privilege, the exclusive judge; but it must first decide, and that in a proper judicial character, whether a law is constitutional, before it is passed. It had an opportunity of exercising its judgment in this respect, upon the present subject, not only in the principal acts incorporating the former, and the present bank, but in the various incidental statutes subsequently enacted on the same subject; in all of which, the question of constitutionality was equally open to debate, but in none of which was it agitated.

There are, then, in the present case, the repeated determinations of the three branches of the national legislature, confirmed by the constant acquiescence of the state sovereignties, and of the people, for a considerable length of time.

Their strength is fortified by judicial authority. The decisions in the courts, affirming the constitutionality of

---

[1] A Latin phrase which means to speak under silence. Precedents that pass sub silentio have little or no authority.

[2] A Latin phrase which means evident without proof or reasoning, or obvious.

these laws, passed, indeed, sub silentio; but it was the duty of the judges, especially in criminal cases, to have raised the question; and we are to conclude, from this circumstance, that no doubt was entertained respecting it. And if the question be examined on principle, it will be found not to admit of doubt. Has congress, abstractedly, the authority to erect corporations? This authority is not more a sovereign power, than many other powers which are acknowledged to exist, and which are but means to an end. All the objects of the government are national objects, and the means are, and must be, fitted to accomplish them. These objects are enumerated in the constitution, and have no limits but the constitution itself.

A more perfect union is to be formed; justice to be established; domestic tranquillity insured; the common defence provided for; the general welfare promoted; the blessings of liberty secured to the present generation, and to posterity. For the attainment of these vast objects, the government is armed with powers and faculties corresponding in magnitude. Congress has power to lay and collect taxes and duties, imposts and excises; to pay the debts, and provide for the common defence and general welfare of the United States; to borrow money on the credit of the nation; to regulate commerce; to establish uniform naturalization and bankrupt laws; to coin money, and regulate the circulating medium, and the standard of weights and measures; to establish post-offices and post-roads; to promote the progress of science and the useful arts, by granting patents and copyrights; to constitute tribunals inferior to the Supreme Court, and to define and punish offences against the law of nations; to declare and carry on war; to raise and support armies, and to provide and maintain a navy; to discipline and govern the land and naval forces; to call forth the militia to execute the laws, suppress insurrections and repel invasions; to provide for organizing, arming and disciplining the militia; to exercise exclusive legislation, in all cases, over the district where the seat of government is established, and over such other portions of territory as may be ceded to the Union for the erection of forts, magazines, & c.; to dispose of, and make all needful rules and regulations respecting, the territory or other property belonging to the United States; and to make all laws which shall be necessary and proper for carrying into execution these powers, and all other powers vested in the national government, or any of its departments or officers. The laws thus made are declared to be the supreme law of the land; and the judges in every state are bound thereby, anything in the constitution or laws of any state to the contrary notwithstanding. Yet it is doubted, whether a government invested with such immense powers has authority to erect a corporation within the sphere of its general objects, and in order to accomplish some of those objects! The state powers are much less in point of magnitude, though greater in number; yet it is supposed, the states possess the authority of establishing corporations, whilst it is denied to the general government. It is conceded to the state legislatures, though not specifically granted, because it is said to be an incident of state sovereignty; but it is refused to congress, because it is not specifically granted, though it may be necessary and proper to execute the powers which are specifically granted. But the authority of legislation in the state government is not unlimited; there are several limitations to their legislative authority. First, from the nature of all government, especially, of republican government, in which the residuary powers of sovereignty, not granted specifically, by inevitable implication, are reserved to the people. Secondly, from the express limitations contained in the state constitutions. And thirdly, from the express prohibitions to the states contained in the United States constitution. The power of erecting corporations is nowhere expressly granted to the legislatures of the states in their constitutions; it is taken by necessary implication: but it cannot be exercised to accomplish any of the ends which are beyond the sphere of their constitutional authority. The power of erecting corporations is not an end of any government; it is a necessary means of accomplishing the ends of all governments. It is an authority inherent in, and incident to, all sovereignty.

The history of corporations will illustrate this position. They were transplanted from the Roman law into the common law of England, and all the municipal codes of modern Europe. From England, they were derived to this country. But in the civil law, a corporation could be created by a mere voluntary association of individuals. (1 Bl. Com. 471). And in England, the authority of parliament is not necessary to create a corporate body.

The king may do it, and may communicate his power to a subject (1 Bl. Com. 474), so little is this regarded as a transcendent power of sovereignty, in the British constitution. So also, in our constitution, it ought to be regarded as but a subordinate power to carry into effect the great objects of government.

The state governments cannot establish corporations to carry into effect the national powers given to congress, nor can congress create corporations to execute the peculiar duties of the state governments. But so much of the power or faculty of incorporation as concerns national objects has passed away from the state legislatures, and is vested in the national government. An act of incorporation is but a law, and laws are but means to promote the legitimate end of all government—the felicity of the people. All powers are given to the national government, as the people will. The reservation in the 10th amendment to the constitution, of 'powers not delegated to the United States,' is not confined to powers not expressly delegated. Such an amendment was indeed proposed; but it was perceived, that it would strip the government of some of its most essential powers, and it was rejected. Unless a specific means be expressly prohibited to the general government, it has it, within the sphere of its specified powers. Many particular means are, of course, involved in the general means necessary to carry into effect the powers expressly granted, and in that case, the general means become the end, and the smaller objects the means.

It was impossible for the framers of the constitution to specify, prospectively, all these means, both because it would have involved an immense variety of details, and because it would have been impossible for them to foresee the infinite variety of circumstances, in such an unexampled state of political society as ours, for ever changing and for ever improving. How unwise would it have been, to legislate immutably for exigencies which had not then occurred, and which must have been foreseen but dimly and imperfectly! The security against abuse is to be found in the constitution and nature of the government, in its popular character and structure. The statute book of the United States is filled with powers derived from implication. The power to lay and collect taxes will not execute itself. Congress must designate in detail all the means of collection. So also, the power of establishing post-offices and post-roads, involves that of punishing the offence of robbing the mail. But there is no more necessary connection between the punishment of mail-robbers, and the power to establish post-roads, than there is between the institution of a bank, and the collection of the revenue and payment of the public debts and expenses. So, light-houses, beacons, buoys and public piers, have all been established, under the general power to regulate commerce. But they are not indispensably necessary to commerce. It might linger on, without these aids, though exposed to more perils and losses. So, congress has authority to coin money, and to guard the purity of the circulating medium, by providing for the punishment of counterfeiting the current coin; but laws are also made for punishing the offence of uttering and passing the coin thus counterfeited.

It is the duty of the court to construe the constitutional powers of the national government liberally, and to mould them so as to effectuate its great objects. Whence is derived the power to punish smuggling? It does not collect the impost, but it is a means more effectually to prevent the collection from being diminished in amount, by frauds upon the revenue laws. Powers, as means, may then be implied in many cases. And if so, why not in this case as well as any other?

The power of making all needful rules and regulations respecting the territory of the United States, is one of the specified powers of congress. Under this power, it has never been doubted, that congress had authority to establish corporations in the territorial governments. But this power is derived entirely from implication. It is assumed, as an incident to the principal power. If it may be assumed, in that case, upon the ground, that it is a necessary means of carrying into effect the power expressly granted, why may it not be assumed, in the present case, upon a similar ground? It is readily admitted, there must be a relation, in the nature and fitness of things between the means used and the end to be accomplished. But the question is, whether the necessity which will justify a resort to a certain means, must be an absolute, indispensable, inevitable necessity? The power of passing all laws necessary and proper to carry into effect the other powers specifically granted, is a political power; it is a matter of legislative discretion, and those who exercise it, have a wide range of choice in selecting means. In its exercise, the mind must compare means with each other. But absolute necessity excludes all choice; and therefore, it cannot be this species of necessity which is required. Congress alone has the fit means of inquiry and decision. The more or less of necessity never can enter as an ingredient into judicial decision. Even absolute necessity cannot be judged of here; still less, can practical necessity be determined in a judicial forum. The judiciary may, indeed, and must, see that what has been done is not a mere evasive pretext, under which the national legislature travels out of the prescribed bounds of its authority, and encroaches upon state sovereignty, or the rights of the people. For this purpose, it must inquire, whether the means assumed have a connection, in the nature and fitness of things, with the end to be accomplished. The vast variety of possible means, excludes the practicability of judicial determination as to the fitness of a particular means. It is sufficient, that it does not appear to be violently and unnaturally forced into the service, or fraudulently assumed, in order to usurp a new substantive power of sovereignty. A philological analysis of the terms 'necessary and proper' will illustrate the argument.

Compare these terms as they are used in that part of the constitution now in question, with the qualified manner in which they are used in the 10th section of the same article. In the latter, it is provided that 'no state shall, without the consent of congress, lay any imposts or duties on imports or exports, except what may be absolutely necessary for executing its inspection laws.' In the clause in question, congress is invested with the power 'to make all laws which shall be necessary and proper for carrying into execution the foregoing powers,' &c. There is here then, no qualification of the necessity; it need not be absolute; it may be taken in its ordinary grammatical sense. The word necessary, standing by itself, has no inflexible meaning; it is used in a sense more or less strict, according to the subject.

This, like many other words, has a primitive sense, and another figurative and more relaxed; it may be qualified by the addition of adverbs of diminution or enlargement, such as very, indispensably, more, less, or absolutely necessary; which last is the sense in which it is used in the 10th section of this article of the constitution. But that it is not always used in this strict and rigorous sense, may be proved, by tracing its definition, and etymology in every human language.

If, then, all the powers of the national government are sovereign and supreme; if the power of incorporation is incidental, and involved in the others; if the degree of political necessity which will justify a resort to a particular means, to carry into execution the other powers of the government, can never be a criterion of judicial determination, but must be left to legislative discretion, it only remains to inquire, whether a bank has a natural and obvious connection with other express or implied powers, so as to become a necessary and proper means of carrying them into execution. A bank might be established as a branch of the public administration, without incorporation. The government might issue paper, upon the credit of the public faith, pledged for its redemption, or upon the credit of its property and funds. Let the office where this paper is issued be made a place of deposit for the money of individuals, and authorize its officers to discount, and a bank is created. It only wants the forms of incorporation. But, surely, it will not be pretended, that clothing it with these forms would make such an establishment unconstitutional. In the bank which is actually established and incorporated, the United States are joint stockholders, and appoint joint directors; the secretary of the secretary of the treasury has a supervising authority over its affairs; it is bound, upon his requisition, to transfer the funds of the government wherever they may be wanted; it performs all the duties of commissioners of the loan-office; it is bound to loan the government a certain amount of money, on demand; its notes are receivable in payment for public debts and duties; it is intimately connected, according to the usage of the whole world, with the power of borrowing money, and with all the financial operations of the government. It has, also, a close connection with the power of regulating foreign commerce, and that between the different states. It provides a circulating medium, by which that commerce can be more conveniently carried on, and exchanges may be facilitated. It is true, there are state banks by which a circulating medium to a certain extent is provided. But that only diminishes the quantum of necessity, which is no criterion by which to test the constitutionality of a measure. It is also connected with the power of making all needful regulations for the government of the territory, 'and other property of the United States.' If they may establish a corporation to regulate their territory, they may establish one to regulate their property. Their treasure is their property, and may be invested in this mode. It is put in partnership; but not for the purpose of carrying on the trade of banking as one of the ends for which the government was established; but only as an instrument or means for executing its sovereign powers. This instrument could not be rendered effectual for this purpose, but by mixing the property of individuals with that of the public. The bank could not otherwise acquire a credit for its notes. Universal experience shows, that, if, altogether a government bank, it could not acquire, or would soon lose, the confidence of the community.

2. As to the branches, they are identical with the parent bank. The power to establish them is that species of subordinate power, wrapped up in the principal power, which congress may place at its discretion.
3. The last and greatest, and only difficult question in the cause, is that which respects the assumed right of the states to tax this bank, and its branches, thus established by congress? This is a question, comparatively of no importance to the individual states, but of vital importance to the Union. Deny this exemption to the bank as an instrument of government, and what is the consequence? There is no express provision in the constitution, which exempts any of the national institutions or property from state taxation.

It is only by implication that the army and navy, and treasure, and judicature of the Union are exempt from state taxation. Yet they are practically exempt; and they must be, or it would be in the power of any one state to destroy their use. Whatever the United States have a right to do, the individual states have no right to undo. The power of congress to establish a bank, like its other sovereign powers, is supreme, or it would be nothing. Rising out of an exertion of paramount authority, it cannot be subject to any other power. Such a power in the states, as that contended for on the other side, is manifestly repugnant to the power of congress; since a power to establish, implies a power to continue and preserve.

There is a manifest repugnancy between the power of Maryland to tax, and the power of congress to preserve, this institution. A power to build up, what another may pull down at pleasure, is a power which may provoke a smile, but can do nothing else. This law of Maryland acts directly on the operations of the bank, and may destroy it. There is no limit or check in this respect, but in the discretion of the state legislature. That discretion cannot be controlled by the national councils. Whenever the local councils of Maryland will it, the bank must be expelled from that state. A right to tax, without limit or control, is essentially a power to destroy. If one national institution may be destroyed in this manner, all may be destroyed in the same manner. If this power to tax the national property and institutions exists in the state of Maryland, it is unbounded in extent. There can be no check upon it, either by congress, or the people of the other states. Is there then any intelligible, fixed, defined boundary of this taxing power? If any, it must be found in this court. If it does not exist here, it is a nonentity. But the court cannot say what is an abuse, and what is a legitimate use of the power. The legislative intention may be so masked, as to defy the scrutinizing eye of the court. How will the court ascertain, a priori, that the given amount of tax will crush the bank? It is essentially a question of political economy, and there are always a vast variety of facts bearing upon it. The facts may be mistaken. Some important considerations belonging to the subject may be kept out of sight; they must all vary with times and circumstances. The result, then, must determine, whether the tax is destructive. But the bank may linger on for some time, and that result cannot be known, until the work of destruction is consummated. A criterion which has been proposed, is to see whether the tax has been laid, impartially, upon the state banks, as well as the Bank of the United States. Even this is an unsafe test; for the state governments may wish, and intend, to destroy their own banks. The existence of any national institution ought not to depend upon so frail a security. But this tax is leveled exclusively at the branch of the United States Bank established in Maryland. There is, in point of fact, a branch of no other bank within that state, and there can legally be no other.

It is a fundamental article of the state constitution of Maryland, that taxes shall operate on all the citizens impartially and uniformly, in proportion to their property, with the exception, however, of taxes laid for political purposes. This is a tax laid for a political purpose; for the purpose of destroying a great institution of the national government; and if it were not imposed for that purpose, it would be repugnant to the state constitution, as not being laid uniformly on all the citizens, in proportion to their property. So that the legislature cannot disavow this to be its object, without, at the same time, confessing a manifest violation of the state constitution. Compare this act of Maryland with that of Kentucky, which is yet to come before the court, and the absolute necessity of repressing such attempts in their infancy, will be evident. Admit the constitutionality of the Maryland tax, and that of Kentucky follows inevitably. How can it be said, that the office of discount and deposit in Kentucky cannot bear a tax of $60,000 per annum, payable monthly? Probably, it could not; but judicial certainty is essential; and the court has no means of arriving at that certainty. There is, then, here, an absolute repugnancy of power to power; we are not bound to show, that the particular exercise of the power in the present case is absolutely repugnant. It is sufficient, that the same power may be thus exercised.

There certainly may be some exceptions out of the taxing power of the states, other than those created by the taxing power of congress; because, if there were no implied exceptions, then, the navy, and other exclusive property of the United States, would be liable to state taxation. If some of the powers of congress, other than its taxing power, necessarily involve incompatibility with the taxing power of the states, this may be incompatible.

This is incompatible; for a power to impose a tax ad libitum[1] upon the notes of the bank, is a power to repeal the law, by which the bank was created. The bank cannot be useful, it cannot act at all, unless it issues notes. If the present tax does not disable the bank from issuing its notes, another may; and it is the authority itself which is questioned, as being entirely repugnant to the power which established and preserves the bank. Two powers thus hostile and incompatible cannot co-exist. There must be, in this case, an implied exception to the general taxing power of the states, because it is a tax upon the legislative faculty of congress, upon the national property, upon the national institutions. Because the taxing powers of the two governments are concurrent in some respects, it does not follow, that there may not be limitations on the taxing power of the states, other than those which are imposed by the taxing power of congress. Judicial proceedings are practically a subject of taxation in many countries, and in some of the states of this Union. The states are not expressly prohibited in the constitution, from taxing the judicial proceedings of the United States. Yet such a prohibition must be implied, or the administration of justice in the national courts might be obstructed by a prohibitory tax. But such a tax is no more a tax on the legislative faculty

1 A Latin phrase which means at will or without advanced notice.

of congress than this. The branch bank in Maryland is as much an institution of the sovereign power of the Union, as the circuit court of Maryland. One is established in virtue of an express power; the other by an implied authority; but both are equal, and equally supreme. All the property and all the institutions of the United States are, constructively, without the local, territorial jurisdiction of the individual states, in every respect, and for every purpose, including that of taxation. This immunity must extend to this case, because the power of taxation imports the power of taxation for the purpose of prohibition and destruction. The immunity of foreign public vessels from the local jurisdiction, whether state or national, was established in the case of (The Exchange, 7 Cranch 116), not upon positive municipal law, nor upon conventional law; but it was implied, from the usage of nations, and the necessity of the case. If, in favor of foreign governments, such an edifice of exemption has been built up, independent of the letter of the constitution, or of any other written law, shall not a similar edifice be raised on the same foundations, for the security of our own national government? So also, the jurisdiction of a foreign power, holding a temporary possession of a portion of national territory, is nowhere provided for in the constitution; but is derived from inevitable implication. United States v. Rice (ante, p. 246). These analogies show, that there may be exemptions from state jurisdiction, not detailed in the constitution, but arising out of general considerations. If congress has power to do a particular act, no state can impede, retard or burden it. Can there be a stronger ground, to infer a cessation of state jurisdiction?

The Bank of the United States is as much an instrument of the government for fiscal purposes, as the courts are its instruments for judicial purposes. They both proceed from the supreme power, and equally claim its protection. Though every state in the Union may impose a stamp tax, yet no state can lay a stamp tax upon the judicial proceedings or custom-house papers of the United States.

But there is no such express exception to the general taxing power of the states contained in the constitution. It arises from the general nature of the government, and from the principle of the supremacy of the national powers, and the laws made to execute them, over the state authorities and state laws.

It is objected, however, that the act of congress, incorporating the bank, withdraws property from taxation by the state, which would be otherwise liable to state taxation. We answer, that it is immaterial, if it does thus withdraw certain property from the grasp of state taxation, if congress had authority to establish the bank, since the power of congress is supreme. But, in fact, it withdraws nothing from the mass of taxable property in Maryland, which that state could tax. The whole capital of the bank, belonging to private stockholders, is drawn from every state in the Union, and the stock belonging to the United States, previously constituted a part of the public treasure.

Neither the stock belonging to citizens of other states, nor the privileged treasure of the United States, mixed up with this private property, were previously liable to taxation in Maryland; and as to the stock belonging to its own citizens, it still continues liable to state taxation, as a portion of their individual property, in common with all the other private property in the state. The establishment of the bank, so far from withdrawing anything from taxation by the state, brings something into Maryland which that state may tax.

It produces revenue to the citizens of Maryland, which may be taxed equally and uniformly, with all their other private property. The materials of which the ships of war, belonging to the United States, are constructed, were previously liable to state taxation. But the instant they are converted into public property, for the public defence, they cease to be subject to state taxation.

So, here, the treasure of the United States, and that of individuals, citizens of Maryland, and of other states, are undistinguishably confounded in the capital stock of this great national institution, which, it has been before shown, could be made useful as an instrument of finance, in no other mode than by thus blending together the property of the government and of private merchants. This partnership is, therefore, one of necessity, on the part of the United States. Either this tax operates upon the franchise of the bank, or upon its property. If upon the former, then it comes directly in conflict with the exercise of a great sovereign authority of congress; if upon the latter, then it is a tax upon the property of the United States; since the law does not, and cannot, in imposing a stamp tax, distinguish their interest from that of private stockholders.

But it is said, that congress possesses and exercises the unlimited authority of taking the state banks; and therefore, the states ought to have an equal right to tax the Bank of the United States. The answer to this objection is, that, in taxing the state banks, the states in congress exercise their power of taxation. Congress exercises the power of the people; the whole acts on the whole. But the state tax is a part acting on the whole. Even if the two cases were the same, it would rather exempt the state banks from federal taxation, than subject the Bank of the United States to taxation by a particular state.

But the state banks are not machines essential to execute the powers of the state sovereignties, and therefore, this is out of the question. The people of the United States, and the sovereignties of the several states, have no control over the taxing power of a particular state. But they have a control over the taxing power of the United States, in the responsibility of the members of the house of representatives to the people of the state which sends them, and of the senators, to the legislature by whom they are chosen. But there is no correspondent responsibility of the local legislature of Maryland, for example, to the people of the other states of the Union. The people of other states are not represented in the legislature of Maryland, and can have no control, directly or indirectly, over its proceedings. The legislature of Maryland is responsible only to the people of that state. The national government can withdraw nothing from the taxing power of the states, which is not for the purpose of national benefit and the common welfare, and within its defined powers. But the local interests of the states are in perpetual conflict with the interests of the Union; which shows the danger of adding power to the partial views and local prejudices of the states. If the tax imposed by this law be not a tax on the property of the United States, it is not a tax on any property; and it must, consequently, be a tax on the faculty or franchise. It is, then, a tax on the legislative faculty of the Union, on the charter of the bank. It imposes a stamp duty upon the notes of the bank, and thus stops the very source of its circulation and life. It is as much a direct interference with the legislative faculty of congress, as would be a tax on patents, or copyrights, or custom-house papers or judicial proceedings.

Since, then, the constitutional government of this republican empire cannot be practically enforced, so as to secure the permanent glory, safety and felicity of this great country, but by a fair and liberal interpretation of its powers; since those powers could not all be expressed in the constitution, but many of them must be taken by implication; since the sovereign powers of the Union are supreme, and, wherever they come in direct conflict and repugnancy with those of the state governments, the latter must give way; since it has been proved, that this is the case as to the institution of the bank, and the general power of taxation by the states; since this power unlimited and unchecked, as it necessarily must be, by the very nature of the subject, is absolutely inconsistent with, and repugnant to, the right of the United States to establish a national bank; if the power of taxation be applied to the corporate property, or franchise, or property of the bank, and might be applied in the same manner, to destroy any other of the great institutions and establishments of the Union, and the whole machine of the national government might be arrested in its motions, by the exertion, in other cases, of the same power which is here attempted to be exerted upon the bank: no other alternative remains, but for this court to interpose its authority, and save the nation from the consequences of this dangerous attempt.

JEAN-JACQUES ROUSSEAU

1712-1778

THE SOCIAL CONTRACT

1762

Rousseau was born in Geneva in the French-speaking part of Switzerland but he spent most of his disorderly life in France. He was a prolific and influential author with a gift for a vivid turn of phrase, as is demonstrated by the line which begins the first chapter of *The Social Contract,* "Man is born free; and everywhere he is in chains." But he never established a stable personal life, quarreled with collaborators, and continually had to seek patrons. He began his writing career on impulse, winning a prize for his *Discourse on the Sciences and the Arts* in 1749. His continuing concern was how to bring out what he considered the innate goodness of people, which continually brought him into conflict with authorities who saw themselves as the agents of a morality that struggled against the fallen nature of man. *The Social Contract* (1762) was his argument outlining the political conditions for his project. It has been said that *Émile* (1762) should be read as the companion volume on the education that would be necessary for citizens who would freely act for the public good, as opposed to learning to obey authority. Since Rousseau's arguments undermined the role of government as the protector of the faith and promoter of a better life, the royal government sought suppress his work. The alternative government envisaged by Rousseau would be one where free and equal citizens would work together, exercising the "general will," without being drawn into pursuing their private interests at the expense of others. Rousseau's work, like Diderot's, was a great influence on the thinking of leaders of the French Revolution.

SOURCE:

Rousseau, Jean Jacques. 1762. *The Social Contract & Discourses.* G.D.H. Cole, Trans. New York: E. P. Dutton & Co. 1913.

Selections from:

BOOK I

I Mean to inquire if, in the civil order, there can be any sure and legitimate rule of administration, men being taken as they are and laws as they might be. In this inquiry I shall endeavour always to unite what right sanctions with what is prescribed by interest, in order that justice and utility may in no case be divided.

I enter upon my task without proving the importance of the subject. I shall be asked if I am a prince or a legislator, to write on politics. I answer that I am neither, and that is why I do so. If I were a prince or a legislator, I should not waste time in saying what wants doing; I should do it, or hold my peace.

As I was born a citizen of a free State, and a member of the Sovereign, I feel that, however feeble the influence my voice can have on public affairs, the right of voting on them makes it my duty to study them: and I am happy, when I reflect upon governments, to find my inquiries always furnish me with new reasons for loving that of my own country.

CHAPTER I

SUBJECT OF THE FIRST BOOK

MAN is born free; and everywhere he is in chains. One thinks himself the master of others, and still remains a greater slave than they. How did this change come about? I do not know. What can make it legitimate? That question I think I can answer.

If I took into account only force, and the effects derived from it, I should say: "As long as a people is compelled to obey, and obeys, it does well; as soon as it can shake off the yoke, and shakes it off, it does still better; for, regaining its liberty by the same right as took it away, either it is justified in resuming it, or there was no justification for those who took it away?" But the social order is a sacred right which is the basis of all other rights. Nevertheless, this right does not come from nature, and must therefore be founded on conventions. Before coming to that, I have to prove what I have just asserted.

CHAPTER II

THE FIRST SOCIETIES

The most ancient of all societies, and the only one that is natural, is the family: and even so the children remain attached to the father only so long as they need him for their preservation. As soon as this need ceases, the natural bond is dissolved. The children, released from the obedience they owed to the father, and the father, released from the care he owed his children, return equally to independence. If they remain united, they continue so no longer naturally, but voluntarily; and the family itself is then maintained only by convention.

This common liberty results from the nature of man. His first law is to provide for his own preservation, his first cares are those which he owes to himself; and, as soon as he reaches years of discretion, he is the sole judge of the proper means of preserving himself, and consequently becomes his own master.

The family then may be called the first model of political societies: the ruler corresponds to the father, and the people to the children; and all, being born free and equal, alienate their liberty only for their own advantage. The whole difference is that, in the family, the love of the father for his children repays him for the care he takes of them, while, in the State, the pleasure of commanding takes the place of the love which the chief cannot have for the peoples under him. . . .

CHAPTER III

THE RIGHT OF THE STRONGEST

The strongest is never strong enough to be always the master, unless he transforms strength into right, and obedience into duty. Hence the right of the strongest, which, though to all seeming meant ironically, is really laid down as a fundamental principle. But are we never to have an explanation of this phrase? Force is a physical power, and I fail to see what moral effect it can have. To yield to force is an act of necessity, not of will—at the most, an act of prudence. In what sense can it be a duty?

Suppose for a moment that this so-called "right" exists. I maintain that the sole result is a mass of inexplicable nonsense. For, if force creates right, the effect changes with the cause: every force that is greater than the first succeeds to its right. As soon as it is possible to disobey with impunity, disobedience is legitimate; and, the strongest being always in the right, the only thing that matters is to act so as to become the strongest. But what kind of right is that which perishes when force fails? If we must obey perforce, there is no need to obey because we ought; and if we are not forced to obey, we are under no obligation to do so. Clearly, the word "right" adds nothing to force: in this connection, it means absolutely nothing.

Obey the powers that be. If this means yield to force, it is a good precept, but superfluous: I can answer for its never being violated. All power comes from God, I admit; but so does all sickness: does that mean that we are forbidden to call in the doctor? A brigand surprises me at the edge of a wood: must I not merely surrender my purse on compulsion; but, even if I could withhold it, am I in conscience bound to give it up? For certainly the pistol he holds is also a power.

Let us then admit that force does not create right, and that we are obliged to obey only legitimate powers. In that case, my original question recurs.

CHAPTER VI

THE SOCIAL COMPACT

I SUPPOSE men to have reached the point at which the obstacles in the way of their preservation in the state of nature show their power of resistance to be greater than the resources at the disposal of each individual for his maintenance in that state. That primitive condition can then subsist no longer; and the human race would perish unless it changed its manner of existence.

But, as men cannot engender new forces, but only unite and direct existing ones, they have no other means of preserving themselves than the formation, by aggregation, of a sum of forces great enough to overcome the resistance. These they have to bring into play by means of a single motive power, and cause to act in concert.

This sum of forces can arise only where several persons come together: but, as the force and liberty of each man are the chief instruments of his self-preservation, how can he pledge them without harming his own interests, and neglecting the care he owes to himself? This difficulty, in its bearing on my present subject, may be stated in the following terms—

"The problem is to find a form of association which will defend and protect with the whole common force the person and goods of each associate, and in which each, while uniting himself with all, may still obey himself alone, and remain as free as before." This is the fundamental problem of which the *Social Contract* provides the solution.

The clauses of this contract are so determined by the nature of the act that the slightest modification would make them vain and ineffective; so that, although they have perhaps never been formally set forth, they are everywhere the same and everywhere tacitly admitted and recognised, until, on the violation of the social compact, each regains his original rights and resumes his natural liberty, while losing the conventional liberty in favour of which he renounced it.

These clauses, properly understood, may be reduced to one—the total alienation of each associate, together with all his rights, to the whole community; for, in the first place, as each gives himself absolutely, the conditions are the same for all; and, this being so, no one has any interest in making them burdensome to others.

Moreover, the alienation being without reserve, the union is as perfect as it can be, and no associate has anything more to demand: for, if the individuals retained certain rights, as there would be no common superior to decide between them and the public, each, being on one point his own judge, would ask to be so on all; the state of nature would thus continue, and the association would necessarily become inoperative or tyrannical.

Finally, each man, in giving himself to all, gives himself to nobody; and as there is no associate over whom he does not acquire the same right as he yields others over himself, he gains an equivalent for everything he loses, and an increase of force for the preservation of what he has.

If then we discard from the social compact what is not of its essence, we shall find that it reduces itself to the following terms—

"Each of us puts his person and all his power in common under the supreme direction of the general will, and, in our corporate capacity, we receive each member as an indivisible part of the whole.". . .

CHAPTER VII

THE SOVEREIGN

. . . As soon as [the] multitude is so united in one body, it is impossible to offend against one of the members without attacking the body, and still more to offend against the body without the members resenting it. Duty and interest therefore equally oblige the two contracting parties to give each other help; and the same men should seek to combine, in their double capacity, all the advantages dependent upon that capacity.

Again, the Sovereign, being formed wholly of the individuals who compose it, neither has nor can have any interest contrary to theirs; and consequently the sovereign power need give no guarantee to its subjects, because it is impossible for the body to wish to hurt all its members. We shall also see later on that it cannot hurt any in particular. The Sovereign, merely by virtue of what it is, is always what it should be.

This, however, is not the case with the relation of the subjects to the Sovereign, which, despite the common interest, would have no security that they would fulfill their undertakings, unless it found means to assure itself of their fidelity.

In fact, each individual, as a man, may have a particular will contrary or dissimilar to the general will which he has as a citizen. His particular interest may speak to him quite differently from the common interest: his absolute and naturally independent existence may make him look upon what he owes to the common cause as a gratuitous contribution, the loss of which will do less harm to others than the payment of it is burdensome to himself; and, regarding the moral person which constitutes the State as a persona ficta, because not a man, he may wish to enjoy the rights of citizenship without being ready to fulfill the duties of a subject. The continuance of such an injustice could not but prove the undoing of the body politic.

In order then that the social compact may not be an empty formula, it tacitly includes the undertaking, which alone can give force to the rest, that whoever refuses to obey the general will shall be compelled to do so by the whole body. This means nothing less than that he will be forced to be free; for this is the condition which, by giving each citizen to his country, secures him against all personal dependence. In this lies the key to the working of the political machine; this alone legitimises civil undertakings, which, without it, would be absurd, tyrannical, and liable to the most frightful abuses.

BOOK II

CHAPTER I

THAT SOVEREIGNTY IS INALIENABLE

The first and most important deduction from the principles we have so far laid down is that the general will alone can direct the State according to the object for which it was instituted, i. e. the common good: for if the clashing of particular interests made the establishment of societies necessary, the agreement of these very interests made it possible. The common element in these different interests is what forms the social tie; and, were there no point of agreement between them all, no society could exist. It is solely on the basis of this common interest that every society should be governed.

I hold then that Sovereignty, being nothing less than the exercise of the general will, can never be alienated, and that the Sovereign, who is no less than a collective being, cannot be represented except by himself: the power indeed may be transmitted, but not the will.

In reality, if it is not impossible for a particular will to agree on some point with the general will, it is at least impossible for the agreement to be lasting and constant; for the particular will tends, by its very nature, to partiality, while the general will tends to equality. It is even more impossible to have any guarantee of this agreement; for even if it should always exist, it would be the effect not of art, but of chance. The Sovereign may indeed say: "I now will actually what this man wills, or at least what he says he wills"; but it cannot say: "What he wills tomorrow, I too shall will" because it is absurd for the will to bind itself for the future, nor is it incumbent on any will to consent to anything that is not for the good of the being who wills. If then the people promises simply to obey, by that very act it dissolves itself and loses what makes it a people; the moment a master exists, there is no longer a Sovereign, and from that moment the body politic has ceased to exist. . . .

CHAPTER II

THAT SOVEREIGNTY IS INDIVISIBLE

Sovereignty, for the same reason as makes it inalienable, is indivisible; for will either is, or is not, general;[1] it is the will either of the body of the people, or only of a part of it. In the first case, the will, when declared, is an act of Sovereignty and constitutes law: in the second, it is merely a particular will, or act of magistracy—at the most a decree.

But our political theorists, unable to divide Sovereignty in principle, divide it according to its object: into force and will; into legislative power and executive power; into rights of taxation, justice and war; into internal administration and power of foreign treaty. Sometimes they confuse all these sections, and sometimes they distinguish them; they turn the Sovereign into a fantastic being composed of several connected pieces: it is as if they were making man of several bodies, one with eyes, one with arms, another with feet, and each with nothing besides. We are told that the jugglers of Japan dismember a child before the eyes of the spectators; then they throw all the members into the air one after another, and the child falls down alive and whole. The conjuring tricks of our political theorists are very like that; they first dismember the body politic by an illusion worthy of a fair, and then join it together again we know not how.

This error is due to a lack of exact notions concerning the Sovereign authority, and to taking for parts of it what are only emanations from it. Thus, for example, the acts of declaring

---

1 to be general, a will need not always be unanimous; but every vote must be counted: any exclusion is a breach of generality. [G.D.H.C.]

war and making peace have been regarded as acts of Sovereignty; but this is not the case, as these acts do not constitute law, but merely the application of a law, a particular act which decides how the law applies, as we shall see clearly when the idea attached to the word law has been defined.

If we examined the other divisions in the same manner, we should find that, whenever Sovereignty seems to be divided, there is an illusion: the rights which are taken as being part of Sovereignty are really all subordinate, and always imply supreme wills of which they only sanction the execution. . . .

CHAPTER III

WHETHER THE GENERAL WILL IS FALLIBLE

IT follows from what has gone before that the general will is always right and tends to the public advantage; but it does not follow that the deliberations of the people are always equally correct. Our will is always for our own good, but we do not always see what that is; the people is never corrupted, but it is often deceived, and on such occasions only does it seem to will what is bad.

There is often a great deal of difference between the will of all and the general will; the latter considers only the common interest, while the former takes private interest into account, and is no more than a sum of particular wills: but take away from these same wills the pluses and minuses that cancel one another,[1] and the general will remains as the sum of the differences.

---

1 "Every interest," says the Marguis d'Argenson, "has different principles. The agreement of two particular interests is formed by opposition to a third." He might have added that the agreement of all interests is formed by opposition to that of each. If there were no different interests, the common interest would be barely felt, as it would encounter no obstacle; all would go on of its own accord, and politics would cease to be an art. (J. J. Rousseau)

If, when the people, being furnished with adequate information, held its deliberations, the citizens had no communication one with another, the grand total of the small differences would always give the general will, and the decision would always be good. But when factions arise, and partial associations are formed at the expense of the great association, the will of each of these associations becomes general in relation to its members, while it remains particular in relation to the State: it may then be said that there are no longer as many votes as there are men, but only as many as there are associations. The differences become less numerous and give a less general result. Lastly, when one of these associations is so great as to prevail over all the rest, the result is no longer a sum of small differences, but a single difference; in this case there is no longer a general will, and the opinion which prevails is purely particular.

It is therefore essential, if the general will is to be able to express itself, that there should be no partial society within the State, and that each citizen should think only his own thoughts:[1] which was indeed the sublime and unique system established by the great Lycurgus. But is there are partial societies, it is best to have as many as possible and to prevent them from being unequal, as was done by Solon, Numa and Servius. These precautions are the only ones that can guarantee that the general will shall be always enlightened, and that the people shall in no way deceive itself.

---

1 "In fact," says Macchiavelli, "there are some divisions that are harmful to a Republic and some that are advantageous. Those which stir up sects and parties are harmful; those attended by neither are advantageous. Since, then, the founder of a Republic cannot help enmities arising, he ought at least to prevent them from growing into sects." (*History of Florence,* Book vii). [Rousseau quotes the Italian. G.D.H.C.]

CHAPTER IV

THE LIMITS OF THE SOVEREIGN POWER

IF the State is a moral person whose life is in the union of its members, and if the most important of its cares is the care for its own preservation, it must have a universal and compelling force, in order to move and dispose each part as may be most advantageous to the whole. As nature gives each man absolute power over all his members, the social compact gives the body politic absolute power over all its members also; and it is this power which, under the direction of the general will, bears, as I have said, the name of Sovereignty.

But, besides the public person, we have to consider the private persons composing it, whose life and liberty are naturally independent of it. We are bound then to distinguish clearly between the respective rights of the citizens and the Sovereign,[1] and between the duties the former have to fulfill as subjects, and the natural rights they should enjoy as men.

Each man alienates, I admit, by the social compact, only such part of his powers, goods and liberty as it is important for the community to control; but it must also be granted that the Sovereign is sole judge of what is important.

Every service a citizen can render the State he ought to render as soon as the Sovereign demands it; but the Sovereign, for its part, cannot impose upon its subjects any fetters that are useless to the Community, nor can it even wish to do so; for no more by the law of reason than by the law of nature can anything occur without a cause.

The undertakings which bind us to the social body are obligatory only because they are mutual; and their nature is such that in fulfilling them we cannot work for others without

---

1 Attentive readers, do not, I pray, be in a hurry to charge me with contradicting myself. The terminology made it unavoidable, considering the poverty of the language; but wait and see. (J. J. Rousseau)

working for ourselves. Why is it that the general will is always in the right, and that all continually will the happiness of each one, unless it is because there is not a man who does not think of "each" as meaning him, and consider himself in voting for all? This proves that equality of rights and the idea of justice which such equality creates originate in the preference each man gives to himself, and accordingly in the very nature of man. It proves that the general will, to be really such, must be general in its object as well as its essence; that it must both come from all and apply to all; and that it loses its natural rectitude when it is directed to some particular and determinate object, because in such a case we are judging of something foreign to us, and have no true principle of equity to guide us. . . .

. . . It should be seen from the foregoing that what makes the will general is less the number of voters than the common interest uniting them; for, under this system, each necessarily submits to the conditions he imposes on others: and this admirable agreement between interest and justice gives to the common deliberations an equitable character which at once vanishes when any particular question is discussed, in the absence of a common interest to unite and identify the ruling of the judge with that of the party.

From whatever side we approach our principle, we reach the same conclusion, that the social compact sets up among the citizens an equality of such a kind, that they all bind themselves to observe the same conditions and should therefore all enjoy the same rights. Thus, from the very nature of the compact, every act of Sovereignty, *i.e.* every authentic act of the general will, binds or favours all the citizens equally; so that the Sovereign recognises only the body of the nation, and draws no distinctions between those of whom it is made up. What, then, strictly speaking, is an act of Sovereignty? It is not a convention between a superior and an inferior, but a convention between the body and each of its members. It is legitimate, because based on the social contract, and equitable, because common to all; useful, because it can have no other object than the general good, and stable, because guaranteed by the public force and the supreme power. So long as the subjects have to submit only to conventions of this sort, they obey no-one but their own will; and to ask how far the respective rights of the Sovereign and the citizens extend, is to ask up to what point the latter can enter into undertakings with themselves, each with all, and all with each.

We can see from this that the sovereign power, absolute, sacred and inviolable as it is, does not and cannot exceed the limits of general conventions, and that every man may dispose at will of such goods and liberty as these conventions leave him; so that the Sovereign never has a right to lay more charges on one subject than on another, because, in that case, the question becomes particular, and ceases to be within its competency.

When these distinctions have once been admitted, it is seen to be so untrue that there is, in the social contract, any real renunciation on the part of the individuals, that the position in which they find themselves as a result of the contract is really preferable to that in which they were before. Instead of a renunciation, they have made an advantageous exchange: instead of an uncertain and precarious way of living they have got one that is better and more secure; instead of natural independence they have got liberty, instead of the power to harm others security for themselves, and instead of their strength, which others might overcome, a right which social union makes invincible. Their very life, which they have devoted to the State, is by it constantly protected; and when they risk it in the State's defence, what more are they doing than giving back what they have received from it? What are they doing that they would not do more often and with greater danger in the state of nature, in which they would inevitably have to fight battles at the peril of their lives in defence of that which is the means of their preservation? All have indeed to fight when their country needs them; but then no one has ever to fight for himself. Do we not gain something by running, on behalf of what gives us our security, only some of the risks we should have to run for ourselves, as soon as we lost it?

CHAPTER V

THE RIGHT OF LIFE AND DEATH

THE question is often asked how individuals, having no right to dispose of their own lives, can transfer to the Sovereign a right which they do not possess. The difficulty of answering this question seems to me to lie in its being wrongly stated. Every man has a right to risk his own life in order to preserve it. Has it ever been said that a man who throws himself out of the window to escape from a fire is guilty of suicide? Has such a crime ever been laid to the charge of him who perishes in a storm because, when he went on board, he knew of the danger?

The social treaty has for its end the preservation of the contracting parties. He who wills the end wills the means also, and the means must involve some risks, and even some losses. He who wishes to preserve his life at others' expense should also, when it is necessary, be ready to give it up for their sake. Furthermore, the citizen is no longer the judge of the dangers to which the law desires him to expose himself; and when the prince says to him: "It is expedient for the State that you should die," he ought to die, because it is only on that condition that he has been living in security up to the present, and because his life is no longer a mere bounty of nature, but a gift made conditionally by the State.

The death-penalty inflicted upon criminals may be looked on in much the same light: it is in order that we may not fall victims to an assassin that we consent to die if we ourselves turn assassins. In this treaty, so far from disposing of our own lives, we think only of securing them, and it is not to be assumed that any of the parties then expects to get hanged. Again, every malefactor, by attacking social rights, becomes on forfeit a rebel and a traitor to his country; by violating its laws he ceases to be a member of it; he even makes war upon it. In such a case the preservation of the State is inconsistent with his own, and one or the other must perish; in putting the guilty to death, we slay not so much the citizen as an enemy. The trial and the judgment are the proofs that he has broken the social treaty, and is in consequence no longer a member of the State. Since, then, he has recognised himself to be such by living there, he must be removed by exile as a violator of the compact, or by death as a public enemy; for such an enemy is not a moral person, but merely a man; and in such a case the right of war is to kill the vanquished.

But, it will be said, the condemnation of a criminal is a particular act. I admit it: but such condemnation is not a function of the Sovereign; it is a right the Sovereign can confer without being able itself to exert it. All my ideas are consistent, but I cannot expound them all at once.

We may add that frequent punishments are always a sign of weakness or remissness on the part of the government. There is not a single ill-doer who could not be turned to some good. The State has no right to put to death, even for the sake of making an example, any one whom it can leave alive without danger.

The right of pardoning or exempting the guilty from a penalty imposed by the law and pronounced by the judge belongs only to the authority which is superior to both judge and law, *i.e.* the Sovereign; even its right in this matter is far from clear, and the cases for exercising it are extremely rare. In a well-governed State, there are few punishments, not because there are many pardons but because criminals are rare; it is when a State is in decay that the multitude of crimes is a guarantee of impunity. Under the Roman Republic, neither the Senate nor the Consuls ever attempted to pardon; even the people never did so, though it sometimes revoked its own decision. Frequent pardons mean that crime will soon need them no longer, and no-one can help seeing whither that leads. But I feel my heart protesting and restraining my pen; let us leave these questions to the just man who has never offended, and would himself stand in no need of pardon.

CHAPTER VI

LAW

BY the social compact we have given the body politic existence and life; we have now by legislation to give it movement and will. For the original act by which the body is formed and united still in no respect determines what it ought to do for its preservation.

What is well and in conformity with order is so by the nature of things and independently of human conventions. All justice comes from God, who is its sole source; but if we knew how to receive so high an inspiration, we should need neither government nor laws. Doubtless, there is a universal justice emanating from reason alone; but this justice, to be admitted among us, must be mutual. Humanly speaking, in default of natural sanctions, the laws of justice are ineffective among men: they merely make for the good of the wicked and the undoing of the just, when the just man observes them towards everybody and nobody observes them towards him. Conventions and laws are therefore needed to join rights to duties and refer justice to its object. In the state of nature, where everything is common, I owe nothing to him whom I have promised nothing; I recognise as belonging to others only what is of no use to me. In the state of society all rights are fixed by law, and the case becomes different.

But what, after all, is a law? As long as we remain satisfied with attaching purely metaphysical ideas to the word, we shall go on arguing without arriving at an understanding; and when we have defined a law of nature, we shall be no nearer the definition of a law of the State.

I have already said that there can be no general will directed to a particular object. Such an object must be either within or outside the State. If outside, a will which is alien to it cannot be, in relation to it, general; if within, it is part of the State, and in that case there arises a relation between whole and part which makes them two separate beings, of which the part is one, and the whole minus the part the other. But the whole minus a part cannot be the whole; and while this relation persists, there can be no whole, but only two unequal parts; and it follows that the will of one is no longer in any respect general in relation to the other.

But when the whole people decrees for the whole people, it is considering only itself; and if a relation is then formed, it is between two aspects of the entire object, without there being any division of the whole. In that case the matter about which the decree is made is, like the decreeing will, general. This act is what I call a law. . . .

. . . Laws are, properly speaking, only the conditions of civil association. The people, being subject to the laws, ought to be their author: the conditions of the society ought to be regulated solely by those who come together to form it. But how are they to regulate them? Is it to be by common agreement, by a sudden inspiration? Has the body politic an organ to declare its will? Who can give it the foresight to formulate and announce its acts in advance? Or how is it to announce them in the hour of need? How can a blind multitude, which often does not know what it wills, because it rarely knows what is good for it, carry out for itself so great and difficult an enterprise as a system of legislation? Of itself the people wills always the good, but of itself it by no means always sees it. The general will is always in the right, but the judgment which guides it is not always enlightened. It must be got to see objects as they are, and sometimes as they ought to appear to it; it must be shown the good road it is in search of, secured from the seductive influences of individual wills, taught to see times and spaces as a series, and made to weigh the attractions of present and sensible advantages against the danger of distant and hidden evils. The individuals see the good they reject; the public wills the good it does not see. All stand equally in need of guidance. The former must be compelled to bring their wills into conformity with their reason; the latter must be taught to know what it wills. If that is done, public enlightenment leads to the union of understanding and will in the social body: the parts are made to work exactly together, and the whole is raised to its highest power. This makes a legislator necessary.

THOMAS HOBBES

1588-1679

LEVIATHAN

1651

Consider the relation of the description of authority below with the excerpt containing Hobbes' account of man's natural state found on p. 57 in the Freedom section. To what extent does this understanding of the purpose of government logically follow from the conviction that without authoritative power, life would be a "war of all, against all"?

Selections from: Hobbes, Thomas. 1651. *Leviathan.* Oxford: Oxford UP, 1909.

Chapter XVII: Of the Causes, Generation, and Definition of a Commonwealth (128-132)

Chapter XXI: Of the Liberty of Subjects (161-171)

CHAPTER XVII

OF THE CAUSES, GENERATION, AND DEFINITION OF A COMMONWEALTH

THE final cause, end, or design of men (who naturally love liberty, and dominion over others) in the introduction of that restraint upon themselves, in which we see them live in Commonwealths, is the foresight of their own preservation, and of a more contented life thereby; that is to say, of getting themselves out from that miserable condition of war which is necessarily consequent, as hath been shown, to the natural passions of men when there is no visible power to keep them in awe, and tie them by fear of punishment to the performance of their covenants, and observation of those laws of nature set down in the fourteenth and fifteenth chapters.

For the laws of nature, as justice, equity, modesty, mercy, and, in sum, doing to others as we would be done to, of themselves, without the terror of some power to cause them to be observed, are contrary to our natural passions, that carry us to partiality, pride, revenge, and the like. And covenants, without the sword, are but words and of no strength to secure a man at all. Therefore, notwithstanding the laws of nature (which every one hath then kept, when he has the will to keep them, when he can do it safely), if there be no power erected, or not great enough for our security, every man will and may lawfully rely on his own strength and art for caution against all other men. And in all places, where men have lived by small families, to rob and spoil one another has been a trade, and so far from being reputed against the law of nature that the greater spoils they gained, the greater was their honour; and men observed no other laws therein but the laws of honour; that is, to abstain from cruelty, leaving to men their lives and instruments of husbandry. And as small families did then; so now do cities and kingdoms, which are but greater families (for their own security), enlarge their dominions upon all pretences of danger, and fear of invasion, or assistance that may be given to invaders; endeavour as much as they can to subdue or weaken their neighbours by open force, and secret arts, for want of other caution, justly; and are remembered for it in after ages with honour.

Nor is it the joining together of a small number of men that gives them this security; because in small numbers, small additions on the one side or the other make the advantage of strength so great as is sufficient to carry the victory, and therefore gives encouragement to an invasion. The multitude sufficient to confide in for our security is not determined by any certain number, but by comparison with the enemy we fear; and is then sufficient when the odds of the enemy is not of so visible and conspicuous moment to determine the event of war, as to move him to attempt.

And be there never so great a multitude; yet if their actions be directed according to their particular judgements, and particular appetites, they can expect thereby no defence, nor protection, neither against a common enemy, nor against the injuries of one another. For being distracted in opinions concerning the best use and application of their strength, they do not help, but hinder one another, and reduce their strength by mutual opposition to nothing: whereby they are easily, not only subdued by a very few that agree together, but also, when there is no common enemy, they make war upon each other for their particular interests. For if we could suppose a great multitude of men to consent in the observation of justice, and other laws of nature, without a common power to keep them all in awe, we might as well suppose all mankind to do the same; and then there neither would be, nor need to be, any civil government or Commonwealth at all, because there would be peace without subjection.

Nor is it enough for the security, which men desire should last all the time of their life, that they be governed and directed by one judgement for a limited time; as in one battle, or one war. For though they obtain a victory by their unanimous endeavour against a foreign enemy, yet afterwards, when either they have no common enemy, or he that by one part is held for an enemy is by another part held for a friend, they must needs by the difference of their interests dissolve, and fall again into a war amongst themselves.

It is true that certain living creatures, as bees and ants, live sociably one with another (which are therefore by Aristotle numbered amongst political creatures), and yet have no other direction than their particular judgements and appetites; nor speech, whereby one of them can signify to another what he thinks expedient for the common benefit: and therefore some man may perhaps desire to know why mankind cannot do the same. To which I answer,

First, that men are continually in competition for honour and dignity, which these creatures are not; and consequently amongst men there ariseth on that ground, envy, and hatred, and finally war; but amongst these not so.

Secondly, that amongst these creatures the common good differeth not from the private; and being by nature inclined to their private, they procure thereby the common benefit. But man, whose joy consisteth in comparing himself with other men, can relish nothing but what is eminent.

Thirdly, that these creatures, having not, as man, the use of reason, do not see, nor think they see, any fault in the administration of their common business: whereas amongst men there are very many that think themselves wiser and abler to govern the public better than the rest, and these strive to reform and innovate, one this way, another that way; and thereby bring it into distraction and civil war.

Fourthly, that these creatures, though they have some use of voice in making known to one another their desires and other affections, yet they want that art of words by which some men can represent to others that which is good in the likeness of evil; and evil, in the likeness of good; and augment or diminish the apparent greatness of good and evil, discontenting men and troubling their peace at their pleasure.

Fifthly, irrational creatures cannot distinguish between injury and damage; and therefore as long as they be at ease, they are not offended with their fellows: whereas man is then most troublesome when he is most at ease; for then it is that he loves to show his wisdom, and control the actions of them that govern the Commonwealth.

Lastly, the agreement of these creatures is natural; that of men is by covenant only, which is artificial: and therefore it is no wonder if there be somewhat else required, besides covenant, to make their agreement constant and lasting; which is a common power to keep them in awe and to direct their actions to the common benefit.

The only way to erect such a common power, as may be able to defend them from the invasion of foreigners, and the injuries of one another, and thereby to secure them in such sort as that by their own industry and by the fruits of the earth they may nourish themselves and live contentedly, is to confer all their power and strength upon one man, or upon one assembly of men, that may reduce all their wills, by plurality of voices, unto one will: which is as much as to say, to appoint one man, or assembly of men, to bear their person; and every one to own and acknowledge himself to be author of whatsoever he that so beareth their person shall act, or cause to be acted, in those things which concern the common peace and safety; and therein to submit their wills, every one to his will, and their judgements to his judgement. This is more than consent, or concord; it is a real unity of them all in one and the same person, made by covenant of every man with every man, in such manner as if every man should say to every man: I authorise and give up my right of governing myself to this man, or to this assembly of men, on this condition; that thou give up, thy right to him, and authorise all his actions in like manner. This done, the multitude so united in one person is called a

COMMONWEALTH; in Latin, CIVITAS. This is the generation of that great LEVIATHAN, or rather, to speak more reverently, of that mortal god to which we owe, under the immortal God, our peace and defence. For by this authority, given him by every particular man in the Commonwealth, he hath the use of so much power and strength conferred on him that, by terror thereof, he is enabled to form the wills of them all, to peace at home, and mutual aid against their enemies abroad. And in him consisteth the essence of the Commonwealth; which, to define it, is: one person, of whose acts a great multitude, by mutual covenants one with another, have made themselves every one the author, to the end he may use the strength and means of them all as he shall think expedient for their peace and common defence.

And he that carryeth this person is called sovereign, and said to have sovereign power; and every one besides, his subject.

The attaining to this sovereign power is by two ways. One, by natural force: as when a man maketh his children to submit themselves, and their children, to his government, as being able to destroy them if they refuse; or by war subdueth his enemies to his will, giving them their lives on that condition. The other, is when men agree amongst themselves to submit to some man, or assembly of men, voluntarily, on confidence to be protected by him against all others. This latter may be called a political Commonwealth, or Commonwealth by Institution; and the former, a Commonwealth by acquisition. And first, I shall speak of a Commonwealth by institution.

CHAPTER XXI

OF THE LIBERTY OF SUBJECTS

LIBERTY, or freedom, signifieth properly the absence of opposition (by opposition, I mean external impediments of motion); and may be applied no less to irrational and inanimate creatures than to rational. For whatsoever is so tied, or environed, as it cannot move but within a certain space, which space is determined by the opposition of some external body, we say it hath not liberty to go further. And so of all living creatures, whilst they are imprisoned, or restrained with walls or chains; and of the water whilst it is kept in by banks or vessels that otherwise would spread itself into a larger space; we use to say they are not at liberty to move in such manner as without those external impediments they would. But when the impediment of motion is in the constitution of the thing itself, we use not to say it wants the liberty, but the power, to move; as when a stone lieth still, or a man is fastened to his bed by sickness.

And according to this proper and generally received meaning of the word, a freeman is he that, in those things which by his strength and wit he is able to do, is not hindered to do what he has a will to. But when the words free and liberty are applied to anything but bodies, they are abused; for that which is not subject to motion is not to subject to impediment: and therefore, when it is said, for example, the way is free, no liberty of the way is signified, but of those that walk in it without stop. And when we say a gift is free, there is not meant any liberty of the gift, but of the giver, that was not bound by any law or covenant to give it. So when we speak freely, it is not the liberty of voice, or pronunciation, but of the man, whom no law hath obliged to speak otherwise than he did. Lastly, from the use of the words free will, no liberty can be inferred of the will, desire, or inclination, but the liberty of the man; which consisteth in this, that he finds no stop in doing what he has the will, desire, or inclination to do.

Fear and liberty are consistent: as when a man throweth his goods into the sea for fear the ship should sink, he doth it nevertheless very willingly, and may refuse to do it if he will; it is therefore the action of one that was free: so a man sometimes pays his debt, only for fear of imprisonment, which, because no body hindered him from detaining, was the action of a man at liberty. And generally all actions which men do in Commonwealths, for fear of the law, are actions which the doers had liberty to omit.

Liberty and necessity are consistent: as in the water that hath not only liberty, but a necessity of descending by the channel; so, likewise in the actions which men voluntarily do, which, because they proceed their will, proceed from liberty, and yet because every act of man's will and every desire and inclination proceedeth from some cause, and that from another cause, in a continual chain (whose first link is in the hand of God, the first of all causes), proceed from necessity. So that to him that could see the connexion of those causes, the necessity of all men's voluntary actions would appear manifest. And therefore God, that seeth and disposeth all things, seeth also that the liberty of man in doing what he will is accompanied with the necessity of doing that which God will and no more, nor less. For though men may do many things which God does not command, nor is therefore author of them; yet they can have no passion, nor appetite to anything, of which appetite God's will is not the cause. And did not His will assure the necessity of man's will, and consequently of all that on man's will dependeth, the liberty of men would be a contradiction and impediment to the omnipotence and liberty of God. And this shall suffice, as to the matter in hand, of that natural liberty, which only is properly called liberty.

But as men, for the attaining of peace and conservation of themselves thereby, have made an artificial man, which we call a Commonwealth; so also have they made artificial chains, called civil laws, which they themselves, by mutual covenants, have fastened at one end to the lips of that man, or assembly, to whom they have given the sovereign power, and at the other to their own ears. These bonds, in their own nature but weak, may nevertheless be made to hold, by the danger, though not by the difficulty of breaking them.

In relation to these bonds only it is that I am to speak now of the liberty of subjects. For seeing there is no Commonwealth in the world wherein there be rules enough set down for the regulating of all the actions and words of men (as being a thing impossible): it followeth necessarily that in all kinds of actions, by the laws pretermitted, men have the liberty of doing what their own reasons shall suggest for the most profitable to themselves. For if we take liberty in the proper sense, for corporal liberty; that is to say, freedom from chains and prison, it were very absurd for men to clamour as they do for the liberty they so manifestly enjoy. Again, if we take liberty for an exemption from laws, it is no less absurd for men to demand as they do that liberty by which all other men may be masters of their lives. And yet as absurd as it is, this is it they demand, not knowing that the laws are of no power to protect them without a sword in the hands of a man, or men, to cause those laws to be put in execution. The liberty of a subject lieth therefore only in those things which, in regulating their actions, the sovereign hath pretermitted: such as is the liberty to buy, and sell, and otherwise contract with one another; to choose their own abode, their own diet, their own trade of life, and institute their children as they themselves think fit; and the like.

Nevertheless we are not to understand that by such liberty the sovereign power of life and death is either abolished or limited. For it has been already shown that nothing the sovereign representative can do to a subject, on what pretence soever, can properly be called injustice or injury; because every subject is author of every act the sovereign doth, so that he never wanteth right to any thing, otherwise than as he himself is the subject of God, and bound thereby to observe the laws of nature. And therefore it may and doth often happen in Commonwealths that a subject may be put to death by the command of the sovereign power, and yet neither do the other wrong; as when Jephthah caused his daughter to be sacrificed: in which, and the like cases, he that so dieth had liberty to do the action, for which he is nevertheless, without injury, put to death. And the same holdeth also in a sovereign prince that putteth to death an innocent subject. For though the action be against the law of nature, as being contrary to equity (as was the killing of Uriah by David); yet it was not an injury to Uriah, but to God. Not to Uriah, because the right to do what he pleased was given him by Uriah himself; and yet to God, because David was God's subject and prohibited all iniquity by the law of nature. Which distinction, David himself, when he repented the fact, evidently confirmed, saying, "To thee only have I sinned." In the same manner, the people of Athens, when they banished the most potent of their Commonwealth for ten years, thought they committed no injustice; and yet they never questioned what crime he had done, but what hurt he would do: nay, they commanded the banishment of they knew not whom; and every citizen bringing his oyster shell into the market place, written with the name of him he desired should be banished, without actually accusing him sometimes banished an Aristides, for his reputation of justice; and sometimes a scurrilous jester, as Hyperbolus, to make a jest of it. And yet a man cannot say the sovereign people of Athens wanted right to banish them; or an Athenian the liberty to jest, or to be just.

The liberty whereof there is so frequent and honourable mention in the histories and philosophy of the ancient Greeks and Romans, and in the writings and discourse of those that from them have received all their learning in the politics, is not the liberty of particular men, but the liberty of the Commonwealth: which is the same with that which every man then should have, if there were no civil laws nor Commonwealth at all. And the effects of it also be the same. For as amongst masterless men, there is perpetual war of every man against his neighbour; no inheritance to transmit to the son, nor to expect from the father; no propriety of goods or lands; no security; but a full and absolute liberty in every particular man: so in states and Commonwealths not dependent on one another, every Commonwealth, not every man, has an absolute liberty to do what it shall judge, that is to say, what that man or assembly that representeth it shall judge, most conducing to their benefit. But withal, they live in the condition of a perpetual war, and upon the confines of battle, with their frontiers armed, and cannons planted against their neighbours round about. The Athenians and Romans were free; that is, free Commonwealths: not that any particular men had the liberty to resist their own representative, but that their representative had the liberty to resist, or invade, other people. There is written on the turrets of the city of Luca in great characters at this day, the word LIBERTAS; yet no man can thence infer that a particular man has more liberty or immunity from the service of the Commonwealth there than in Constantinople. Whether a Commonwealth be monarchical or popular, the freedom is still the same.

But it is an easy thing for men to be deceived by the specious name of liberty; and, for want of judgement to distinguish, mistake that for their private inheritance and birthright which is the right of the public only. And when the same error is confirmed by the authority of men in reputation for their writings on this subject, it is no wonder if it produce sedition and change of government. In these western parts of the world we are made to receive our opinions concerning the institution and rights of Commonwealths from Aristotle, Cicero, and other men, Greeks and Romans, that, living under popular states, derived those rights, not from the principles of nature, but transcribed them into their books out of the practice of their own Commonwealths, which were popular; as the grammarians describe the rules of language out of the practice of the time; or the rules of poetry out of the poems of Homer and Virgil. And because the Athenians were taught (to keep them from desire of changing their government) that they were freemen, and all that lived under monarchy were slaves; therefore Aristotle puts it down in his Politics "In democracy, liberty is to be supposed: for it is commonly held that no man is free in any other government." [Aristotle, *Politics*, Bk VI] And as Aristotle, so Cicero and other writers have grounded their civil doctrine on the opinions of the Romans, who were taught to hate monarchy: at first, by them that, having deposed their sovereign, shared amongst them the sovereignty of Rome; and afterwards by their successors. And by reading of these Greek and Latin authors, men from their childhood have gotten a habit, under a false show of liberty, of favouring tumults, and of licentious controlling the actions of their sovereigns; and again of controlling those controllers; with the effusion of so much blood, as I think I may truly say there was never anything so dearly bought as these western parts have bought the learning of the Greek and Latin tongues.

To come now to the particulars of the true liberty of a subject; that is to say, what are the things which, though commanded by the sovereign, he may nevertheless without injustice refuse to do; we are to consider what rights we pass away when we make a Commonwealth; or, which is all one, what liberty we deny ourselves by owning all the actions, without exception, of the man or assembly we make our sovereign. For in the act of our submission consisteth both our obligation and our liberty; which must therefore be inferred by arguments taken from thence; there being no obligation on any man which ariseth not from some act of his own; for all men equally are by nature free. And because such arguments must either be drawn from the express words, "I authorise all his actions," or from the intention of him that submitteth himself to his power (which intention is to be understood by the end for which he so submitteth), the obligation and liberty of the subject is to be derived either from those words, or others equivalent, or else from the end of the institution of sovereignty; namely, the peace of the subjects within themselves, and their defence against a common enemy.

First therefore, seeing sovereignty by institution is by covenant of every one to every one; and sovereignty by acquisition, by covenants of the vanquished to the victor, or child to the parent; it is manifest that every subject has liberty in all those things the right whereof cannot by covenant be transferred. I have shown before, in the fourteenth Chapter, that covenants not to defend a man's own body are void. Therefore, If the sovereign command a man, though justly condemned, to kill, wound, or maim himself; or not to resist those that assault him; or to abstain from the use of food, air, medicine, or any other thing without which he cannot live; yet hath that man the liberty to disobey.

If a man be interrogated by the sovereign, or his authority, concerning a crime done by himself, he is not bound (without assurance of pardon) to confess it; because no man, as I have shown in the same chapter, can be obliged by covenant to accuse himself.

Again, the consent of a subject to sovereign power is contained in these words, "I authorise, or take upon me, all his actions"; in which there is no restriction at all of his own former natural liberty: for by allowing him to kill me, I am not bound to kill myself when he commands me. It is one thing to say, "Kill me, or my fellow, if you please"; another thing to say, "I will kill myself, or my fellow." It followeth, therefore, that No man is bound by the words themselves, either to kill himself or any other man; and consequently, that the obligation a man may sometimes have, upon the command of the sovereign, to execute any dangerous or dishonourable office, dependeth not on the words of our submission, but on the intention; which is to be understood by the end thereof. When therefore our refusal to obey frustrates the end for which the sovereignty was ordained, then there is no liberty to refuse; otherwise, there is.

Upon this ground a man that is commanded as a soldier to fight against the enemy, though his sovereign have right enough to punish his refusal with death, may nevertheless in many cases refuse, without injustice; as when he substituteth a sufficient soldier in his place: for in this case he deserteth not the service of the Commonwealth. And there is allowance to be made for natural timorousness, not only to women (of whom no such dangerous duty is expected), but also to men of feminine courage. When armies fight, there is on one side, or both, a running away; yet when they do it not out of treachery, but fear, they are not esteemed to do it unjustly, but dishonourably. For the same reason, to avoid battle is not injustice, but cowardice. But he that enrolleth himself a soldier, or taketh impressed money, taketh away the excuse of a timorous nature, and is obliged, not only to go to the battle, but also not to run from it without his captain's leave. And when the defence of the Commonwealth requireth at once the help of all that are able to bear arms, every one is obliged; because otherwise the institution of the Commonwealth, which they have not the purpose or courage to preserve, was in vain.

To resist the sword of the Commonwealth in defence of another man, guilty or innocent, no man hath liberty; because such liberty takes away from the sovereign the means of protecting us, and is therefore destructive of the very essence of government. But in case a great many men together have already resisted the sovereign power unjustly, or committed some capital crime for which every one of them expecteth death, whether have they not the liberty then to join together, and assist, and defend one another? Certainly they have: for they but defend their lives, which the guilty man may as well do as the innocent. There was indeed injustice in the first breach of their duty: their bearing of arms subsequent to it, though it be to maintain what they have done, is no new unjust act. And if it be only to defend their persons, it is not unjust at all. But the offer of pardon taketh from them to whom it is offered the plea of self-defence, and maketh their perseverance in assisting or defending the rest unlawful.

As for other liberties, they depend on the silence of the law. In cases where the sovereign has prescribed no rule, there the subject hath the liberty to do, or forbear, according to his own discretion. And therefore such liberty is in some places more, and in some less; and in some times more, in other times less, according as they that have the sovereignty shall think most convenient. As for example, there was a time when in England a man might enter into his own land, and dispossess such as wrongfully possessed it, by force. But in after times that liberty of forcible entry was taken away by a statute made by the king in Parliament. And in some places of the world men have the liberty of many wives: in other places, such liberty is not allowed.

If a subject have a controversy with his sovereign of debt, or of right of possession of lands or goods, or concerning any service required at his hands, or concerning any penalty, corporal or pecuniary, grounded on a precedent law, he hath the same liberty to sue for his right as if it were against a subject, and before such judges as are appointed by the sovereign. For seeing the sovereign demandeth by force of a former law, and not by virtue of his power, he declareth thereby that he requireth no more than shall appear to be due by that law. The suit therefore is not contrary to the will of the sovereign, and consequently the subject hath the liberty to demand the hearing of his cause, and sentence according to that law. But if he demand or take anything by pretence of his power, there lieth, in that case, no action of law: for all that is done by him in virtue of his power is done by the authority of every subject, and consequently, he that brings an action against the sovereign brings it against himself.

If a monarch, or sovereign assembly, grant a liberty to all or any of his subjects, which grant standing, he is disabled to provide for their safety; the grant is void, unless he directly renounce or transfer the sovereignty to another. For in that he might openly (if it had been his will), and in plain terms, have renounced or transferred it and did not, it is to be understood it was not his will, but that the grant proceeded from ignorance of the repugnancy between such a liberty and the sovereign power: and therefore the sovereignty is still retained, and consequently all those powers which are necessary to the exercising thereof; such as are the power of war and peace, of judicature, of appointing officers and counsellors, of levying money, and the rest named in the eighteenth Chapter.

The obligation of subjects to the sovereign is understood to last as long, and no longer, than the power lasteth by which he is able to protect them. For the right men have by nature to protect themselves, when none else can protect them, can by no covenant be relinquished. The sovereignty is the soul of the Commonwealth; which, once departed from the body, the members do no more receive their motion from it. The end of obedience is protection; which, wheresoever a man seeth it, either in his own or in another's sword, nature applieth his obedience to it, and his endeavour to maintain it. And though sovereignty, in the intention of them that make it, be immortal; yet is it in its own nature, not only subject to violent death by foreign war, but also through the ignorance and passions of men it hath in it, from the very institution, many seeds of a natural mortality, by intestine discord.

If a subject be taken prisoner in war, or his person or his means of life be within the guards of the enemy, and hath his life and corporal liberty given him on condition to be subject to the victor, he hath liberty to accept the condition; and, having accepted it, is the subject of him that took him; because he had no other way to preserve himself. The case is the same if he be detained on the same terms in a foreign country. But if a man be held in prison, or bonds, or is not trusted with the liberty of his body, he cannot be understood to be bound by covenant to subjection, and therefore may, if he can, make his escape by any means whatsoever.

If a monarch shall relinquish the sovereignty, both for himself and his heirs, his subjects return to the absolute liberty of nature; because, though nature may declare who are his sons, and who are the nearest of his kin, yet it dependeth on his own will, as hath been said in the precedent chapter, who shall be his heir. If therefore he will have no heir, there is no sovereignty, nor subjection. The case is the same if he die without known kindred, and without declaration of his heir. For then there can no heir be known, and consequently no subjection be due.

If the sovereign banish his subject, during the banishment he is not subject. But he that is sent on a message, or hath leave to travel, is still subject; but it is by contract between sovereigns, not by virtue of the covenant of subjection. For whosoever entereth into another's dominion is subject to all the laws thereof, unless he have a privilege by the amity of the sovereigns, or by special license.

If a monarch subdued by war render himself subject to the victor, his subjects are delivered from their former obligation, and become obliged to the victor. But if he be held prisoner, or have not the liberty of his own body, he is not understood to have given away the right of sovereignty; and therefore his subjects are obliged to yield obedience to the magistrates formerly placed, governing not in their own name, but in his. For, his right remaining, the question is only of the administration; that is to say, of the magistrates and officers; which if he have not means to name, he is supposed to approve those which he himself had formerly appointed.

VLADIMIR LENIN

1870-1924

THE STATE AND REVOLUTION

1917

Born Vladimir Ilich Ulyanov, Lenin was the son of a conservative Russian school official. His commitment to revolutionary politics was influenced by his older brother Alexander, who was executed in 1887 for conspiring to assassinate Czar Alexander III. Lenin studied Marxism and became a professional revolutionary, writing a number of works. His group, the Bolsheviks, opposed World War I and deplored the socialists of various countries who supported it. He spent the war in Switzerland, and when Russia was on the point of collapse in 1917, the Germans allowed him passage through Germany to return to Russia. His booklet *State and Revolution* laid out his strategy for creating a Marxist revolution, a dictatorship of the proletariat" in Russia's chaos. His success in doing so is one of the most remarkable stories of that era. He took a small, extreme faction and made it into the ruling class of the new Russia, the Union of Soviet Socialist Republics. His counter-intuitive strategy of pursuing conflict when the country was exhausted from war and, confident that the old regime was disintegrating, attacking socialists who would not follow him was brilliant. He died in

1924 after having made Josef Stalin General Secretary of the Communist Party.

Selections from: Lenin, Vladimir. 1917. *The State and Revolution.* In the *Collected Works 25.* 381-492. Marxist Internet Archive <www.marxists.org/archive/lenin/works/1917/staterev/index.htm[1]

Chapter I: Class Society and The State.

- [Section] 1: The State: A Product of the Irreconcilability of Class Antagonisms
- [Section] 2: Special Bodies of Armed Men, Prisons, etc.,
- [Section] 3: The "Withering Away" of the State, and Violent Revolution

1. THE STATE: A PRODUCT OF THE IRRECONCILABILITY OF CLASS ANTAGONISMS

What is now happening to Marx's theory has, in the course of history, happened repeatedly to the theories of revolutionary thinkers and leaders of oppressed classes fighting for emancipation. During the lifetime of great revolutionaries, the oppressing classes constantly hounded them, received their theories with the most savage malice, the most furious hatred and the most unscrupulous campaigns of lies and slander. After their death, attempts are made to convert them into harmless icons, to canonize them, so to say, and to hallow their *names* to a certain extent for the "consolation" of the oppressed classes and with the object of duping the latter, while at the same time robbing the revolutionary theory of its *substance*, blunting its revolutionary edge and vulgarizing it. Today, the bourgeoisie and the opportunists within the labor movement concur in this doctoring of Marxism. They omit, obscure, or distort the revolutionary side of this theory, its revolutionary soul. They push to the foreground and extol what is or seems acceptable to the bourgeoisie. All the social-chauvinists are now "Marxists" (don't laugh!). And more and more frequently German bourgeois scholars, only yesterday specialists in the annihilation of Marxism, are speaking of the "national-German" Marx, who, they claim, educated the labor unions which are so splendidly organized for the purpose of waging a predatory war!

In these circumstances, in view of the unprecedently widespread distortion of Marxism, our prime task is to re-establish what Marx really taught on the subject of the state. This will necessitate a number of long quotations from the works of Marx and Engels themselves. Of course, long quotations will render the text cumbersome and not help at all to make it popular reading, but we cannot possibly dispense with them. All, or at any rate all the most essential passages in the works of Marx and Engels on the subject of the state must by all means be quoted as fully as possible so that the reader may form an independent opinion of the totality of the views of the founders of scientific socialism, and of the evolution of those views, and so that their distortion by the "Kautskyism" now prevailing may be documentarily proved and clearly demonstrated.

Let us being with the most popular of Engels'[s] works, *The Origin of the Family, Private Property and the State*, the sixth edition of which was published in Stuttgart as far back as 1894. We have to translate the quotations from the German originals, as the Russian translations, while very numerous, are for the most part either incomplete or very unsatisfactory.

Summing up his historical analysis, Engels says:

> "The state is, therefore, by no means a power forced on society from without; just as little is it 'the reality of the ethical idea', 'the image and reality of reason', as Hegel maintains. Rather, it is a product of society at a certain stage of development; it is the admission that this society has become entangled in an insoluble contradiction with itself, that it has split into irreconcilable antagonisms which it is powerless to dispel. But in order that these antagonisms, these classes with conflicting economic interests, might not consume themselves and society in fruitless struggle, it became necessary to have a power, seemingly standing above society, that would alleviate the conflict and keep it within the bounds of 'order'; and this power, arisen out of society but placing itself above it, and alienating itself more and more from it, is the state." (Pp.177-78, sixth edition)[1]

This expresses with perfect clarity the basic idea of Marxism with regard to the historical role and the meaning of the state. The state is a product and a manifestation of the irreconcilability of class antagonisms. The state arises where, when and insofar as class antagonism objectively cannot be reconciled. And, conversely, the existence of the state proves that the class antagonisms are irreconcilable.

It is on this most important and fundamental point that the distortion of Marxism, proceeding along two main lines, begins.

On the one hand, the bourgeois, and particularly the petty-bourgeois, ideologists, compelled under the weight of indisputable historical facts to admit that the state only exists where there are class antagonisms and a class struggle, "correct" Marx in such a way as to make it appear that the state is an organ for the reconciliation of classes. According to Marx, the state could neither have arisen nor maintained itself had it been possible to reconcile classes. From what the petty-bourgeois and philistine professors and publicists say, with quite frequent and benevolent references to Marx, it appears that the state does reconcile classes. According to Marx, the state is an organ of class rule, an organ for the oppression of one class by another; it is the creation of "order," which legalizes and perpetuates this oppression by moderating the conflict between classes. In the opinion of the petty-bourgeois politicians, however, order means the reconciliation of classes, and not the oppression of one class by another; to alleviate the conflict means reconciling classes and not depriving the oppressed classes of definite means and methods of struggle to overthrow the oppressors.

For instance, when, in the revolution of 1917, the question of the significance and role of the state arose in all its magnitude as a practical question demanding immediate action, and, moreover, action on a mass scale, all the Social-Revolutionaries and Mensheviks descended at once to the petty-bourgeois theory that the "state" "reconciles" classes. Innumerable resolutions and articles by politicians of both these parties are thoroughly saturated with this petty-bourgeois and philistine "reconciliation" theory. That the state is an organ of the rule of a definite class which cannot be reconciled with its antipode (the class opposite to it) is something the petty-bourgeois democrats will never be able to understand. Their attitude to the state is one of the most striking manifestations of the fact that our Socialist-Revolutionaries and Mensheviks are not socialists at all (a point that we Bolsheviks have always maintained), but petty-bourgeois democrats using near-socialist phraseology.

On the other hand, the "Kautskyite" distortion of Marxism is far more subtle. "Theoretically," it is not denied that the state is an organ of class rule, or that class antagonisms are irreconcilable. But what is overlooked or glossed over is this: if the state is the product of the irreconcilability of class antagonisms, if it is a power standing above society and "alienating itself more and more from it," it is clear that the liberation of the oppressed class is impossible not only without a violent revolution, but also without the destruction of the apparatus of state power which was created by the ruling class and which is the embodiment of this "alienation." As we shall see later, Marx very explicitly drew this theoretically self-evident conclusion on the strength of a concrete historical analysis of the tasks of the revolution. And—as we shall show in detail further on—it is this conclusion which Kautsky has "forgotten" and distorted.

2. SPECIAL BODIES OF ARMED MEN, PRISONS, ETC.

Engels continues:

> "As distinct from the old gentile [tribal or clan] order,[2] the state, first, divides its subjects according to territory . . . ."

This division seems "natural" to us, but it costs a prolonged struggle against the old organization according to generations or tribes.

> "The second distinguishing feature is the establishment of a public power which no longer directly coincides with the population organizing itself as an armed force. This special, public power is necessary because a self-acting armed organization of the population has become impossible since the split into classes . . . . This public power exists

> in every state; it consists not merely of armed men but also of material adjuncts, prisons, and institutions of coercion of all kinds, of which gentile [clan] society knew nothing . . . ."

Engels elucidates the concept the concept of the "power" which is called the state, a power which arose from society but places itself above it and alienates itself more and more from it. What does this power mainly consist of? It consists of special bodies of armed men having prisons, etc., at their command.

We are justified in speaking of special bodies of armed men, because the public power which is an attribute of every state "does not directly coincide" with the armed population, with its "self-acting armed organization."

Like all great revolutionary thinkers, Engels tries to draw the attention of the class-conscious workers to what prevailing philistinism regards as least worthy of attention, as the most habitual thing, hallowed by prejudices that are not only deep-rooted but, one might say, petrified. A standing army and police are the chief instruments of state power. But how can it be otherwise?

From the viewpoint of the vast majority of Europeans of the end of the 19th century, whom Engels was addressing, and who had not gone through or closely observed a single great revolution, it could not have been otherwise. They could not understand at all what a "self-acting armed organization of the population" was. When asked why it became necessary to have special bodies of armed men placed above society and alienating themselves from it (police and a standing army), the West-European and Russian philistines are inclined to utter a few phrases borrowed from Spencer of Mikhailovsky, to refer to the growing complexity of social life, the differentiation of functions, and so on.

Such a reference seems "scientific," and effectively lulls the ordinary person to sleep by obscuring the important and basic fact, namely, the split of society into irreconcilable antagonistic classes.

Were it not for this split, the "self-acting armed organization of the population" would differ from the primitive organization of a stick-wielding herd of monkeys, or of primitive men, or of men united in clans, by its complexity, its high technical level, and so on. But such an organization would still be possible.

It is impossible because civilized society is split into antagonistic, and, moreover, irreconcilably antagonistic classes, whose "self-acting" arming would lead to an armed struggle between them. A state arises, a special power is created, special bodies of armed men, and every revolution, by destroying the state apparatus, shows us the naked class struggle, clearly shows us how the ruling class strives to restore the special bodies of armed men which serve it, and how the oppressed class strives to create a new organization of this kind, capable of serving the exploited instead of the exploiters.

In the above argument, Engels raises theoretically the very same question which every great revolution raises before us in practice, palpably and, what is more, on a scale of mass action, namely, the question of the relationship between "special" bodies of armed men and the "self-acting armed organization of the population." We shall see how this question is specifically illustrated by the experience of the European and Russian revolutions.

But to return to Engels'[s] exposition.

He points out that sometimes—in certain parts of North America, for example—this public power is weak (he has in mind a rare exception in capitalist society, and those parts of North America in its pre-imperialist days where the free colonists predominated), but that, generally speaking, it grows stronger:

> "It [the public power] grows stronger, however, in proportion as class antagonisms

> within the state become more acute, and as adjacent states become larger and more populous. We have only to look at our present-day Europe, where class struggle and rivalry in conquest have tuned up the public power to such a pitch that it threatens to swallow the whole of society and even the state."

This was written not later than the early nineties of the last century, Engels'[s] last preface being dated June 16, 1891. The turn towards imperialism—meaning the complete domination of the trusts, the omnipotence of the big banks, a grand-scale colonial policy, and so forth—was only just beginning in France, and was even weaker in North America and in Germany. Since then "rivalry in conquest" has taken a gigantic stride, all the more because by the beginning of the second decade of the 20th century the world had been completely divided up among these "rivals in conquest," i.e., among the predatory Great Powers. Since then, military and naval armaments have grown fantastically and the predatory war of 1914-17 for the domination of the world by Britain or Germany, for the division of the spoils, has brought the "swallowing" of all the forces of society by the rapacious state power close to complete catastrophe.

Engels could, as early as 1891, point to "rivalry in conquest" as one of the most important distinguishing features of the foreign policy of the Great Powers, while the social-chauvinist scoundrels have ever since 1914, when this rivalry, many time intensified, gave rise to an imperialist war, been covering up the defence of the predatory interests of "their own" bourgeoisie with phrases about "defence of the fatherland," "defence of the republic and the revolution," etc.!

4. THE "WITHERING AWAY" OF THE STATE, AND VIOLENT REVOLUTION

Engels'[s] words regarding the "withering away" of the state are so widely known, they are often quoted, and so clearly reveal the essence of the customary adaptation of Marxism to opportunism that we must deal with them in detail. We shall quote the whole argument from which they are taken.

> "The proletariat seizes from state power and turns the means of production into state property to begin with. But thereby it abolishes itself as the proletariat, abolishes all class distinctions and class antagonisms, and abolishes also the state as state. Society thus far, operating amid class antagonisms, needed the state, that is, an organization of the particular exploiting class, for the maintenance of its external conditions of production, and, therefore, especially, for the purpose of forcibly keeping the exploited class in the conditions of oppression determined by the given mode of production (slavery, serfdom or bondage, wage-labor). The state was the official representative of society as a whole, its concentration in a visible corporation. But it was this only insofar as it was the state of that class which itself represented, for its own time, society as a whole: in ancient times, the state of slave-owning citizens; in the Middle Ages, of the feudal nobility; in our own time, of the bourgeoisie. When at last it becomes the real representative of the whole of society, it renders itself unnecessary. As soon as there is no longer any social class to be held in

> subjection, as soon as class rule, and the individual struggle for existence based upon the present anarchy in production, with the collisions and excesses arising from this struggle, are removed, nothing more remains to be held in subjection—nothing necessitating a special coercive force, a state. The first act by which the state really comes forward as the representative of the whole of society—the taking possession of the means of production in the name of society—is also its last independent act as a state. State interference in social relations becomes, in one domain after another, superfluous, and then dies down of itself. The government of persons is replaced by the administration of things, and by the conduct of processes of production. The state is not 'abolished.' It withers away. This gives the measure of the value of the phrase 'a free people's state,' both as to its justifiable use for a long time from an agitational point of view, and as to its ultimate scientific insufficiency; and also of the so-called anarchists' demand that the state be abolished overnight." (Herr Eugen Duhring's Revolution in Science [Anti-Duhring*]*, pp. 301-03, third German edition.)[3]

It is safe to say that of this argument of Engels'[s], which is so remarkably rich in ideas, only one point has become an integral part of socialist thought among modern socialist parties, namely, that according to Marx that state "withers away"—as distinct from the anarchist doctrine of the "abolition" of the state. To prune Marxism to such an extent means reducing it to opportunism, for this "interpretation" only leaves a vague notion of a slow, even, gradual change, of absence of leaps and storms, of absence of revolution. The current, widespread, popular, if one may say so, conception of the "withering away" of the state undoubtedly means obscuring, if not repudiating, revolution.

Such an "interpretation," however, is the crudest distortion of Marxism, advantageous only to the bourgeoisie. In point of theory, it is based on disregard for the most important circumstances and considerations indicated in, say, Engels'[s] "summary" argument we have just quoted in full.

In the first place, at the very outset of his argument, Engels says that, in seizing state power, the proletariat thereby "abolishes the state as state." It is not done to ponder over the meaning of this. Generally, it is either ignored altogether, or is considered to be something in the nature of "Hegelian weakness" on Engels'[s] part. As a matter of fact, however, these words briefly express the experience of one of the greatest proletarian revolutions, the Paris Commune of 1871, of which we shall speak in greater detail in its proper place. As a matter of fact, Engels speaks here of the proletariat revolution "abolishing" the *bourgeois* state, while the words about the state withering away refer to the remnants of the *proletarian* state *after* the socialist revolution. According to Engels, the bourgeois state does not "wither away," but is "abolished" by the proletariat in the course of the revolution. What withers away after this revolution is the proletarian state or semi-state.

Secondly, the state is a "special coercive force." Engels gives this splendid and extremely profound definition here with the utmost lucidity. And from it follows that the "special coercive force" for the suppression of the proletariat by the bourgeoisie, of millions of working people by handfuls of the rich, must be replaced by a "special coercive force" for the suppression of the bourgeoisie by the proletariat (the dictatorship of the proletariat). This is precisely what is meant by "abolition of the state as state." This is precisely the "act" of taking possession of the means of production in the name of society. And it is self-evident that such a replacement of one (bourgeois) "special force" by another (proletarian) "special force" cannot possibly take place in the form of "withering away."

Thirdly, in speaking of the state "withering away," and the even more graphic and colorful "dying down of itself," Engels refers quite clearly and definitely to the period after "the state has taken possession of the means of production in the name of the whole of society," that is, after the socialist revolution. We all know that the political form of the "state" at that time is the most complete democracy. But it never enters the head of any of the opportunists, who shamelessly distort Marxism, that Engels is consequently speaking here of democracy "dying down of itself," or "withering away." This seems very strange at first sight. But is is "incomprehensible" only to those who have not thought about democracy also being a state and, consequently, also disappearing when the state disappears. Revolution alone can "abolish" the bourgeois state. The state in general, i.e., the most complete democracy, can only "wither away."

Fourthly, after formulating his famous proposition that "the state withers away," Engels at once explains specifically that this proposition is directed against both the opportunists and the anarchists. In doing this, Engels puts in the forefront that conclusion, drawn from the proposition that "the state withers away," which is directed against the opportunists.

One can wager that out of every 10,000 persons who have read or heard about the "withering away" of the state, 9,990 are completely unaware, or do not remember, that Engels directed his conclusions from that proposition not against anarchists alone. And of the remaining 10, probably nine do not know the meaning of a "free people's state" or why an attack on this slogan means an attack on opportunists. This is how history is written! This is how a great revolutionary teaching is imperceptibly falsified and adapted to prevailing philistinism. The conclusion directed against the anarchists has been repeated thousands of times; it has been vulgarized, and rammed into people's heads in the shallowest form, and has acquired the strength of a prejudice, whereas the conclusion directed against the opportunists has been obscured and "forgotten"!

The "free people's state" was a programme demand and a catchword current among the German Social-Democrats in the seventies. This catchword is devoid of all political content except that it describes the concept of democracy in a pompous philistine fashion. Insofar as it hinted in a legally permissible manner at a democratic republic, Engels was prepared to "justify" its use "for a time" from an agitational point of view. But it was an opportunist catchword, for it amounted to something more than prettifying bourgeois democracy, and was also failure to understand the socialist criticism of the state in general. We are in favor of a democratic republic as the best form of state for the proletariat under capitalism. But we have no right to forget that wage slavery is the lot of the people even in the most democratic bourgeois republic. Furthermore, every state is a "special force" for the suppression of the oppressed class. Consequently, every state is not "free and not a "people's state." Marx and Engels explained this repeatedly to their party comrades in the seventies.

Fifthly, the same work of Engels, whose arguments about the withering away of the state everyone remembers, also contains an argument of the significance of violent revolution. Engels'[s] historical analysis of its role becomes a veritable panegyric on violent revolution. This, "no one remembers." It is not done in modern socialist parties to talk or even think about the significance of this idea, and it plays no part whatever in their daily propaganda and agitation among the people. And yet it is inseparably bound up with the "withering away" of the state into one harmonious whole.

Here is Engels'[s] argument:

> "... That force, however, plays yet another role [other than that of a diabolical power] in history, a revolutionary role; that, in the words of Marx, it is the midwife of every old society which is pregnant with a new one, that it is the instrument with which social movement forces its way through and shatters the dead, fossilized political forms—of this there is not a word in Herr Duhring. It is only with sighs and groans that he admits the possibility that force will perhaps be necessary for the overthrow of an economy based on exploitation—unfortunately, because all use of force demoralizes, he says, the person who uses it. And this in Germany, where a violent collision—which may, after all, be forced on the people—would at least have the advantage of wiping out the servility which has penetrated the nation's mentality following the humiliation of the Thirty Years' War.[4] And this person's mode of thought—dull, insipid, and impotent—presumes to impose itself on the most revolutionary party that history has ever known!" (p.193, third German edition, Part II, end of Chap. IV)

How can this panegyric on violent revolution, which Engels insistently brought to the attention of the German Social-Democrats between 1878 and 1894, i.e., right up to the time of his death, be combined with the theory of the "withering away" of the state to form a single theory?

Usually the two are combined by means of eclecticism, by an unprincipled or sophistic selection made arbitrarily (or to please the powers that be) of first one, then another argument, and in 99 cases out of 100, if not more, it is the idea of the "withering away" that is placed in the forefront. Dialectics are replaced by eclecticism—this is the most usual, the most wide-spread practice to be met with in present-day official Social-Democratic literature in relation to Marxism. This sort of substitution is, of course, nothing new; it was observed even in the history of classical Greek philosophy. In falsifying Marxism in opportunist fashion, the substitution of eclecticism for dialectics is the easiest way of deceiving the people. It gives an illusory satisfaction; it seems to take into account all sides of the process, all trends of development, all the conflicting influences, and so forth, whereas in reality it provides no integral and revolutionary conception of the process of social development at all.

We have already said above, and shall show more fully later, that the theory of Marx and Engels of the inevitability of a violent revolution refers to the bourgeois state. The latter cannot be superseded by the proletarian state (the dictatorship of the proletariat) through the process of "withering away," but, as a general rule, only through a violent revolution. The panegyric Engels sang in its honor, and which fully corresponds to Marx's repeated statements (see the concluding passages of *The Poverty of Philosophy*[5] and the *Communist Manifesto,* [6]with their proud and open proclamation of the inevitability of a violent revolution; see what Marx wrote nearly 30 years later, in criticizing the *Gotha Programme of 1875,*[7] when he mercilessly castigated the opportunist character of that programme)—this panegyric is by no means a mere "impulse," a mere declamation or a polemical sally. The necessity of systematically imbuing the masses with this and precisely this view of violent revolution lies at the root of the entire theory of Marx and Engels. The betrayal of their theory by the now prevailing social-chauvinist and Kautskyite trends expresses itself strikingly in both these trends ignoring such propaganda and agitation.

The supersession of the bourgeois state by the proletarian state is impossible without a violent revolution. The abolition of the proletarian state, i.e., of the state in general, is impossible except through the process of "withering away."

A detailed and concrete elaboration of these views was given by Marx and Engels when they studied each particular revolutionary situation, when they analyzed the lessons of the experience of each particular revolution. We shall now pass to this, undoubtedly the most important, part of their theory.

---

[1] See Frederick Engels, *The Origin of the Family, Private Property and the State* (Karl Marx and Frederick Engels, Selected Works, Vol. 3, Moscow, 1973, pp. 326-27). Further below, on pp. 393-95, 395-99 of the volume, Lenin is quoting from the same work by Engels (op. cit., pp. 327-30).

[2] Gentile, or tribal, organisation of society-the primitive communal system, or the first socio-economic formation in history. The tribal commune was a community of blood relatives linked by economic and social ties. The tribal system went through the matriarchal and the patriarchal periods. The patriarchate culminated in primitive society becoming a class society and in the rise of the state. Relations of production under the primitive communal system were based on social ownership of the means of production and equalitarian distribution of all products. This corresponded in the main to the low level of the productive forces and to their character at the time.

For the primitive communal system, see Karl Marx, Conspectus of Lewis Morgan's "Ancient Society", and Frederick Engels. *The Origin of the Family, Private Property and the State* (Karl Marx and Frederick Engels, Selected Works, Vol. 3, Moscow, 1973, pp. 204-334).

[3] See Frederick Engels, Anti-Duhring, Moscow, 1969, pp. 332-33.
Further down, on p. 404 of this volume, Lenin is quoting from the same work by Engels (op. cit., p. 220).

[4] Thirty Years' War (1618-48), the first European war, resulted from an aggravation of the antagonisms between various alignments of European states, and took the form of a struggle between Protestants and Catholics. It began with a revolt in Bohemia against the tyranny of the Hapsburg monarchy

and the onslaught of Catholic reaction. The states which then entered the war formed two camps. The Pope, the Spanish and Austrian Hapsburgs and the Catholic princes of Germany, who rallied to the Catholic Church, opposed the Protestant countries—Bohemia, Denmark, Sweden, the Dutch Republic, and a number of German states that had accepted the Reformation. The Protestant countries were backed by the French kings, enemies of the Hapsburgs. Germany became the chief battlefield and object of military plunder and predatory claims. The war ended in 1648 with the signing of the Peace Treaty of Westphalia, which completed the political dismemberment of Germany.

[5] See Karl Marx, The Poverty of Philosophy, Moscow, 1973, pp. 151-52.

[6] See Karl Marx and Frederick Engels, Selected Works, Vol. 1, Moscow, 1973, p. 137.

[7] Gotha Programme—the programme adopted by the Socialist Workers' Party of Germany in 1875, at the Gotha Congress, which united two German socialist parties, namely, the Eisenachers—led by August Bebel and Wilhelm Liebknecht and influenced by Marx and Engels—and the Lassalleans. The programme betrayed eclecticism and was opportunist, because the Eisenachers had made concessions to the Lassalleans on major issues and accepted Lassallean formulations. Marx in his Critique of the Gotha Programme, and Engels in his letter to Bebel of March 18-28, 11475, devastated the Gotha Programme, which they regarded as a serious step backwards compared with the Eisenach programme of 1869.

Adolf Hitler

1889-1945

Hitler's Table Talk[1]

1942

The theatrical, brutal, and mesmerizing dictator who ruled Germany from 1933 to 1945 was a master in the use of mass media to manipulate public opinion. He rose to power in the disorder of post-World War I Germany promising a revival of Germany and revenge for Germany's defeat. He left Germany destroyed and divided, committing suicide in Berlin as it was devastated by the Red Army of the USSR. His education was incomplete. He aspired to be an artist, but he was refused admission to art school. A veteran of World War I, he embarked on a career as a right-wing political activist, especially devoted to anti-Semitism. He maneuvered his way to the position of Chancellor in 1933 and six years later started World War II. During the war he ordered the execution of Jews in the infamous death camps where millions were killed, as well as others the Nazi ideology deemed undesirable. He remains a reminder that tyranny can overwhelm even an advanced and highly civilized country.

---

1 Reprinted by permission of Enigma Books

Selected from: *Hitler's Table Talk: 1941-1944.* New York: Enigma Books, 2000. 481-483.

MAY 14, 1942, AT DINNER

. . . When you regard the rôle of the press from this angle, you will realise at once that the profession of the journalist now is very different from that of the journalist of yore. There was, indeed, a time when the profession of journalism was one without any real importance, for rarely had the individual journalist any opportunity to give proof of personal character. To-day, the journalist knows that he is no mere scribbler, but a man with the sacred mission of defending the highest interests of the State. This evolution has been in progress throughout the years following our taking power, and to-day the journalist is conscious of his responsibilities, and his profession appears to him in a new light.

Viewed in this way, the rôle of the press must be guided by certain principles, which must be rigorously applied.

For example, when there are problems, over which men of eminence are scratching their heads without being able to find the solution, it is unwise in the extreme to air them in public; much better wait till the thing is settled. Before a military operation, no one would dream of communicating the orders to the troops, so that the rank and file could discuss them among themselves and express their opinion of the best way of carrying out the operation. To act in such a manner would be tantamount to a surrender of all sense of responsibility, all sense of authority, and a negation of all reason. In the same way, when a choice between two models of tanks is under consideration, it is not the rank and file who are asked to decide which shall be put into production.

Whatever the sphere of activity, when the experts are in doubt, higher authority alone must make the decision. A nation desires leadership, and once it sees that its Chiefs are hesitant about what should be done, then all authority goes by the board. For those in whom authority by is vested it is an honour to have to take decisions and to accept the responsibility for the results thereof. The people will more readily forgive the mistakes made by a Government—which, as of often as not, by the way, escape their notice—than any evidence of hesitancy or lack of assurance. When the leaders recoil from the responsibility of taking a decision, the people become uneasy.

Obviously, then, those in authority must never permit their decisions to be criticised by those subordinate to them. The people themselves have never claimed such a right. Only an inveterate tubthumper would think of such a thing.

A people submits thus voluntarily to authority primarily because its instincts are of a feminine rather than a dominant nature. In the married state a woman will sometimes perhaps reconnoitre a bit, to see whether she could impose her will, but deep within her she has no desire at all to wear the trousers. It's the same thing with the people. Sticking to military simile, a company does not expect its commander to consult it on all points. This explains how the populace came to cut off the head of a being so pusillanimous as Louis XVI—for the attitude of this King towards the people was far less severe than that of Napoleon; but in the latter the people had recognised a leader—and a man worthy of their veneration.

In short, the people expect not only that their leaders should govern them, but also that they should look after them. For the same reason the officer wielding the greatest authority is he who succeeds in deserving the confidence of his men by paying attention to their well-being. Let him but fuss about their food, their sleeping quarters and their little family worries, and his men will go through fire for him, even though in other respects he may be an exceptionally severe and hard taskmaster. The whole gamut of human conduct depends on simple ideas such as these; it is only the scale that varies.

During the showing of a film of Tibet, Reichsleiter Dietrich was struck with the way in which the wild horses of the high Tibetan plains followed the stallion who was guiding them. And what is true of wild horses applies equally to every community of creatures desirous of safe-guarding its survival. If the ram leader is not in his place, the flock of sheep disintegrates. This undoubtedly explains why monkeys put to death any members of their community who show a desire to live apart. And what the apes do, men do, too, in their own manner. Bismarck was perfectly right when he said that any human society which suppressed the death penalty, the ultimate expression of human defence against the a-social, merely from fear of a possible error of justice, was simply destroying itself. However one lives, whatever one does or undertakes, one is invariably exposed to the danger of making mistakes. And so, what, indeed, would become of the individual and of the community, if those in whom authority was vested were paralysed by fear of a possible error, and refused to take the decisions that were called for?

Holocaust Documents[1]

1943

The selections below are a very small sample of the documentary evidence of the Nazi campaign to kill the Jewish population of the areas they controlled during World War II. These selections include official Nazi pronouncements and first-hand accounts of the persecuted.

The "Frank" who authored the second document was Hans Frank (1900-1946), a leading Nazi. Hitler appointed him Governor-General of Poland after Germany conquered Poland in 1939. Frank was tried at the Nuremberg War Crimes Trial for crimes against humanity and executed in October, 1946. The "Himmler" in the fifth selection was Heinrich Himmler (1900-1945), the head of the SS and the Gestapo. He was probably the most powerful figure in the Nazi regime after Hitler. He committed suicide after being captured by British troops.

The International Military Tribunal, composed of American, British, French, and Russian officials conducted the Nuremberg War Crimes Trials. They lasted for several years. The first trials were of the top Nazi leadership and held in 1945-1946. Ten of the accused were hanged on October 16, 1946.

1 Reprinted by permission of Yad Vashem Publishing, Yad Vashem, Jerusalem, Israel.

Selected from: *Documents on the Holocaust: Selected Sources on the Destruction of the Jews of Germany and Austria, Poland, and the Soviet Union.* Eds. Yitzhak Arad, Yisrael Gutman, and Abraham Margaliot. Jerusalem: Yad Vashem Publishing, 1981.

D 88: 201-204
D 116: 247-249
D 122: 272-273
D 130: 284-286
D 161: 344-345
D 163: 347-350
D 165: 353-355
D 167: 358-361
D 168: 362-364

88

EXTRACTS FROM THE WARSAW GHETTO DIARY OF CHAIM A. KAPLAN, 1940

March 10, 1940

The gigantic catastrophe which has descended on Polish Jewry has no parallel, even in the darkest periods of Jewish history. Firstly—the depth of the hatred. This is not hatred whose source is simply in a party platform, invented for political purposes. It is a hatred of emotion, whose source is some psychopathic disease. in its outward manifestation it appears as physiological hatred, which sees the objcct of its hatred as tainted in body, as lepers who have no place in society.

The masses have accepted this sort of objective hatred. Their limited understanding does not grasp ideological hatred; psychology is beyond them, and they are incapable of understanding it. They have absorbed their masters' teaching in a concrete bodily form. The Jew is filthy; the Jew is a swindler and evil; the Jew is the enemy of Germany and undermines its existence; the Jew was the prime mover in the Versailles Treaty, which reduced Germany to a shambles; the Jew is Satan, who sows dissension between the nations, arousing them to bloodshed in order to profit from their destruction. These are easily understood concepts whose effect on day-to-day life can be felt immediately.

But the founders of Nazism and the party leaders created a theoretical ideology with deeper frustrations. They have a complete doctrine which represents the Jewish spirit inside and out. Judaism and Nazism are two attitudes to the world that are incompatible, and for this reason they cannot co-exist side by side. For 2,000 years Judaism has left its imprint, culturally and spiritually, on the nations of the world. It stood fast, blocking the spread of German paganism, whose teaching was different and whose culture was drawn from a different source. Two kings cannot wear one crown. Either humanity would be Judaic, or it would be pagan-German. Up until now it was Judaic. Even Catholicism is a child of Judaism, and the fruit of its spirit, and thus afflicted by all the shortcomings inherited from its mother. The new world which Nazism would fashion would be pagan, primordial, in all its attitudes. It is therefore ready to fight Judaism to the finish. . .

It is our good fortune that the conquerors failed to understand the nature and strength of Polish Jewry. Logically, we are obliged to die. According to the laws of nature, our end is destruction and total annihilation. How can an entire community feed itself when it has no grip on life? For there is no occupation, no trade which is not limited and circumscribed for us.

But even this time we did not comply with the laws of nature. There is within us some hidden power, mysterious and secret, which keeps us going, keeps us alive, despite the natural law. If we cannot live on what is permitted, we live on what is forbidden. That is no disgrace for us. What is permitted is no more than an agreement, and what is forbidden derives from the same agreement. If we do not accept the agreement, it is not binding on us. And particularly where this forbidden and permitted comes from a barbarous conqueror, who limits life to one made in his image, his murderous and larcenous views.

. . . The Jews of Poland—oppressed and broken, shamed and debased, still love life, and do not wish to leave this world before their time. Say what you like, the will to live amidst terrible suffering is the manifestation of some hidden power whose nature we do not yet know. It is a marvelous, life-preserving power that only the most firmly established and strongest of the communities of our people have received as a blessing.

The fact that we have hardly any suicides is worthy of special emphasis.

We have remained naked. But as long as that secret power is concealed within us, we shall not yield to despair. The strength of this power lies in the very nature of the Polish Jew, which is rooted in our eternal tradition that commands us to live. . . .

October 2, 1940
Eve of the New Year, 5701

We have no public prayers even on the High Holy Days. . . .

Even for the High Holy Days permission was not received for public prayers, although I do not know whether the Community [Council] tried to get it. And if it did not try that is only because it knew that its request would be refused. Even in the darkest days of our exile we did not suffer this trial. . . .

The wonder is that despite all this we go on living. Our life may be one of scorn and debasement as it is seen from outside, but our human emotions have become so numbed that we no longer feel, and the awareness of insult that is concealed within every human being no longer rises up in protest against even the most barbarous and cruel of such insults.

To what can this matter be compared? To a vicious dog who does not treat you with respect; would you, then, be insulted? Is not that why he is a dog?

Again: everything is forbidden to us; and yet we do everything! We make our "living" in ways that are forbidden, and not by permission.

It is the same with community prayers: secret *minyamin** in their hundreds all over Warsaw hold prayers together and do not leave out even the most difficult hymns. Neither preachers nor sermons are missing; everything is in accordance with the ancient traditions of Israel. Where there is no informer the enemy does not know what is going on. And surely no member of the Community of Israel, even if he was born in Poland, will go to lay information against Jews standing before their Maker.

Near the main synagogue some side room is chosen with windows facing the courtyard, and there hearts are poured out to the God of Israel in whispered supplications. This time it is without cantors and without choirs; there are only whispered prayers, but the prayer comes from the heart; even tears may be wept secretly, and the gates of the tears cannot be locked. . . .

C. A. Kaplain, *Megilat Yissurin—Yoman Getto Varsha* ("Scroll of Agony—Warsaw Ghetto Diary"), *September 1, 1939—August 4, 1942,* Tel Aviv-Jerusalem, 1966, pp. 201-202, 350.

* The Group of ten adult males making a quorum for Jewish community prayers.

116

FROM A SPEECH BY FRANK ON THE EXTERMINATION OF THE JEWS, DECEMBER 16, 1941

[Hans Frank (1900-1946) was Nazi German's Governor General of Poland.]

. . . One way or another—I will tell you that quite openly—

we must finish off the Jews. The Führer put it into words once: should united Jewry again succeed in setting off a world war, then the blood sacrifice shall not be made only by the peoples driven into war, but then the Jew of Europe will have met his end. I know that there is criticism of many of the measures now applied to the Jews in the Reich. There are always deliberate attempts to speak again and again of cruelty, harshness, etc.; this emerges from the reports on the popular mood. I appeal to you: before I now continue speaking first agree with me on a formula: we will have pity, on principle, only for the German people, and for nobody else in the world. The others had no pity for us either. As an old National-Socialist I must also say that if the pack of Jews (*Judensippschaft*) were to survive the war in Europe while we sacrifice the best of our blood for the preservation of Europe, then this war would still be only a partial success. I will therefore, on principle, approach Jewish affairs in the expectation that the Jews will disappear. They must go. I have started negotiations for the purpose of having them pushed off to the East. In January there will be a major conference on this question in Berlin,* to which I shall send State Secretary Dr. Bühler. The conference is to be held in the office of SS *Obergruppenführer* Heydrich at the Reich Security Main Office (*Reichssicherheitshauptamt*). A major Jewish migration will certainly begin.

But what should be done with the Jews? Can you believe that they will be accommodated in settlements in the *Ostland*? In Berlin we were told: why are you making all this trouble? We don't want them either, not in the *Ostland* nor in the *Reichskommissariat*; liquidate them yourselves! Gentlemen, I must ask you to steel yourselves against all considerations of compassion. We must destroy the Jews wherever we find them, and wherever it is at all possible, in order to maintain the whole structure of the Reich . . . The views that were acceptable up to now cannot be applied to

---

* See Document 17.

such gigantic, unique events. In any case we must find a way that will lead us to our goal, and I have my own ideas on this.

The Jews are also exceptionally harmful feeders for us. In the Government-General we have approximately 2.5 million [Jews], and now perhaps 3.5 million together with persons who have Jewish kin, and so on. We cannot shoot these 3.5 million Jews,** we cannot poison them, but we will be able to take measures that will lead somehow to successful destruction; and this in connection with the large-scale procedures which are to be discussed in the Reich. The Government-General must become as free of Jews as the Reich. Where and how this is to be done is the affair of bodies which we will have to appoint and create, and on whose work I will report to you when the time comes. . . .

122

PROPOSAL FOR THE STERILIZATION OF 2-3 MILLION JEWISH WORKERS, JUNE 23, 1942

Reich Secret Document
Honorable Mr. *Reichsführer*!

On instructions from *Reichsleiter* Bouhler I placed a part of my men at the disposal of *Brigadeführer* Globocnik some considerable time ago for his Special Task. Following a further request from him, I have now made available more personnel. On this occasion *Brigadeführer* Globocnik pressed the view that the whole *Aktion* against the Jews should be carried out as quickly as it is in any way possible, so that we will not some day be stuck in the middle should any kind of difficulty make it necessary to stop the *Aktion*. You yourself, Mr. *Reichsführer*, expressed the view to me

** The figures are not based on facts.

at an earlier time that one must work as fast as possible, if only for reasons of concealment. Both views are more than justified according to my own experience, and basically they produce the same results. Nevertheless I beg to be permitted to present the following consideration of my own in this connection:

According to my impression there are at least 2-3 million men and women well fit for work among the approx. 10 million European Jews. In consideration of the exceptional difficulties posed for us by the question of labor, I am of the opinion that these 2-3 million could in any case be taken out and kept. Of course this can only be done if they are at the same time rendered incapable of reproduction. I reported to you about a year ago that persons under my instruction have completed the necessary experiments for this purpose. I wish to bring up these facts again. The type of sterilization which is normally carried out on persons with genetic disease is out of the question in this case, as it takes too much time and is expensive. Castration by means of X-rays, however, is not only relatively cheap, but can be carried out on many thousands in a very short time. I believe that it has become unimportant at the present time whether those affected will then in the course of a few weeks or months realize by the effects that they are castrated.

In the event, Mr. *Reichsführer*, that you decide to choose these means in the interest of maintaining labor-material, *Reichsleiter* Bouhler will be ready to provide the doctors and other personnel needed to carry out this work. He also instructed me to inform you that I should then order the required equipment as quickly as possible.

Viktor Brack
SS *Oberführer*

---

* See Document 177.

130

NOTES BY A JEWISH OBSERVER IN THE LODZ GHETTO FOLLOWING THE DEPORTATION OF THE CHILDREN*

Lodz Ghetto September 16, 1942

On September 5 the situation became clearer, and the frightening whispers of the past days became terrifying fact. The evacuation of children and old people look on the shape of reality. A small piece of paper on the wall in a busy part of the city announced an address by the President in an urgent matter. A huge crowd in Fire Brigade Square. The "Jewish Elder" will reveal the truth in the rumors. For it concerns the young, for whom he has great love, and the aged, for whom he has much respect. "It cannot be that they will tear the babes from their mothers' breasts, and drag old fathers and old mothers to some unknown place. The German is without mercy, he wages a terrible war, but he will not go as far as that in cruelty." Everybody has faith in the President** and hopes for words of comfort from him

The representative of the ghetto is speaking. His voice fails him, the words stick in his throat. His personal appearance also mirrors the tragedy. One thing was understood by everybody: 20,000 persons must leave the ghetto, children under 10 and old people over 65. . . .

Everybody is convinced that the Jews who are deported are taken to destruction . . . People ran here and there, crazed by the desire to hide the beloved victims. But nobody knew who would direct the *Aktion*: the Jewish Police, the Gestapo in the ghetto, or a mobile unit of the SS. The President, in coordination with the German authorities (Biebow) decided in his area of responsibility to carry out the deportation (with his own forces). It was the Jewish Police that had to tear the children from the mothers, to take the parents from their children . . . It was to be expected that parents and relatives would try in this situation to make changes and corrections in registered ages. Errors and inaccuracies that had not been corrected up to now did exist. Something that gives you the right to live today may well decide your fate tomorrow. There was a tendency to raise the age of the children, because a child from the age of 10 up could go to work and so be entitled to a portion of soup. Other parents lowered the age, because a younger child had a prospect of getting milk. Yesterday the milk and the soup were the most important things, today there is literally a question of staying alive. The age of the old people also moved up and down for various reasons.

An unprecedented migration began to the Registration Office. The officials tried to manage the situation. They worked without stopping, day and night. The pressure of the people at the office windows increased all the time. The applicants yelled, wept and went wild. Every second could bring the death sentence, and hours passed in the struggle to restrain their passion . . . On Saturday the Gestapo already began on the operation [deportation], without paying any attention to the feverish work of registration that had been going on at No. 4 Church Square. Everyone had supposed that the Order Police [Jewish Police] would not stand the test. It could not itself carry out the work of the hangmen. . . .

The little ones who were loaded on the cart behaved quietly, in submission, or yelling, according to their ages. The children of the ghetto, boys and girls less than 10 years old, are already mature and familiar with poverty and suffering. The young look around them with wide-open eyes and do not know what to do. They are on a cart for the first time in their lives, a cart that will be pulled by a real horse, a proper horse. They are looking forward to a gay ride. More than one of the little ones jumps for joy on the floor of the wagon as long as there is enough space. And at the same time his mother has almost gone out of her mind, twisting about on the ground and tearing the hair from her head in despair. It is difficult to overcome several thousand mothers. It is difficult to persuade them to give their children up willingly to death, as a sacrifice. It is difficult to take out the old people who hide in the smallest and most hidden corners.

All this was to be expected. The President imposed a general curfew which came into force at 5 o'clock on Sunday afternoon. Anyone who broke it was threatened with deportation.

Dokumenty i materially, II *Akcje i wysiedlenia* ("Documents and Records, II, *Aktionen* and Deportations"), Warsaw . . ., 1946, pp. 243-246.

* From the description written by O.S. (Oscar Singer), a refugee from Czechoslovakia, a journalist who managed the Jewish archives in Lodz at the time of the Occupation.

** The reference is to Rumkowski

161

FROM A SPEECH BY HIMMLER BEFORE SENIOR SS OFFICERS IN POZNAN, OCTOBER 4, 1943

[Heinrich Himmler (1900-1945) was chief of the Gestapo and the SS in Nazi Germany.]

EVACUATION OF THE JEWS. . .

I also want to speak to you here, in complete frankness, of a really grave chapter. Amongst ourselves, for once, it shall be said quite openly, but all the same we will never speak about it in public. Just as we did not hesitate on June 30, 1934,* to do our duty as we were ordered, and to stand comrades who had erred against the wall and shoot them, and we never spoke about it and we never will speak about it. It was a matter of natural tact that is alive in us, thank

God, that we never talked about it amongst ourselves, that we never discussed it. Each of us shuddered and yet each of us knew clearly that the next time he would do it again if it were an order, and if it were necessary.

I am referring here to the evacuation of the Jews, the extermination of the Jewish people. This is one of the things that is easily said: "The Jewish people are going to be exterminated," that's what every Party member says, "sure, it's in our program, elimination of the Jews, extermination—it'll be done." And then they all come along, the 80 million worthy Germans, and each one has his one decent Jew. Of course, the others are swine, but this one, he is a first-rate Jew. Of all those who talk like that, not one has seen it happen, not one has had to go through with it. Most of you men know what it is like to see 100 corpses side by side, or 500 or 1,000. To have stood fast through this and—except for cases of human weakness—to have stayed decent that has made us hard. This is an unwritten and never-to-be-written page of glory in our history, for we know how difficult it would be for us if today—under bombing raids and the hardships and deprivations of war—if we were still to have the Jews in every city as secret saboteurs, agitators, and inciters. If the Jews were still lodged in the body of the German nation, we would probably by now have reached the stage of 1916-17.

The wealth they possessed we took from them. I gave a strict order, which has been carried out by SS *Obergruppenführer* Pohl, that this wealth will of course be turned over to the Reich in its entirety. We have taken none of it for ourselves. Individuals who have erred will be punished in accordance with the order given by me at the start, threatening that anyone who takes as much as a single Mark of this money is a dead man. A number of SS men—they are not very many—committed this offense, and they shall die. There will be no mercy. We had the moral right, we had the duty towards our people, to destroy this people that wanted to destroy us. But we do not have the right to enrich ourselves by so much as a fur, as a watch, by one Mark or a cigarette or anything else. We do not want, in the end, because we destroyed a bacillus, to be infected by this bacillus and to die. I will never stand by and watch while even a small rotten spot develops or takes hold. Wherever it may form we will together burn it away. All in all, however, we can say that we have carried out this most difficult of tasks in a spirit of love for our people. And we have suffered no harm to our inner being, our soul, our character. . .

PS—1919.

* The reference is to the "night of the long knives,"— murder of Röhm, SA leaders and other purges.

163

FROM NOTES MADE BY KURT GERSTEIN, AN ENGINEER WORKING FOR THE SS, ON THE EXTERMINATION CAMP AT BELZEC*

. . . In Lublin, SS *Gruppenführer* Globocnik was waiting for us. He said: This is one of the most highly secret matters there are, perhaps the most secret. Anybody who speaks about it is shot dead immediately. Two talkative people died yesterday. Then he explained to us that, at the present moment—August 17, 1942—there were the following installations:

1. Belzec, on the Lublin-Lvov road in the sector of the Soviet Demarcation Line. Maximum per day: 15,000 persons (I saw it!).
2. Sobibor, I am not familiar with the exact situation, I did not visit it. 20,000 persons per day.
3. Treblinka, 120 km. NNE of Warsaw, 25,000 per day, saw it!
4. Majdanek, near Lublin, which I saw when it was being built.

Globocnik said: You will have very large quantities of clothes to disinfect, 10 or 20 times as much as the "Textiles Collection," which is only being carried out in order to camouflage the origin of the Jewish, Polish, Czech and other items of clothing. Your second job is to convert the gas-chambers, which have up to now been operated with exhaust gases from an old Diesel engine, to a more poisonous and quicker means, cyanide. But the Führer and Himmler, who were here on August 15, the day before yesterday, that is, gave orders that I am myself to accompany all persons who visit the installations. Professor Pfannenstiel replied "But what does the Führer say?" Then Globocnik, who is now Higher SS and Police Leader in Trieste on the Adriatic Coast, said "The whole *Aktion* must be carried out much faster." Ministerial Director Dr. Herbert Lindner [Linden] of the Ministry of the Interior suggested. "Would it not be better to incinerate the bodies instead of burying them? Another generation might perhaps think differently about this?" Then Globocnik, "But, Gentlemen, if we should ever be succeeded by so cowardly and weak a generation that it does not understand our work, which is so good and so necessary, then, Gentlemen, the whole of National Socialism will have been in vain. On the contrary, one should bury bronze plaques [with the bodies], on which is inscribed that it was we, we who had the courage to complete this gigantic task." Hitler said to this, "Well my good Globocnik, you have said it, and that is my opinion, too."

The next day we moved on to Belzec. There is a separate little station with two platforms, at the foot of the hill of yellow standstone, due north of the Lublin-Lvov road and rail line. To the south of the station, near the main road, there are several office buildings with the inscription "Belzec Office of the *Waffen*-SS" [Military Unit of the SS].

Globocnik introduced me to SS *Hauptsturmführer* Obermeyer from Pirmasens, who showed me the installations very much against his will. There were no dead to be seen that day, but the stench in the whole area, even on the main road, was pestilent. Next to the small station there was a large barrack labelled "Dressing Room," with a window that said "Valuables," and also a hall with 100 "Barbers Chairs." Then there was a passage 150 m. long, in the open, enclosed with barbed wire on either side, and signs inscribed "To the Baths and Inhalation Installations." In front of us there was a house, the bath house, and to the right and left large concrete flower pots with geraniums or other flowers. After climbing a few steps there were three rooms each, on the right and on the left. They looked like garages, 4 by 5 m. and 1.90 m. high. At the back, out of sight, there were doors of wood. On the roof there was a Star of David made of copper. The front of the building bore a notice "Heckenholt Institution." That is all I saw that afternoon.

Next morning, a few minutes before 7 o'clock, I was told that the first train would arrive in 10 minutes. And in fact the first train from Lvov arrived a few minutes later. There were 45 carriages with 6,700 persons, of whom 1,450 were already dead on arrival. Through small openings closed with barbed wire one could see yellow, frightened children, men and women. The train stopped, and 200 Ukrainians, who were forced to perform this service, tore open the doors and chased the people from the carriages with whips. Then instructions were given through a large loud-speaker: The people are to take off all their clothes out of doors—and a few of them in the barracks—including artificial limbs and glasses. Shoes must be tied in pairs with a little piece of string handed out by a small four-year-old Jewish boy. All valuables and money are to be handed in at the window marked "Valuables." without any document or receipt being given. The women and girls must then go to the barber, who cuts off their hair with one or two snips. The hair disappears into large potato sacks, "to make something special for the submarines, to seal them and so on," the duty SS *Unterscharführer* explained to me.

Then the march starts: Barbed wire to the right and left and two dozen Ukrainians with rifles at the rear. They came on, led by an exceptionally pretty girl. I myself was standing with Police Captain Wirth in front of the death chambers. Men, women, children, infants, people with amputated legs, all naked, completely naked, moved past us. In one corner there is a whimsical SS man who tells these poor people in an unctuous voice, "Nothing at all will happen to you. You must just breathe deeply, that strengthens the lungs; this inhalation is necessary because of the infectious diseases, it is good disinfection!" When somebody asks what their fate will be, he explains that the men will of course have to work, building streets and houses. But the women will not have to work. If they want to, they can help in the house or the kitchen. A little glimmer of hope flickers once more in some of these poor people, enough to make them march unresisting into the death chambers. But most of them understand what is happening; the smell reveals their fate! Then they climb up a little staircase and see the truth. Nursing mothers with an infant at the breast, naked; many children of all ages, naked. They hesitate, but they enter the death chambers, most of them silent, forced on by those behind them, who are driven by the whip lashes of the SS men. A Jewish woman of about 40, with flaming eyes, calls down [revenge] for the blood of her children on the head of the murderers. Police Captain Wirth in person strikes her in the face 5 times with his whip, and she disappears into the gas chamber. . . .

PS—1553.

* Gerstein wrote down his evidence on May 26, 1945.

165

EXTRACT FROM THE WRITTEN EVIDENCE BY JACOB WIERNIK ON THE EXTERMINATION CAMP AT TREBLINKA*

. . . I stood in the line opposite my house in Wolynska Street, and from there we were taken to Zamenhof Street. The Ukrainians divided up the loot amongst themselves before our eyes. They fought amongst themselves, valued and sorted everything. Despite the great number of people there was silence in the street. A silent and cruel despair fell upon all. Oh what despair it was! They photographed us as though we were animals from before the Flood. There were also some who remained calm. I myself hoped that we would go home again. I thought they would check our documents. An order was given, and we moved off from our places. Woe to us! The naked truth was revealed before our eyes. Railway cars. Cars that were empty. That day was a fine, hot summer's day. It seemed as though the sun was protesting against the injustice. What was the guilt of our wives, our children, our mothers? What was it? The sun disappeared behind thick clouds. It is beautiful, warms and shines and does not wish to witness our suffering and humiliation.

An order is given to get into the cars. Eighty are pushed into each car. The way back is sealed off. I had on my body only trousers, a shirt and shoes. A back-pack with other things and high boots had stayed at home. I had prepared it because there were rumors that we would be sent to the Ukraine for work. The train was shunted from one siding to another. I knew this rail junction well and realized that we were staying in the same place. Meanwhile we could hear the Ukrainians amusing themselves, the sound of their shouting and cheerful laughter reaching us. It was becoming increasingly suffocating inside the car, and from minute to minute there was less air to breathe; it was all despair, blackness and horror . . . With indescribable suffering we finally arrived at Malkinia. We stopped there all night. Ukrainians came into the car and demanded valuables. Everybody gave them up in order in preserve their lives a little while longer.

. . . In the morning the train moved and we reached Treblinka station. I saw a train that passed us and in it people who were hungry, ragged and half naked. They said something to us but we did not understand them. The day was burning hot. The lack of air was terrible. As a result we were very thirsty. I looked out of the window. The peasants brought water and charged 100 zloty for each bottle. I had no money, apart from 10 gold coins. Also a 2, a 5 and a 10 in silver, with a portrait of the Marshal,** that I had kept for a memento. So I was forced to do without the water. Others bought it. They paid 500 zloty for a kilogram of black bread. I was tortured by thirst until mid-day. Then the future *Hauptsturmführer* came in and picked 10 men who brought us water. I assuaged my thirst a little. An order was given to take out the dead, but there were none. At four in the afternoon the train moved off. We arrived at Treblinka in a few minutes. It was only there that the blinkers dropped from our eyes. Ukrainians with rifles and machine-guns stood on the roofs of the huts. The whole area was strewn with bodies, some dressed and some naked. Their faces were distorted with fear and horror. They were black and swollen. Their eyes were frozen wide open. Their tongues hung out, brains were spattered around and the bodies twisted. There was blood everywhere. Our innocent blood. The blood of our children, our brothers and sisters. The blood or our fathers and mothers. And we are without hope, we realize that we will not escape our fate. . . .

There is an order to get out of the cars. Belongings are to be left behind. We are taken to the yard. There were huts on either side. There were two large notice boards with orders to hand over gold, silver, precious stones and all valuables. Failure to do so would bring the death penalty. On the roofs of the huts were Ukrainians with machine-guns. The women and children were ordered off to the left and the men told to sit down in the yard, on the right. Some distance away from us people were working: they were sorting the belongings taken from the train. I managed to steal over among the workers, and began to work; I suffered the first lash from the whip of a German whom we called Frankenstein. The women and children were told to take off their clothes.

. . . When we carried, or more correctly, dragged, the bodies away we were made to run, and were beaten for the least delay. The dead had been lying there for a long time. They had already begun to decompose. There was a stench of death and decomposition in the air. Worms crawled on the wretched bodies. When we tied on the belts, an arm or a leg would frequently drop off. We also labored on graves for ourselves until dusk, without food or drink. The day was hot, and thirst plagued us greatly. When we reached the huts in the evening each one of us began to search for the people he had known the day before—in vain—they were not to be found, they were no longer among the living. . . .

Shana be-Treblinka (Mi-pi Ed Re'iya) ("A Year in Treblinka by an Eye Witness"), Jerusalem, 1945, pp. 5-14.

* Wiernik took part in the uprising at the Treblinka camp. He succeeded in escaping and reached Warsaw in 1944. He recorded his evidence there, and it was first published by the Underground in Poland.

** The reference is to Marshal Jozef Pilsudski.

167

EXTRACT FROM EVIDENCE GIVEN AT THE NUREMBERG TRIALS ON THE AUSCHWITZ EXTERMINATION CAMP*

M. Dubost: What do you know about the Jewish transport that arrived from Romainville about the same time as you?

Vaillant-Couturier: When we left Romainville the Jewish women who were together with us remained behind. They were sent to Drancy, and finally arrived in Auschwitz, where we saw them again three weeks later. Of 1,200 who left, only 125 arrived in the camp. The rest were taken to the gas chambers immediately, and of the 125 not a single one was left by the end of a month.

The transports were carried out as follows: at the beginning, when we arrived, when a Jewish transport came there was a "selection." First the old women, the mothers and the children. They were told to get on trucks, together with the sick and people who looked weak. They kept only young girls, young women and young men; the latter were sent to the men's camp.

In general, it was rare for more than 250 out of a transport of 1,000 to 1,500 to reach the camp, and that was the maximum; the others were sent to the gas chambers straight away.

At this "selection" healthy women between 20 and 30 years old were also chosen, and sent to the Experimental Block. Girls and women, who were a little older or not chosen for this purpose, were sent to the camp and, like us, had their heads shaved and they were tattooed.

In the spring of 1944 there was also a block for twins. That was at the time of the immense transport of Hungarian Jews, about 700,000** persons. Dr. Mengele, who was carrying out the experiments, kept back the twin children from all transports, as well as twins of any age, so long as both twins were there. Both children and adults slept on the floor in this block. I don't know what experiments were made apart from blood tests and measurements.

M. Dubost: Did you actually see the "selection" when transports arrived?

Vaillant-Couturier: Yes, because when we were working in the Sewing Block in 1944, the block in which we lived was situated just opposite the place where the trains arrived. The whole process had been improved: Instead of carrying out the "selection" where the trains arrived, a siding took the carriages practically to the gas chamber, and the train stopped about 100 m. from the gas chamber. That was right in front of our block, but of course there were two rows of barbed wire between. Then we saw how the seals were taken off the trucks and how women, men and children were pulled out of the trucks by soldiers. We were present at the most terrible scenes when old couples were separated. Mothers had to leave their daughters, because they were taken to the camp, while the mothers and children went to the gas chambers. All these people knew nothing of the fate that awaited them. They were only confused because they were being separated from each other, but they did not know that they were going to their death.

To make the reception pleasanter there was then—in June and July 1944, that is—an orchestra made up of prisoners, girls in white blouses and dark blue skirts, all of them pretty and young, who played gay tunes when the trains arrived, the "Merry Widow," the Barcarolle from the "Tales of Hoffman," etc. They were told it was a labor camp, and as they never entered the camp they saw nothing but the small platform decorated with greenery, where the orchestra played. They could not know what awaited them.

Those who were taken to the gas chambers—that is, the old people, children and others—were taken to a red brick building.

M. Dubost: Then they were not registered?

Vaillant Couturier: No.

Dubost: They were not tattooed?

Vaillant-Couturier: No, they were not even counted.

Dubost: Were you yourself tattooed?

Vaillant-Couturier: Yes.

(The witness shows her arm)

They were taken to a red brick building with a sign that said Baths. There they were told to get undressed and given a towel before they were taken to the so-called shower room. Later, at the time of the large transports from Hungary, there was no time left for any degree of concealment. They were undressed brutally. I know of these particulars because I was acquainted with a little Jewess from France, who had lived on the Place de la Republique. . . .

Dubost: In Paris?

Vaillant-Couturier: In Paris; she was known as "little Marie" and was the only survivor of a family of nine. Her mother and her seven sisters and brothers had been taken to the gas chambers as soon as they arrived. When I got to know her she worked on undressing the small children before they were taken into the gas chamber.

After the people were undressed they were taken into a room that looked like a shower room, and the capsules were thrown down into the room through a hole in the ceiling. An SS man observed the effect through a spy-hole. After about 5 to 7 minutes, when the gas had done its job, he gave a signal for the opening of the doors. Men with gas-masks, these were prisoners too, came in and took the bodies out. They told us that the prisoners must have suffered before they died, because they clung together in bunches like grapes so that it was difficult to separate them. . . .

Trial of the Major War Criminals before the International Military Tribunal, Nuremberg 14 November 1945-1 October 1946, VI, Nuremberg, 1947, pp. 214-216.

* From the evidence of a Frenchwoman, Marie-Claude Vaillant-Couturier, who was a prisoner in the Auschwitz concentration camp, where she arrived on January 1, 1943.

** The correct number of Hungarian Jews sent to Auschwitz was about 430,000.

168

"THE FACE OF THE FUTURE," EDITORIAL FROM THE NEWSPAPER OF A JEWISH UNDERGROUND YOUTH ORGANIZATION IN CRACOW*

In view of the tragic existence of the Jews, where the life of the individual depends on chance, and the life of the community as a whole has long been on the brink of cessation, one must, more than ever, see the situation comprehensively. An individual point of view—everyone will surely understand that now—is of no significance today. As individuals, we are all lost. The likelihood of staying alive is minute. Broken and alone—there is not much we can expect of life. Dying together with Polish Jewry we must clearly visualize for ourselves the historic character of this time and tell ourselves with courage that our death does not spell the end of the world. The record of humanity and of the Jewish people will continue at its own speed in the future, even after we are safely under the ground.

The numerical balance-sheet of the Jews will be sad when peace finally comes to the world after the historical blood-bath. This is indeed not the first defeat of a defenseless people scattered over the face of the earth. Slaughter, murders, confiscation of property, and the burning alive of people—all these have been known to us for generations as the essential elements of our martyrology. But there has never been such wholesale extermination. Never did a situation develop like this, where there is no way out. Never before did great numbers of people armed with the most modern technology move against the Jews. Of 16 million Jews in the world, we shall scarcely reach 9 million after the war. And, most important of all, the Jews of Europe will no longer be there, those who up to now made up the healthiest part of the nation. . .

Nobody held out a helping hand to the Jews who were destroyed, nobody made any effort to help them to the extent that they could escape from the danger of extermination. They looked on our destruction as on the death of maggots, and not as the loss of a nation with high cultural values. When the question of the Jews came up even the hatred towards the Germans lessened. There was solidarity with the enemy in the joy over the fall of the Jews. Only a few retained any degree of humanity, and even they did not dare to give this public expression. The truth of aloneness was again confirmed.

We shall carry the heavy burden of this isolation until the end of our days, and it points to the fact that the only proper approach is that of self-liberation: We have nobody on whom to depend except ourselves. All other political concepts will lead us astray. We have paid the highest possible price because we were lulled asleep by the prosperity of Europe, or guided by false hopes of rescue that would come from outside. We lost our sense of reality and instead of planning our independence we scattered invaluable forces in alien fields. Who knows what would have been the future of the Jewish people if there were no *Yishuv* (Community) of half a million in Palestine, that built its foundations before the war broke out and which has now reached a million souls? Only this nucleus of a Jewish State now offers assurance for the survival of the people. It makes us believe that an independent Jewish nation will rise again, a well-spring of profound spiritual values as always. It is easier to die, therefore, in the knowledge that a genuine Jewish life still throbs there, that in that one small corner of the wide world we were not undesirables, lonely victims. There would be no sense in our death but for the feeling that, after we have gone, they will be the only ones who will think about us with genuine emotion.

Therefore, despite certain death, we join them in their struggle for the future. Every one of our deeds paved the way for freedom, and furthers the building of an independent homeland. Our revolt is a protest against the evil that is engulfing the world. To counter the terror that has crushed our people we shall stand prepared for the struggle for justice and freedom that should light up the life of humanity as a whole. We are willing to die in order that the shame of death in slavery shall not burden the future of the Jews, and that these Jews shall not have to recall the Jews of Europe with shame because they allowed themselves to be led unresisting to slaughter, and they had not the spirit and courage to defend themselves against destruction. As we had not been allowed to make our contributions to the creative work of building, we shall at least fulfill our historic duty here: it is we who must raise up the name of the lost people to wipe away the mark of shame of slavery, and to place it among the ranks of people free in spirit . . . .

Yad Vashem, 0-6/59.

* From the Underground newspaper of the Fighting Organization of the Jewish Prioneer Youth (Akiva) in Cracow, He-Halutz ha-Lohem ("Fighting Pioneer"), No. 29, August 13, 1943.

CHIEF JOSEPH

1840?-1904

AN INDIAN'S VIEWS OF INDIAN AFFAIRS

1879

Chief Joseph was chief of the Native American nation known as the Nez Percé. The ancestral lands of his people were in the Wallowa Valley in eastern Oregon. Joseph's ambition was only the simple one of securing that land for his people, but the settlement of the area by whites would make that impossible. A series of disputes over treaties led to an outbreak of armed hostilities in 1877. After initial success, the Nez Percé tried to make their way to refuge in Canada. They traveled over a thousand miles in the attempt, and almost half died along the way. The U.S. Army brought reinforcements in and caught them thirty miles from their goal. Overwhelmed, Joseph surrendered, still convinced of the rightness of his cause as well as the futility of further resistance.

Selected from: Chief Joseph. 1879. "Chief Joseph's Own Story." In Cyrus Townsend Brady, LL. D., Ed. *Northwestern Fights and Fighters.* New York: Doubleday, Page & Co., 1913. 38, 48-52, 55-56, 63-75.

An Indian's Views of Indian Affairs

My friends, I have been asked to show you my heart. I am glad to have a chance to do so. I want the white people to understand my people. Some of you think an Indian is like a wild animal. This is a great mistake. I will tell you all about our people, and then you can judge whether an Indian is a man or not. I believe much trouble and blood would be saved if we opened our hearts more. I will tell you in my way how the Indian sees things. The white man has more words to tell you how they look to him, but it does not require many words to speak the truth. What I have to say will come from my heart, and I will speak with a straight tongue. Ah-cum-kin-i-ma-me-hut (the Great Spirit) is looking at me, and will hear me.

My name is In-mut-too-yah-lat-lat (Thunder-traveling-over-the-Mountains). I am chief of the Wal-lam-wat-kin band of Chute-pa-lu, or Nez Percés (nose-pierced Indians). I was born in eastern Oregon, thirty-eight winters ago. My father was chief before me. When a young man, he was called Joseph by Mr. Spaulding, a missionary. He died a few years ago. He left a good name on earth. He advised me well for my people.

Our fathers gave us many laws, which they had learned from their fathers. These laws were good. They told us to treat all men as they treated us: that we should never be the first to break a bargain; that it was a disgrace to tell a lie; that we should speak only the truth; that it was a shame for one man to take from another his wife or his property without paying for it. We were taught to believe that the Great Spirit sees and hears everything, and that He never forgets, that hereafter He will give every man a spirit-home according to his desserts; if he has been a good man, he will have a good home; if he has been a bad man, he will have a bad home. This I believe, and all my people believe the same.

We did not know there were other people besides the Indian until about one hundred winters ago, when some men with white faces came to our country. They brought many things with them to trade for furs and skins. They brought tobacco, which was new to us. They brought guns with flint stones on them, which frightened our women and children. Our people could not talk with these white-faced men, but they used signs which all people understand. These men were Frenchmen, and they called our people "Nez Percés," because they wore rings in their noses for ornaments. Although very few of our people wear them now, we are still called by the same name. These French trappers said a great many things to our fathers, which have been planted in our hearts. Some were good for us, but some were bad. Our people were divided in opinion about these men. Some thought they taught more bad than good. An Indian respects a brave man, but he despises a coward. He loves a straight tongue, but he hates a forked tongue. The French trappers told us some truths and some lies.

The first white men of your people who came to our country were named Lewis and Clarke. They also brought many things that our people had never seen. They talked straight, and our people gave them a great feast, as a proof that their hearts were friendly. These men were very kind. They made presents to our chiefs and our people made presents to them. We had a great many horses, of which we gave them what they needed, and they gave us guns and tobacco in return. All the Nez Percés made friends with Lewis and Clarke, and agreed to let them pass through their country, and never to make war on white men. This promise the Nez Percés have never broken. No white man can accuse them of bad faith, and speak with a straight tongue. It has always been the pride of the Nez Percés that they were the friends of the white men. When my father was a young man there came to our country a white man (Rev. Mr. Spaulding) who talked spirit law. He won the affections of our people because he spoke good things to them. At first he did not say any thing about white men wanting to settle on our lands.

Nothing was said about that until about twenty winters ago, when a number of white people came into our country and built houses and made farms. At first our people made no complaint. They thought there was room enough for all to live in peace, and they were learning many things from the white men that seemed to be good. But we soon found that the white men were growing rich very fast, and were greedy to possess everything the Indian had. My father was the first to see through the schemes of the white men, and he warned his tribe to be careful about trading with them. He had suspicion of men who seemed anxious to make money. I was a boy then, but I remember well my father's caution. He had sharper eyes than the rest of our people.

Next there came a white officer (Governor Stevens), who invited all the Nez Percés to a treaty council. After the council was opened he made known his heart. He said there were a great many white people in our country, and many more would come; that he wanted the land marked out so that the Indians and white men could be separated. If they were to live in peace it was necessary, he said, that the Indians should have a country set apart for them, and in that country they must stay. My father, who represented his band, refused to have anything to do with the council, because he wished to be a free man. He claimed that no man owned any part of the earth, and a man could not sell what he did not own.

Mr. Spaulding took hold of my father's arm and said, "Come and sign the treaty." My father pushed him away, and said: "Why do you ask me to sign away my country? It is your business to talk to us about spirit matters, and not to talk to us about parting with our land." Governor Stevens urged my father to sign his treaty, but he refused. "I will not sign your paper," he said; "you go where you please, so do I; you are not a child, I am no child; I can think for myself. No man can think for me. I have no other home than this. I will not give it up to any man. My people would have no home. Take away your paper. I will not touch it with my hand."

My father left the council. Some of the chiefs of the other bands of the Nez Percés signed the treaty, and then Governor Stevens gave them presents of blankets. My father cautioned his people to take no presents, for "after a while" he said, "they will claim that you have accepted pay for your country." Since that time four bands of the Nez Percés have received annuities from the United States. My father was invited to many councils, and they tried hard to make him sign the treaty, but he was firm as the rock, and would not sign away his home. His refusal caused a difference among the Nez Percés.

Eight years later (1863) was the next treaty council. A chief called Lawyer, because he was a great talker, took the lead in this council, and sold nearly all the Nez Percés country. My father was not there. He said to me: "When you go into council with the white man, always remember your country. Do not give it away. The white man will cheat you out of your home. I have taken no pay from the United States. I have never sold our land." In this treaty Lawyer acted without authority from our band. He had no right to sell the Wallowa (*winding water*) country. That had always belonged to my father's own people, and the other bands had never disputed our right to it. No other Indians ever claimed Wallowa.

In order to have all people understand how much land we owned, my father planted poles around it and said:

"Inside is the home of my people—the white man may take the land outside. Inside this boundary all our people were born. It circles around the graves of our fathers, and we will never give up these graves to any man."

The United States claimed they had bought all the Nez Percés country outside the Lapwai Reservation, from Lawyer and other chiefs, but we continued to live on this land in peace until eight years ago, when white men began to come inside the bounds my father had set. We warned them against this great wrong, but they would not leave our land,

and some bad blood was raised. The white men represented that we were going upon the warpath. They reported many things that were false.

The United States Government again asked for a treaty council. My father had become blind and feeble. He could no longer speak for his people. It was then that I took my father's place as chief. In this council I made my first speech to white men. I said to the agent who held the council:

"I did not want to come to this council, but I came hoping that we could save blood. The white man has no right to come here and take our country. We have never accepted any presents from the Government. Neither Lawyer nor any other chief had authority to sell this land. It has always belonged to my people. It came unclouded to them from our fathers, and we will defend this land as long as a drop of Indian blood warms the hearts of our men."

The agent said he had orders, from the Great White Chief at Washington, for us to go upon the Lapwai Reservation, and that if we obeyed he would help us in many ways. "You must move to the agency," he said. I answered him "I will not. I do not need your help; we have plenty, and we are contented and happy if the white man will let us alone. The reservation is too small for so many people with all their stock. You can keep your presents; we can go to your towns and pay for all we need; we have plenty of horses and cattle to sell, and we won't have any help from you; we are free now: we can go where we please. Our fathers were born here. Here they lived; here they died, here are their graves. We will never leave them." The agent went away, and we had peace for a little while.

Soon after this my father sent for me. I saw he was dying. I took his hand in mine. He said: "My son, my body is returning to my mother earth, and my spirit is going very soon to see the Great Spirit Chief. When I am gone, think of your country. You are the chief of these people. They look to you to guide them. Always remember that your father never sold this country. You must stop your ears whenever you are asked to sign a treaty selling your home. A few years more, and white men will be all around you. They have their eyes on this land. My son, never forget my dying words. This country holds your father's body. Never sell the bones of your father and your mother." I pressed my father's hand and told him I would protect his grave with my life. My father smiled and passed away to the spirit-land.

I buried him in that beautiful valley of winding waters. I love that land more than all the rest of the world. A man who would not love his father's grave is worse than a wild animal.

For a short time we lived quietly. But this could not last. White men had found gold in the mountains around the land of winding water. They stole a great many horses from us, and we could not get them back because we were Indians. The white men told lies for each other. They drove off a great many of our cattle. Some white men branded our young cattle so they could claim them. We had no friend who would plead our cause before the law councils. It seemed to me that some of the white men in Wallowa were doing these things on purpose to get up a war. They knew that we were not strong enough to fight them. I labored hard to avoid trouble and bloodshed. We gave up some of our country to the white men, thinking that then we could have peace. We were mistaken. The white man would not let us alone. We could have avenged our wrongs many times, but we did not. Whenever the Government has asked us to help them against other Indians, we have never refused. When the white men were few and we were strong we could have killed them all off, but the Nez Percés wished to live at peace.

If we have not done so, we have not been to blame. I believe that the old treaty has never been correctly reported. If we ever owned the land we own it still, for we never sold it. In the treaty councils the commissioners have claimed that our country had been sold to the Government. Suppose a white man should come to me and say, "Joseph, I like your horses, and I want to buy them." I say to him, "No, my horses suit me, I will not sell them." Then he goes to my neighbor, and says to him: "Joseph has some good horses. I want to buy them, but he refuses to sell." My neighbor answers, "Pay me the money, and I will sell you Joseph's horses." The white man returns to me, and says, "Joseph, I have bought your horses, and you must let me have them." If we sold our lands to the Government, this is the way they were bought.

On account of the treaty made by the other bands of the Nez Percés, the white men claimed my lands. We were troubled greatly by white men crowding over the line. Some of these were good men, and we lived on peaceful terms with them, but they were not all good.

Nearly every year the agent came over from Lapwai and ordered us on to the reservation. We always replied that we were satisfied to live in Wallowa. We were careful to refuse presents or annuities which he offered.

Through all the years since the white men came to Wallowa we have been threatened and taunted by them and the treaty Nez Percés. They have given us no rest. We have had a few good friends among white men, and they have always advised my people to bear these taunts without fighting. Our young men were quick-tempered, and I have had great trouble in keeping them from doing rash things. I have carried a heavy load on my back ever since I was a boy. I learned then that we were but few, while the white men were many, and that we could not hold our own with them. We were like deer. They were like grizzly bears. We had a small country. Their country was large. We were contented to let things remain as the Great Spirit Chief made them. They were not; and would change the rivers and mountains if they did not suit them.

Year after year we have been threatened, but no war was made upon my people until General Howard came to our country two years ago and told us he was the white war-chief of all that country. He said: "I have a great many soldiers at my back. I am going to bring them up here, and then I will talk to you again. I will not let white men laugh at me the next time I come. The country belongs to the Government, and I intend to make you go upon the reservation."

I remonstrated with him against bringing more soldiers to the Nez Percés country. He had one house full of troops all the time at Fort Lapwai.

The next spring the agent at Umatilla Agency sent an Indian runner to tell me to meet General Howard at Walla Walla. I could not go myself, but I sent my brother and five other head men to meet him, and they had a long talk.

General Howard said: "You have talked straight, and it is all right. You can stay at Wallowa." He insisted that my brother and his company should go with him to Fort Lapwai. When the party arrived there General Howard sent out runners and called all the Indians to a grand council. I was in that council. I said to General Howard, "We are ready to listen." He answered that he would not talk then, but would hold a council next day, when he would talk plainly. I said to general Howard: "I am ready to talk to-day. I have been in a great many councils, but I am no wiser. We are all sprung from a woman, although we are unlike in many things. We cannot be made over again. You are as you were made, and as you were made you can remain. We are just as we were made by the Great Spirit, and you cannot change us; then why should children of one mother and one father quarrel?—why should one try to cheat the other? I do not believe that the Great Spirit Chief gave one kind of men the right to tell another kind of men what they must do."

General Howard replied: "You deny my authority, do you? You want to dictate to me, do you?"

Then one of my chiefs—Too-hool-hool-suit—rose in the council and said to General Howard: "The Great Spirit Chief made the world as it is, and as He wanted it, and He made a part of it for us to live upon. I do not see where you get authority to say that we shall not live where He placed us."

General Howard lost his temper and said: "Shut up! I don't want to hear any more of such talk. The law says you shall go upon the reservation to live, and I want you to do so, but you persist in disobeying the law" (meaning the treaty). "If you do not move, I will take the matter into my own hand, and make you suffer for your disobedience."

Too-hool-hool-suit answered: "Who are you, that you ask us to talk, and then tell me I shan't talk? Are you the Great Spirit? Did you make the world? Did you make the sun? Did you make the rivers to run for us to drink? Did you make the grass to grow? Did you make all these things that you talk to us as though we were boys? If you did, then you have the right to talk as you do."

General Howard replied: "You are an impudent fellow, and I will put you in the guard-house," and then ordered a soldier to arrest him.

Too-hool-hool-suit made no resistance. He asked General Howard: "Is that your order? I don't care. I have expressed my heart to you. I have nothing to take back. I have spoken for my country. You can arrest me, but you cannot change me or make me take back what I have said."

The soldiers came forward and seized my friend and took him to the guard-house. My men whispered among themselves whether they would let this thing be done. I counseled them to submit. I knew if we resisted that all the white men present, including General Howard, would be killed in a moment, and we would be blamed. If I had said nothing, General Howard would never have given an unjust order against my men. I saw the danger and while they dragged Too-hool-hool-suit to prison, I arose and said: "*I am going to talk now.* I don't care whether you arrest me or not." I turned to my people and said: "The arrest of Too-hool-hool-suit was wrong, but we will not resent the insult. We were invited to this council to express our hearts, and we have done so." Too-hool-hool-suit was prisoner for five days before he was released.

The council broke up that day. On the next morning General Howard came to my lodge, and invited me to go with him and White Bird and Looking Glass, to look for land for my people. As we rode along we came to some good land that was already occupied by Indians and white people. General Howard, pointing to this land, said: "If you will come on to the reservation, I will give you these lands and move these people off."

I replied: "No. It would be wrong to disturb these people. I have no right to take their homes. I have never taken what did not belong to me. I will not now."

We rode all day upon the reservation, and found no good land unoccupied. I have been informed by men who do not lie that General Howard sent a letter that night telling the soldiers at Walla Walla to go to Wallowa Valley, and drive us out upon our return home.

In the council next day General Howard informed us in a haughty spirit that he would give my people *thirty days* to go back home, collect all their stock, and move on to the reservation, saying, "If you are not here in that time, I shall consider that you want to fight, and will send my soldiers to drive you on."

I said: "War can be avoided and it ought to be avoided. I want no war. My people have always been the friends of the white man. Why are you in such a hurry? I cannot get ready to move in thirty days. Our stock is scattered, and Snake River is very high. Let us wait until fall, then the river will be low. We want time to hunt our stock and gather our supplies for winter."

General Howard replied, "If you let the time run over one day, the soldiers will be there to drive you on to the reservation, and all your cattle and horses outside of the reservation at that time will fall into the hands of the white men."

I knew I had never sold my country, and that I had no land in Lapwai; but I did not want bloodshed. I did not want my people killed. I did not want anybody killed. Some of my people had been murdered by white men, and the white murderers were never punished for it. I told General Howard about this, and again said I wanted no war. I wanted the people who live upon the lands I was to occupy at Lapwai to have time to gather their harvest.

I said in my heart that, rather than have war I would give up my country. I would rather give up my father's grave. I would give up everything rather than have the blood of white men upon the hands of my people.

General Howard refused to allow me more than thirty days to move my people and their stock. I am sure that he began to prepare for war at once.

When I returned to Wallowa I found my people very much excited upon discovering that the soldiers were already in the Wallowa Valley. We held a council, and decided to move immediately to avoid bloodshed.

Too-hool-hool-suit, who felt outraged by his imprisonment, talked for war, and made many of my young men willing to fight rather than be driven like dogs from the land where they were born. He declared that blood alone would wash out the disgrace General Howard had put upon him. It required a strong heart to stand up against such talk, but I urged my people to be quiet, and not to begin a war.

We gathered all the stock we could find, and made an attempt to move. We left many of our horses and cattle in Wallowa, and we lost several hundred in crossing the river. All my people succeeded in getting across in safety. Many of the Nez Percés came together in Rocky Cañon to hold a grand council. I went with all my people. This council lasted ten days. There was a great deal of war talk, and a great deal of excitement. There was one young brave present whose father had been killed by a white man five years before. This man's blood was bad against white men and he left the council calling for revenge.

Again I counseled peace, and I thought the danger was past. We had not complied with General Howard's order because we could not, but we intended to do so as soon as possible. I was leaving the council to kill beef for my family, when news came that the young man whose father had been killed had gone out with several hot-blooded young braves and killed four white men. He rode up to the council and shouted: "Why do you sit here like women? The war has begun already." I was deeply grieved. All the lodges were moved except my brother's and my own. I saw clearly that the war was upon us when I learned that my young men had been secretly buying ammunition. I heard then that Too-hool-hool-suit, who had been imprisoned by General Howard, had succeeded in organizing a war party. I knew that their acts would involve all my people. I saw that the war could not then be prevented. The time had passed. I counseled peace from the beginning. I knew that we were too weak to fight the United States. We had many grievances, but I knew that war would bring more. We had good white friends, who advised us against taking the war-path. My friend and brother, Mr. Chapman, who has been with us since the surrender, told us just how the war would end. Mr. Chapman took sides against us and helped General Howard. I do not blame him for doing so. He tried hard to prevent bloodshed. We hoped the white settlers would not join the soldiers. Before the war commenced we had discussed this matter all over, and many of my people were in favor of warning them that if they took no part against us they should not be molested in the event of war being begun by General Howard. This plan was voted down in the war-council.

There were bad men among my people who had quarreled with white men, and they talked of their wrongs until they roused all the bad hearts in the council. Still I could not believe that they would begin the war. I know that my young men did a great wrong, but I ask, Who was first to blame? They had been insulted a thousand times; their fathers and brothers had been killed; their mothers and wives had been disgraced; they had been driven to madness by whisky sold to them by the white men; they had been told by General Howard that all their horses and cattle which they had been unable to drive out of Wallowa were to fall into the hands of white men; and, added to all this, they were homeless and desperate.

I would have given my own life if I could have undone the killing of white men by my people. I blame my young men and I blame the white men. I blame General Howard for not giving my people time to get their stock away from Wallowa. I do not acknowledge that he had the right to order me to leave Wallowa at any time. I deny that either my father or myself ever sold that land. It is still our land. It may never again be our home, but my father sleeps there, and I love it as I love my mother. I left there, hoping to avoid bloodshed.

If General Howard had given me plenty of time to gather up my stock, and treated Too-hool-hool-suit as a man should be treated, there *would have been no war.* My friends among white men have blamed me for the war. I am not to blame. When my young men began the killing, my heart was hurt. Although I did not justify them, I remembered all the insults I had endured, and my blood was on fire. Still I would have taken my people to the buffalo country without fighting, if possible.

I could see no other way to avoid a war. We moved over to White Bird Creek, sixteen miles away, and there encamped, intending to collect our stock before leaving; but the soldiers attacked us and the first battle was fought. We numbered in that battle sixty men, and the soldiers a hundred. The fight lasted but a few minutes, when the soldiers retreated before us for twelve miles. They lost thirty-three killed, and had seven wounded. When an Indian fights, he only shoots to kill; but soldiers shoot at random. None of the soldiers were scalped. We do not believe in scalping, nor in killing wounded men. Soldiers do not kill many Indians unless they are wounded and left upon the battle-field. Then they kill Indians.

Seven days after the first battle General Howard arrived in the Nez Percés country, bringing seven hundred more soldiers. It was now war in earnest. We crossed the Salmon River, hoping General Howard would follow. We were not disappointed. He did follow us, and we got back between him and his supplies, and cut him off for three days. He sent out two companies to open the way. We attacked them, killing one officer, two guides, and ten men.

We withdrew, hoping the soldiers would follow, but they had got fighting enough for that day. They intrenched themselves, and next day we attacked again. The battle lasted all day, and was renewed next morning. We killed four and wounded seven or eight.

About this time General Howard found out that we were in his rear. Five days later he attacked us with three hundred and fifty soldiers and settlers. We had two hundred and fifty warriors. The fight lasted twenty-seven hours. We lost four killed and several wounded. General Howard's loss was twenty-nine men killed and sixty wounded.

The following day the soldiers charged upon us, and we retreated with our families and stock a few miles, leaving eighty lodges to fall into General Howard's hands.

Finding that we were outnumbered, we retreated to Bitter Root Valley. Here another body of soldiers came upon us and demanded our surrender. We refused. They said, "You cannot get by us." We answered, "We are going by you without fighting if you will let us, but we are going by you anyhow." We then made a treaty with these soldiers. We agreed not to molest any one and they agreed that we might pass through the Bitter Root country in peace. We bought provisions and traded stock with white men there.

We understood that there was to be no war. We intended to go peaceably to the buffalo country, and leave the question of returning to our country to be settled afterward.

With this understanding we traveled for four days, and, thinking that the trouble was all over, we stopped and prepared tent-poles to take with us. We started again, and at the end of two days we saw three white men passing our camp. Thinking that peace had been made, we did not molest them. We could have killed, or taken them prisoners, but we did not suspect them of being spies, which they were.

That night the soldiers surrounded our camp. About daybreak one of my men went out to look after his horses. The soldiers saw him and shot him down like a coyote. I have since learned that these soldiers were not those we had left behind. They had come upon us from another direction. The new white war-chief's name was Gibbon. He charged upon us while some of my people were still asleep. We had a hard fight. Some of my men crept around and attacked the soldiers from the rear. In this battle we lost nearly all our lodges, but we finally drove General Gibbon back.

Finding that he was not able to capture us, he sent to his camp a few miles away for his big guns (cannons), but my men had captured them and all the ammunition. We damaged the big guns all we could, and carried away the powder and lead. In the fight with General Gibbon we lost fifty women and children and thirty fighting men. We remained long enough to bury our dead. The Nez Percés never make war on women and children; we could have killed a great many women and children while the war lasted, but we would feel ashamed to do so cowardly an act.

We never scalped our enemies, but when General Howard came up and joined General Gibbon, their Indian scouts dug up our dead and scalped them. I have been told that General Howard did not order this great shame to be done.

We retreated as rapidly as we could toward the buffalo country. After six days General Howard came close to us, and we went out and attacked him, and captured nearly all his horses and mules (about two hundred and fifty head). We then marched on to the Yellowstone Basin.

On the way we captured one white man and two white women. We released them at the end of three days. They were treated kindly. The women were not insulted. Can the white soldiers tell me of one time when Indian women were taken prisoners, and held three days and then released without being insulted? Were the Nez Percés women who fell into the hands of General Howard's soldiers treated with as much respect? I deny that a Nez Percé was ever guilty of such a crime.

A few days later we captured two more white men. One of them stole a horse and escaped. We gave the other a poor horse and told him that he was free.

Nine days' march brought us to the mouth of Clarke's Fork of the Yellowstone. We did not know what had become of General Howard, but we supposed that he had sent for more horses and mules. He did not come up, but another new war-chief (General Sturgis) attacked us. We held him in check while we moved all our women and children and stock out of danger, leaving a few men to cover our retreat.

Several days passed, and we heard nothing of General Howard, or Gibbon, or Sturgis. We had repulsed each in turn, and began to feel secure, when another army, under General Miles, struck us. This was the fourth army, each of which outnumbered our fighting force, that we had encountered within sixty days.

We had no knowledge of General Miles's army until a short time before he made a charge upon us, cutting our camp in two, and capturing nearly all of our horses. About seventy men, myself among them, were cut off. My little daughter, twelve years of age, was with me. I gave her a rope, and told her to catch a horse and join the others who were cut off from the camp. I have not seen her since, but I have learned that she is alive and well.

I thought of my wife and children, who were now surrounded by soldiers, and I resolved to go to them or die. With a prayer in my mouth to the Great Spirit Chief who rules above, I dashed unarmed through the line of soldiers. It seemed to me that there were guns on every side, before and behind me. My clothes were cut to pieces and my horse was wounded, but I was not hurt. As I reached the door of my lodge, my wife handed me my rifle, saying: "Here's your gun. Fight!"

The soldiers kept up a continuous fire. Six of my men were killed in one spot near me. Ten or twelve soldiers charged into our camp and got possession of two lodges, killing three Nez Percés and losing three of their men, who fell inside our lines. I called my men to drive them back. We fought at close range, not more than twenty steps apart, and drove the soldiers back upon their main line, leaving their dead in our hands. We secured their arms and ammunition. We lost, the first day and night, eighteen men and three women. General Miles lost twenty-six killed and forty wounded. The following day General Miles sent a messenger into my camp under protection of a white flag. I sent my friend Yellow Bull to meet him.

Yellow Bull understood the messenger to say that General Miles wished me to consider the situation; that he did not want to kill my people unnecessarily. Yellow Bull understood this to be a demand for me to surrender and save blood. Upon reporting this message to me, Yellow Bull said he wondered whether General Miles was in earnest. I sent him back with my answer, that I had not made up my mind, but would think about it and send word soon. A little later he sent some Cheyenne scouts with another message. I went out to meet them. They said they believed that General Miles was sincere and really wanted peace. I walked on to General Miles's tent. He met me and we shook hands. He said, "Come, let us sit down by the fire and talk this matter over." I remained with him all night; next morning, Yellow Bull came over to see if I was alive, and why I did not return.

General Miles would not let me leave the tent to see my friend alone.

Yellow Bull said to me: "They have got you in their power, and I am afraid they will never let you go again. I have an officer in our camp, and I will hold him until they let you go free."

I said: "I do not know what they mean to do with me, but if they kill me you must not kill the officer. It will do no good to avenge my death by killing him."

Yellow Bull returned to my camp. I did not make any agreement that day with General Miles. The battle was renewed while I was with him. I was very anxious about my people. I knew that we were near Sitting Bull's camp in King George's land, and I thought maybe the Nez Percés who had escaped would return with assistance. No great damage was done to either party during the night.

On the following morning I returned to my camp by agreement, meeting the officer who had been held a prisoner in my camp at the flag of truce. My people were divided about surrendering. We could have escaped from Bear Paw Mountain if we had left our wounded, old women, and children behind. We were unwilling to do this. We had never heard of a wounded Indian recovering while in the hands of white men.

On the evening of the fourth day, General Howard came in with a small escort, together with my friend Chapman. We could now talk understandingly. General Miles said to me in plain words, "If you will come out and give up your arms, I will spare your lives and send you back to the reservation." I do not know what passed between General Miles and General Howard.

I could not bear to see my wounded men and women suffer any longer; we had lost enough already. General Miles had promised that we might return to our country with what stock we had left. I thought we could start again. I believed General Miles, *or I never would have surrendered.* I have heard that he has been censured for making the promise to return us to Lapwai. He could not have made any other terms with me at that time. I would have held him in check until my friends came to my assistance, and then neither of the generals nor their soldiers would have ever left Bear Paw Mountain alive.

On the fifth day I went to General Miles and gave up my gun, and said, "From where the sun now stands I will fight no more." My people needed rest—we wanted peace.

> [The complete text of the surrender speech of October 5, 1877, is as follows: "Tell General Howard I know his heart. What he told me before—I have in my heart. I am tired of fighting. Our chiefs are killed. Looking Glass is dead. *Too-hul-hul-suit*[1] is dead. The old men are all dead. It is the young men now, who say "yes" or "no" [that is, vote in council]. He who led the young men [Joseph's brother Ollicut] is dead. It is cold, and we have no blankets. The little children are freezing to death. My people—some of them—have run away to the hills, and have no blankets, no food. No one knows where they are—perhaps freezing to death. I want to have time to look for my children, and see how many of them I can find; maybe I shall find them among the dead. Hear me, my chiefs, my heart is sick and sad. From where the sun *now* stands, I will fight no more forever." (Brady, 38)]

I was told we could go with General Miles to Tongue River and stay there until spring, when we would be sent back to our country. Finally it was decided that we were to be taken to Tongue River. We had nothing to say about it. After our arrival at Tongue River, General Miles received orders to take us to Bismarck. The reason given was, that subsistence would be cheaper there.

General Miles was opposed to this order. He said: "You

---

1 Too-hool-hool-suit. Some people spell his name differently, probably due to phonetic spellings

must not blame me. I have endeavored to keep my word, but the chief who is over me has given the order, and I must obey it or resign. That would do you no good. Some other officer would carry out the order."

I believe General Miles would have kept his word if he could have done so. I do not blame him for what we have suffered since the surrender. I do not know who is to blame. We gave up all our horses—over eleven hundred—and all our saddles—over one hundred—and we have not heard from them since. Somebody has got our horses.

General Miles turned my people over to another soldier, and we were taken to Bismarck. Captain Johnson, who now had charge of us, received an order to take us to Fort Leavenworth. At Leavenworth we were placed in on a low river bottom, with no water except river water to drink and cook with. We had always lived in a healthy country, where the mountains were high and the water was cold and clear. Many of our people sickened and died, and we buried them in this strange land.* I cannot tell how much my heart suffered for my people while at Leavenworth. The Great Spirit Chief who rules above seemed to be looking some other way, and did not see what was being done to my people.

During the hot days (July, 1878) we received notice that we were to be moved farther away from our own country. We were not asked if we were willing to go. We were ordered to get into railroad-cars. Three of my people died on the way to Baxter Springs. It was worse to die there than to die fighting in the mountains.

We were moved from Baxter Springs (Kansas) to the Indian Territory, and set down without our lodges. We had but little medicine and we were nearly all sick. Seventy of my people have died since we moved there.

We had a great many visitors who have talked many ways. Some of the chiefs (General Fish and Colonel Stickney) from

---

* I can corroborate this. I saw them there often.—C.T.B.

Washington came to see us, and selected land for us to live upon. We have not moved to that land, for it is not a good place to live.

The Commissioner Chief (E. A. Hayt) came to see us. I told him, as I told every one, that I expected General Miles's word would be carried out. He said it "could not be done; that white men now lived in my country and all the land was taken up; that, if I returned to Wallowa, I could not live in peace; that law-papers were out against my young men who began the war, and that the Government could not protect my people." This talk fell like a heavy stone upon my heart. I saw that I could not gain anything by talking to him. Other law chiefs (Congressional Committee) came to see me and said they would help me to get a healthy country. I did not know whom to believe. The white people have too many chiefs. They do not understand each other. They do not all talk alike.

The Commissioner Chief (Mr. Hayt) invited me to go with him and hunt for a better home than we have now. I like the land we found (west of the Osage Reservation) better than any place I have seen in that country; but it is not a healthy land. There are no mountains and rivers. The water is warm. It is not a good country for stock. I do not believe my people can live there. I am afraid they will all die. The Indians who occupy that country are dying off. I promised Chief Hayt to go there, and do the best I could until the Government got ready to make good General Miles' word. I was not satisfied, but I could not help myself.

Then the Inspector Chief (General McNiel) came to my camp and we had a long talk. He said I ought to have a home in the mountain country north, and that he would write a letter to the Great Chief at Washington. Again the hope of seeing the mountains of Idaho and Oregon grew up in my heart.

At last I was granted permission to come to Washington and bring my friend Yellow Bull and our interpreter with me. I am glad we came. I have shaken hands with a great many friends, but there are some things I want to know which no one seems able to explain. I cannot understand how the Government sends a man out to fight us, as it did General Miles, and then breaks his word. Such a government has something wrong about it. I cannot understand why so many chiefs are allowed to talk so many different ways, and promise so many different things. I have seen the Great Father Chief (the President); the next Great Chief (Secretary of the Interior); the Commissioner Chief (Hayt); the Law Chief (General Butler), and many other law chiefs (Congressmen), and they all say they are my friends, and that I shall have justice, but while their mouths all talk right I do not understand why nothing is done for my people. I have heard talk and talk, but nothing is done. Good words do not last long unless they amount to something. Words do not pay for my dead people. They do not pay for my country, now overrun by white men. They do not protect my father's grave. They do not pay for my horses and cattle. Good words will not give me back my children. Good words will not make good the promise of your War Chief, General Miles. Good words will not give my people good health and stop them from dying. Good words will not get my people a home where they can live in peace and take care of themselves. I am tired of talk that comes to nothing. It makes my heart sick when I remember all the good words and all the broken promises. There has been too much talking by men who had no right to talk. Too many misrepresentations have been made, too many misunderstandings have come up between the white men about the Indians. If the white man wants to live in peace with the Indian he can live in peace. There need be no trouble. Treat all men alike. Give them the same law. Give them all an even chance to live and grow. All men were made by the same Great Spirit Chief. They are all brothers. The earth is the mother of all people, and all people should have equal rights upon it. You might as well expect the rivers to run backward as that any man who was born a free man should be contented penned up and denied liberty to go where he pleases. If you tie a horse to a stake, do you expect he will grow fat? If you pen an Indian up on a small spot of earth, and compel him to stay there, he will not be contented nor will he grow and prosper. I have asked some of the great white chiefs where they get their authority to say to the Indian that he shall stay in one place, while he sees white men going where they please. They cannot tell me.

I only ask of the Government to be treated as all other men are treated. If I cannot go to my own home, let me have a home in some country where my people will not die so fast. I would like to go to Bitter Root Valley. There my people would be healthy; where they are now they are dying. Three have died since I left my camp to come to Washington.

When I think of our condition my heart is heavy. I see men of my race treated as outlaws and driven from country to country, or shot down like animals.

I know that my race must change. We cannot hold our own with the white men as we are. We only ask an even chance to live as other men live. We ask to be recognized as men. We ask that the same law shall work alike on all men. If the Indian breaks the law, punish him by the law. If the white man breaks the law, punish him also.

Let me be a free man—free to travel, free to stop, free to work, free to trade, where I choose, free to choose my own teachers, free to follow the religion of my fathers, free to think and talk and act for myself—and I will obey every law, or submit to the penalty.

Whenever the white man treats the Indian as they treat each other, then we will have no more wars. We shall all be alike—brothers of one father and one mother, with one sky above us and one country around us, and one government for all. Then the Great Spirit Chief who rules above will smile upon this land, and send rain to wash out the bloody spots made by brothers' hands from the face of the earth. For this time the Indian race are waiting and praying. I hope that no more groans of wounded men and women will ever go to the ear of the Great Spirit Chief above, and that all people may be one people.

In-mut-too-yah-lat-lat has spoken for his people.

YOUNG JOSEPH.

Resistance

Introduction

More people tolerate overbearing authorities than resist them. We can, and do, allow ourselves to be bullied and deprived of our freedom. Philosophers offer standards for determining when resistance can be justified, but an actual decision to resist is a practical decision. Someone must decide in a particular place and at a particular time to do something that will, in fact, constitute resistance to authority. Antigone must confront Creon. Socrates must challenge the crowd that is trying to threaten him into silence. From somewhere inside himself, Douglass must find the determination to fight Covey. The tasks for Thoreau and King were not as much personal confrontations, as finding ways to challenge institutions and laws, in Thoreau's case taxes and in King's the system of legal racial segregation. Havel's situation was still more complex. What does one do to when the institutions are so powerful and ruthless, as they were in Communist bloc of eastern and central Europe from the end of World War II until 1989, that they can resist challenge and the public are so resigned that demonstrations and revolt are impossible? His prescription to "live in truth" speaks beyond the immediate circumstances of his time and place to concerns that plague mankind with unhappy regularity.

Sophocles

495-406 B.C.E.

ANTIGONE

441 B.C.E.

Of an estimated one hundred and twenty-five plays that Sophocles wrote, only seven have come down to us, but these have been enough to support his reputation as a master of tragic drama. He lived in Athens at the height of that city's accomplishments and died before it was finally defeated in the Peloponnesian War. Like his fellow Athenians, Sophocles participated in civic life in addition to pursuing his profession. *Antigone* is the concluding play in the series of three tragic plays about Oedipus and his family that we know as the "Oedipus Cycle." The classical Greek understanding of tragedy includes a strong sense of a person having a fate that was beyond control. The curse on Oedipus and his family provides that element, which makes Antigone's defiance of King Creon all the more powerful.

Selected from: Sophocles. 441 B.C.E. *The Tragedies of Sophocles.* Trans. Richard C. Jebb. London: Cambridge at the University Press. 1917. 125-172.

CHARACTERS

Ismene , *daughter of Oedipus*
Antigone , *daughter of Oedipus*
Creon, *King of Thebes*
Haemon, *son of Creon*
Teiresias, *a blind prophet*
A Sentry
A Messenger
Eurydice, *wife of Creon*
Chorus of *Theban elders*

SCENE: Before the Royal Palace at Thebes

Polyneices, supported by an Argive army, had marched against Thebes, in order to wrest the sovereignty from his brother Eteocles. The day before that on which the drama opens had been disastrous for the invaders. At six of the city's seven gates, a Theban champion slew his Argive opponent: at the seventh, Eteocles met Polyneices, and each fell by the other's hand. The Argive army fled in the night. Creon, now King of Thebes, has just issued an edict, proclaiming that Eteocles shall be interred with public honours, but that the corpse of Polyneices shall be left unburied.

ANTIGONE.

Ismene, sister, mine own dear sister, knowest thou what ill there is, of all bequeathed by Oedipus, that Zeus fulfils not for us twain while we live? Nothing painful is there, nothing fraught with ruin, no shame, no dishonour, that I have not seen in thy woes and mine.

And now what new edict is this of which they tell, that our Captain hath just published to all Thebes? Knowest thou aught? Hast thou heard? Or is it hidden from thee that our friends are threatened with the doom of our foes?

ISMENE.

No word of friends, Antigone, gladsome or painful, hath come to me, since we two sisters were bereft of brothers twain, killed in one day by a twofold blow; and since in this last night the Argive host hath fled, I know no more, whether my fortune be brighter, or more grievous.

AN. I knew it well, and therefore sought to bring thee beyond the gates of the court, that thou mightest hear alone.

IS. What is it? 'Tis plain that thou art brooding on some dark tidings.

AN. What, hath not Creon destined our brothers, the one to honoured burial, the other to unburied shame? Eteocles, they say, with due observance of right and custom, he hath laid in the earth, for his honour among the dead below. But the hapless corpse of Polyneices—as rumour saith, it hath been published to the town that none shall entomb him or mourn, but leave unwept, unsepulchred, a welcome store for the birds, as they espy him, to feast on at will.

Such, 'tis said, is the edict that the good Creon hath set forth for thee and for me,—yes, for *me*,—and is coming hither to proclaim it clearly to those who know it not; nor counts the matter light, but, who so disobeys in aught, his doom is death by stoning before all the folk. Thou knowest it now; and thou wilt soon show whether thou art nobly bred, or the base daughter of a noble line.

IS. Poor sister,—and if things stand thus, what could I help to do or undo?

AN. Consider if thou wilt share the toil and the deed.

IS. In what venture? What can be thy meaning?

AN. Wilt thou aid this hand to lift the dead?

IS. Thou wouldst bury him,—when 'tis forbidden to Thebes?

AN. I will do my part,—and thine, if thou wilt not,—to a brother. False to him will I never be found.

IS. Ah, over-bold! when Creon hath forbidden?

AN. Nay, he hath no right to keep me from mine own.

IS. Ah me! think, sister, how our father perished, amid hate and scorn, when sins bared by his own search had moved him to strike both eyes with self-blinding hand; then the mother wife, two names in one, with twisted noose did despite unto her life; and last, our two brothers in one day,—each shedding, hapless one, a kinsman's blood,—wrought out with mutual hands their common doom. And now *we* in turn—we two left all alone—think how we shall perish, more miserably than all the rest, if, in defiance of the law, we brave a king's decree or his powers. Nay, we must remember, first, that we were born women, as who should not strive with men; next, that we are ruled of the stronger, so that we must obey in these things, and in things yet sorer. I, therefore, asking the Spirits Infernal to pardon, seeing that force is put on me herein, will hearken to our rulers; for 'tis witless to be over busy.

AN. I will not urge thee,—no, nor, if thou yet shouldst have the mind, wouldst thou be welcome as a worker with *me*. Nay, be what thou wilt; but I will bury him: well for me to die in doing that. I shall rest, a loved one with him whom I have loved, sinless in my crime; for I owe a longer allegiance to the dead than to the living: in that world I shall abide for ever. But if *thou* wilt, be guilty of dishonouring laws which the gods have stablished in honour.

IS. I do them no dishonour; but to defy the State,—I have no strength for that.

AN. Such be thy plea: I,—then, will go to heap the earth above the brother whom I love.

IS. Alas, unhappy one! How I fear for thee!

AN. Fear not for me: guide thine own fate aright.

IS. At least, then, disclose this plan to none, but hide it closely,—and so, too, will I.

AN. Oh, denounce it! Thou wilt be far more hateful for thy silence, if thou proclaim not these things to all.

IS. Thou hast a hot heart for chilling deeds.

AN. I know that I please where I am most bound to please.

IS. Aye, if thou canst; but thou wouldst what thou canst not.

AN. Why, then, when my strength fails, I shall have done.

IS. A hopeless quest should not be made at all.

AN. If thus thou speakest, thou wilt have hatred from me, and will justly be subject to the lasting hatred of the dead. But leave me, and the folly that is mine alone, to suffer this dread thing; for I shall not suffer aught so dreadful as an ignoble death.

IS. Go, then, if thou must; and of this be sure, that, though thine errand is foolish, to thy dear ones thou art truly dear.

[*Exit* ANTIGONE *on the spectators' left.* ISMENE *retires into the palace by one of the two side-doors.*

CHORUS.

Beam of the sun, fairest light that ever dawned on Thebé of the seven gates, thou hast shone forth at last, eye of golden day, arisen above Dircè's streams! The warrior of the white shield, who came from Argos in his panoply, hath been stirred by thee to headlong flight, in swifter career; who set forth against our land by reason of the vexed claims of Polyneices; and, like shrill-screaming eagle, he flew over into our land, in snow-white pinion sheathed, with an armed throng, and with plumage of helms.

He paused above our dwellings; he ravened around our sevenfold portals with spears athirst for blood; but he went hence, or ever his jaws were glutted with our gore, or the Fire-god's pine-fed flame had seized our crown of towers. So fierce was the noise of battle raised behind him, a thing too hard for him to conquer, as he wrestled with his dragon foe.

For Zeus utterly abhors the boasts of a proud tongue; and when he beheld them coming on in a great stream, in the haughty pride of clanging gold, he smote with brandished fire one who was now hasting to shout victory at his goal upon our ramparts.

Swung down, he fell on the earth with a crash, torch in hand, he who so lately, in the frenzy of the mad onset, was raging against us with the blasts of his tempestuous hate. But those threats fared not as he hoped; and to other foes the mighty War-god dispensed their several dooms, dealing havoc around, a mighty helper at our need.

For seven captains at seven gates, matched against seven, left the tribute of their panoplies to Zeus who turns the battle; save those two of cruel fate, who, born of one sire and one mother, set against each other their twain conquering spears, and are sharers in a common death.

But since Victory of glorious name hath come to us, with joy responsive to the joy of Thebé whose chariots are many, let us enjoy forgetfulness after the late wars, and visit all the temples of the gods with night-long dance and song; and may Bacchus be our leader, whose dancing shakes the land of Thebé.

But lo, the king of the land comes yonder, Creon, son of Menoeceus, our new ruler by the new fortunes that the gods have given; what counsel is he pondering, that he hath proposed this special conference of elders, summoned by his general mandate?

Enter CREON, *from the central doors of the palace, in the garb of king, with two attendants.*

CR. Sirs, the vessel of our State, after being tossed on wild waves, hath once more been safely steadied by the gods:

and ye, out of all the folk, have been called apart by my summons, because I knew, first of all, how true and constant was your reverence for the royal power of Laiüs; how, again, when Oedipus was ruler of our land, and when he had perished, your steadfast loyalty still upheld their children. Since, then, his sons have fallen in one day by a twofold doom,—each smitten by the other, each stained with a brother's blood,—I now possess the throne and all its powers, by nearness of kinship to the dead.

No man can be fully known, in soul and spirit and mind, until he hath been seen versed in rule and law-giving. For if any, being supreme guide of the State, cleaves not to the best counsels, but, through some fear, keeps his lips locked, I hold, and have ever held, him most base; and if any makes a friend of more account than his fatherland, that man hath no place in my regard. For I—be Zeus my witness, who sees all things always—would not be silent if I saw ruin, instead of safety, coming to the citizens; nor would I ever deem the country's foe a friend to myself; remembering this, that our country is the ship that bears us safe, and that only while she prospers in our voyage can we make true friends.

Such are the rules by which I guard this city's greatness. And in accord with them is the edict which I have now published to the folk touching the sons of Oedipus;—that Eteocles, who hath fallen fighting for our city, in all renown of arms, shall be entombed, and crowned with every rite that follows the noblest dead to their rest. But for his brother, Polyneices,—who came back from exile, and sought to consume utterly with fire the city of his fathers and the shrines of his fathers' gods,—sought to taste of kindred blood, and to lead the remnant into slavery;—touching this man, it hath been proclaimed to our people that none shall grace him with sepulture or lament, but leave him unburied, a corpse for birds and dogs to eat, a ghastly sight of shame.

Such the spirit of my dealing; and never, by deed of mine, shall the wicked stand in honour before the just; but whoso hath good will to Thebes, he shall be honoured of me, in his life and in his death.

CH. Such is thy pleasure, Creon, son of Menoeceus, touching this city's foe, and its friend; and thou hast power, I ween, to take what order thou wilt, both for the dead, and for all us who live.

CR. See, then, that ye be guardians of the mandate.

CH. Lay the burden of this task on some younger man.

CR. Nay, watchers of the corpse have been found.

CH. What, then, is this further charge that thou wouldst give?

CR. That ye side not with the breakers of these commands.

CH. No man is so foolish that he is enamoured of death.

CR. In sooth, that is the meed; yet lucre hath oft ruined men through their hopes.

Enter GUARD.

GU. My liege, I will not say that I come breathless from speed, or that I have plied a nimble foot; for often did my thoughts make me pause, and wheel round in my path, to return. My mind was holding large discourse with me; 'Fool, why goest thou to thy certain doom?' 'Wretch, tarrying again? And if Creon hears this from another, must not thou smart for it?' So debating, I went on my way with lagging steps, and thus a short road was made long. At last, however, it carried the day that I should come hither—to thee; and, though my tale be nought, yet will I tell it; for I come with a good grip on one hope,—that I can suffer nothing but what is my fate.

CR. And what is it that disquiets thee thus?

GU. I wish to tell thee first about myself—I did not do the deed—I did not see the doer—it were not right that I should come to any harm.

CR. Thou hast a shrewd eye for thy mark; well dost thou

fence thyself round against the blame:—clearly thou hast some strange thing to tell.

GU. Aye, truly; dread news makes one pause long.

CR Then tell it, wilt thou, and so get thee gone?

GU. Well, this is it.—The corpse—some one hath just given it burial, and gone away, after sprinkling thirsty dust on the flesh, with such other rites as piety enjoins.

CR. What sayest thou? What living man hath dared this deed?

GU. I know not; no stroke of pickaxe was seen there, no earth thrown up by mattock; the ground was hard and dry, unbroken, without track of wheels; the doer was one who had left no trace. And when the first day-watchman showed it to us, sore wonder fell on all. The dead man was veiled from us; not shut within a tomb, but lightly strewn with dust, as by the hand of one who shunned a curse. And no sign met the eye as though any beast of prey or any dog had come nigh to him, or torn him.

Then evil words flew fast and loud among us, guard accusing guard; and it would e'en have come to blows at last, nor was there any to hinder. Every man was the culprit, and no one was convicted, but all disclaimed knowledge of the deed. And we were ready to take red-hot iron in our hands;—to walk through fire;—to make oath by the gods that we had not done the deed,—that we were not privy to the planning or the doing.

At last, when all our searching was fruitless, one spake, who made us all bend our faces on the earth in fear; for we saw not how we could gainsay him, or escape mischance if we obeyed. His counsel was that this deed must be reported to thee, and not hidden. And this seemed best; and the lot doomed my hapless self to win this prize. So here I stand,—as unwelcome as unwilling, well I wot; for no man delights in the bearer of bad news.

CH. O king, my thoughts have long been whispering, can this deed, perchance, be e'en the work of gods?

CR. Cease, ere thy words fill me utterly with wrath, lest thou be found at once an old man and foolish. For thou sayest what is not to be borne, in saying that the gods have care for this corpse. Was it for high reward of trusty service that they sought to hide his nakedness, who came to burn their pillared shrines and sacred treasures, to burn their land, and scatter its laws to the winds? Or dost thou behold the gods honouring the wicked? It cannot be. No! From the first there were certain in the town that muttered against me, chafing at this edict, wagging their heads in secret; and kept not their necks duly under the yoke, like men contented with my sway.

'Tis by them, well I know, that these have been beguiled and bribed to do this deed. Nothing so evil as money ever grew to be current among men. This lays cities low, this drives men from their homes, this trains and warps honest souls till they set themselves to works of shame; this still teaches folk to practise villainies, and to know every godless deed. But all the men who wrought this thing for hire have made it sure that, soon or late, they shall pay the price. Now, as Zeus still hath my reverence, know this—I tell it thee on my oath:—If ye find not the very author of this burial, and produce him before mine eyes, death alone shall not be enough for you, till first, hung up alive, ye have revealed this outrage,—that henceforth ye may thieve with better knowledge whence lucre should be won, and learn that it is not well to love gain from every source. For thou wilt find that ill-gotten pelf[1] brings more men to ruin than to weal.[2]

GU. May I speak? Or shall I just turn and go?

CR. Knowest thou not that even now thy voice offends?

GU. Is thy smart in the ears, or in the soul?

CR. And why wouldst thou define the seat of my pain

GU. The doer vexes thy mind, but I, thine ears.

1 Dishonestly acquired wealth or riches.

2 prosperity

CR. Ah, thou art a born babbler, 'tis well seen.

GU. May be, but never the doer of this deed.

CR. Yea, and more,—the seller of thy life for silver.

GU. Alas! 'Tis sad, truly, that he who judges should misjudge.

CR. Let thy fancy play with 'judgment' as it will; but,—if ye show me not the doers of these things, ye shall avow that dastardly gains work sorrows.

[*Exit.*

GU. Well, may he be found! so 'twere best. But, be he caught or be he not—fortune must settle—that truly thou wilt not see me here again. Saved, even now, beyond hope and thought, I owe the gods great thanks.

[*Exit.*

CHORUS

Wonders are many, and none is more wonderful than man; the power that crosses the white sea, driven by the stormy south-wind, making a path under surges that threaten to engulf him; and Earth, the eldest of the gods, the immortal, the unwearied, doth he wear, turning the soil with the offspring of horses, as the ploughs go to and fro from year to year.

And the light-hearted race of birds, and the tribes of savage beasts, and the sea-brood of the deep, he snares in the meshes of his woven toils, he leads captive, man excellent in wit. And he masters by his arts the beast whose lair is in the wilds, who roams the hills; he tames the horse of shaggy mane, he puts the yoke upon its neck, he tames the tireless mountain bull.

And speech, and wind-swift thought, and all the moods that mould a state, hath he taught himself; and how to flee the arrows of the frost, when 'tis hard lodging under the clear sky, and the arrows of the rushing rain; yea, he hath resource for all; without resource he meets nothing that must come: only against Death shall he call for aid in vain; but from baffling maladies he hath devised escapes.

Cunning beyond fancy's dream is the fertile skill which brings him, now to evil, now to good. When he honours the laws of the land, and that justice which he hath sworn by the gods to uphold, proudly stands his city: no city hath he who, for his rashness, dwells with sin. Never may he share my hearth, never think my thoughts, who doth these things!

Enter the GUARD *on the spectators' left, leading in* ANTIGONE.

What portent from the gods is this?—my soul is amazed. I know her!—how can I deny that yon maiden is Antigone?

O hapless, and child of hapless sire,—of Oedipus! What means this? Thou brought a prisoner?—thou, disloyal to the king's laws, and taken in folly?

GUARD.

Here she is, the doer of the deed:—we caught this girl burying him:—but where is Creon?

CH. Lo, he comes forth again from the house, at our need.

CR. What is it? What hath chanced, that makes my coming timely?

GU. O king, against nothing should men pledge their word; for the afterthought belies the first intent. I could have vowed that I should not soon be here again,—scared by thy threats, with which I had just been lashed: but,—since the joy that surprises and transcends our hopes is like in fulness to no other pleasure,—I have come, though 'tis in breach of my sworn oath, bringing this maid; who was taken showing grace to the dead. This time there was no casting of lots; no, this luck hath fallen to me, and to none else. And now, sire, take her thyself, question her, examine her, as thou wilt; but I have a right to free and final quittance of this trouble.

CR. And thy prisoner here—how and whence hast thou taken her?

GU. She was burying the man; thou knowest all.

CR. Dost thou mean what thou sayest? Dost thou speak aright?

GU. I saw her burying the corpse that thou hadst forbidden to bury. Is that plain and clear?

CR. And how was she seen? how taken in the act?

GU. It befell on this wise. When we had come to the place,—with those dread menaces of thine upon us,—we swept away all the dust that covered the corpse, and bared the dank body well; and then sat us down on the brow of the hill, to windward, heedful that the smell from him should not strike us; every man was wide awake, and kept his neighbour alert with torrents of threats, if anyone should be careless of this task.

So went it, until the sun's bright orb stood in mid heaven, and the heat began to burn: and then suddenly a whirlwind lifted from the earth a storm of dust, a trouble in the sky, and filled the plain, marring all the leafage of its woods; and the wide air was choked therewith: we closed our eyes, and bore the plague from the gods.

And when, after a long while, this storm had passed, the maid was seen, and she cried aloud with the sharp cry of a bird in its bitterness,—even as when, within the empty nest, it sees the bed stripped of its nestlings. So she also, when she saw the corpse bare, lifted up a voice of wailing, and called down curses on the doers of that deed. And straightway she brought thirsty dust in her hands; and from a shapely ewer of bronze, held high, with thrice-poured drink-offering she crowned the dead.

We rushed forward when we saw it, and at once closed upon our quarry, who was in no wise dismayed. Then we taxed her with her past and present doings; and she stood not on denial of aught,—at once to my joy and to my pain. To have escaped from ills one's self is a great joy; but 'tis painful to bring friends to ill. Howbeit, all such things are of less account to me than mine own safety.

CR. Thou,—thou whose face is bent to earth—dost thou avow, or disavow, this deed?

AN. I avow it; I make no denial. CR. *(To GUARD.)* Thou canst betake thee whither thou wilt, free and clear of a grave charge.

[*Exit* GUARD.

(To ANTIGONE.) Now, tell me thou—not in many words, but briefly—knewest thou that an edict had forbidden this?

AN. I knew it: could I help it? It was public.

CR. And thou didst indeed dare to transgress that law?

AN. Yes; for it was not Zeus that had published me that edict; not such are the laws set among men by the Justice who dwells with the gods below; nor deemed I that thy decrees were of such force, that a mortal could override the unwritten and unfailing statutes of heaven. For their life is not of to-day or yesterday, but from all time, and no man knows when they were first put forth.

Not through dread of any human pride could I answer to the gods for breaking *these*. Die I must,—I knew that well (how should I not?) even without thy edicts. But if I am to die before my time, I count that a gain: for when any one lives, as I do, compassed about with evils, can such an one find aught but gain in death?

So for me to meet this doom is trifling grief; but if I had suffered my mother's son to lie in death an unburied corpse, that would have grieved me; for this, I am not grieved. And if my present deeds are foolish in thy sight, it may be that a foolish judge arraigns my folly.

CH. The maid shows herself passionate child of passionate sire, and knows not how to bend before troubles.

CR. Yet I would have thee know that o'er-stubborn spirits are most often humbled; 'tis the stiffest iron, baked to hardness in the fire, that thou shalt oftenest see snapped and shivered; and I have known horses that show temper brought to order by a little curb; there is no room for pride, when thou art thy neighbour's slave.—This girl was already versed in insolence when she transgressed the laws that had been set forth; and, that done, lo, a second insult,—to vaunt of this, and exult in her deed.

Now verily I am no man, she is the man, if this victory shall rest with her, and bring no penalty. No! be she sister's child, or nearer to me in blood than any that worships Zeus at the altar of our house,—she and her kinsfolk shall not avoid a doom most dire; for indeed I charge that other with a like share in the plotting of this burial.

And summon her—for I saw her e'en now within,—raving, and not mistress of her wits. So oft, before the deed, the mind stands self-convicted in its treason, when folks are plotting mischief in the dark. But verily this, too, is hateful,—when one who hath been caught in wickedness then seeks to make the crime a glory.

AN. Wouldst thou do more than take and slay me?

CR. No more, indeed; having that, I have all.

AN. Why then dost thou delay? In thy discourse there is nought that pleases me,—never may there be!—and so my words must needs be unpleasing to thee. And yet, for glory—whence could I have won a nobler, than by giving burial to mine own brother? All here would own that they thought it well, were not their lips sealed by fear. But royalty, blest in so much besides, hath the power to do and say what it will.

CR. Thou differest from all these Thebans in that view.

AN. These also share it; but they curb their tongues for thee.

CR And art thou not ashamed to act apart from them?

AN. No; there is nothing shameful in piety to a brother.

CR. Was it not a brother, too, that died in the opposite cause?

AN. Brother by the same mother and the same sire.

CR. Why, then, dost thou render a grace that is impious in his sight?

AN. The dead man will not say that he so deems it.

CR. Yea, if thou makest him but equal in honour with the wicked.

AN. It was his brother, not his slave, that perished.

CR. Wasting this land; while *he* fell as its champion.

AN. Nevertheless, Hades desires these rites.

CR. But the good desires not a like portion with the evil.

AN. Who knows but this seems blameless in the world below?

CR. A foe is never a friend—not even in death.

AN. 'Tis not my nature to join in hating, but in loving.

CR. Pass, then, to the world of the dead, and, if thou must needs love, love them. While I live, no woman shall rule me.

Enter ISMENE *from the house, led in by two attendants.*

CH. Lo, yonder Ismene comes forth, shedding such tears as fond sisters weep; a cloud upon her brow casts its shadow over her darkly-flushing face, and breaks in rain on her fair cheek.

CR. And thou, who, lurking like a viper in my house, wast secretly draining my life-blood, while I knew not that I was nurturing two pests, to rise against my throne—come, tell me now, wilt thou also confess thy part in this burial, or wilt thou forswear all knowledge of it?

IS. I have done the deed,—if she allows my claim,—and share the burden of the charge.

AN. Nay, justice will not suffer thee to do that: thou didst not consent to the deed, nor did I give thee part in it.

IS. But, now that ills beset thee, I am not ashamed to sail the sea of trouble at thy side.

AN. Whose was the deed, Hades and the dead are witnesses: a friend in words is not the friend that I love.

IS. Nay, sister, reject me not, but let me die with thee, and duly honour the dead.

AN. Share not thou my death, nor claim deeds to which thou hast not put thy hand: my death will suffice.

IS. And what life is dear to me, bereft of thee?

AN. Ask Creon; all thy care is for him.

IS. Why vex me thus, when it avails thee nought?

AN. Indeed, if I mock, 'tis with pain that I mock thee.

IS. Tell me,—how can I serve thee, even now?

AN. Save thyself: I grudge not thy escape.

IS. Ah, woe is me! And shall I have no share in thy fate?

AN. Thy choice was to live; mine, to die.

IS. At least thy choice was not made without my protest.

AN. One world approved thy wisdom; another, mine.

IS. Howbeit, the offence is the same for both of us.

AN. Be of good cheer; thou livest ; but my life hath long been given to death, that so I might serve the dead.

CR. Lo, one of these maidens hath newly shown herself foolish, as the other hath been since her life began.

IS. Yea, O king, such reason as nature may have given abides not with the unfortunate, but goes astray.

CR. Thine did, when thou chosest vile deeds with the vile.

IS. What life could I endure, without her presence?

CR. Nay, speak not of her 'presence;' she lives no more.

IS. But wilt thou slay the betrothed of thine own son?

CR. Nay, there are other fields for him to plough.

IS. But there can never be such love as bound him to her.

CR. I like not an evil wife for my son.

AN. Haemon, beloved! How thy father wrongs thee!

CR. Enough, enough of thee and of thy marriage!

CH. Wilt thou indeed rob thy son of this maiden?

CR. 'Tis Death that shall stay these bridals for me.

CH. 'Tis determined, it seems, that she shall die.

CR. Determined, yes, for thee and for me.—*(To the two attendants.)* No more delay—servants, take them within! Henceforth they must be women, and not range at large; for verily even the bold seek to fly, when they see Death now closing on their life.

[*Exeunt attendants, guarding* ANTIGONE *And* ISMENE,—CREON *remains.*

CH. Blest are they whose days have not tasted of evil. For when a house hath once been shaken from heaven, there the curse fails nevermore, passing from life to life of the race; even as, when the surge is driven over the darkness of the deep by the fierce breath of Thracian sea-winds, it rolls up the black sand from the depths, and there is a sullen roar from wind-vexed headlands that front the blows of the storm.

I see that from olden time the sorrows in the house of the Labdacidae are heaped upon the sorrows of the dead; and generation is not freed by generation, but some god strikes them down, and the race hath no deliverance.

For now that hope of which the light had been spread above the last root of the house of Oedipus—that hope, in turn, is brought low—by the blood-stained dust due to the gods infernal, and by folly in speech, and frenzy at the heart.

Thy power, O Zeus, what human trespass can limit? That power which neither Sleep, the all-ensnaring, nor the untiring months of the gods can master; but thou, a ruler to whom time brings not old age, dwellest in the dazzling splendour of Olympus.

And through the future, near and far, as through the past, shall this law hold good: Nothing that is vast enters into the life of mortals without a curse.

For that hope whose wanderings are so wide is to many men a comfort, but to many a false lure of giddy desires; and the disappointment comes on one who knoweth nought till he burn his foot against the hot fire.

For with wisdom hath some one given forth the famous saying, that evil seems good, soon or late, to him whose mind the god draws to mischief; and but for the briefest space doth he fare free of woe.

But lo, Haemon, the last of thy sons;—comes he grieving for the doom of his promised bride, Antigone, and bitter for the baffled hope of his marriage?

Enter HAEMON

CR. We shall know soon, better than seers could tell us.— My son, hearing the fixed doom of thy betrothed, art thou come in rage against thy father? Or have I thy good will, act how I may?

HAE. Father, I am thine; and thou, in thy wisdom, tracest for me rules which I shall follow. No marriage shall be deemed by me a greater gain than thy good guidance.

CR. Yea, this, my son, should be thy heart's fixed law— in all things to obey thy father's will. 'Tis for this that men pray to see dutiful children grow up around them in their homes—that such may requite their father's foe with evil, and honour, as their father doth, his friend. But he who begets unprofitable children—what shall we say that he hath sown, but troubles for himself, and much triumph for his foes? Then do not thou, my son, at pleasure's beck, dethrone thy reason for a woman's sake; knowing that this is a joy that soon grows cold in clasping arms,—an evil woman to share thy bed and thy home. For what wound could strike deeper than a false friend? Nay, with loathing, and as if she were thine enemy, let this girl go to find a husband in the house of Hades. For since I have taken her, alone of all the city, in open disobedience, I will not make myself a liar to my people— I will slay her.

So let her appeal as she will to the majesty of kindred blood. If I am to nurture mine own kindred in naughtiness, needs must I bear with it in aliens. He who does his duty in his own household will be found righteous in the State also. But if any one transgresses, and does violence to the laws, or thinks to dictate to his rulers, such an one can win no praise from me. No, whomsoever the city may appoint, that man must be obeyed, in little things and great, in just things and unjust; and I should feel sure that one who thus obeys would be a good ruler no less than a good subject, and in the storm of spears would stand his ground where he was set, loyal and dauntless at his comrade's side.

But disobedience is the worst of evils. This it is that ruins cities; this makes homes desolate; by this, the ranks of allies are broken into headlong rout; but, of the lives whose course is fair, the greater part owes safety to obedience. Therefore we must support the cause of order, and in no wise suffer a woman to worst us. Better to fall from power, if we must, by a man's hand; then we should not be called weaker than a woman.

CH. To us, unless our years have stolen our wit, thou seemest to say wisely what thou sayest.

HAE. Father, the gods implant reason in men, the highest of all things that we call our own. Not mine the skill—far from me be the quest!—To say wherein thou speakest not aright; and yet another man, too, might have some useful thought. At least, it is my natural office to watch, on thy behalf, all that men say, or do, or find to blame. For the dread of thy frown forbids the citizen to speak such words as would offend thine ear; but I can hear these murmurs in the dark, these moanings of the city for this maiden; 'no woman,' they say, 'ever merited her doom less,—none ever was to die so shamefully for deeds so glorious as hers; who, when her own brother had fallen in bloody strife, would not leave him unburied, to be devoured by carrion dogs, or by any bird: deserves not *she* the meed of golden honour?'

Such is the darkling rumour that spreads in secret. For me, my father, no treasure is so precious as thy welfare. What, indeed, is a nobler ornament for children than a prospering sire's fair fame, or for sire than son's? Wear not, then, one mood only in thyself; think not that thy word, and thine alone, must be right. For if any man thinks that he alone is wise,—that in speech, or in mind, he hath no peer,—such a soul, when laid open, is ever found empty.

No, though a man be wise, 'tis no shame for him to learn many things, and to bend in season. Seest thou, beside the wintry torrent's course, how the trees that yield to it save every twig, while the stiff-necked perish root and branch? And even thus he who keeps the sheet of his sail taut, and never slackens it, upsets his boat, and finishes his voyage with keel uppermost.

Nay, forego thy wrath; permit thyself to change. For if I, a younger man, may offer my thought, it were far best, I ween, that men should be all-wise by nature; but, otherwise—and oft the scale inclines not so—'tis good also to learn from those who speak aright.

CH. Sire, 'tis meet that thou shouldest profit by his words, if he speaks aught in season, and thou, Haemon, by thy father's; for on both parts there hath been wise speech.

CR. Men of my age—are we indeed to be schooled, then, by men of his?

HAE. In nothing that is not right; but if I am young, thou shouldest look to my merits, not to my years.

CR. Is it a merit to honour the unruly?

HAE. I could wish no one to show respect for evil-doers.

CR. Then is not she tainted with that malady?

HAE. Our Theban folk, with one voice, denies it.

CR. Shall Thebes prescribe to me how I must rule? HAE. See, there thou hast spoken like a youth indeed.

CR. Am I to rule this land by other judgment than mine own?

HAE. That is no city which belongs to one man.

CR. Is not the city held to be the ruler's?

HAE. Thou wouldst make a good monarch of a desert.

CR. This boy, it seems, is the woman's champion.

HAE. If thou art a woman; indeed, my care is for thee.

CR Shameless, at open feud with thy father!

HAE. Nay, I see thee offending against justice.

CR. Do I offend, when I respect mine own prerogatives?

HAE. Thou dost not respect them, when thou tramplest on the gods' honours.

CR. O dastard nature, yielding place to woman!

HAE. Thou wilt never find me yield to baseness.

CR. All thy words, at least, plead for that girl.

HAE. And for thee, and for me, and for the gods below.

CR. Thou canst never marry her, on this side the grave.

HAE. Then she must die, and in death destroy another.

CR. How! Doth thy boldness run to open threats?

HAE. What threat is it, to combat vain resolves?

CR. Thou shalt rue thy witless teaching of wisdom.

HAE. Wert thou not my father, I would have called thee unwise.

CR. Thou woman's slave, use not wheedling speech with me.

HAE. Thou wouldest speak, and then hear no reply?

CR. Sayest thou so? Now, by the heaven above us—be sure of it—thou shalt smart for taunting me in this opprobrious strain. Bring forth that hated thing, that she may die forthwith in his presence—before his eyes—at her bridegroom's side!

HAE. No, not at my side—never think it—shall she perish; nor shalt thou ever set eyes more upon my face:—rave, then, with such friends as can endure thee.

[*Exit* HAEMON.

CH. The man is gone, O king, in angry haste; a youthful mind, when stung, is fierce.

CR. Let him do, or dream, more than man—good speed to him!—But he shall not save these two girls from their doom.

CH. Dost thou indeed purpose to slay both?

CR. Not her whose hands are pure: thou sayest well.

CH. And by what doom mean'st thou to slay the other?

CR. I will take her where the path is loneliest, and hide her, living, in a rocky vault, with so much food set forth as piety prescribes, that the city may avoid a public stain. And there, praying to Hades, the only god whom she worships, perchance she will obtain release from death; or else will learn, at last, though late, that it is lost labour to revere the dead.

[*Exit* CREON.

CH. Love, unconquered in the fight, Love, who makest havoc of wealth, who keepest thy vigil on the soft cheek of a maiden; thou roamest over the sea, and among the homes of dwellers in the wilds; no immortal can escape thee, nor any among men whose life is for a day; and he to whom thou hast come is mad.

The just themselves have their minds warped by thee to wrong, for their ruin: 'tis thou that hast stirrer up this present strife of kinsmen; victorious is the love-kindling light from the eyes of the fair bride; it is a power enthroned in sway beside the eternal laws; for there the goddess Aphrodite is working her unconquerable will.

But now I also am carried beyond the bounds of loyalty, and can no more keep back the streaming tears, when I see Antigone thus passing to the bridal chamber where all are laid to rest.

AN. See me, citizens of my fatherland, setting forth on my last way, looking my last on the sunlight that is for me no more; no, Hades who gives sleep to all leads me living to Acheron's shore; who have had no portion in the chant that brings the bride, nor hath any song been mine for the crowning of bridals; whom the lord of the Dark Lake shall wed.

CH. Glorious, therefore, and with praise, thou departest to that deep place of the dead: wasting sickness hath not smitten thee; thou hast not found the wages of the sword;

no, mistress of thine own fate, and still alive, thou shalt pass to Hades, as no other of mortal kind hath passed.

AN. I have heard in other days how dread a doom befell our Phrygian guest, the daughter of Tantalus, on the Sipylian heights; how, like clinging ivy, the growth of stone subdued her; and the rains fail not, as men tell, from her wasting form, nor fails the snow, while beneath her weeping lids the tears bedew her bosom; and most like to hers is the fate that brings me to my rest.

CH. Yet she was a goddess, thou knowest, and born of gods; we are mortals, and of mortal race. But 'tis great renown for a woman who hath perished that she should have shared the doom of the godlike, in her life, and afterward in death.

AN. Ah, I am mocked! In the name of our fathers' gods, can ye not wait till I am gone,—must ye taunt me to my face, O my city, and ye, her wealthy sons? Ah, fount of Dircê, and thou holy ground of Thebé whose chariots are many; ye, at least, will bear me witness, in what sort, unwept of friends, and by what laws I pass to the rock-closed prison of my strange tomb, ah me unhappy! who have no home on the earth or in the shades, no home with the living or with the dead.

CH. Thou hast rushed forward to the utmost verge of daring; and against that throne where Justice sits on high thou hast fallen, my daughter, with a grievous fall. But in this ordeal thou art paying, haply, for thy father's sin.

AN. Thou hast touched on my bitterest thought,—awaking the ever-new lament for my sire and for all the doom given to us, the famed house of Labdacus. Alas for the horrors of the mother's bed! alas for the wretched mother's slumber at the side of her own son,—and my sire! From what manner of parents did I take my miserable being! And to them I go thus, accursed, unwed, to share their home. Alas, my brother, ill-starred in thy marriage, in thy death thou hast undone my life!

CH. Reverent action claims a certain praise for reverence; but an offence against power cannot be brooked by him who hath power in his keeping. Thy self-willed temper hath wrought thy ruin.

AN. Unwept, unfriended, without marriage-song, I am led forth in my sorrow on this journey that can be delayed no more. No longer, hapless one, may I behold yon day-star's sacred eye; but for my fate no tear is shed, no friend makes moan.

CR. Know ye not that songs and wailings before death would never cease, if it profited to utter them? Away with her—away! And when ye have enclosed her, according to my word, in her vaulted grave, leave her alone, forlorn—whether she wishes to die, or to live a buried life in such a home. Our hands are clean as touching this maiden. But this is certain—she shall be deprived of her sojourn in the light.

AN. Tomb, bridal-chamber, eternal prison in the caverned rock, whither I go to find mine own, those many who have perished, and whom Persephone hath received among the dead! Last of all shall I pass thither, and far most miserably of all, before the term of my life is spent. But I cherish good hope that my coming will be welcome to my father, and pleasant to thee, my mother, and welcome, brother, to thee; for, when ye died, with mine own hands I washed and dressed you, and poured drink-offerings at your graves; and now, Polyneices, 'tis for tending thy corpse that I win such recompense as this.

[And yet I honoured thee, as the wise will deem, rightly. Never, had I been a mother of children, or if a husband had been mouldering in death, would I have taken this task upon me in the city's despite. What law, ye ask, is my warrant for that word? The husband lost, another might have been found, and child from another, to replace the first-born; but, father and mother hidden with Hades, no brother's life could ever bloom for me again. Such was the law whereby

I held thee first in honour; but Creon deemed me guilty of error therein, and of outrage, ah brother mine! And now he leads me thus, a captive in his hands; no bridal bed, no bridal song hath been mine, no joy of marriage, no portion in the nurture of children; but thus, forlorn of friends, unhappy one, I go living to the vaults of death.]

And what law of heaven have I transgressed? Why, hapless one, should I look to the gods any more,—what ally should I invoke,—when by piety I have earned the name of impious? Nay, then, if these things are pleasing to the gods, when I have suffered my doom, I shall come to know my sin; but if the sin is with my judges, I could wish them no fuller measure of evil than they, on their part, mete wrongfully to me.

CH. Still the same tempest of the soul vexes this maiden with the same fierce gusts. CR. Then for this shall her guards have cause to rue their slowness.

AN. Ah me! that word hath come very near to death. CR. I can cheer thee with no hope that this doom is not thus to be fulfilled.

AN. O city of my fathers in the land of Thebè! O ye gods, eldest of our race!—they lead me hence—now, now—they tarry not! Behold me, princes of Thebes, the last daughter of the house of your kings,—see what I suffer, and from whom, because I feared to cast away the fear of Heaven!

[ANTIGONE *is led away by the guards.*

CH. Even thus endured Danaë in her beauty to change the light of day for brass-bound walls; and in that chamber, secret as the grave, she was held close prisoner; yet was she of a proud lineage, O my daughter, and charged with the keeping of the seed of Zeus, that fell in the golden rain.

But dreadful is the mysterious power of fate; there is no deliverance from it by wealth or by war, by fenced city, or dark, sea-beaten ships.

And bonds tamed the son of Dryas, swift to wrath, that

king of the Edonians; so paid he for his frenzied taunts, when, by the will of Dionysus, he was pent in a rocky prison. There the fierce exuberance of his madness slowly passed away. That man learned to know the god, whom in his frenzy he had provoked with mockeries; for he had sought to quell the god-possessed women, and the Bacchanalian fire; and he angered the Muses that love the flute.

And by the waters of the Dark Rocks, the waters of the twofold sea, are the shores of Bosporus, and Thracian Salmydessus; where Ares, neighbour to the city, saw the accurst, blinding wound dealt to the two sons of Phineus by his fierce wife,—the wound that brought darkness to those vengeance-craving orbs, smitten with her bloody hands, smitten with her shuttle for a dagger.

Pining in their misery, they bewailed their cruel doom, those sons of a mother hapless in her marriage; but she traced her descent from the ancient line of the Erechtheidae; and in far-distant caves she was nursed amid her father's storms, that child of Boreas, swift as a steed over the steep hills, a daughter of gods; yet upon her also the gray Fates bore hard, my daughter.

Enter TEIRESIAS, *led by a Boy, on the spectators' right.*

TE. Princes of Thebes, we have come with linked steps, both served by the eyes of one; for thus, by a guide's help, the blind must walk.

CR. And what, aged Teiresias, are thy tidings?

TE. I will tell thee; and do thou hearken to the seer.

CR. Indeed, it has not been my wont to slight thy counsel.

TE. Therefore didst thou steer our city's course aright.

CR. I have felt, and can attest, thy benefits.

TE. Mark that now, once more, thou standest on fate's fine edge.

CR. What means this? How I shudder at thy message!

TE. Thou wilt learn, when thou hearest the warnings of

mine art. As I took my place on mine old seat of augury, where all birds have been wont to gather within my ken, I heard a strange voice among them; they were screaming with dire, feverish rage, that drowned their language in a jargon; and I knew that they were rending each other with their talons, murderously; the whirr of wings told no doubtful tale.

Forthwith, in fear, I essayed burnt-sacrifice on a duly kindled altar: but from my offerings the Fire-god showed no flame; a dank moisture, oozing from the thigh-flesh, trickled forth upon the embers, and smoked, and sputtered; the gall was scattered to the air; and the streaming thighs lay bared of the fat that had been wrapped round them.

Such was the failure of the rites by which I vainly asked a sign, as from this boy I learned; for he is my guide, as I am guide to others. And 'tis thy counsel that hath brought this sickness on our State. For the altars of our city and of our hearths have been tainted, one and all, by birds and dogs, with carrion from the hapless corpse, the son of Oedipus: and therefore the gods no more accept prayer and sacrifice at our hands, or the flame of meat-offering; nor doth any bird give a clear sign by its shrill cry, for they have tasted the fatness of a slain man's blood.

Think, then, on these things, my son. All men are liable to err; but when an error hath been made, that man is no longer witless or unblest who heals the ill into which he hath fallen, and remains not stubborn.

Self-will, we know, incurs the charge of folly. Nay, allow the claim of the dead; stab not the fallen; what prowess is it to slay the slain anew? I have sought thy good, and for thy good I speak: and never is it sweeter to learn from a good counsellor than when he counsels for thine own gain.

CR. Old man, ye all shoot your shafts at me, as archers at the butts;—ye must needs practise on me with seer-craft also;—aye, the seer-tribe hath long trafficked in me, and made me their merchandise. Gain your gains, drive your trade, if ye list, in the silver-gold of Sardis and the gold of

India; but ye shall not hide that man in the grave,—no, though the eagles of Zeus should bear the carrion morsels to their Master's throne—no, not for dread of that defilement will I suffer his burial:—for well I know that no mortal can defile the gods.—But, aged Teiresias, the wisest fall with a shameful fall, when they clothe shameful thoughts in fair words, for lucre's sake.

TE. Alas! Doth any man know, doth any consider . . .

CR. Whereof? What general truth dost thou announce?

TE. How precious, above all wealth, is good counsel.

CR. As folly, I think, is the worst mischief.

TE. Yet thou art tainted with that distemper.

CR. I would not answer the seer with a taunt.

TE.But thou dost, in saying that I prophesy falsely.

CR. Well, the prophet-tribe was ever fond of money.

TE. And the race bred of tyrants loves base gain.

CR. Knowest thou that thy speech is spoken of thy king?

TE. I know it; for through me thou hast saved Thebes.

CR. Thou art a wise seer; but thou lovest evil deeds.

TE. Thou wilt rouse me to utter the dread secret in my soul.

CR. Out with it!—Only speak it not for gain.

TE. Indeed, methinks, I shall not,—as touching thee.

CR. Know that thou shalt not trade on my resolve.

TE. Then know thou—aye, know it well—that thou shalt not live through many more courses of the sun's swift chariot, ere one begotten of thine own loins shall have been given by thee, a corpse for corpses; because thou hast thrust children of the sunlight to the shades, and ruthlessly lodged a living soul in the grave; but keepest in this world one who belongs to the gods infernal, a corpse unburied, unhonoured, all unhallowed. In such thou hast no part, nor have the gods above, but this is a violence done to them by thee. Therefore the avenging destroyers lie in wait for thee, the Furies of Hades and of the gods, that thou mayest be taken in these same ills.

And mark well if I speak these things as a hireling. A time not long to be delayed shall awaken the wailing of men and of women in thy house. And a tumult of hatred against thee stirs all the cities whose mangled sons had the burial-rite from dogs, or from wild beasts, or from some winged bird that bore a polluting breath to each city that contains the hearths of the dead.

Such arrows for thy heart—since thou provokest me—have I launched at thee, archer-like, in my anger,—sure arrows, of which thou shalt not escape the smart.—Boy, lead me home, that he may spend his rage on younger men, and learn to keep a tongue more temperate, and to bear within his breast a better mind than now he bears.

[*Exit* Teiresias.

CH. The man hath gone, O King, with dread prophecies. And, since the hair on this head, once dark, hath been white, I know that he hath never been a false prophet to our city.

CR. I, too, know it well, and am troubled in soul. 'Tis dire to yield; but, by resistance, to smite my pride with ruin—this, too, is a dire choice.

CH. Son of Menoeceus, it behoves thee to take wise counsel.

CR. What should I do, then? Speak, and I will obey.

CH. Go thou, and free the maiden from her rocky chamber, and make a tomb for the unburied dead.

CR. And this is thy counsel? Thou wouldst have me yield?

CH. Yea, King, and with all speed; for swift harms from the gods cut short the folly of men.

CR. Ah me, 'tis hard, but I resign my cherished resolve,—I obey. We must not wage a vain war with destiny.

CH. Go, thou, and do these things; leave them not to others.

CR. Even as I am I'll go:—on, on, my servants, each and all of you,—take axes in your hands, and hasten to the ground that ye see yonder! Since our judgment hath taken this turn, I will be present to unloose her, as I myself bound her. My heart misgives me, 'tis best to keep the established laws, even to life's end.

CH. O thou of many names, glory of the Cadmeian bride, offspring of loud-thundering Zeus! thou who watchest over famed Italia, and reignest, where all guests are welcomed, in the sheltered plain of Eleusinian Deô! O Bacchus, dweller in Thebè, mother-city of Bacchants, by the softly-gliding stream of Ismenus, on the soil where the fierce dragon's teeth were sown!

Thou hast been seen where torch-flames glare through smoke, above the crests of the twin peaks, where move the Corycian nymphs, thy votaries, hard by Castalia's stream.

Thou comest from the ivy-mantled slopes of Nysa's hills, and from the shore green with many-clustered vines, while thy name is lifted up on strains of more than mortal power, as thou visitest the ways of Thebè:

Thebè, of all cities, thou holdest first in honour, thou, and thy mother whom the lightning smote; and now, when all our people is captive to a violent plague, come thou with healing feet over the Parnassian height, or over the moaning strait!

O thou with whom the stars rejoice as they move, the stars whose breath is fire; O master of the voices of the night; son begotten of Zeus; appear, O king, with thine attendant Thyiads, who in night-long frenzy dance before thee, the giver of good gifts, Iacchus!

Enter MESSENGER, *on the spectators' left hand*

ME. Dwellers by the house of Cadmus and of Amphion, there is no estate of mortal life that I would ever praise or blame as settled. Fortune raises and Fortune humbles the lucky or unlucky from day to day, and no one can prophesy to men concerning those things which are established. For Creon was blest once, as I count bliss; he had saved this land of Cadmus from its foes; he was clothed with sole dominion in the land; he reigned, the glorious sire of princely children.

And now all hath been lost. For when a man hath forfeited his pleasures, I count him not as living,—I hold him but a breathing corpse. Heap up riches in thy house, if thou wilt; live in kingly state; yet, if there be no gladness therewith, I would not give the shadow of a vapour for all the rest, compared with joy.

CH. And what is this new grief that thou hast to tell for our princes?

ME. Death; and the living are guilty for the dead.

CH. And who is the slayer? Who the stricken? Speak.

ME. Haemon hath perished; his blood hath been shed by no stranger.

CH. By his father's hand, or by his own? ME. By his own, in wrath with his sire for the murder.

CH. O prophet, how true, then, hast thou proved thy word!

ME. These things stand thus; ye must consider of the rest. CH. Lo, I see the hapless Eurydicè, Creon's wife, approaching; she comes from the house by chance, haply,—or because she knows the tidings of her son.

Enter EURYDICÈ *from the palace.*

EU. People of Thebes, I heard your words as I was going forth, to salute the goddess Pallas with my prayers. Even as I was loosing the fastenings of the gate, to open it, the message of a household woe smote on mine ear: I sank back, terror-stricken, into the arms of my handmaids, and my senses fled. But say again what the tidings were; I shall hear them as one who is no stranger to sorrow.

ME. Dear lady, I will witness of what I saw, and will leave no word of the truth untold. Why, indeed, should I soothe thee with words in which I must presently be found false? Truth is ever best.—I attended thy lord as his guide to the furthest part of the plain, where the body of Polyneices, torn by dogs, still lay unpitied. We prayed the goddess of the roads, and Pluto, in mercy to restrain their wrath; we washed the dead with holy washing; and with freshly-plucked boughs we solemnly burned such relics as there were. We raised a high mound of his native earth; and then we turned away to enter the maiden's nuptial chamber with rocky couch, the caverned mansion of the bride of Death. And, from afar off, one of us heard a voice of loud wailing at that bride's unhallowed bower; and came to tell our master Creon.

And as the king drew nearer, doubtful sounds of a bitter cry floated around him; he groaned, and said in accents of anguish, 'Wretched that I am, can my foreboding be true? Am I going on the wofullest way that ever I went? My son's voice greets me.—Go, my servants,—haste ye nearer, and when ye have reached the tomb, pass through the gap, where the stones have been wrenched away, to the cell's very mouth,—and look, and see if 'tis Haemon's voice that I know, or if mine ear is cheated by the gods.'

This search, at our despairing master's word, we went to make; and in the furthest part of the tomb we descried *her* hanging by the neck, slung by a thread-wrought halter of fine linen; while *he* was embracing her with arms thrown around her waist,—bewailing the loss of his bride who is with the dead, and his father's deeds, and his own ill-starred love.

But his father, when he saw him, cried aloud with a dread cry and went in, and called to him with a voice of wailing:—'Unhappy, what a deed hast thou done! What thought hath come to thee? What manner of mischance hath marred thy reason? Come forth, my child! I pray thee—I implore!' But the boy glared at him with fierce eyes, spat in his face, and, without a word of answer, drew his cross-hilted sword:—as his father rushed forth in flight, he missed his aim;—then, hapless one, wroth with himself, he straightway leaned with all his weight against his sword, and drove it, half its length, into his side; and, while sense lingered, he clasped the maiden to his faint embrace, and, as he gasped, sent forth on her pale cheek the swift stream of the oozing blood.

Corpse enfolding corpse he lies; he hath won his nuptial rites, poor youth, not here, yet in the halls of Death; and he hath witnessed to mankind that, of all curses which cleave to man, ill counsel is the sovereign curse.

[EURYDICÈ *retires into the house.*

CH. What wouldst thou augur from this? The lady hath turned back, and is gone, without a word, good or evil.

ME. I, too, am startled; yet I nourish the hope that, at these sore tidings of her son, she cannot deign to give her sorrow public vent, but in the privacy of the house will set her handmaids to mourn the household grief. For she is not untaught of discretion, that she should err.

CH. I know not; but to me, at least, a strained silence seems to portend peril, no less than vain abundance of lament.

ME. Well, I will enter the house, and learn whether indeed she is not hiding some repressed purpose in the depths of a passionate heart. Yea, thou sayest well: excess of silence, too, may have a perilous meaning.

[*Exit* MESSENGER.

Enter CREON, *on the spectators' left, with attendants, carrying the shrouded body of* HAEMON *on a bier.*

CH. Lo, yonder the king himself draws near, bearing that which tells too clear a tale, the work of no stranger's madness,—if we may say it,—but of his own misdeeds.

CR. Woe for the sins of a darkened soul, stubborn sins, fraught with death! Ah, ye behold us, the sire who hath slain, the son who hath perished! Woe is me, for the wretched blindness of my counsels! Alas, my son, thou hast died in thy youth, by a timeless doom, woe is me!—thy spirit hath fled,—not by thy folly, but by mine own!

CH. Ah me, how all too late thou seemest to see the right!

CR. Ah me, I have learned the bitter lesson! But then,

methinks, oh then, some god smote me from above with crushing weight, and hurled me into ways of cruelty, woe is me,—overthrowing and trampling on my joy! Woe, woe, for the troublous toils of men!

Enter MESSENGER *from the house.*

ME. Sire, thou hast come, methinks, as one whose hands are not empty, but who hath store laid up besides; thou bearest yonder burden with thee; and thou art soon to look upon the woes within thy house.

CR. And what worse ill is yet to follow upon ills? ME. Thy queen hath died, true mother of yon corpse—ah, hapless lady!—by blows newly dealt.

CR. Oh Hades, all-receiving, whom no sacrifice can appease! Hast thou, then, no mercy for me? O thou herald of evil, bitter tidings, what word dost thou utter? Alas, I was already as dead, and thou hast smitten me anew! What sayest thou, my son? What is this new message that thou bringest woe, woe is me!—Of a wife's doom,—of slaughter heaped on slaughter?

CH. Thou canst behold: 'tis no longer hidden within.

[*The doors of the palace are opened, and the corpse of* EURYDICÈ is *disclosed.*

CR. Ah me,—yonder I behold a new, a second woe! What destiny, ah what, can yet await me? I have but now raised my son in my arms,—and there, again, I see a corpse before me! Alas, alas, unhappy mother! Alas, my child!

ME. There, at the altar, self-stabbed with a keen knife, she suffered her darkening eyes to close, when she had wailed for the noble fate of Megareus who died before, and then for his fate who lies there,—and when, with her last breath, she had invoked evil fortunes upon thee, the slayer of thy sons.

CR. Woe, woe! I thrill with dread. Is there none to strike me to the heart with two-edged sword?—O miserable that I am, and steeped in miserable anguish!

ME. Yea, both this son's doom, and that other's, were laid to thy charge by her whose corpse thou seest.

CR. And what was the manner of the violent deed by which she passed away?

ME. Her own hand struck her to the heart, when she had learned her son's sorely lamented fate.

CR. Ah me, this guilt can never be fixed on any other of mortal kind, for my acquittal I, even I, was thy slayer, wretched that I am—I own the truth. Lead me away, O my servants, lead me hence with all speed, whose life is but as death!

CH. Thy counsels are good, if there can be good with ills; briefest is best, when trouble is in our path.

CR. Oh, let it come, let it appear, that fairest of fates for me, that brings my last day,—aye, best fate of all! Oh, let it come, that I may never look upon to-morrow's light.

CH. These things are in the future; present tasks claim our care: the ordering of the future rests where it should rest.

CR. All my desires, at least, were summed in that prayer.

CH. Pray thou no more; for mortals have no escape from destined woe.

CR. Lead me away, I pray you; a rash, foolish man; who have slain thee, ah my son, unwittingly, and thee, too, my wife—unhappy that I am! I know not which way I should bend my gaze, or where I should seek support; for all is amiss with that which is in my hands,—and yonder, again, a crushing fate hath leapt upon my head.

[*As* Creon *is being conducted into the house, the Coryphaeus speaks the closing verses.*

CH. Wisdom is the supreme part of happiness; and reverence towards the gods must be inviolate. Great words of prideful men are ever punished with great blows, and, in old age, teach the chastened to be wise.

Plato

427-347 B.C.E.

APOLOGY

399 B.C.E.

The American philosopher Alfred North Whitehead paid tribute to Plato by declaring that all subsequent philosophy was merely a footnote to him. Curiously, the central figure in Plato's philosophy is not Plato, but his mentor Socrates (469-399 B.C.E.). Socrates did no writing at all, but confined himself to asking questions of his fellow Athenians. In the superheated politics of Athens that followed its defeat in the Peloponnesian War, Socrates was charged with atheism and corrupting the youth and brought before the huge democratic jury that would decide his guilt or innocence. The "Apology" should not be understood to mean he is apologizing in the modern sense of the term. He is explaining why he questions others so persistently, why what he does is legal, and why he will continue, no matter what his fellow citizens think. He lost the case and died by taking hemlock. Plato left Athens to travel, and on his return founded the Academy, the school that has been regarded as the first university.

Selected from: Plato. 399 B.C.E. "Apology." *The Works of Plato: Four Volumes in One*. Vol. 3. Benjamin Jowett, Trans., New York: Tudor [1936?]. 101-134.

How you have felt, O men of Athens, at hearing the speeches of my accusers, I can not tell; but I know that their persuasive words almost made me forget who I was:—such was the effect of them; and yet they have hardly spoken a word of truth. But many as their falsehoods were, there was one of them which quite amazed me;—I mean when they told you to be upon your guard, and not to let yourself be deceived by the force of my eloquence. They ought to have been ashamed of saying this, because they were sure to be detected as soon as I opened my lips and displayed my deficiency: they certainly did appear to be most shameless in saying this, unless by the force of eloquence they mean the force of truth; for then I do indeed admit that I am eloquent. But in how different a way from theirs! Well, as I was saying, they have hardly uttered a word, or not more than a word, of truth; but you shall hear from me the whole truth: not, however, delivered after their manner, in a set oration duly ornamented with words and phrases. No, indeed! but I shall use the words and arguments which occur to me at the moment; for I am certain that this is right, and that at my time of life I ought not to be appearing before you, O men of Athens, in the character of a juvenile orator:—let no one expect this of me. And I must beg of you to grant me one favor, which is this—If you hear me using the same words in my defence which I have been in the habit of using, and which most of you may have heard in the agora, and at the tables of the money-changers, or anywhere else, I would ask you not to be surprised at this, and not to interrupt me. For I am more than seventy years of age, and this is the first time that I have ever appeared in a court of law, and I am quite a stranger to the ways of the place; and therefore I would have you regard me as if I were really a stranger, whom you would excuse if he spoke in his native tongue, and after the fashion of his country:—that I think is not an unfair request. Never mind the manner, which may or may not be good; but think only of the justice of my cause, and give heed to that: let the judge decide justly and the speaker speak truly.

And first, I have to reply to the older charges and to my first accusers, and then I will go on to the later ones. For I have had many accusers, who accused me of old, and their false charges have continued during many years; and I am more afraid of them than of Anytus and his associates, who are dangerous, too, in their own way. But far more dangerous are these, who began when you were children, and took possession of your minds with their falsehoods, telling of one Socrates, a wise man, who speculated about the heaven above, and searched into the earth beneath, and made the worse appear the better cause. These are the accusers whom I dread; for they are the circulators of this rumor, and their hearers are too apt to fancy that speculators of this sort do not believe in the gods. And they are many, and their charges against me are of ancient date, and they made them in days when you were impressible—in childhood, or perhaps in youth—and the cause when heard went by default, for there was none to answer. And hardest of all, their names I do not know and can not tell; unless in the chance case of a comic poet. But the main body of these slanderers who from envy and malice have wrought upon you—and there are some of them who are convinced themselves, and impart their convictions to others—all these, I say, are most difficult to deal with; for I can not have them up here, and examine them, and therefore I must simply fight with shadows in my own defence, and examine when there is no one who answers. I will ask you then to assume with me, as I was saying, that my opponents are of two kinds; one recent, the other ancient: and I hope that you will see the propriety of my answering the latter first, for these accusations you heard long before the others, and much oftener.

Well, then, I will make my defence, and I will endeavor in the short time which is allowed to do away with this evil opinion of me which you have held for such a long time;

and I hope I may succeed, if this be well for you and me, and that my words may find favor with you. But I know that to accomplish this is not easy—I quite see the nature of the task. Let the event be as God wills: in obedience to the law I make my defence.

I will begin at the beginning, and ask what the accusation is which has given rise to this slander of me, and which has encouraged Meletus to proceed against me. What do the slanderers say? They shall be my prosecutors, and I will sum up their words in an affidavit. "Socrates is an evil-doer, and a curious person, who searches into things under the earth and in heaven, and he makes the worse appear the better cause; and he teaches the aforesaid doctrines to others." That is the nature of the accusation, and that is what you have seen yourselves in the comedy of Aristophanes, who has introduced a man whom he calls Socrates, going about and saying that he can walk in the air, and talking a deal of nonsense concerning matters of which I do not pretend to know either much or little—not that I mean to say anything disparaging of any one who is a student of natural philosophy. I should be very sorry if Meletus could lay that to my charge. But the simple truth is, O Athenians, that I have nothing to do with these studies. Very many of those here present are witnesses to the truth of this, and to them I appeal. Speak then, you who have heard me, and tell your neighbors whether any of you have ever known me hold forth in few words or in many upon matters of this sort . . . . You hear their answer. And from what they say of this you will be able to judge of the truth of the rest.

As little foundation is there for the report that I am a teacher, and take money; that is no more true than the other. Although, if a man is able to teach, I honor him for being paid. There is Gorgias of Leontium, and Prodicus of Ceos, and Hippias of Elis, who go the round of the cities, and are able to persuade the young men to leave their own citizens, by whom they might be taught for nothing, and come to them, whom they not only pay, but are thankful if they may be allowed to pay them. There is actually a Parian philosopher residing in Athens, of whom I have heard; and I came to hear of him in this way:—I met a man who has spent a world of money on the Sophists, Callias the son of Hipponicus, and knowing that he had sons, I asked him: "Callias," I said, "if your two sons were foals or calves, there would be no difficulty in finding someone to put over them; we should hire a trainer of horses or a farmer probably who would improve and perfect them in their own proper virtue and excellence; but as they are human beings, whom are you thinking of placing over them? Is there any one who understands human and political virtue? You must have thought about this as you have sons; is there any one?" "There is," he said. "Who is he?" said I; "and of what country? and what does he charge?" "Evenus the Parian," he replied; "he is the man, and his charge is five minae." Happy is Evenus, I said to myself, if he really has this wisdom, and teaches at such a modest charge. Had I the same, I should have been very proud and conceited; but the truth is that I have no knowledge of the kind, O Athenians.

I dare say that some one will ask the question, "Why is this, Socrates, and what is the origin of these accusations of you: for there must have been something strange which you have been doing? All this great fame and talk about you would never have arisen if you had been like other men: tell us, then, why this is, as we should be sorry to judge hastily of you." Now I regard this as a fair challenge, and I will endeavor to explain to you the origin of this name of "wise," and of this evil fame. Please to attend then. And although some of you may think I am joking, I declare that I will tell you the entire truth. Men of Athens, this reputation of mine has come of a certain sort of wisdom which I possess. If you ask me what kind of wisdom, I reply, such wisdom as is attainable by man, for to that extent I am inclined to believe that I am wise; whereas the persons of whom I was speaking have a superhuman wisdom, which I may fail to describe, because I have it not myself; and he who says that I have, speaks falsely, and is taking away my character. And here, O men of Athens, I must beg you not to interrupt me, even if I seem to say something extravagant. For the word which I will speak is not mine. I will refer you to a wisdom who is worthy of credit, and will tell you about my wisdom—whether I have any, and of what sort—and that witness shall be the God of Delphi. You must have known Chaerephon; he was early a friend of mine, and also a friend of yours, for he shared in the exile of the people, and returned with you. Well, Chaerephon, as you know, was very impetuous in all his doings, and he went to Delphi and boldly asked the oracle to tell him whether—as I was saying, I must beg you not to interrupt—he asked the oracle to tell him whether there was any one wiser than I was, and the Pythian prophetess answered, that there was no man wiser. Chaerephon is dead himself; but his brother, who is in court, will confirm the truth of this story.

Why do I mention this? Because I am going to explain to you why I have such an evil name. When I heard the answer, I said to myself, What can the god mean? and what is the interpretation of this riddle? for I know that I have no wisdom, small or great. What then can he mean when he says that I am the wisest of men? And yet he is a god, and can not lie; that would be against his nature. After long consideration, I at last thought of a method of trying the question. I reflected that if I could only find a man wiser than myself, then I might go to the god with a refutation in my hand. I should say to him, "Here is a man who is wiser than I am; but you said that I was the wisest." Accordingly I went to one who had the reputation of wisdom, and observed him—his name I need not mention; he was a politician whom I selected for examination—and the result was as follows: When I began to talk with him, I could not help thinking that he was not really wise, although he was thought wise by many, and wiser still by himself; and I went and tried to explain to him that he thought himself wise, but was not really wise; and the consequence was that he hated me, and his enmity was shared by several who were present and heard me. So I left him, saying to myself, as I went away: Well, although I do not suppose that either of us knows anything really beautiful and good, I am better off than he is,—for he knows nothing, and thinks that he knows. I neither know nor think that I know. In this latter particular, then, I seem to have slightly the advantage of him. Then I went to another, who had still higher philosophical pretensions, and my conclusion was exactly the same. I made another enemy of him, and of many others besides him.

After this I went to one man after another, being not unconscious of the enmity which I provoked, and I lamented and feared this: but necessity was laid upon me,—the word of God, I thought, ought to be considered first. And I said to myself, Go I must to all who appear to know, and find out the meaning of the oracle. And I swear to you, Athenians, by the dog I swear!—for I must tell you the truth—the result of my mission was just this: I found that the men most in repute were all but the most foolish; and that some inferior men were really wiser and better. I will tell you the tale of my wanderings and of the "Herculean" labors, as I may call them, which I endured only to find at last the oracle irrefutable. When I left the politicians, I went to the poets; tragic, dithyrambic, and all sorts. And there, I said to myself, you will be detected; now you will find out that you are more ignorant than they are. Accordingly, I took them some of the most elaborate passages in their own writings, and asked what was the meaning of them—thinking that they would teach me something. Will you believe me? I am almost ashamed to speak of this, but still I must say that there is hardly a person present who would not have talked better about their poetry than they did themselves. That showed me in an instant that not by wisdom do poets write poetry, but by a sort of genius and inspiration; they are like diviners or soothsayers who also say many fine things, but do not understand the meaning of them. And the poets appeared to me to be much in the same case; and I further observed that upon the strength of their poetry they believed themselves to be the wisest of men in other things in which they were not wise. So I departed, conceiving myself to be superior to them for the same reason that I was superior to the politicians.

At last I went to the artisans, for I was conscious that I knew nothing at all, as I may say, and I was sure that they knew many fine things; and in this I was not mistaken, for they did know many things of which I was ignorant, and in this they certainly were wiser than I was. But I observed that even the good artisans fell into the same error as the poets;—because they were good workmen they thought that they also knew all sorts of high matters, and this defect in them overshadowed their wisdom—therefore I asked myself on behalf of the oracle, whether I would like to be as I was, neither having their knowledge nor their ignorance, or like them in both; and I made answer to myself and the oracle that I was better off as I was.

This investigation has led to my having many enemies of the worst and most dangerous kind, and has given occasion also to many calumnies. And I am called wise, for my hearers always imagine that I myself possess the wisdom which I find wanting in others: but the truth is, O men of Athens, that God only is wise; and in this oracle he means to say that the wisdom of men is little or nothing; he is not speaking of Socrates, he is only using my name as an illustration, as if he said, He, O men, is the wisest who, like Socrates, knows that his wisdom is in truth worth nothing. And so I go my way, obedient to the god, and make inquisition into the wisdom of any one, whether citizen or stranger, who appears to be wise; and if he is not wise, then in vindication of the oracle I show him that he is not wise; and this occupation quite absorbs me, and I have no time to give either to any public matter of interest or to any concern of my own, but I am in utter poverty by reason of my devotion to the god.

There is another thing:—young men of the richer classes, who have not much to do, come about me of their own accord; they like to hear the pretenders examined, and they often imitate me, and examine others themselves; there are plenty of persons, as they soon enough discover, who think that they know something, but really know little or nothing; and then those who are examined by them instead of being angry with themselves are angry with me: This confounded Socrates, they say; this villainous misleader of youth!—and then if somebody asks them, Why, what evil does he practice or teach? they do not know, and can not tell; but in order that they may not appear to be at a loss, they repeat the ready-made charges which are used against all philosophers about teaching things up in the clouds and under the earth, and having no gods, and making the worse appear the better cause; for they do not like to confess that their pretence of knowledge has been detected—which is the truth; and as they are numerous and ambitious and energetic, and are all in battle array and have persuasive tongues, they have filled your ears with their loud and inveterate calumnies. And this is the reason why my three accusers, Meletus and Anytus and Lycon, have set upon me; Meletus, who has a quarrel with me on behalf of the poets; Anytus, on behalf of the craftsmen; Lycon, on behalf of the rhetoricians: and as I said at the beginning, I can not expect to get rid of this mass of calumny all in a moment. And this, O men of Athens, is the truth and the whole truth; I have concealed nothing, I have dissembled nothing. And yet I know that this plainness of speech makes them hate me, and what is their hatred but a proof that I am speaking the truth?—this is the occasion and reason of their slander of me, as you will find out either in this or in any future inquiry.

I have said enough in my defence against the first class of my accusers; I turn to the second class who are headed by Meletus, that good and patriotic man, as he calls himself. And now I will try to defend myself against them: these new accusers must also have their affidavit read. What do they say? Something of this sort:—That Socrates is a doer of evil, and corrupter of the youth, and he does not believe in the gods of the State, and has other new divinities of his own. That is the sort of charge; and now let us examine the particular counts. He says that I am a doer of evil, who corrupt the youth; but I say, O men of Athens, that Meletus is a doer of evil, and the evil is that he makes a joke of a serious matter, and is too ready at bringing other men to trial from a pretended zeal and interest about matters in which he really never had the smallest interest. And the truth of this I will endeavor to prove.

Come hither, Meletus, and let me ask a question of you. You think a great deal about the improvement of youth?

Yes I do.

Tell the judges, then, who is their improver; for you must know, as you have taken the pains to discover their corrupter, and are citing and accusing me before them. Speak, then, and tell the judges who their improver is. Observe, Meletus, that you are silent, and have nothing to say. But is not this rather disgraceful, and a very considerable proof of what I was saying, that you have no interest in the matter? Speak up, friend, and tell us who their improver is.

The laws.

But that, my good sir, is not my meaning. I want to know who the person is, who, in the first place, knows the laws.

The judges, Socrates, who are present in court.

What, do you mean to say, Meletus, that they are able to instruct and improve youth?

Certainly they are.

What, all of them, or some only and not others?

All of them.

By the goddess Here, that is good news! There are plenty of improvers, then. And what do you say of the audience,—do they improve them?

Yes, they do.

And the senators?

Yes, the senators improve them.

But perhaps the ecclesiasts [members of the citizen assembly] corrupt them?—or do they too improve them?

They improve them.

Then every Athenian improves and elevates them; all with the exception of myself; and I alone am their corrupter? Is that what you affirm?

That is what I stoutly affirm.

I am very unfortunate if that is true. But suppose I ask you a question: Would you say that this also holds true in the case of horses? Does one man do them harm and all the world good? Is not the exact opposite of this true? One man is able to do them good, or at least not many;—the trainer of horses, that is to say, does them good, and others who have to do with them rather injure them? Is not that true, Meletus, of horses, or any other animals? Yes, certainly. Whether you and Anytus say yes or no, that is no matter. Happy indeed would be the condition of youth if they had one corrupter only, and all the rest of the world were their improvers. And you, Meletus, have sufficiently shown that you never had a thought about the young: your carelessness is seen in your not caring about matters spoken of in this very indictment.

And now, Meletus, I must ask you another question: Which is better, to live among bad citizens, or among good ones? Answer, friend, I say; for that is a question which may be easily answered. Do not the good do their neighbors good, and the bad do them evil?

Certainly.

And is there any one who would rather be injured than benefited by those who live with him? Answer, my good friend; the law requires you to answer—does any one like to be injured?

Certainly not.

And when you accuse me of corrupting and deteriorating the youth, do you allege that I corrupt them intentionally or unintentionally?

Intentionally, I say.

But you have just admitted that the good do their neighbors good, and the evil do them evil. Now, is that a truth which your superior wisdom has recognized thus early in life, and am I, at my age, in such darkness and ignorance as not to know that if a man with whom I have to live is corrupted by me. I am very likely to be harmed by him, and yet I corrupt him, and intentionally, too;—that is what you are saying, and of that you will never persuade me or any other human being. But either I do not corrupt them, or I corrupt them unintentionally, so that on either view of the case you lie. If my offence is unintentional, the law has no cognizance of unintentional offences: you ought to have taken me privately, and warned and admonished me; for if I had been better advised, I should have left off doing what I only did unintentionally—no doubt I should; whereas you hated to converse with me or teach me, but you indicted me in this court, which is a place not of instruction, but of punishment.

I have shown, Athenians, as I was saying, that Meletus has no care at all, great or small, about the matter. But still I should like to know, Meletus, in what I am affirmed to corrupt the young. I suppose you mean, as I infer from your indictment, that I teach them not to acknowledge the gods which the state acknowledges, but some other new divinities or spiritual agencies in their stead. These are the lessons which corrupt the youth, as you say.

Yes, that I say emphatically.

Then, by the gods, Meletus, of whom we are speaking, tell me and the court, in somewhat plainer terms, what you mean! for I do not as yet understand whether you affirm that I teach others to acknowledge some gods, and therefore do believe in gods and am not an entire atheist—this you do not lay to my charge;—but only that they are not the same gods which the city recognizes—the charge is that they are different gods. Or, do you mean to say that I am an atheist simply, and a teacher of atheism?

I mean the latter—that you are a complete atheist.

That is an extraordinary statement, Meletus. Why do you say that? Do you mean that I do not believe in the godhead of the sun or moon, which is the common creed of all men?

I assure you, judges, that he does not believe in them; for he says that the sun is stone, and the moon earth.

Friend Meletus, you think that you are accusing Anaxagoras: and you have but a bad opinion of the judges, if you fancy them ignorant to such a degree as not to know that those doctrines are found in the books of Anaxagoras the Clazomenian, who is full of them. And these are the doctrines which the youth are said to learn of Socrates, when there are not unfrequently exhibitions of them at the theatre[1] (price of admission one drachma at the most); and they might cheaply purchase them, and laugh at Socrates if he pretends to father such eccentricities. And so, Meletus, you really think that I do not believe in any god?

I swear by Zeus that you believe absolutely in none at all.

You are a liar, Meletus, not believed even by yourself. For I can not help thinking, O men of Athens, that Meletus is reckless and impudent, and that he has written this indictment in a spirit of mere wantonness and youthful bravado. Has he not compounded a riddle, thinking to try me? He said to himself:—I shall see whether this wise Socrates will discover my ingenious contradiction, or whether I shall be able to deceive him and the rest of them. For he certainly does appear to me to contradict himself in the indictment as much as if he said that Socrates is guilty of not believing in

1 Probably in allusion to Aristophanes who caricatured, and to Euripides who borrowed the notions of Anaxagoras, as well to other dramatic poets. [BJ]

the gods, and yet of believing in them—but this surely is a piece of fun.

I should like you, O men of Athens, to join me in examining what I conceive to be his inconsistency; and do you, Meletus, answer. And I must remind you that you are not to interrupt me if I speak in my accustomed manner.

Did ever man, Meletus, believe in the existence of human things, and not of human beings? . . . I wish, men of Athens, that he would answer, and not be always trying to get up an interruption. Did ever any man believe in horsemanship, and not in horses? or in flute-playing, and not in flute-players? No, my friend; I will answer to you and to the court, as you refuse to answer for yourself. There is no man who ever did. But now please to answer the next question: Can a man believe in spiritual and divine agencies, and not in spirits or demigods?

He can not.

I am glad that I have extracted that answer, by the assistance of the court; nevertheless you swear in the indictment that I teach and believe in divine or spiritual agencies (new or old, no matter for that); at any rate, I believe in spiritual agencies, as you say and swear in the affidavit; but if I believe in divine beings, I must believe in spirits or demigods;—is not that true? Yes, that is true, for I may assume that your silence gives assent to that. Now what are spirits or demigods? are they not either gods or the sons of gods? Is that true?

Yes, that is true.

But this is just the ingenious riddle of which I was speaking: the demigods or spirits are gods, and you say first that I don't believe in gods, and then again that I do believe in gods; that is, if I believe in demigods. For if the demigods are the illegitimate sons of gods, whether by the nymphs or by any other mothers, as is thought, that, as all men will allow, necessarily implies the existence of their parents. You might as well affirm the existence of mules, and deny that of horses and asses. Such nonsense, Meletus, could only have been intended by you as a trial of me. You have put this into the indictment because you had nothing real of which to accuse me. But no one who has a particle of understanding will ever be convinced by you that the same man can believe in divine and superhuman things, and yet not believe that there are gods and demigods and heroes.

I have said enough in answer to the charge of Meletus: any elaborate defence is unnecessary; but as I was saying before, I certainly have many enemies, and this is what will be my destruction if I am destroyed; of that I am certain;—not Meletus, nor yet Anytus, but the envy and detraction of the world, which has been the death of many good men, and will probably be the death of many more; there is no danger of my being the last of them.

Some one will say: And are you not ashamed, Socrates, of a course of life which is likely to bring you to an untimely end? To him I may fairly answer: There you are mistaken: a man who is good for anything ought not to calculate the chance of living or dying; he ought only to consider whether in doing anything he is doing right or wrong—acting the part of a good man or of a bad. Whereas, according to your view, the heroes who fell at Troy were not good for much, and the son of Thetis above all, who altogether despised danger in comparison with disgrace; and when his goddess mother said to him, in his eagerness to slay Hector, that if he avenged his companion Patroclus, and slew Hector, he would die himself—"Fate," as she said, "waits upon you next after Hector;" he, hearing this, utterly despised danger and death, and instead of fearing them, feared rather to live in dishonor, and not to avenge his friend. "Let me die next," he replies, "and be avenged of my enemy, rather than abide here by the beaked ships, a scorn and a burden of the earth." Had Achilles any thought of death and danger? For wherever a man's place is, whether the place which he has chosen or that in which he has been placed by a commander, there he ought to remain in the hour of danger; he should not think of death or of anything, but of disgrace. And this, O men of Athens, is a true saying.

Strange, indeed, would be my conduct, O men of Athens, if I who, when I was ordered by the generals whom you chose to command me at Potidaea and Amphipolis and Delium, remained where they placed me, like any other man, facing death;—if, I say, now, when, as I conceive and imagine, God orders me to fulfil the philosopher's mission of searching into myself and other men, I were to desert my post through fear of death, or any other fear; that would indeed be strange, and I might justly be arraigned in court for denying the existence of the gods, if I disobeyed the oracle because I was afraid of death: then I should be fancying that I was wise when I was not wise. For this fear of death is indeed the pretence of wisdom, and not real wisdom, being the appearance of knowing the unknown; since no one knows whether death, which they in their fear apprehend to be the greatest evil, may not be the greatest good. Is there not here conceit of knowledge, which is a disgraceful sort of ignorance? And this is the point in which, as I think, I am superior to men in general, and in which I might perhaps fancy myself wiser than other men,—that whereas I know but little of the world below, I do not suppose that I know: but I do know that injustice and disobedience to a better, whether God or man, is evil and dishonorable, and I will never fear or avoid a possible good rather than a certain evil. And therefore if you let me go now, and reject the counsels of Anytus, who said that if I were not put to death I ought not to have been prosecuted, and that if I escape now, your sons will all be utterly ruined by listening to my words—if you say to me, Socrates, this time we will not mind Anytus, and will let you off, but upon one condition, that you are not to inquire and speculate in this way any more, and that if you are caught doing this again you shall die;—if this was the condition on which you let me go, I should reply: Men of Athens, I honor and love you; but I shall obey God rather than you, and while I have life and strength I shall never cease from the practice and teaching of philosophy, exhorting any one whom I meet after my manner, and convincing him, saying: O my friend, why do you, who are a citizen of the great and mighty and wise city of Athens, care so much about laying up the greatest amount of money and honor and reputation, and so little about wisdom and truth and the greatest improvement of the soul, which you never regard or heed at all? Are you not ashamed of this? And if the person with whom I am arguing says: Yes, but I do care; I do not depart or let him go at once; I interrogate and examine and cross-examine him, and if I think that he has no virtue, but only says that he has, I reproach him with undervaluing the greater, and overvaluing the less. And this I should say to everyone whom I meet, young and old, citizen and alien, but especially to the citizens, inasmuch as they are my brethren. For this is the command of God, as I would have you know; and I believe that to this day no greater good has ever happened in the state than my service to the God. For I do nothing but go about persuading you all, old and young alike, not to take thought for your persons and your properties, but first and chiefly to care about the greatest improvement of the soul. I tell you that virtue is not given by money, but that from virtue come money and every other good of man, public as well as private. This is my teaching, and if this is the doctrine which corrupts the youth, my influence is ruinous indeed. But if any one says that this is not my teaching, he is speaking an untruth. Wherefore, O men of Athens, I say to you, do as Anytus bids or not as Anytus bids, and either acquit me or not; but whatever you do, know that I shall never alter my ways, not even if I have to die many times.

Men of Athens, do not interrupt, but hear me; there was an agreement between us that you should hear me out. And I think that what I am going to say will do you good: for I have something more to say, at which you may be inclined to cry out; but I beg that you will not do this. I would have you know, that if you kill such an one as I am, you will injure yourselves more than you will injure me. Meletus and Anytus will not injure me: they can not; for it is not in the nature of things that a bad man should injure a better than himself. I do not deny that he may, perhaps, kill him, or drive him into exile, or deprive him of civil rights; and he may imagine, and others may imagine, that he is doing him a great injury: but in that I do not agree with him; for the evil of doing as Anytus is doing—of unjustly taking away another man's life is greater far. And now, Athenians, I am not going to argue for my own sake, as you may think, but for yours, that you may not sin against the God, or lightly reject his boon by condemning me. For if you kill me you will not easily find another like me, who, if I may use such a ludicrous figure of speech, am a sort of gadfly, given to the state by the God; and the state is like a great and noble steed who is tardy in his motions owing to his very size, and requires to be stirred into life. I am that gadfly which God has given the state, and all day long and in all places am always fastening upon you, arousing and persuading and reproaching you. And as you will not easily find another like me, I would advise you to spare me. I dare say that you may feel irritated at being suddenly awakened when you are caught napping; and you may think that if you were to strike me dead, as Anytus advises, which you easily might, then you would sleep on for the remainder of your lives, unless God in his care of you gives you another gadfly. And that I am given to you by God is proved by this:—that if I had been like other men, I should not have neglected all my own concerns, or patiently seen the neglect of them during all these years, and have been doing yours, coming to you individually like a father or elder brother, exhorting you to regard virtue; this, I say, would not be like human nature. And had I gained anything, or if my exhortations had been paid, there would have been some sense in that; but now, as you will perceive, not even the impudence of my accusers dares to say that I have ever exacted or sought pay of any one; they have no witness of that. And I have a witness of the truth of what I say; my poverty is a sufficient witness.

Some one may wonder why I go about in private giving advice and busying myself with the concerns of others, but do not venture to come forward in public and advise the state. I will tell you the reason of this. You have often heard me speak of an oracle or sign which comes to me, and is the divinity which Meletus ridicules in the indictment. This sign I have had ever since I was a child. The sign is a voice which comes to me and always forbids me to do something which I am going to do, but never commands me to do anything, and this is what stands in the way of my being a politician. And rightly, as I think. For I am certain, O men of Athens, that if I had engaged in politics, I should have perished long ago and done no good either to you or to myself. And don't be offended at my telling you the truth: for the truth is, that no man who goes to war with you or any other multitude, honestly struggling against the commission of unrighteousness and wrong in the state, will save his life; he who will really fight for the right, if he would live even for a little while, must have a private station and not a public one.

I can give you as proofs of this, not words only, but deeds, which you value more than words. Let me tell you a passage of my own life which will prove to you that I should never have yielded to injustice from any fear of death, and that if I had not yielded I should have died at once. I will tell you a story—tasteless perhaps and commonplace, but nevertheless true. The only office of state which I ever held, O men of Athens, was that of senator: the tribe Antiochis, which is my tribe, had the presidency at the trial of the generals who had not taken up the bodies of the slain after the battle of Arginusae; and you proposed to try them all together, which was illegal, as you all thought afterwards; but at the time I was the only one of the Prytanes who was opposed to the illegality, and I gave my vote against you; and when the orators threatened to impeach and arrest me, and have me taken away, and you called and shouted, I made up my mind that I would run the risk, having law and justice with me, rather than take part in your injustice because I feared imprisonment and death. This happened in the days of the democracy. But when the oligarchy of the Thirty was in power, they sent for me and four others into the rotunda, and bade us bring Leon the Salaminian from Salamis, as they wanted to execute him. This was a specimen of the sort of commands which they were always giving with the view of implicating as many as possible in their crimes; and then I showed, not in words only, but in deed, that, if I may be allowed to use such an expression, I cared not a straw for death, and that my only fear was the fear of doing an unrighteous or unholy thing. For the strong arm of that oppressive power did not frighten me into doing wrong; and when we came out of the rotunda the other four went to Salamis and fetched Leon, but I went quietly home. For which I might have lost my life, had not the power of the Thirty shortly afterwards come to an end. And to this many will witness.

Now do you really imagine that I could have survived all these years, if I had led a public life, supposing that like a good man I had always supported the right and had made justice, as I ought, the first thing? No, indeed, men of Athens, neither I nor any other. But I have been always the same in all my actions, public as well as private, and never have I yielded any base compliance to those who are slanderously termed my disciples, or to any other. For the truth is that I have no regular disciples: but if any one likes to come and hear me while I am pursuing my mission, whether he be young or old, he may freely come. Nor do I converse with those who pay only, and not with those who do not pay; but any one, whether he be rich or poor, may ask and answer me and listen to my words; and whether he turns out to be a bad man or a good one, that can not be justly laid to my charge, as I never taught him anything. And if any one says that he has ever learned or heard anything from me in private which all the world has not heard, I should like you to know that he is speaking an untruth.

But I shall be asked, Why do people delight in continually conversing with you? I have told you already, Athenians, the whole truth about this: they like to hear the cross-examination of the pretenders to wisdom; there is amusement in this. And this is a duty which the God has imposed upon me, as I am assured by oracles, visions, and in every sort of way in which the will of divine power was ever signified to any one. This is true, O Athenians; or, if not true, would be soon refuted. For if I am really corrupting the youth, and have corrupted some of them already, those of them who have grown up and have become sensible that I gave them bad advice in the days of their youth should come forward as accusers and take their revenge; and if they do not like to come themselves, some of their relatives, fathers, brothers, or other kinsmen, should say what evil their families suffered at my hands. Now is their time. Many of them I see in the court. There is Crito, who is of the same age and of the same deme with myself, and there is Critobulus his son, whom I also see. Then again there is Lysanias of Sphettus, who is the father of Aeschines—he is present; and also there is Antiphon of Cephisus, who is the father of Epigenes; and there are the brothers of several who have associated with me. There is Nicostratus the son of Theosdotides, and the brother of Theodotus (now Theodotus himself is dead, and therefore he, at any rate, will not seek to stop him); and there is Paralus the son of Demodocus, who had a brother Theages; and Adeimantus the son of Ariston, whose brother Plato is present; and Areantodorus, who is the brother of Apollodorus, whom I also see. I might mention a great many others, any of whom Meletus should have produced as witnesses in the course of his speech; and let him still produce them, if he has forgotten—I will make way for him. And let him say, if he has any testimony of the sort which he can produce. Nay, Athenians, the very opposite is the truth. For all these are ready to witness on behalf of the corrupter, of the destroyer of their kindred, as Meletus and Anytus call me; not the corrupted youth only—there might have been a motive for that—but their uncorrupted elder relatives. Why should they too support me with their testimony? Why, indeed, except for the sake of truth and justice, and because they know that I am speaking the truth, and that Meletus is lying.

Well, Athenians, this and the like of this is nearly all the defence which I have to offer. Yet a word more. Perhaps there may be some one who is offended at me, when he calls to mind how himself, on a similar or even a less serious occasion, had recourse to prayers and supplications with many tears, and how he produced his children in court, which was a moving spectacle, together with a posse of his relations and friends; whereas I, who am probably in danger of my life, will do none of these things. Perhaps this may come into his mind, and he may be set against me, and vote in anger because he is displeased at this. Now if there be such a person among you, which I am far from affirming, I may fairly reply to him: My friend, I am a man, and like other men, a creature of flesh and blood, and not of wood or stone, as Homer says; and I have a family, yes, and sons, O Athenians, three in number, one of whom is growing up, and the two others are still young; and yet I will not bring any of them hither in order to petition you for an acquittal. And why not? Not from any self-will or disregard of you. Whether I am or am not afraid of death is another question, of which I will not now speak. But my reason simply is, that I feel such conduct to be discreditable to myself, and you, and the whole state. One who has reached my years, and who has a name for wisdom, whether deserved or not, ought not to debase himself. At any rate, the world has decided that Socrates is in some way superior to other men. And if those among you who are said to be superior in wisdom and courage, and any other virtue, demean themselves in this way, how shameful is their conduct! I have seen men of reputation, when they have been condemned, behaving in the strangest manner: they seemed to fancy that they were going to suffer something dreadful if they died, and that they could be immortal if you only allowed them to live; and I think that they were a dishonor to the state, and that any stranger coming in would say of them that the most eminent men of Athens, to whom the Athenians themselves give honor and command, are no better than women. And I say that these things ought not to be done by those of us who are of reputation; and if they are done, you ought not to permit them; you ought rather to show that you are more inclined to condemn, not the man who is quiet, but the man who gets up a doleful scene, and makes the city ridiculous.

But, setting aside the question of dishonor, there seems to be something wrong in petitioning a judge, and thus procuring an acquittal instead of informing and convincing him. For his duty is, not to make a present of justice, but to give judgment; and he has sworn that he will judge according to the laws, and not according to his own good pleasure; and neither he nor we should get into the habit of perjuring ourselves—there can be no piety in that. Do not then require me to do what I consider dishonorable and impious and wrong, especially now, when I am being tried for impiety on the indictment of Meletus. For if, O men of Athens, by force of persuasion and entreaty, I could overpower your oaths, then I should be teaching you to believe that there are no gods, and convict myself, in my own defence, of not believing in them. But that is not the case; for I do believe that there are gods, and in a far higher sense than that in which any of my accusers believe in them. And to you and to God I commit my cause, to be determined by you as is best for you and me.[1]

There are many reasons why I am not grieved, O men of Athens, at the vote of condemnation. I expected this, and am only surprised that the votes are so nearly equal; for I had thought that the majority against me would have been far larger; but now, had thirty votes gone over to the other side, I should have been acquitted. And I may say that I have escaped Meletus. And I may say more; for without the assistance of Anytus and Lycon, he would not have had a fifth part of the votes, as the law requires, in which case he would have incurred a fine of a thousand drachma, as is evident.

And so he proposes death as the penalty. And what shall I propose on my part, O men of Athens? Clearly that which is my due. And what is that which I ought to pay or to receive? What shall be done to the man who has never had the wit to be idle during his whole life; but has been careless of what the many care about—wealth, and family interests, and military offices, and speaking in the assembly, and magistracies, and plots, and parties. Reflecting that I was really too honest a man to follow in this way and live I did not go where I could do no good to you or to myself; but where I could do the greatest good privately to every one of you, thither I went, and sought to persuade every man among you that he must look to himself, and seek virtue and wisdom before he looks to his private interests, and look to the state before he looks to the interests of the state; and that this should be the order which he observes in all his actions. What shall be done to such an one? Doubtless some good thing, O men of Athens, if he has his reward; and the good should be of a kind suitable to him. What would be a reward suitable to a poor man who is your benefactor, who desires leisure that he may instruct you? There can be no more

---

1 Socrates is convicted by 281 votes to 220.

fitting reward than maintenance in the Prytaneum, O men of Athens, a reward which be deserves far more than the citizen who has won the prize at Olympia in the horse or chariot race, whether the chariots were drawn by two horses or by many. For I am in want, and he has enough; and he only gives you the appearance of happiness, and I give you the reality. And if I am to estimate the penalty justly, I say that maintenance in the Prytaneum is the just return.

Perhaps you may think that I am braving you in saying this, as in what I said before about the tears and prayers. But that is not the case. I speak rather because I am convinced that I never intentionally wronged any one, although I can not convince you of that—for we have had a short conversation only; but if there were a law at Athens, such as there is in other cities, that a capital cause should not be decided in one day, then I believe that I should have convinced you; but now the time is too short. I can not in a moment refute great slanders; and, as I am convinced that I never wronged another, I will assuredly not wrong myself. I will not say of myself that I deserve any evil, or propose any penalty. Why should I? Because I am afraid of the penalty of death which Meletus proposes? When I do not know whether death is a good or an evil, why should I propose a penalty which would certainly be an evil? Shall I say imprisonment? And why should I live in prison, and be the slave of the magistrates of the year—of the eleven? Or shall the penalty be a fine, and imprisonment until the fine is paid? There is the same objection. I should have to lie in prison, for money I have none, and I can not pay. And if I say exile (and this may possibly be the penalty which you will affix), I must indeed be blinded by the love of life if I were to consider that when you, who are my own citizens, can not endure my discourses and words, and have found them so grievous and odious that you would fain have done with them, others are likely to endure me. No indeed, men of Athens, that is not very likely. And what a life should I lead, at my age, wandering from city to city, living in ever-changing exile, and always being driven out! For I am quite sure that into whatever place I go, as here so also there, the young men will come to me; and if I drive them away, their elders will drive me out at their desire; and if I let them come, their fathers and friends will drive me out for their sakes.

Some one will say: Yes, Socrates, but can not you hold your tongue, and then you may go into a foreign city, and no one will interfere with you? Now I have great difficulty in making you understand my answer to this. For if I tell you that this would be a disobedience to a divine command, and therefore that I can not hold my tongue, you will not believe that I am serious; and if I say again that the greatest good of man is daily to converse about virtue, and all that concerning which you hear me examining myself and others, and that the life which is unexamined is not worth living—that you are still less likely to believe. And yet what I say is true, although a thing of which it is hard for me to persuade you. Moreover, I am not accustomed to think that I deserve any punishment. Had I money I might have proposed to give you what I had, and have been none the worse. But you see that I have none, and can only ask you to proportion the fine to my means. However, I think that I could afford a mina, and therefore I propose that penalty: Plato, Crito, Critobulus, and Apollodorus, my friends here, bid me say thirty minae, and they will be the sureties. Well, then, say thirty minae, let that be the penalty; for that they will be ample security to you.[1]

Not much time will be gained, O Athenians, in return for the evil name which you will get from the detractors of the city, who will say that you killed Socrates, a wise man; for they will call me wise even although I am not wise when they want to reproach you. If you had waited a little while, your desire would have been fulfilled in the course of nature.

---

1 Socrates is condemned to death.

For I am far advanced in years, as you may perceive, and not far from death. I am speaking now only to those of you who have condemned me to death. And I have another thing to say to them: You think that I was convicted through deficiency of words—I mean, that if I had thought fit to leave nothing undone, nothing unsaid, I might have gained an acquittal. Not so; the deficiency which led to my conviction was not of words—certainly not. But I had not the boldness or impudence or inclination to address you as you would have liked me to address you, weeping and wailing and lamenting, and saying and doing many things which you have been accustomed to hear from others, and which, as I say, are unworthy of me. But I thought that I ought not to do anything common or mean in the hour of danger: nor do I now repent of the manner of my defence, and I would rather die having spoken after my manner, than speak in your manner and live. For neither in war nor yet at law ought any man to use every way of escaping death. For often in battle there is no doubt that if a man will throw away his arms, and fall on his knees before his pursuers, he may escape death; and in other dangers there are other ways of escaping death, if a man is willing to say and do anything. The difficulty, my friends, is not in avoiding death, but in avoiding unrighteousness; for that runs faster than death. I am old and move slowly, and the slower runner has overtaken me, and my accusers are keen and quick, and the faster runner, who is unrighteousness, has overtaken them. And now I depart hence condemned by you to suffer the penalty of death, and they, too, go their ways condemned by the truth to suffer the penalty of villainy and wrong; and I must abide by my award—let them abide by theirs. I suppose that these things may be regarded as fated,—and I think that they are well.

And now, O men who have condemned me, I would fain prophesy to you; for I am about to die, and that is the hour in which men are gifted with prophetic power. And I prophesy to you who are my murderers, that immediately after my death punishment far heavier than you have inflicted on me will surely await you. Me you have killed because you wanted to escape the accuser, and not to give an account of your lives. But that will not be as you suppose: far otherwise. For I say that there will be more accusers of you than there are now; accusers whom hitherto I have restrained: and as they are younger they will be more severe with you, and you will be more offended at them. For if you think that by killing men you can avoid the accuser censuring your lives, you are mistaken; that is not a way of escape which is either possible or honorable; the easiest and noblest way is not to be crushing others, but to be improving yourselves. This is the prophecy which I utter before my departure, to the judges who have condemned me.

Friends, who would have acquitted me, I would like also to talk with you about this thing which has happened, while the magistrates are busy, and before I go to the place at which I must die. Stay then awhile, for we may as well talk with one another while there is time. You are my friends, and I should like to show you the meaning of this event which has happened to me. O my judges—for you I may truly call judges—I should like to tell you of a wonderful circumstance. Hitherto the familiar oracle within me has constantly been in the habit of opposing me even about trifles, if I was going to make a slip or error about anything; and now as you see there has come upon me that which may be thought, and is generally believed to be, the last and worst evil. But the oracle made no sign of opposition, either as I was leaving my house and going out in the morning, or when I was going up into this court, or while I was speaking, at anything which I was going to say; and yet I have often been stopped in the middle of a speech, but now in nothing I either said or did touching this matter has the oracle opposed me. What do I take to be the explanation of this? I will tell you. I regard this as a proof that what has happened to me is a good, and that those of us who think that death is an evil are in error. This is a great proof to me of what I am saying, for the customary sign would surely have opposed me had I been going to evil and not to good.

Let us reflect in another way, and we shall see that there is great reason to hope that death is a good, for one of two things:—either death is a state of nothingness and utter unconsciousness, or, as men say, there is a change and migration of the soul from this world to another. Now if you suppose that there is no consciousness, but a sleep like the sleep of him who is undisturbed even by the sight of dreams, death will be an unspeakable gain. For if a person were to select the night in which his sleep was undisturbed even by dreams, and were to compare with this the other days and nights of his life, and then were to tell us how many days and nights he had passed in the course of his life better and more pleasantly than this one, I think that any man, I will not say a private man, but even the great king, will not find many such days or nights, when compared with the others. Now if death is like this, I say that to die is gain; for eternity is then only a single night. But if death is the journey to another place, and there, as men say, all the dead are, what good, O my friends and judges, can be greater than this? If indeed when the pilgrim arrives in the world below, he is delivered from the professors of justice in this world, and finds the true judges who are said to give judgment there, Minos and Rhadamanthus and Aeacus and Triptolemus, and other sons of God who were righteous in their own life, that pilgrimage will be worth making. What would not a man give if he might converse with Orpheus and Musaeus and Hesiod and Homer? Nay, if this be true, let me die again and again. I, too, shall have a wonderful interest in a place where I can converse with Palamedes, and Ajax the son of Telamon, and other heroes of old, who have suffered death through an unjust judgment; and there will be no small pleasure, as I think, in comparing my own sufferings with theirs. Above all, I shall be able to continue my search into true and false knowledge; as in this world, so also in that; I shall find out who is wise, and who pretends to be wise, and is not. What would not a man give, O judges, to be able to examine the leader of the great Trojan expedition; or Odysseus or Sisyphus, or numberless others, men and women too! What infinite delight would there be in conversing with them and asking them questions! For in that world they do not put a man to death for this; certainly not. For besides being happier in that world than in this, they will be immortal, if what is said is true.

Wherefore, O judges, be of good cheer about death, and know this of a truth—that no evil can happen to a good man, either in life or after death. He and his are not neglected by the gods; nor has my own approaching end happened by mere chance. But I see clearly that to die and be released was better for me; and therefore the oracle gave no sign. For which reason also, I am not angry with my accusers, or my condemners; they have done me no harm, although neither of them meant to do me any good; and for this I may gently blame them.

Still I have a favor to ask of them. When my sons are grown up. I would ask you, O my friends, to punish them; and I would have you trouble them, as I have troubled you, if they seem to care about riches, or anything, more than about virtue; or if they pretend to be something when they are really nothing,—then reprove them, as I have reproved you, for not caring about that for which they ought to care, and thinking that they are something when they are really nothing. And if you do this, I and my sons will have received justice at your hands.

The hour of departure has arrived, and we go our ways—I to die, and you to live. Which is better, God only knows.

Plato

427-347 B.C.E.

CRITO

399 B.C.E.

This dialogue directly follows the Apology. Socrates has been confined to the Athenian jail and is awaiting his death, which will come when the holiday, referred to in the text, is over. Crito was one of the friends of Socrates and is deeply distressed. Possibly at some risk to himself, he has arranged to bribe the jailer and smuggle Socrates out of the jail and out of town. But Socrates refuses to escape and tries to convince Crito that this is the correct course of action.

Selected from: Plato. 399 B.C.E. "Crito." *The Works of Plato: Four Volumes in One.* Vol. 3. Benjamin Jowett, Trans., New York: Tudor [1936?]. 141-157.

CRITO
PERSONS OF THE DIALOGUE
SOCRATES **CRITO**
SCENE: The Prison of Socrates

Socrates. Why have you come at this hour, Crito? it must be quite early?

Crito. Yes, certainly.

Soc. What is the exact time?

Cr. The dawn is breaking.

Soc. I wonder the keeper of the prison would let you in.

Cr. He knows me, because I often come, Socrates, moreover, I have done him a kindness.

Soc. And are you only just come?

Cr. No, I came some time ago.

Soc. Then why did you sit and say nothing, instead of awakening me at once?

Cr. Why, indeed, Socrates, I myself would rather not have all this sleeplessness and sorrow. But I have been wondering at your peaceful slumbers, and that was the reason why I did not awaken you, because I wanted you to be out of pain. I have always thought you happy in the calmness of your temperament; but never did I see the like of the easy, cheerful way in which you bear this calamity.

Soc. Why, Crito, when a man has reached my age he ought not to be repining at the prospect of death.

Cr. And yet other old men find themselves in similar misfortunes and age does not prevent them from repining.

Soc. That may be. But you have not told me why you come at this early hour.

Cr. I come to bring you a message which is sad and painful; not, as l believe, to yourself, but to all of us who are your friends, and saddest of all to me.

Soc. What! I suppose that the ship has come from Delos, on the arrival of which I am to die?

Cr. No, the ship has not actually arrived, but she will probably be here today, as persons who have come from Sunium tell me that they have left her there; and therefore to-morrow, Socrates, will be the last day of your life.

Soc.: Very well, Crito; if such is the will of God, I am willing; but my belief is that there will be a delay of a day.

Cr. Why do you say this?

Soc. I will tell you. I am to die on the day after the arrival of the ship?

Cr. Yes; that is what the authorities say.

Soc. But I do not think that the ship will be here until to-morrow; this I gather from a vision which I had last night, or rather only just now, when you fortunately allowed me to sleep.

Cr. And what was the nature of the vision?

Soc. There came to me the likeness of a woman, fair and comely, clothed in white raiment, who called to me and said: O Socrates,

"The third day hence, to Phthia shalt thou go."

Cr. What a singular dream, Socrates!

Soc. There can be no doubt about the meaning Crito, I think.

Cr. Yes; the meaning is only too clear. But, Oh! my beloved Socrates, let me entreat you once more to take my advice and escape. For if you die I shall not only lose a friend who can never be replaced, but there is another evil: people who do not know you and me will believe that I might have saved you if I had been willing to give money, but that I did not care. Now, can there be a worse disgrace than this—that I should be thought to value money more than the life of a friend? For the many will not be persuaded that I wanted you to escape, and that you refused.

Soc. But why, my dear Crito, should we care about the opinion of the many? Good men, and they are the only persons who are worth considering, will think of these things truly as they happened.

Cr. But do you see, Socrates, that the opinion of the many must be regarded, as is evident in your own case, because they can do the very greatest evil to any one who has lost their good opinion.

Soc. I only wish, Crito, that they could; for then they could also do the greatest good, and that would be well. But the truth is, that they can do neither good nor evil; they can not make a man wise or make him foolish; and whatever they do is the result of chance.

Cr. Well, I will not dispute about that; but please to tell me, Socrates, whether you are not acting out of regard to me and your other friends: are you not afraid that if you escape hence we may get into trouble with the informers for having stolen you away, and lose either the whole or a great part of our property; or that even a worse evil may happen to us? Now, if this is your fear, be at ease; for in order to save you, we ought surely to run this or even a greater risk; be persuaded, then, and do as I say.

Soc. Yes, Crito, that is one fear which you mention, but by no means the only one.

Cr. Fear not. There are persons who at no great cost are willing to save you and bring you out of prison; and as for the informers, you may observe that they are far from being exorbitant in their demands; a little money will satisfy them. My means, which, as I am sure, are ample, are at your service, and if you have a scruple about spending all mine, here are strangers who will give you the use of theirs; and one of them, Simmias the Theban, has brought a sum of money for this very purpose; and Cebes and many others are willing to spend their money too. I say, therefore, do not on that account hesitate about making your escape, and do not say, as you did in the court, that you will have a difficulty in knowing what to do with yourself if you escape. For men will love you in other places to which you may go, and not in Athens only; there are friends of mine in Thessaly, if you like to go to them, who will value and protect you, and no Thessalian will give you any trouble. Nor can I think that you are justified, Socrates, in betraying your own life when you might be saved; this is playing into the hands of your enemies and destroyers; and moreover I should say that you were betraying your children; for you might bring them up and educate them; instead of which you go away and leave them, and they will have to take their chance; and if they do not meet with the usual fate of orphans, there will be small thanks to you. No man should bring children into the world who is unwilling to persevere to the end in their nurture and education. But you are choosing the easier part, as I think, not the better and manlier, which would rather have become one who professes virtue in all his actions, like yourself. And, indeed, I am ashamed not only of you, but of us who are your friends, when I reflect that this entire business of yours will be attributed to our want of courage. The trial need never have come on, or might have been brought to another issue; and the end of all, which is the crowning absurdity, will seem to have been permitted by us, through cowardice and baseness, who might have saved you, as you might have saved yourself, if we had been good for anything (for there was no difficulty in escaping); and we did not see how disgraceful, Socrates, and also miserable all this will be to us as well as to you. Make your mind up then, or rather have your mind already made up, for the time of deliberation is over, and there is only one thing to be done, which must be done, if at all, this very night, and which any delay will render all but impossible; I beseech you therefore, Socrates, to be persuaded by me, and to do as I say.

Soc. Dear Crito, your zeal is invaluable, if a right one; but if wrong, the greater the zeal the greater the evil; and therefore we ought to consider whether these things shall be done or not. For I am and always have been one of those natures who must be guided by reason, whatever the reason may be which upon reflection appears to me to be the best; and now that this fortune has come upon me, I can not put away the reasons which I have before given: the principles which I have hitherto honored and revered I still honor, and unless we can find other and better principles on the instant, I am certain not to agree with you; no, not even if the power of the multitude could inflict many more imprisonments, confiscations, deaths, frightening us like children with hobgoblin terrors. But what will be the fairest way of considering the question? Shall I return to your old argument about the opinions of men? some of which are to be regarded, and others, as we are saying, are not to be regarded. Now were we right in maintaining this before I was condemned? And has the argument which was once good now proved to be talk for the sake of talking;—in fact an amusement only, and altogether vanity? That is what I want to consider with your help, Crito:—whether, under my present circumstances, the argument appears to be in any way different or not; and is to be allowed by me or disallowed. That argument, which, as I believe, is maintained by many who assume to be authorities, was to the effect, as I was saying, that the opinions of some men are to be regarded, and of other men not to be regarded. Now you, Crito, are a disinterested person who are not going to die to-morrow—at least, there is no human probability of this, and you are therefore not liable to be deceived by the circumstances in which you are placed. Tell me, then, whether I am right in saying that some opinions, and the opinions of some men only, are to be valued, and other opinions, and the opinions of other men, are not to be valued. I ask you whether I was right in maintaining this?

Cr. Certainly.

Soc. The good are to be regarded, and not the bad?

Cr. Yes.

Soc. And the opinions of the wise are good, and the opinions of the unwise are evil?

Cr. Certainly.

Soc. And what was said about another matter? Was the disciple in gymnastics supposed to attend to the praise and blame and opinion of every man, or of one man only—his physician or trainer, whoever that was?

Cr. Of one man only.

Soc. And he ought to fear the censure and welcome the praise of that one only, and not of the many?

Cr. That is clear.

Soc. And he ought to live and train, and eat and drink in the way which seems good to his single master who has understanding, rather than according to the opinion of all other men put together?

Cr. True.

Soc. And if he disobeys and disregards the opinion and approval of the one, and regards the opinion of the many who have no understanding, will he not suffer evil?

Cr. Certainly he will.

Soc. And what will the evil be, whither tending and what affecting, in the disobedient person?

Cr. Clearly, affecting the body; that is what is destroyed by the evil.

Soc. Very good; and is not this true, Crito, of other things which we need not separately enumerate? In the matter of just and unjust, fair and foul, good and evil, which are the subjects of our present consultation, ought we to follow the opinion of the many and to fear them; or the opinion of the one man who has understanding, and whom we ought to fear and reverence more than all the rest of the world: and whom deserting we shall destroy and injure that principle in us which may be assumed to be improved by justice and deteriorated by injustice;—is there not such a principle?

Cr. Certainly there is, Socrates.

Soc. Take a parallel instance:—if, acting under the advice of men who have no understanding, we destroy that which is improvable by health and deteriorated by disease—when that has been destroyed, I say, would life be worth having? And that is—the body?

Cr. Yes.

Soc. Could we live, having an evil and corrupted body?

Cr. Certainly not.

Soc. And will life be worth having, if that higher part of man be depraved, which is improved by justice and deteriorated by injustice? Do we suppose that principle, whatever it may be in man, which has to do with justice and injustice, to be inferior to the body?

Cr. Certainly not.

Soc. More honored, then?

Cri. Far more honored.

Soc. Then, my friend, we must not regard what the many say of us: but what he, the one man who has understanding of just and unjust, will say, and what the truth will say. And therefore you begin in error when you suggest that we should regard the opinion of the many about just and unjust, good and evil, honorable and dishonorable.—Well, someone will say, "but the many can kill us."

Cr. Yes, Socrates; that will clearly be the answer.

Soc. That is true: but still I find with surprise that the old argument is, as I conceive, unshaken as ever. And I should like to know whether I may say the same of another proposition—that not life, but a good life, is to be chiefly valued?

Cr. Yes, that also remains.

Soc. And a good life is equivalent to a just and honorable one—that holds also?

Cr. Yes, that holds.

Soc. From these premises I proceed to argue the question whether I ought or ought not to try to escape without the consent of the Athenians: and if I am clearly right in escaping, then I will make the attempt; but if not, I will abstain. The other considerations which you mention, of money and loss of character, and the duty of educating children, are, I fear, only the doctrines of the multitude, who would be as ready to call people to life, if they were able, as they are to put them to death—and with as little reason. But now, since the argument has thus far prevailed, the only question which remains to be considered is, whether we shall do rightly either in escaping or in suffering others to aid in our escape and paying them in money and thanks, or whether we shall not do rightly; and if the latter, then death or any other calamity which may ensue on my remaining here must not be allowed to enter into the calculation.

Cr. I think that you are right, Socrates; how then shall we proceed?

Soc. Let us consider the matter together, and do you either refute me if you can, and I will be convinced; or else cease, my dear friend, from repeating to me that I ought to escape against the wishes of the Athenians: for I am extremely desirous to be persuaded by you, but not against my own better judgment. And now please to consider my first position, and do your best to answer me.

Cr. I will do my best.

Soc. Are we to say that we are never intentionally to do wrong, or that in one way we ought and in another way we ought not to do wrong, or is doing wrong always evil and dishonorable, as I was just now saying, and as has been already acknowledged by us? Are all our former admissions which were made within a few days to be thrown away? And have we, at our age, been earnestly discoursing with one another all our life long only to discover that we are no better than children? Or are we to rest assured, in spite of the opinion of the many, and in spite of consequences whether better or worse, of the truth of what was then said, that injustice is always an evil and dishonor to him who acts unjustly? Shall we affirm that?

Cr. Yes.

Soc. Then we must do no wrong?

Cr. Certainly not.

Soc. Nor when injured injure in return, as the many imagine; for we must injure no one at all?

Cr. Clearly not.

Soc. Again, Crito, may we do evil?

Cr. Surely not, Socrates.

Soc. And what of doing evil in return for evil, which is the morality of the many—is that just or not?

Cr. Not just.

Soc. For doing evil to another is the same as injuring him?

Cr. Very true.

Soc. Then we ought not to retaliate or render evil for evil to any one, whatever evil we may have suffered from him.

Cr. Clearly not.

Soc. Again, Crito, may we do evil?

Cr. Surely not, Socrates.

Soc. And what of doing evil in return for evil, which is the morality of the many—is that just or not?

Cr. Not just.

Soc. For doing evil to another is the same as injuring him?

Cr. Very true.

Soc. Then we ought not to retaliate or render evil for evil to any one, whatever evil we may have suffered from him. But I would have you consider, Crito, whether you really mean what you are saying. For this opinion has never been held, and never will be held, by any considerable number of persons; and those who are agreed and those who are not agreed upon this point have no common ground, and can only despise one another, when they see how widely they differ. Tell me, then, whether you agree with and assent to my first principle, that neither injury nor retaliation nor warding off evil by evil is ever right. And shall that be the premise of our agreement? Or do you decline and dissent from this? For this has been of old and is still my opinion; but, if you are of another opinion, let me hear what you have to say. If, however, you remain of the same mind as formerly, I will proceed to the next step.

Cr. You may proceed, for I have not changed my mind.

Soc. Then I will proceed to the next step, which may be put in the form of a question:—Ought a man to do what he admits to be right, or ought he to betray the right?

Cr. He ought to do what he thinks right.

Soc. But if this is true, what is the application? In leaving the prison against the will of the Athenians, do I wrong any?

or rather do I not wrong those whom I ought least to wrong? Do I not desert the principles which were acknowledged by us to be just? What do you say?

Cr. I can not tell, Socrates, for I do not know.

Soc. Consider the matter in this way:—Imagine that I am about to play truant (you may call the proceeding by any name which you like), and the laws and the government come and interrogate me: "Tell us, Socrates," they say; "what are you about? are you going by an act of yours to overturn us—the laws and the whole state, as far as in you lies? Do you imagine that a state can subsist and not be overthrown, in which the decisions of law have no power, but are set aside and overthrown by individuals?" What will be our answer, Crito, to these and the like words? Any one, and especially a clever rhetorician, will have a good deal to urge about the evil of setting aside the law which requires a sentence to be carried out; and we might reply, "Yes; but the state has injured us and given an unjust sentence." Suppose I say that?

Cr. Very good, Socrates.

Soc. "And was that our agreement with you?" the law would say, "or were you to abide by the sentence of the state?" And if I were to express astonishment at their saying this, the law would probably add: "Answer, Socrates, instead of opening your eyes: you are in the habit of asking and answering questions. Tell us what complaint you have to make against us which justifies you in attempting to destroy us and the state? In the first place did we not bring you into existence? Your father married your mother by our aid and begat you. Say whether you have any objection to urge against those of us who regulate marriage?" None, I should reply. "Or against those of us who regulate the system of nurture and education of children in which you were trained? Were not the laws, who have the charge of this, right in commanding your father to train you in music and gymnastic?" Right, I should reply. "Well, then, since you were brought into the world and nurtured and educated by us, can you deny in the first place that you are our child and slave as your fathers were before you? And if this is true you are not on equal terms with us; nor can you think that you have a right to do to us what we are doing to you. Would you have any right to strike or revile or do any other evil to a father or to your master, if you had one, when you have been struck or reviled by him, or received some other evil at his hands?"—you would not say this? And because we think right to destroy you, do you think that you have any right to destroy us in return, and your country as far as in you lies? And will you, O professor of true virtue, say that you are justified in this? Has a philosopher like you failed to discover that our country is more to be valued and higher and holier far than mother or father or any ancestor, and more to be regarded in the eyes of the gods and of men of understanding? also to be soothed, and gently and reverently entreated when angry, even more than a father, and if not persuaded, obeyed? And when we are punished by her, whether with imprisonment or stripes, the punishment is to be endured in silence; and if she leads us to wounds or death in battle, thither we follow as is right; neither may any one yield or retreat or leave his rank, but whether in battle or in a court of law, or in any other place, he must do what his city and his country order him; or he must change their view of what is just: and if he may do no violence to his father or mother, much less may he do violence to his country." What answer shall we make to this, Crito? Do the laws speak truly, or do they not?

Cr. I think that they do.

Soc. Then the laws will say: "Consider, Socrates, if this is true, that in your present attempt you are going to do us wrong. For, after having brought you into the world, and nurtured and educated you, and given you and every other citizen a share in every good that we had to give, we further proclaim and give the right to every Athenian, that if he does not like us when he has come of age and has seen the ways of the city, and made our acquaintance, he may go where he pleases and take his goods with him; and none of us laws will forbid him or interfere with him. Any of you who does not like us and the city, and who wants to go to a colony or to any other city, may go where he likes, and take his goods with him. But he who has experience of the manner in which we order justice and administer the state, and still remains, has entered into an implied contract that he will do as we command him. And he who disobeys us is, as we maintain, thrice wrong; first, because in disobeying us he is disobeying his parents; secondly, because we are the authors of his education; thirdly, because he has made an agreement with us that he will duly obey our commands; and he neither obeys them nor convinces us that our commands are wrong; and we do not rudely impose them, but give him the alternative of obeying or convincing us;—that is what we offer, and he does neither. These are the sort of accusations to which, as we were saying, you, Socrates, will be exposed if you accomplish your intentions; you, above all other Athenians." Suppose I ask, why is this? they will justly retort upon me that I above all other men have acknowledged the agreement. "There is clear proof," they will say, "Socrates, that we and the city were not displeasing to you. Of all Athenians you have been the most constant resident in the city, which, as you never leave, you may be supposed to love. For you never went out of the city either to see the games, except once when you went to the Isthmus, or to any other place unless when you were on military service; nor did you travel as other men do. Nor had you any curiosity to know other states or their laws: your affections did not go beyond us and our state; we were your especial favorites, and you acquiesced in our government of you; and this is the state in which you begat your children, which is a proof of your satisfaction. Moreover, you might, if you had liked, have fixed the penalty at banishment in the course of the trial—the state which refuses to let you go now would have let you go then. But you pretended that you preferred death to exile, and that you were not grieved at death. And now you have forgotten these fine sentiments, and pay no respect to us, the laws, of whom you are the destroyer; and are doing what only a miserable slave would do, running away and turning your back upon the compacts and agreements which you made as a citizen. And first of all answer this very question: Are we right in saying that you agreed to be governed according to us in deed, and not in word only? Is that true or not?" How shall we answer that, Crito? Must we not agree?

Cr. There is no help, Socrates

Soc. Then will they not say: "You, Socrates, are breaking the covenants and agreements which you made with us at your leisure, not in any haste or under any compulsion or deception, but having had seventy years to think of them, during which time you were at liberty to leave the city, if we were not to your mind, or if our covenants appeared to you to be unfair. You had your choice, and might have gone either to Lacedamon or Crete, which you often praise for their good government, or to some other Hellenic or foreign state. Whereas you, above all other Athenians, seemed to be so fond of the state, or, in other words, of us her laws (for who would like a state that has no laws?), that you never stirred out of her: the halt, the blind, the maimed, were not more stationary in her than you were. And now you run away and forsake your agreements. Not so, Socrates, if you will take our advice; do not make yourself ridiculous by escaping out of the city.

"For just consider, if you transgress and err in this sort of way, what good will you do, either to yourself or to your friends? That your friends will be driven into exile and deprived of citizenship, or will lose their property, is tolerably certain; and you yourself, if you fly to one of the neighboring cities, as, for example, Thebes or Megara, both of which are well-governed cities, will come to them as an enemy, Socrates, and their government will be against you, and all patriotic citizens will cast an evil eye upon you as a subverter of the laws, and you will confirm in the minds of the judges the justice of their own condemnation of you. For he who is a corrupter of the laws is more than likely to be corrupter of the young and foolish portion of mankind. Will you then flee from well-ordered cities and virtuous men? and is existence worth having on these terms? Or will you go to them without shame, and talk to them, Socrates? And what will you say to them? What you say here about virtue and justice and institutions and laws being the best things among men? Would that be decent of you? Surely not. But if you go away from well-governed states to Crito's friends in Thessaly, where there is great disorder and license, they will be charmed to have the tale of your escape from prison, set off with ludicrous particulars of the manner in which you were wrapped in a goatskin or some other disguise, and metamorphosed as the fashion of runaways is—that is very likely; but will there be no one to remind you that in your old age you violated the most sacred laws from a miserable desire of a little more life? Perhaps not, if you keep them in a good temper; but if they are out of temper you will hear many degrading things; you will live, but how?—as the flatterer of all men, and the servant of all men; and doing what?—eating and drinking in Thessaly, having gone abroad in order that you may get a dinner. And where will be your fine sentiments about justice and virtue then? Say that you wish to live for the sake of your children, that you may bring them up and educate them—will you take them into Thessaly and deprive them of Athenian citizenship? Is that the benefit which you would confer upon them? Or are you under the impression that they will be better cared for and educated here if you are still alive, although absent from them; for that your friends will take care of them? Do you fancy that if you are an inhabitant of Thessaly they will take care of them, and if you are an inhabitant of the other world they will not take care of them? Nay; but if they who call themselves friends are truly friends, they surely will.

"Listen, then, Socrates, to us who have brought you up. Think not of life and children first, and of justice afterwards, but of justice first, that you may be justified before the princes of the world below. For neither will you nor any that belong to you be happier or holier or juster in this life, or happier in another, if you do as Crito bids. Now you depart in innocence, a sufferer and not a doer of evil; a victim, not of the laws, but of men. But if you go forth, returning evil for evil, and injury for injury, breaking the covenants and agreements which you have made with us, and wronging those whom you ought least to wrong, that is to say, yourself, your friends, your country, and us, we shall be angry with you while you live, and our brethren, the laws in the world below, will receive you as an enemy; for they will know that you have done your best to destroy us. Listen, then, to us and not to Crito."

This is the voice which I seem to hear murmuring in my ears, like the sound of the flute in the ears of the mystic; that voice, I say, is humming in my ears, and prevents me from hearing any other. And I know that anything more which you will say will be in vain. Yet speak, if you have anything to say.

Cr. I have nothing to say, Socrates.

Soc. Then let me follow the intimations of the will of God.

THOMAS JEFFERSON

1743-1826

THE DECLARATION OF INDEPENDENCE

JULY 4, 1776

Though he was a key figure in the War of Independence, an enormously influential political figure in the early history of the Republic, and the third President of the United States, Jefferson wanted only three accomplishments listed on his tombstone: authoring the Virginia Statute for Religious Freedom, founding the University of Virginia, and writing the *Declaration of Independence.* The *Declaration*'s succinct expression of its key ideas has contributed to the vitality of those ideas in American public life and continues to be an enduring expression of the ideal of national freedom.

THE UNANIMOUS DECLARATION OF THE THIRTEEN UNITED STATES OF AMERICA

WHEN IN THE COURSE OF HUMAN EVENTS, it becomes necessary for one people to dissolve the political bands which have connected them with another, and to assume among the Powers of the earth, the separate and equal station to which the Laws of Nature and of Nature's God entitle them, a decent respect to the opinions of mankind requires that they should declare the causes which impel them to the separation.

We hold these truths to be self-evident, that all men are created equal, that they are endowed by their Creator with certain unalienable Rights, that among these are Life, Liberty, and the pursuit of Happiness. That to secure these rights, Governments are instituted among Men, deriving their just powers from the consent of the governed; That whenever any Form of Government becomes destructive of these ends, it is the Right of the People to alter or to abolish it, and to institute new Government, laying its foundation on such principles and organizing its powers in such form, as to them shall seem most likely to effect their Safety and Happiness. Prudence, indeed, will dictate that Governments long established should not be changed for light and transient causes; and accordingly all experience hath shown, that mankind are more disposed to suffer, while evils are sufferable, than to right themselves by abolishing the forms to which they are accustomed. But when a long train of abuses and usurpations, pursuing invariably the same Object evinces a design to reduce them under absolute Despotism, it is their right, it is their duty, to throw off such Government, and to provide new Guards for their future security. Such has been the patient sufferance of these Colonies; and such is now the necessity which constrains them to alter their former Systems of Government. The history of the present King of Great Britain is a history of repeated injuries and usurpations, all having in direct object the establishment of an absolute Tyranny over these States. To prove this, let Facts be submitted to a candid world.

He has refused his Assent to Laws, the most wholesome and necessary for the public good.

He has forbidden his Governors to pass Laws of immediate and pressing importance, unless suspended in their operation till his Assent should be obtained; and when so suspended, he has utterly neglected to attend to them.

He has refused to pass other Laws for the accommodation of large districts of people, unless those people would relinquish the right of Representation in the Legislature, a right inestimable to them and formidable to tyrants only.

He has called together legislative bodies at places unusual, uncomfortable, and distant from the depository of their Public Records, for the sole purpose of fatiguing them into compliance with his measures.

He has dissolved Representative Houses repeatedly, for opposing with manly firmness his invasions on the rights of the people.

He has refused for a long time, after such dissolutions, to cause others to be elected; whereby the Legislative Powers, incapable of Annihilation, have returned to the People at large for their exercise; the State remaining in the meantime exposed to all the dangers of invasion from without, and convulsions within.

He has endeavoured to prevent the population of these states; for that purpose obstructing the Laws of Naturalization of Foreigners; refusing to pass others to encourage their migration hither, and raising the conditions of new Appropriations of Lands.

He has obstructed the Administration of Justice, by refusing his Assent to Laws for establishing Judiciary Powers.

He has made Judges dependent on his Will alone, for the tenure of their offices, and the amount and payment of their salaries.

He has erected a multitude of New Offices, and sent hither swarms of Officers to harass our People, and eat out their substance.

He has kept among us, in times of peace, Standing Armies without the Consent of our legislature.

He has affected to render the Military independent of and superior to the Civil Power.

He has combined with others to subject us to a jurisdiction foreign to our constitution, and unacknowledged by our laws; giving his Assent to their acts of pretended legislation:

For quartering large bodies of armed troops among us:

For protecting them, by a mock Trial, from Punishment for any Murders which they should commit on the Inhabitants of these states:

For cutting off our Trade with all parts of the world:

For imposing taxes on us without our Consent:

For depriving us in many cases, of the benefits of Trial by Jury:

For transporting us beyond Seas to be tried for pretended offences:

For abolishing the free System of English Laws in a neighbouring Province, establishing therein an Arbitrary government, and enlarging its Boundaries so as to render it at once an example and fit instrument for introducing the same absolute rule into these Colonies:

For taking away our Charters, abolishing our most valuable Laws, and altering fundamentally the Forms of our Governments:

For suspending our own Legislature, and declaring themselves invested with Power to legislate for us in all cases whatsoever.

He has abdicated Government here, by declaring us out of his Protection and waging War against us.

He has plundered our seas, ravaged our Coasts, burnt our towns, and destroyed the lives of our people.

He is at this time transporting large armies of foreign mercenaries to compleat the works of death, desolation and tyranny, already begun with circumstances of Cruelty & perfidy scarcely paralleled in the most barbarous ages, and totally unworthy the Head of a civilized nation.

He has constrained our fellow Citizens taken Captive on the high Seas to bear Arms against their Country, to become the executioners of their friends and Brethren, or to fall themselves by their Hands.

He has excited domestic insurrections amongst us, and has endeavoured to bring on the inhabitants of our frontiers, the merciless Indian Savages, whose known rule of warfare, is an undistinguished destruction of all ages, sexes and conditions.

In every stage of these Oppressions We have Petitioned for Redress in the most humble terms: Our repeated Petitions have been answered only by repeated injury. A Prince, whose character is thus marked by every act which may define a Tyrant, is unfit to be the ruler of a free People.

Nor have We been wanting in attention to our British brethren. We have warned them from time to time of attempts by their legislature to extend an unwarrantable jurisdiction over us. We have reminded them of the circumstances of our emigration and settlement here. We have appealed to their native justice and magnanimity, and we have conjured them by the ties of our common kindred to disavow these usurpations, which would inevitably interrupt our connections and correspondence. They too have been deaf to the voice of justice and of consanguinity. We must, therefore, acquiesce in the necessity, which denounces our Separation, and hold them, as we hold the rest of mankind, Enemies in War, in Peace Friends.

We, therefore, the Representatives of the United States of America, in General Congress, Assembled, appealing to the Supreme Judge of the world for the rectitude of our intentions, do, in the Name, and by Authority of the good People of these Colonies, solemnly publish and declare, That these United Colonies are, and of Right ought to be Free and Independent States; that they are Absolved from all Allegiance to the British Crown, and that all political connection between them and the State of Great Britain, is and ought to be totally dissolved; and that as Free and Independent States, they have full Power to levy War, conclude Peace, contract Alliances, establish Commerce, and to do all other Acts and Things which Independent States may of right do. And for the support of this Declaration, with a firm reliance on the Protection of Divine Providence, we mutually pledge to each other our Lives, our Fortunes and our sacred Honor.

JOHN HANCOCK

NEW HAMPSHIRE

JOSIAH BARTLETT
WM. WHIPPLE
MATTHEW THORNTON

MASSACHUSETTS BAY

SAML. ADAMS
JOHN ADAMS
ELBRIDGE GERRY
ROBT. TREAT PAINE

RHODE ISLAND

STEP. HOPKINS
WILLIAM ELLERY

CONNECTICUT

ROGER SHERMAN WM.
SAM'EL HUNTINGTON
WILLIAMS
OLIVER WOLCOTT

NEW YORK

WM. FLOYD
PHIL. LIVINGSTON
FRANS. LEWIS
LEWIS MORRIS

NEW JERSEY

RICHD. STOCKTON
JNO. WITHERSPOON
FRAS. HOPKINSON
JOHN HART
ABRA. CLARK

PENNSYLVANIA

ROBT. MORRIS
BENJAMIN RUSH
BENJA. FRANKLIN
JAS. SMITH
GEO. TAYLOR
JAMES WILSON

JOHN MORTON
GEO. CLYMER
GEO. ROSS

DELAWARE
CAESAR RODNEY
GEO. READ
THO. M'KEAN

MARYLAND
SAMUEL CHASE
WM. PACA
THOS. STONE
CHARLES CARROLL of Carrollton

VIRGINIA
GEORGE WYTHE
RICHARD HENRY LEE
TH. JEFFERSON
BENJA. HARRISON
THOS. NELSON, Jr.
FRANCIS LIGHTFOOT LEE
CARTER BRAXTON

NORTH CAROLINA
WM. HOOPER
JOSEPH HEWES
JOHN PENN

SOUTH CAROLINA
EDWARD RUTLEDGE
THOS. HEYWARD, junr.
ARTHUR MIDDLETON
THOMAS LYNCH, junr.

GEORGIA
BUTTON GWINNETT
LYMAN HALL
GEO. WALTON

Fredrick Douglass

1818-1895

NARRATIVE OF THE LIFE OF FREDRICK DOUGLASS, AN AMERICAN SLAVE

1845

Douglass's life story would make fascinating reading even if he had not become a noted public figure. Born in slavery in Maryland, he started on his distinctive path in life when he learned to read at the age of nine from the wife of his owner. He eventually escaped from slavery and moved to New York, then Boston at the age of twenty. Encouraged by prominent abolitionists, he became a writer, publisher, and speaker on the evils of slavery. The readings here give a sense of his enormous personal determination and inner strength.

Selected from: Douglass, Fredrick. 1845. *Narrative of the Life of Frederick Douglass, an American Slave:* Written by Himself. Boston: Published at the Anti-Slavery Office, No. 25, Cornhill. Reprinted Dolphin Books edition, 1963.

Chapter 10 (excerpted 61-74)

CHAPTER X

I left Master Thomas's house, and went to live with Mr. Covey, on the 1st of January, 1833. I was now, for the first time in my life, a field hand. In my new employment, I found myself even more awkward than a country boy appeared to be in a large city. I had been at my new home but one week before Mr. Covey gave me a very severe whipping, cutting my back causing the blood to run, and raising ridges on my flesh as large as my little finger. The details of this affair are as follows: Mr. Covey sent me, very early in the morning of one of our coldest days in the month of January, to the woods, to get a load of wood. He gave me a team of unbroken oxen. He told me which was the in-hand ox, and which the off-hand one. He then tied the end of a large rope around the horns of the in-hand ox, and gave me the other end of it, and told me, if the oxen started to run, that I must hold on upon the rope. I had never driven oxen before, and of course I was very awkward. I, however, succeeded in getting to the edge of the woods with little difficulty; but I had got a very few rods into the woods, when the oxen took fright, and started full tilt, carrying the cart against trees, and over stumps, in the most frightful manner. I expected every moment that my brains would be dashed out against the trees. After running thus for a considerable distance, they finally upset the cart, dashing it with great force against a tree, and threw themselves into a dense thicket. How I escaped death, I do not know. There I was, entirely alone, in a thick wood, in a place new to me. My cart was upset and shattered, my oxen were entangled among the young trees, and there was none to help me. After a long spell of effort, I succeeded in getting my cart righted, my oxen disentangled, and again yoked to the cart. I now proceeded with my team to the place where I had, the day before, been chopping wood, and loaded my cart pretty heavily, thinking in this way to tame my oxen. I then proceeded on my way home. I had now consumed one half of the day. I got out of the woods safely, and now felt out of danger. I stopped my oxen to open the woods gate; and just as I did so, before I could get hold of my ox-rope, the oxen again started, rushed through the gate, catching it between the wheel and the body of the cart, tearing it to pieces, and coming within a few inches of crushing me against the gate-post. Thus twice, in one short day, I escaped death by the merest chance. On my return, I told Mr. Covey what had happened, and how it happened. He ordered me to return to the woods again immediately. I did so, and he followed on after me. Just as I got into the woods, he came up and told me to stop my cart, and that he would teach me how to trifle away my time, and break gates. He then went to a large gum-tree, and with his axe cut three large switches, and, after trimming them up neatly with his pocket-knife, he ordered me to take off my clothes. I made him no answer, but stood with my clothes on. He repeated his order. I still made him no answer, nor did I move to strip myself. Upon this he rushed at me with the fierceness of a tiger, tore off my clothes, and lashed me till he had worn out his switches, cutting me so savagely as to leave the marks visible for a long time after. This whipping was the first of a number just like it, and for similar offences.

I lived with Mr. Covey one year. During the first six months, of that year, scarce a week passed without his whipping me. I was seldom free from a sore back. My awkwardness was almost always his excuse for whipping me. We were worked fully up to the point of endurance. Long before day we were up, our horses fed, and by the first approach of day we were off to the field with our hoes and ploughing teams. Mr. Covey gave us enough to eat, but scarce time to eat it. We were often less than five minutes taking our meals. We were often in the field from the first approach of day till its last lingering ray had left us; and at saving-fodder time, midnight often caught us in the field binding blades.

Covey would be out with us. The way he used to stand it, was this. He would spend the most of his afternoons in bed. He would then come out fresh in the evening, ready to urge us on with his words, example, and frequently with the whip. Mr. Covey was one of the few slaveholders who could and did work with his hands. He was a hard-working man. He knew by himself just what a man or a boy could do. There was no deceiving him. His work went on in his absence almost as well as in his presence; and he had the faculty of making us feel that he was ever present with us. This he did by surprising us. He seldom approached the spot where we were at work openly, if he could do it secretly. He always aimed at taking us by surprise. Such was his cunning, that we used to call him, among ourselves, "the snake." When we were at work in the cornfield, he would sometimes crawl on his hands and knees to avoid detection, and all at once he would rise nearly in our midst, and scream out, "Ha, ha! Come, come! Dash on, dash on!" This being his mode of attack, it was never safe to stop a single minute. His comings were like a thief in the night. He appeared to us as being ever at hand. He was under every tree, behind every stump, in every bush, and at every window, on the plantation. He would sometimes mount his horse, as if bound to St. Michael's, a distance of seven miles, and in half an hour afterwards you would see him coiled up in the corner of the wood-fence, watching every motion of the slaves. He would, for this purpose, leave his horse tied up in the woods. Again, he would sometimes walk up to us, and give us orders as though he was upon the point of starting on a long journey, turn his back upon us, and make as though he was going to the house to get ready; and, before he would get half way thither, he would turn short and crawl into a fence-corner, or behind some tree, and there watch us till the going down of the sun.

Mr. Covey's *forte* consisted in his power to deceive. His life was devoted to planning and perpetrating the grossest deceptions. Every thing he possessed in the shape of learning or religion, he made conform to his disposition to deceive. He seemed to think himself equal to deceiving the Almighty. He would make a short prayer in the morning, and a long prayer at night; and, strange as it may seem, few men would at times appear more devotional than he. The exercises of his family devotions were always commenced with singing; and, as he was a very poor singer himself, the duty of raising the hymn generally came upon me. He would read his hymn, and nod at me to commence. I would at times do so; at others, I would not. My non-compliance would almost always produce much confusion. To show himself independent of me, he would start and stagger through with his hymn in the most discordant manner. In this state of mind, he prayed with more than ordinary spirit. Poor man! such was his disposition, and success at deceiving, I do verily believe that he sometimes deceived himself into the solemn belief, that he was a sincere worshipper of the most high God; and this, too, at a time when he may be said to have been guilty of compelling his woman slave to commit the sin of adultery. The facts in the case are these: Mr. Covey was a poor man; he was just commencing in life; he was only able to buy one slave; and, shocking as is the fact, he bought her, as he said, for *a breeder*. This woman was named Caroline. Mr. Covey bought her from Mr. Thomas Lowe, about six miles from St. Michael's. She was a large, able-bodied woman, about twenty years old. She had already given birth to one child, which proved her to be just what he wanted. After buying her, he hired a married man of Mr. Samuel Harrison, to live with him one year; and him he used to fasten up with her every night! The result was, that, at the end of the year, the miserable woman gave birth to twins. At this result Mr. Covey seemed to be highly pleased, both with the man and the wretched woman. Such was his joy, and that of his wife, that nothing they could do for Caroline during her confinement was too good, or too hard, to be done. The children were regarded as being quite an addition to his wealth.

If at any one time of my life more than another, I was made to drink the bitterest dregs of slavery, that time was during the first six months of my stay with Mr. Covey. We were worked in all weathers. It was never too hot or too cold; it could never rain, blow, hail, or snow, too hard for us to work in the field. Work, work, work, was scarcely more the order of the day than of the night. The longest days were too short for him, and the shortest nights too long for him. I was somewhat unmanageable when I first went there, but a few months of this discipline tamed me. Mr. Covey succeeded in breaking me. I was broken in body, soul, and spirit. My natural elasticity was crushed, my intellect languished, the disposition to read departed, the cheerful spark that lingered about my eye died; the dark night of slavery closed in upon me; and behold a man transformed into a brute!

Sunday was my only leisure time. I spent this in a sort of beast-like stupor, between sleep and wake, under some large tree. At times I would rise up, a flash of energetic freedom would dart through my soul, accompanied with a faint beam of hope, that flickered for a moment, and then vanished. I sank down again, mourning over my wretched condition. I was sometimes prompted to take my life, and that of Covey, but was prevented by a combination of hope and fear. My sufferings on this plantation seem now like a dream rather than a stern reality.

Our house stood within a few rods of the Chesapeake Bay, whose broad bosom was ever white with sails from every quarter of the habitable globe. Those beautiful vessels, robed in purest white, so delightful to the eye of freemen, were to me so many shrouded ghosts, to terrify and torment me with thoughts of my wretched condition. I have often, in the deep stillness of a summer's Sabbath, stood all alone upon the lofty banks of that noble bay, and traced, with saddened heart and tearful eye, the countless number of sails moving off to the mighty ocean. The sight of these always affected me powerfully. My thoughts would compel utterance; and there, with no audience but the Almighty, I would pour out my soul's complaint, in my rude way, with an apostrophe to the moving multitude of ships:—

"You are loosed from your moorings, and are free; I am fast in my chains, and am a slave! You move merrily before the gentle gale, and I sadly before the bloody whip! You are freedom's swift-winged angels, that fly round the world; I am confined in bands of iron! O that I were free! O, that I were on one of your gallant decks, and under your protecting wing! Alas! betwixt me and you, the turbid waters roll. Go on, go on. O that I could also go! Could I but swim! If I could fly! O, why was I born a man, of whom to make a brute! The glad ship is gone; she hides in the dim distance. I am left in the hottest hell of unending slavery. O God, save me! God, deliver me! Let me be free! Is there any God? Why am I a slave? I will run away. I will not stand it. Get caught, or get clear, I'll try it. I had as well die with ague as the fever. I have only one life to lose. I had as well be killed running as die standing. Only think of it; one hundred miles straight north, and I am free! Try it? Yes! God helping me, I will. It cannot be that I shall live and die a slave. I will take to the water. This very bay shall yet bear me into freedom. The steamboats steered in a north-east course from North Point. I will do the same; and when I get to the head of the bay, I will turn my canoe adrift, and walk straight through Delaware into Pennsylvania. When I get there, I shall not be required to have a pass; I can travel without being disturbed. Let but the first opportunity offer, and, come what will, I am off. Meanwhile, I will try to bear up under the yoke. I am not the only slave in the world. Why should I fret? I can bear as much as any of them. Besides, I am but a boy, and all boys are bound to some one. It may be that my misery in slavery will only increase my happiness when I get free. There is a better day coming."

Thus I used to think, and thus I used to speak to myself; goaded almost to madness at one moment, and at the next reconciling myself to my wretched lot.

I have already intimated that my condition was much worse, during the first six months of my stay at Mr. Covey's, than in the last six. The circumstances leading to the change in Mr. Covey's course toward me form an epoch in my humble history. You have seen how a man was made a slave; you shall see how a slave was made a man. On one of the hottest days of the month of August, 1833, Bill Smith, William Hughes, a slave named Eli, and myself, were engaged in fanning wheat. Hughes was clearing the fanned wheat from before the fan, Eli was turning, Smith was feeding, and I was carrying wheat to the fan. The work was simple, requiring strength rather than intellect; yet, to one entirely unused to such work, it came very hard. About three o'clock of that day, I broke down; my strength failed me; I was seized with a violent aching of the head, attended with extreme dizziness; I trembled in every limb. Finding what was coming, I nerved myself up, feeling it would never do to stop work. I stood as long as I could stagger to the hopper with grain. When I could stand no longer, I fell, and felt as if held down by an immense weight. The fan of course stopped; every one had his own work to do; and no one could do the work of the other, and have his own go on at the same time.

Mr. Covey was at the house, about one hundred yards from the treading-yard where we were fanning. On hearing the fan stop, he left immediately, and came to the spot where we were. He hastily inquired what the matter was. Bill answered that I was sick, and there was no one to bring wheat to the fan. I had by this time crawled away under the side of the post and rail-fence by which the yard was enclosed, hoping to find relief by getting out of the sun. He then asked where I was. He was told by one of the hands. He came to the spot, and, after looking at me awhile, asked me what was the matter. I told him as well as I could, for I scarce had strength to speak. He then gave me a savage kick in the side, and told me to get up. I tried to do so, but fell back in the attempt. He gave me another kick, and again told me to rise. I again tried, and succeeded in gaining my feet; but, stooping to get the tub with which I was feeding the fan, I again staggered and fell. While down in this situation, Mr. Covey took up the hickory slat with which Hughes had been striking off the half-bushel measure, and with it gave me a heavy blow upon the head, making a large wound, and the blood ran freely; and with this again told me to get up. I made no effort to comply, having now made up my mind to let him do his worst. In a short time after receiving this blow, my head grew better. Mr. Covey had now left me to my fate. At this moment I resolved, for the first time, to go to my master, enter a complaint, and ask his protection. In order to [do] this, I must that afternoon walk seven miles; and this, under the circumstances, was truly a severe undertaking. I was exceedingly feeble; made so as much by the kicks and blows which I received, as by the severe fit of sickness to which I had been subjected. I, however, watched my chance, while Covey was looking in an opposite direction, and started for St. Michael's. I succeeded in getting a considerable distance on my way to the woods, when Covey discovered me, and called after me to come back, threatening what he would do if I did not come. I disregarded both his calls and his threats, and made my way to the woods as fast as my feeble state would allow; and thinking I might be overhauled by him if I kept the road, I walked through the woods, keeping far enough from the road to avoid detection, and near enough to prevent losing my way I had not gone far before my little strength again failed me. I could go no farther. I fell down, and lay for a considerable time. The blood was yet oozing from the wound on my head. For a time I thought I should bleed to death; and think now that I should have done so, but that the blood so matted my hair as to stop the wound. After lying there about three quarters of an hour, I nerved myself up again, and started on my way, through bogs and briers, barefooted and bareheaded, tearing my feet sometimes at nearly every step; and after a journey of about seven miles, occupying some five hours to perform it, I arrived at master's store. I then presented an appearance enough to affect any but a heart of iron. From the crown of my head to my feet, I was covered with blood. My hair was all clotted with dust and blood; my shirt was stiff with blood. My legs and feet were torn in sundry places with briers and thorns, and were also covered with blood. I suppose I looked like a man who had escaped a den of wild beasts, and barely escaped them. In this state I appeared before my master, humbly entreating him to interpose his authority for my protection. I told him all the circumstances as well as I could, and it seemed, as I spoke, at times to affect him. He would then walk the floor, and seek to justify Covey by saying he expected I deserved it. He asked me what I wanted. I told him, to let me get a new home; that as sure as I lived with Mr. Covey again, I should live with but to die with him; that Covey would surely kill me; he was in a fair way for it. Master Thomas ridiculed the idea that there was any danger of Mr. Covey's killing me, and said that he knew Mr. Covey; that he was a good man, and that he could not think of taking me from him; that, should he do so, he would lose the whole year's wages; that I belonged to Mr. Covey for one year, and that I must go back to him, come what might; and that I must not trouble him with any more stories, or that he would himself *get hold of me.* After threatening me thus, he gave me a very large dose of salts, telling me that I might remain in St. Michael's that night, (it being quite late,) but that I must be off back to Mr. Covey's early in the morning; and that if I did not, he would *get hold of me,* which meant that he would whip me. I remained all night, and, according to his orders, I started off to Covey's in the morning, (Saturday morning,) wearied in body and broken in spirit. I got no supper that night, or breakfast that morning. I reached Covey's about nine o'clock; and just as I was getting over the fence that divided Mrs. Kemp's fields from ours, out ran Covey with his cowskin, to give me another whipping. Before he could reach me, I succeeded in getting to the cornfield; and as the corn was very high, it afforded me the means of hiding. He seemed very angry, and searched for me a long time. My behavior was altogether unaccountable. He finally gave up the chase, thinking, I suppose, that I must come home for something to eat; he would give himself no further trouble in looking for me. I spent that day mostly in the woods, having the alternative before me,—to go home and be whipped to death, or stay in the woods and be starved to death. That night, I fell in with Sandy Jenkins, a slave with whom I was somewhat acquainted. Sandy had a free wife who lived about four miles from Mr. Covey's; and it being Saturday, he was on his way to see her. I told him my circumstances, and he very kindly invited me to go home with him. I went home with him, and talked this whole matter over, and got his advice as to what course it was best for me to pursue. I found Sandy an old adviser. He told me, with great solemnity, I must go back to Covey; but that before I went, I must go with him into another part of the woods, where there was a certain *root*, which, if I would take some of it with me, carrying it *always on my right side,* would render it impossible for Mr. Covey, or any other white man, to whip me. He said he had carried it for years; and since he had done so, he had never received a blow, and never expected to while he carried it. I at first rejected the idea, that the simple carrying of a root in my pocket would have any such effect as he had said, and was not disposed to take it; but Sandy impressed the necessity with much earnestness, telling me it could do no harm, if it did no good. To please him, I at length took the root, and, according to his direction, carried it upon my right side. This was Sunday morning. I immediately started for home; and upon entering the yard gate, out came Mr. Covey on his way to meeting. He spoke to me very kindly, made me drive the pigs from a lot near by, and passed on towards the church. Now, this singular conduct of Mr. Covey really made me begin to think that there was something in the *root* which Sandy had given me; and had it been on any other day than Sunday, I could have attributed the conduct to no other cause than the influence of that root; and as it was, I was half inclined to think the *root* to be something more than I at first had taken it to be. All went well till Monday morning. On this morning, the virtue of the *root* was fully tested. Long before daylight, I was called to go and rub, curry, and feed, the horses. I obeyed, and was glad to obey. But whilst thus engaged, whilst in the act of throwing down some blades from the loft, Mr. Covey entered the stable with a long rope; and just as I was half out of the loft, he caught hold of my legs, and was about tying me. As soon as I found what he was up to, I gave a sudden spring, and as I did so, he holding to my legs, I was brought sprawling on the stable floor. Mr. Covey seemed now to think he had me, and could do what he pleased; but at this moment—from whence came the spirit I don't know—I resolved to fight; and, suiting my action to the resolution, I seized Covey hard by the throat; and as I did so, I rose. He held on to me, and I to him. My resistance was so entirely unexpected, that Covey seemed taken all aback. He trembled like a leaf. This gave me assurance, and I held him uneasy, causing the blood to run where I touched him with the ends of my fingers. Mr. Covey soon called out to Hughes for help. Hughes came, and, while Covey held me, attempted to tie my right hand. While he was in the act of doing so, I watched my chance, and gave him a heavy kick close under the ribs. This kick fairly sickened Hughes, so that he left me in the hands of Mr. Covey. This kick had the effect of not only weakening Hughes, but Covey also. When he saw Hughes bending over with pain, his courage quailed. He asked me if I meant to persist in my resistance. I told him I did, come what might; that he had used me like a brute for six months, and that I was determined to be used so no longer. With that, he strove to drag me to a stick that was lying just out of the stable door. He meant to knock me down. But just as he was leaning over to get the stick, I seized him with both hands by his collar, and brought him by a sudden snatch to the ground. By this time, Bill came. Covey called upon him for assistance. Bill wanted to know what he could do. Covey said, "Take hold of him, take hold of him!" Bill said his master hired him out to work, and not to help to whip me; so he left Covey and myself to fight our own battle out. We were at it for nearly two hours. Covey at length let me go, puffing and blowing at a great rate, saying that if I had not resisted, he would not have whipped me half so much. The truth was, that he had not whipped me at all. I considered him as getting entirely the worst end of the bargain; for he had drawn no blood from me, but I had from him. The whole six months afterwards, that I spent with Mr. Covey, he never laid the weight of his finger upon me in anger. He would occasionally say, he didn't want to get hold of me again. "No," thought I, "you need not; for you will come off worse than you did before."

This battle with Mr. Covey was the turning-point in my career as a slave. It rekindled the few expiring embers of freedom, and revived within me a sense of my own manhood. It recalled the departed self-confidence, and inspired me again with a determination to be free. The gratification afforded by the triumph was a full compensation for whatever else might follow, even death itself. He only can understand the deep satisfaction which I experienced, who has himself repelled by force the bloody arm of slavery. I felt as I never felt before. It was a glorious resurrection, from the tomb of slavery, to the heaven of freedom. My long-crushed spirit rose, cowardice departed, bold defiance took its place; and I now resolved that, however long I might remain a slave in form, the day had passed forever when I could be a slave in fact. I did not hesitate to let it be known of me, that the white man who expected to succeed in whipping, must also succeed in killing me. . . .

(Frederick Douglass's service to Mr. Covey ended on Christmas Day, 1833, four years after this encounter; Douglass was never whipped again, nor taken to the public whipping post as some slave owners did with slaves who dared to stand up to them. Douglass speculated that for Covey to do so would have cost him a tremendous loss of face as he prided himself on being a first-rate "Negro breaker." Douglass was sold to Mr. William Freeland, a much different master than Covey. Mr. Freeland owned two slaves, but all other hands were hired, including Douglass. While working for Freeland, Douglass taught others to read, and soon slaves from other plantations were attending classes. They studied in secret at St. Michael's, Maryland, allowing their masters to believe that they were spending Sundays wrestling, boxing, and drinking rather than reading and worshiping. A failed escape plan landed Douglass in the service of another master who placed him at the shipyards in Baltimore and took all of his weekly wages. Douglass, who was really William Bailey, planned a successful escape to New York and was then helped by persons there to go to New Bedford where he finally became a free man. His escape was aided by various changes in his name, his final being William Douglass, the name by which history now knows him.)

HENRY DAVID THOREAU

1817-1862

CIVIL DISOBEDIENCE

1849

Thoreau was the archetypal individualist. Born in Concord, Massachusetts, he graduated from Harvard in 1837 and wrote continuously for the rest of his life. Though some of his works were to become classics of American literature, he was never able to make a living from his writing. Intellectually, he was associated with the transcendentalist movement, and Ralph Waldo Emerson was his mentor and, for a time, his patron. Resistance to tyranny and living a life of freedom were, for him, not so much political matters but questions of how we live our lives from day to day by taking responsibility for our own thoughts and actions. The work presented here, "Civil Disobedience," was published in 1849. His famous *Walden*, the account of his retreat to a cabin in the woods, was published in 1854.

Selection from: Thoreau, Henry David. 1849. "Civil Disobedience." *The Maine Woods, Cape Cod, and Miscellanies.* Boston: Houghton Mifflin Company, 1929. (356-387)

CIVIL DISOBEDIENCE

I heartily accept the motto, "That government is best which governs least;" and I should like to see it acted up to more rapidly and systematically. Carried out, it finally amounts to this, which also I believe,—"That government is best which governs not at all;" and when men are prepared for it, that will be the kind of government which they will have. Government is at best but an expedient; but most governments are usually, and all governments are sometimes, inexpedient. The objections which have been brought against a standing army, and they are many and weighty, and deserve to prevail, may also at last be brought against a standing government. The standing army is only an arm of the standing government. The government itself, which is only the mode which the people have chosen to execute their will, is equally liable to be abused and perverted before the people can act through it. Witness the present Mexican war, the work of comparatively a few individuals using the standing government as their tool; for, in the outset, the people would not have consented to this measure.

This American government,—what is it but a tradition, though a recent one, endeavoring to transmit itself unimpaired to posterity, but each instant losing some of its integrity? It has not the vitality and force of a single living man; for a single man can bend it to his own. It is a sort of wooden gun to the people themselves. But it is not the less necessary for this; for the people must have some complicated machinery or other, and hear its din, to satisfy that idea of government which they have. Governments show thus how successfully men can be imposed on, even impose on themselves, for their own advantage. It is excellent, we must all allow. Yet this government never of itself furthered any enterprise, but by the alacrity with which it got out of its way. *It* does not keep the country free. *It* does not settle the West. *It* does not educate. The character inherent in the American people has done all that has been accomplished; and it would have done somewhat more, if the government had not sometimes got in its way. For government is an expedient by which men would fain succeed in letting one another alone; and, as has been said, when it is most expedient, the governed are most let alone by it. Trade and commerce, if they were not made of india-rubber, would never manage to bounce over the obstacles which legislators are continually putting in their way; and, if one were to judge these men wholly by the effects of their actions and not partly by their intentions, they would deserve to be classed and punished with those mischievous persons who put obstructions on the railroads.

But, to speak practically and as a citizen, unlike those who call themselves no-government men, I ask for, not at once no government, but *at once* a better government. Let every man make known what kind of government would command his respect, and that will be one step toward obtaining it.

After all, the practical reason why, when the power is once in the hands of the people, a majority are permitted, and for a long period continue, to rule is not because they are most likely to be in the right, nor because this seems fairest to the minority, but because they are physically the strongest. But a government in which the majority rule in all cases cannot be based on justice, even as far as men understand it. Can there not be a government in which majorities do not virtually decide right and wrong, but conscience?—in which majorities decide only those questions to which the rule of expediency is applicable? Must the citizen ever for a moment, or in the least degree, resign his conscience to the legislator? Why has every man a conscience, then? I think that we should be men first, and subjects afterward. It is not desirable to cultivate a respect for the law, so much as for the right. The only obligation which I have a right to assume is to do at any time what I think right. It is truly enough said that a corporation has no conscience; but a corporation of conscientious men is a corporation *with* a conscience. Law never made men a whit more just; and, by means of their respect for it, even the well-disposed are daily made the agents of injustice. A common and natural result of an undue respect for law is, that you may see a file of soldiers, colonel, captain, corporal, privates, powder-monkeys, and all, marching in admirable order over hill and dale to the wars, against their wills, ay, against their common sense and consciences, which makes it very steep marching indeed, and produces a palpitation of the heart. They have no doubt that it is a damnable business in which they are concerned; they are all peaceably inclined. Now, what are they? Men at all? or small movable forts and magazines, at the service of some unscrupulous man in power? Visit the Navy-Yard, and behold a marine, such a man as an American government can make, or such as it can make a man with its black arts,—a mere shadow and reminiscence of humanity, a man laid out alive and standing, and already, as one may say, buried under arms with funeral accompaniments, though it may be,—

> "Not a drum was heard, not a funeral note,
> As his corse to the rampart we hurried;
> Not a soldier discharged his farewell shot
> O'er the grave where our hero we buried."

The mass of men serve the state thus, not as men mainly, but as machines, with their bodies. They are the standing army, and the militia, jailors, constables, *posse comitatus*, etc. In most cases there is no free exercise whatever of the judgment or of the moral sense; but they put themselves on a level with wood and earth and stones; and wooden men can perhaps be manufactured that will serve the purpose as well. Such command no more respect than men of straw or a lump of dirt. They have the same sort of worth only as horses and dogs. Yet such as these even are commonly esteemed good citizens. Others—as most legislators, politicians, lawyers, ministers, and office-holders—serve the state chiefly with their heads; and, as they rarely make any moral distinctions, they are as likely to serve the devil, without *intending* it, as God. A very few—as heroes, patriots, martyrs, reformers in the great sense, and *men*—serve the state with their consciences also, and so necessarily resist it for the most part; and they are commonly treated as enemies by it. A wise man will only be useful as a man, and will not submit to be "clay," and "stop a hole to keep the wind away," but leave that office to his dust at least:—

> "I am too high-born to be propertied,
> To be a secondary at control,
> Or useful serving-man and instrument
> To any sovereign state throughout the world."

He who gives himself entirely to his fellow-men appears to them useless and selfish; but he who gives himself partially to them is pronounced a benefactor and philanthropist.

How does it become a man to behave toward this American government to-day? I answer, that he cannot without disgrace be associated with it. I cannot for an instant recognize that political organization as *my* government which is the *slave's* government also.

All men recognize the right of revolution; that is, the right to refuse allegiance to, and to resist, the government, when its tyranny or its inefficiency are great and unendurable. But almost all say that such is not the case now. But such was the case, they think, in the Revolution of '75. If one were to tell me that this was a bad government because it taxed certain foreign commodities brought to its ports, it is most probable that I should not make an ado about it, for I can do without them. All machines have their friction; and possibly this does enough good to counterbalance the evil. At any rate, it is a great evil to make a stir about it. But when the friction comes to have its machine, and oppression and robbery are organized, I say, let us not have such a machine any longer. In other words, when a sixth of the population of a nation which has undertaken to be the refuge of liberty are slaves, and a whole country is unjustly overrun and conquered by a foreign army, and subjected to military law, I think that it is not too soon for honest men to rebel and revolutionize. What makes this duty the more urgent is the fact that the country so overrun is not our own, but ours is the invading army.

Paley, a common authority with many on moral questions, in his chapter on the "Duty of Submission to Civil Government," resolves all civil obligation into expediency; and he proceeds to say that "so long as the interest of the whole society requires it, that is, so long as the established government cannot be resisted or changed without public inconveniency, it is the will of God . . . that the established government be obeyed,—and no longer. This principle being admitted, the justice of every particular case of resistance is reduced to a computation of the quantity of the danger and grievance on the one side, and of the probability and expense of redressing it on the other." Of this, he says, every man shall judge for himself. But Paley appears never to have contemplated those cases to which the rule of expediency does not apply, in which a people, as well as an individual, must do justice, cost what it may. If I have unjustly wrested a plank from a drowning man, I must restore it to him though I drown myself. This, according to Paley, would be inconvenient. But he that would save his life, in such a case, shall lose it. This people must cease to hold slaves, and to make war on Mexico, though it cost them their existence as a people.

In their practice, nations agree with Paley; but does any one think that Massachusetts does exactly what is right at the present crisis?

> "A drab of state, a cloth-o'-silver slut,
> To have her train borne up, and her soul
> trail in the dirt."

Practically speaking, the opponents to a reform in Massachusetts are not a hundred thousand politicians at the South, but a hundred thousand merchants and farmers here, who are more interested in commerce and agriculture than they are in humanity, and are not prepared to do justice to the slave and to Mexico, *cost what it may*. I quarrel not with far-off foes, but with those who, near at home, coöperate with, and do the bidding of, those far away, and without whom the latter would be harmless. We are accustomed to say, that the mass of men are unprepared; but improvement is slow, because the few are not materially wiser or better than the many. It is not so important that many should be as good as you, as that there be some absolute goodness somewhere; for that will leaven the whole lump. There are thousands who are *in opinion* opposed to slavery and to the war, who yet in effect do nothing to put an end to them; who, esteeming themselves children of Washington and Franklin, sit down with their hands in their pockets, and say that they know not what to do, and do nothing; who even postpone the question of freedom to the question of free-trade, and quietly read the prices-current along with the latest advices from Mexico, after dinner, and, it may be, fall asleep over them both. What is the price-current of an honest man and patriot to-day? They hesitate, and they regret, and sometimes they petition; but they do nothing in earnest and with effect. They will wait, well disposed, for others to remedy the evil, that they may no longer have it to regret. At most, they give only a cheap vote, and a feeble countenance and God-speed, to the right, as it goes by them. There are nine hundred and ninety-nine patrons of virtue to one virtuous man. But it is easier to deal with the real possessor of a thing than with the temporary guardian of it.

All voting is a sort of gaming, like checkers or backgammon, with a slight moral tinge to it, a playing with right and wrong, with moral questions; and betting naturally accompanies it. The character of the voters is not staked. I cast my vote, perchance, as I think right; but I am not vitally concerned that right should prevail. I am willing to leave it to the majority. Its obligation, therefore, never exceeds that of expediency. Even voting *for the right* is *doing* nothing for it. It is only expressing to men feebly your desire that it should prevail. A wise man will not leave the right to the mercy of chance, nor wish it to prevail through the power of the majority. There is but little virtue in the action of masses of men. When the majority shall at length vote for the abolition of slavery, it will be because they are indifferent to slavery, or because there is but little slavery left to be abolished by their vote. *They* will then be the only slaves. Only *his* vote can hasten the abolition of slavery who asserts his own freedom by his vote.

I hear of a convention to be held at Baltimore, or elsewhere, for the selection of a candidate for the Presidency, made up chiefly of editors, and men who are politicians by profession; but I think, what is it to any independent, intelligent, and respectable man what decision they may come to? Shall we not have the advantage of his wisdom and honesty, nevertheless? Can we not count upon some independent votes? Are there not many individuals in the country who do not attend conventions? But no: I find that the respectable man, so called, has immediately drifted from his position, and despairs of his country, when his country has more reason to despair of him. He forthwith adopts one of the candidates thus selected as the only *available* one, thus proving that he is himself *available* for any purposes of the demagogue. His vote is of no more worth than that of any unprincipled foreigner or hireling native, who may have been bought. O for a man who is a *man,* and, as my neighbor says, has a bone in his back which you cannot pass your hand through! Our statistics are at fault: the population has been returned too large. How many *men* are there to a square thousand miles in this country? Hardly one. Does not America offer any inducement for men to settle here? The American has dwindled into an Odd Fellow,—one who may be known by the development of his organ of gregariousness, and a manifest lack of intellect and cheerful self-reliance; whose first and chief concern, on coming into the world, is to see that the almshouses are in good repair; and, before yet he has lawfully donned the virile garb, to collect a fund for the support of the widows and orphans that may be; who, in short, ventures to live only by the aid of the Mutual Insurance company, which has promised to bury him decently.

It is not a man's duty, as a matter of course, to devote himself to the eradication of any, even the most enormous wrong; he may still properly have other concerns to engage him; but it is his duty, at least, to wash his hands of it, and, if he gives it no thought longer, not to give it practically his support. If I devote myself to other pursuits and contemplations, I must first see, at least, that I do not pursue them sitting upon another man's shoulders. I must get off him first, that he may pursue his contemplations too. See what gross inconsistency is tolerated. I have heard some of my townsmen say, "I should like to have them order me out to help put down an insurrection of the slaves, or to march to Mexico;—see if I would go;" and yet these very men have each, directly by their allegiance, and so indirectly, at least, by their money, furnished a substitute. The soldier is applauded who refuses to serve in an unjust war by those who do not refuse to sustain the unjust government which makes the war; is applauded by those whose own act and authority he disregards and sets at naught; as if the state were penitent to that degree that it hired one to scourge it while it sinned, but not to that degree that it left off sinning for a moment. Thus, under the name of Order and Civil Government, we are all made at last to pay homage to and support our own meanness. After the first blush of sin comes its indifference; and from immoral it becomes, as it were, *un*moral, and not quite unnecessary to that life which we have made.

The broadest and most prevalent error requires the most disinterested virtue to sustain it. The slight reproach to which the virtue of patriotism is commonly liable, the noble are most likely to incur. Those who, while they disapprove of the character and measures of a government, yield to it their allegiance and support are undoubtedly its most conscientious supporters, and so frequently the most serious obstacles to reform. Some are petitioning the State to dissolve the Union, to disregard the requisitions of the President. Why do they not dissolve it themselves,—the union between themselves and the State,—and refuse to pay their quota into its treasury? Do not they stand in the same relation to the State that the State does to the Union? And have not the same reasons prevented the State from resisting the Union which have prevented them from resisting the State?

How can a man be satisfied to entertain an opinion merely, and enjoy *it*? Is there any enjoyment in it, if his opinion is that he is aggrieved? If you are cheated out of a single dollar by your neighbor, you do not rest satisfied with knowing that you are cheated, or with saying that you are cheated, or even with petitioning him to pay you your due; but you take effectual steps at once to obtain the full amount, and see that you are never cheated again. Action from principle, the perception and the performance of right, changes things and relations; it is essentially revolutionary, and does not consist wholly with anything which was. It not only divides States and churches, it divides families; ay, it divides the *individual,* separating the diabolical in him from the divine.

Unjust laws exist: shall we be content to obey them, or shall we endeavor to amend them, and obey them until we have succeeded, or shall we transgress them at once? Men generally, under such a government as this, think that they ought to wait until they have persuaded the majority to alter them. They think that, if they should resist, the remedy would be worse than the evil. But it is the fault of the government itself that the remedy *is* worse than the evil. *It* makes it worse. Why is it not more apt to anticipate and provide for reform? Why does it not cherish its wise minority? Why does it cry and resist before it is hurt? Why does it not encourage its citizens to be on the alert to point out its faults, and *do* better than it would have them? Why does it always crucify Christ, and excommunicate Copernicus and Luther, and pronounce Washington and Franklin rebels?

One would think, that a deliberate and practical denial of its authority was the only offense never contemplated by government; else, why has it not assigned its definite, its suitable and proportionate, penalty? If a man who has no property refuses but once to earn nine shillings for the State, he is put in prison for a period unlimited by any law that I know, and determined only by the discretion of those who placed him there; but if he should steal ninety times nine shillings from the State, he is soon permitted to go at large again.

If the injustice is part of the necessary friction of the machine of government, let it go, let it go: perchance it will wear smooth,—certainly the machine will wear out. If the injustice has a spring, or a pulley, or a rope, or a crank, exclusively for itself, then perhaps you may consider whether the remedy will not be worse than the evil; but if it is of such a nature that it requires you to be the agent of injustice to another, then, I say, break the law. Let your life be a counter-friction to stop the machine. What I have to do is to see, at any rate, that I do not lend myself to the wrong which I condemn.

As for adopting the ways which the State has provided for remedying the evil, I know not of such ways. They take too much time, and a man's life will be gone. I have other affairs to attend to. I came into this world, not chiefly to make this a good place to live in, but to live in it, be it good or bad. A man has not everything to do, but something; and because he cannot do *everything,* it is not necessary that he should do *something* wrong. It is not my business to be petitioning the Governor or the Legislature any more than it is theirs to petition me; and if they should not hear my petition, what should I do then? But in this case the State has provided no way: its very Constitution is the evil. This may seem to be harsh and stubborn and unconciliatory; but it is to treat with the utmost kindness and consideration the only spirit that can appreciate or deserves it. So is all change for the better, like birth and death, which convulse the body.

I do not hesitate to say, that those who call themselves Abolitionists should at once effectually withdraw their support, both in person and property, from the government of Massachusetts, and not wait till they constitute a majority of one, before they suffer the right to prevail through them. I think that it is enough if they have God on their side, without waiting for that other one. Moreover, any man more right than his neighbors constitutes a majority of one already.

I meet this American government, or its representative, the State government, directly, and face to face, once a year—no more—in the person of its tax-gatherer; this is the only mode in which a man situated as I am necessarily meets it; and it then says distinctly, Recognize me; and the simplest, most effectual, and, in the present posture of affairs, the indispensablest mode of treating with it on this head, of expressing your little satisfaction with and love for it, is to deny it then. My civil neighbor, the tax-gatherer, is the very man I have to deal with,—for it is, after all, with men and not with parchment that I quarrel,—and he has voluntarily chosen to be an agent of the government. How shall he ever know well what he is and does as an officer of the government, or as a man, until he is obliged to consider whether he shall treat me, his neighbor, for whom he has respect, as a neighbor and well-disposed man, or as a maniac and disturber of the peace, and see if he can get over this obstruction to his neighborliness without a ruder and more impetuous thought or speech corresponding with his action. I know this well, that if one thousand, if one hundred, if ten men whom I could name,—if ten *honest* men only,—ay, if *one* HONEST man, in this State of Massachusetts, *ceasing to hold slaves,* were actually to withdraw from this copartnership, and be locked up in the county jail therefore [SIC], it would be the abolition of slavery in America. For it matters not how small the beginning may seem to be: what is once well done is done forever. But we love better to talk about it: that we say is our mission. Reform keeps many scores of newspapers in its service, but not one man. If my esteemed neighbor, the State's ambassador, who will devote his days to the settlement of the question of human rights in the Council Chamber, instead of being threatened with the prisons of Carolina, were to sit down the prisoner of Massachusetts, that State which is so anxious to foist the sin of slavery upon her sister,—though at present she can discover only an act of inhospitality to be the ground of a quarrel with her,—the Legislature would not wholly waive the subject the following winter.

Under a government which imprisons any unjustly, the true place for a just man is also a prison. The proper place to-day, the only place which Massachusetts has provided for her freer and less desponding spirits, is in her prisons, to be put out and locked out of the State by her own act, as they have already put themselves out by their principles. It is there that the fugitive slave, and the Mexican prisoner on parole, and the Indian come to plead the wrongs of his race should find them; on that separate, but more free and honorable, ground, where the State places those who are not *with* her, but *against* her,—the only house in a slave State in which a free man can abide with honor. If any think that their influence would be lost there, and their voices no longer afflict the ear of the State, that they would not be as an enemy within its walls, they do not know by how much truth is stronger than error, nor how much more eloquently and effectively he can combat injustice who has experienced a little in his own person. Cast your whole vote, not a strip of paper merely, but your whole influence. A minority is powerless while it conforms to the majority; it is not even a minority then; but it is irresistible when it clogs by its whole weight. If the alternative is to keep all just men in prison, or give up war and slavery, the State will not hesitate which to choose. If a thousand men were not to pay their tax-bills this year, that would not be a violent and bloody measure, as it would be to pay them, and enable the State to commit violence and shed innocent blood. This is, in fact, the definition of a peaceable revolution, if any such is possible. If the tax-gatherer, or any other public officer, asks me, as one has done, "But what shall I do?" my answer is, "If you really wish to do anything, resign your office." When the subject has refused allegiance, and the officer has resigned his office, then the revolution is accomplished. But even suppose blood should flow. Is there not a sort of blood shed when the conscience is wounded? Through this wound a man's real manhood and immortality flow out, and he bleeds to an everlasting death. I see this blood flowing now.

I have contemplated the imprisonment of the offender, rather than the seizure of his goods,—though both will serve the same purpose,—because they who assert the purest right, and consequently are most dangerous to a corrupt State, commonly have not spent much time in accumulating property. To such the State renders comparatively small service, and a slight tax is wont to appear exorbitant, particularly if they are obliged to earn it by special labor with their hands. If there were one who lived wholly without the use of money, the State itself would hesitate to demand it of him. But the rich man—not to make any invidious comparison—is always sold to the institution which makes him rich. Absolutely speaking, the more money, the less virtue; for money comes between a man and his objects, and obtains them for him; and it was certainly no great virtue to obtain it. It puts to rest many questions which he would otherwise be taxed to answer; while the only new question which it puts is the hard but superfluous one, how to spend it. Thus his moral ground is taken from under his feet. The opportunities of living are diminished in proportion as what are called the "means" are increased. The best thing a man can do for his culture when he is rich is to endeavor to carry out those schemes which he entertained when he was poor. Christ answered the Herodians according to their condition. "Show me the tribute-money," said he;—and one took a penny out of his pocket;—if you use money which has the image of Caesar on it, and which he has made current and valuable, that is, *if you are men of the State,* and gladly enjoy the advantages of Caesar's government, then pay him back some of his own when he demands it. "Render therefore to Caesar that which is Caesar's, and to God those things which are God's,"—leaving them no wiser than before as to which was which; for they did not wish to know.

When I converse with the freest of my neighbors, I perceive that, whatever they may say about the magnitude and seriousness of the question, and their regard for the public tranquillity, the long and the short of the matter is, that they cannot spare the protection of the existing government, and they dread the consequences to their property and families of disobedience to it. For my own part, I should not like to think that I ever rely on the protection of the State. But, if I deny the authority of the State when it presents its tax-bill, it will soon take and waste all my property, and so harass me and my children without end. This is hard. This makes it impossible for a man to live honestly, and at the same time comfortably, in outward respects. It will not be worth the while to accumulate property; that would be sure to go again. You must hire or squat somewhere, and raise but a small crop, and eat that soon. You must live within yourself, and depend upon yourself always tucked up and ready for a start, and not have many affairs. A man may grow rich in Turkey even, if he will be in all respects a good subject of the Turkish government. Confucius said: "If a state is governed by the principles of reason, poverty and misery are subjects of shame; if a state is not governed by the principles of reason, riches and honors are the subjects of shame." No: until I want the protection of Massachusetts to be extended to me in some distant Southern port, where my liberty is endangered, or until I am bent solely on building up an estate at home by peaceful enterprise, I can afford to refuse allegiance to Massachusetts, and her right to my property and life. It costs me less in every sense to incur the penalty of disobedience to the State than it would to obey. I should feel as if I were worth less in that case.

Some years ago, the State met me in behalf of the Church, and commanded me to pay a certain sum toward the support of a clergyman whose preaching my father attended, but never I myself. "Pay," it said, "or be locked up in the jail." I declined to pay. But, unfortunately, another man saw fit to pay it. I did not see why the schoolmaster should be taxed to support the priest, and not the priest the schoolmaster; for I was not the State's schoolmaster, but I supported myself by voluntary subscription. I did not see why the lyceum should not present its tax-bill, and have the State to back its demand, as well as the Church. However, at the request of the selectman, I condescended to make some such statement as this in writing:—"Know all men by these presents, that I, Henry Thoreau, do not wish to be regarded as a member of any incorporated society which I have not joined." This I gave to the town clerk; and he has it. The State, having thus learned that I did not wish to be regarded as a member of that church, has never made a like demand on me since; though it said that it must adhere to its original presumption that time. If I had known how to name them, I should then have signed off in detail from all the societies which I never signed on to; but I did not know where to find a complete list.

I have paid no poll-tax for six years. I was put into a jail once on this account, for one night; and, as I stood considering the walls of solid stone, two or three feet thick, the door of wood and iron, a foot thick, and the iron grating which strained the light, I could not help being struck with the foolishness of that institution which treated me as if I were mere flesh and blood and bones, to be locked up. I wondered that it should have concluded at length that this was the best use it could put me to, and had never thought to avail itself of my services in some way. I saw that, if there was a wall of stone between me and my townsmen, there was a still more difficult one to climb or break through before they could get to be as free as I was. I did not for a moment feel confined, and the walls seemed a great waste of stone and mortar. I felt as if I alone of all my townsmen had paid my tax. They plainly did not know how to treat me, but behaved like persons who are underbred. In every threat and in every compliment there was a blunder; for they thought that my chief desire was to stand the other side of that stone wall. I could not but smile to see how industriously they locked the door on my meditations, which followed them out again without let or hindrance, and *they* were really all that was dangerous. As they could not reach me, they had resolved to punish my body; just as boys, if they cannot come at some person against whom they have a spite, will abuse his dog. I saw that the State was half-witted, that it was timid as a lone woman with her silver spoons, and that it did not know its friends from its foes, and I lost all my remaining respect for it, and pitied it.

Thus the State never intentionally confronts a man's sense, intellectual or moral, but only his body, his senses. It is not armed with superior wit or honesty, but with superior physical strength. I was not born to be forced. I will breathe after my own fashion. Let us see who is the strongest. What force has a multitude? They only can force me who obey a higher law than I. They force me to become like themselves. I do not hear of *men* being *forced* to live this way or that by masses of men. What sort of life were that to live? When I meet a government which says to me, "Your money or your life," why should I be in haste to give it my money? It may be in a great strait, and not know what to do: I cannot help that. It must help itself; do as I do. It is not worth the while to snivel about it. I am not responsible for the successful working of the machinery of society. I am not the son of the engineer. I perceive that, when an acorn and a chestnut fall side by side, the one does not remain inert to make way for the other, but both obey their own laws, and spring and grow and flourish as best they can, till one, perchance, overshadows and destroys the other. If a plant cannot live according to its nature, it dies; and so a man.

The night in prison was novel and interesting enough. The prisoners in their shirt-sleeves were enjoying a chat and the evening air in the doorway, when I entered. But the jailer said, "Come, boys, it is time to lock up;" and so they dispersed, and I heard the sound of their steps returning into the hollow apartments. My room-mate was introduced to me by the jailer as "a first-rate fellow and a clever man." When the door was locked, he showed me where to hang my hat, and how he managed matters there. The rooms were whitewashed once a month; and this one, at least, was the whitest, most simply furnished, and probably the neatest apartment in the town. He naturally wanted to know where I came from, and what brought me there; and, when I had told him, I asked him in my turn how he came there, presuming him to be an honest man, of course; and, as the world goes, I believe he was. "Why," said he, "they accuse me of burning a barn; but I never did it." As near as I could discover, he had probably gone to bed in a barn when drunk, and smoked his pipe there; and so a barn was burnt. He had the reputation of being a clever man, had been there some three months waiting for his trial to come on, and would have to wait as much longer; but he was quite domesticated and contented, since he got his board for nothing, and thought that he was well treated.

He occupied one window, and I the other; and I saw that if one stayed there long, his principal business would be to look out the window. I had soon read all the tracts that were left there, and examined where former prisoners had broken out, and where a grate had been sawed off, and heard the history of the various occupants of that room; for I found that even here there was a history and a gossip which never circulated beyond the walls of the jail. Probably this is the only house in the town where verses are composed, which are afterward printed in a circular form, but not published. I was shown quite a long list of verses which were composed by some young men who had been detected in an attempt to escape, who avenged themselves by singing them.

I pumped my fellow-prisoner as dry as I could, for fear I should never see him again; but at length he showed me which was my bed, and left me to blow out the lamp.

It was like traveling into a far country, such as I had never expected to behold, to lie there for one night. It seemed to me that I never had heard the town-clock strike before, nor the evening sounds of the village; for we slept with the windows open, which were inside the grating. It was to see my native village in the light of the Middle Ages, and our Concord was turned into a Rhine stream, and visions of knights and castles passed before me. They were the voices of old burghers that I heard in the streets. I was an involuntary spectator and auditor of whatever was done and said in the kitchen of the adjacent village inn,—a wholly new and rare experience to me. It was a closer view of my native town. I was fairly inside of it. I never had seen its institutions before. This is one of its peculiar institutions; for it is a shire town. I began to comprehend what its inhabitants were about.

In the morning, our breakfasts were put through the hole in the door, in small oblong-square tin pans, made to fit, and holding a pint of chocolate, with brown bread, and an iron spoon. When they called for the vessels again, I was green enough to return what bread I had left; but my comrade seized it, and said that I should lay that up for lunch or dinner. Soon after he was let out to work at haying in a neighboring field, whither he went every day, and would not be back till noon; so he bade me good-day, saying that he doubted if he should see me again.

When I came out of prison,—for some one interfered, and paid that tax,—I did not perceive that great changes had taken place on the common, such as he observed who went in a youth and emerged a tottering and gray-headed man; and yet a change had to my eyes come over the scene,—the town, and State, and country,—greater than any that mere time could effect. I saw yet more distinctly the State in which I lived. I saw to what extent the people among whom I lived could be trusted as good neighbors and friends; that their friendship was for summer weather only; that they did not greatly propose to do right; that they were a distinct race from me by their prejudices and superstitions, as the Chinamen and Malays are; that in their sacrifices to humanity they ran no risks, not even to their property; that after all they were not so noble but they treated the thief as he had treated them, and hoped, by a certain outward observance and a few prayers, and by walking in a particular straight though useless path from time to time, to save their souls. This may be to judge my neighbors harshly; for I believe that many of them are not aware that they have such an institution as the jail in their village.

It was formerly the custom in our village, when a poor debtor came out of jail, for his acquaintances to salute him, looking through their fingers, which were crossed to represent the grating of a jail window, "How do ye do?" My neighbors did not thus salute me, but first looked at me, and then at one another, as if I had returned from a long journey. I was put into jail as I was going to the shoemaker's to get a shoe which was mended. When I was let out the next morning, I proceeded to finish my errand, and, having put on my mended shoe, joined a huckleberry party, who were impatient to put themselves under my conduct; and in half an hour,—for the horse was soon tackled,—was in the midst of a huckleberry field, on one of our highest hills, two miles off, and then the State was nowhere to be seen.

This is the whole history of "My Prisons."

I have never declined paying the highway tax, because I am as desirous of being a good neighbor as I am of being a bad subject; and as for supporting schools, I am doing my part to educate my fellow-countrymen now. It is for no particular item in the tax-bill that I refuse to pay it. I simply wish to refuse allegiance to the State, to withdraw and stand aloof from it effectually. I do not care to trace the course of my dollar, if I could, till it buys a man or a musket to shoot with,—the dollar is innocent,—but I am concerned to trace the effects of my allegiance. In fact, I quietly declare war with the State, after my fashion, though I will still make what use and get what advantage of her I can, as is usual in such cases.

If others pay the tax which is demanded of me, from a sympathy with the State, they do but what they have already done in their own case, or rather they abet injustice to a greater extent than the State requires. If they pay the tax from a mistaken interest in the individual taxed, to save his property, or prevent his going to jail, it is because they have not considered wisely how far they let their private feelings interfere with the public good.

This, then, is my position at present. But one cannot be too much on his guard in such a case, lest his action be biased by obstinacy or an undue regard for the opinions of men. Let him see that he does only what belongs to himself and to the hour.

I think sometimes, Why, this people mean well, they are only ignorant; they would do better if they knew how: why give your neighbors this pain to treat you as they are not inclined to? But I think again, This is no reason why I should do as they do, or permit others to suffer much greater pain of a different kind. Again, I sometimes say to myself, When many millions of men, without heat, without ill will, without personal feeling of any kind, demand of you a few shillings only, without the possibility, such is their constitution, of retracting or alerting their present demand, and without the possibility, on your side, of appeal to any other millions, why expose yourself to this overwhelming brute force? You do not resist cold and hunger, the winds and the waves, thus obstinately; you quietly submit to a thousand similar necessities. You do not put your head into the fire. But just in proportion as I regard this as not wholly a brute force, but partly a human force, and consider that I have relations to those millions as to so many millions of men, and not of mere brute or inanimate things, I see that appeal is possible, first and instantaneously, from them to the Maker of them, and, secondly, from them to themselves. But if I put my head deliberately into the fire, there is no appeal to fire or to the Maker of fire, and I have only myself to blame. If I could convince myself that I have any right to be satisfied with men as they are, and to treat them accordingly, and not according, in some respects, to my requisitions and expectations of what they and I ought to be, then, like a good Mussulman and fatalist, I should endeavor to be satisfied with things as they are, and say it is the will of God. And, above all, there is this difference between resisting this and a purely brute or natural force, that I can resist this with some effect; but I cannot expect, like Orpheus, to change the nature of the rocks and trees and beasts.

I do not wish to quarrel with any man or nation. I do not wish to split hairs, to make fine distinctions, or set myself up as better than my neighbors. I seek rather, I may say, even an excuse for conforming to the laws of the land. I am but too ready to conform to them. Indeed, I have reason to suspect myself on this head; and each year, as the tax-gatherer comes round, I find myself disposed to review the acts and position of the general and State governments, and the spirit of the people, to discover a pretext for conformity.

> "We must affect our country as our parents,
> And if at any time we alienate
> Our love or industry from doing it honor,
> We must respect effects and teach the soul
> Matter of conscience and religion,
> And not desire of rule or benefit."

I believe that the State will soon be able to take all my work of this sort out of my hands, and then I shall be no better a patriot than my fellow-countrymen. Seen from a lower point of view, the Constitution, with all its faults, is very good; the law and the courts are very respectable; even this State and this American government are, in many respects, very admirable, and rare things, to be thankful for, such as a great many have described them; but seen from a point of view a little higher, they are what I have described them; seen from a higher still, and the highest, who shall say what they are, or that they are worth looking at or thinking of at all?

However, the government does not concern me much, and I shall bestow the fewest possible thoughts on it. It is not many moments that I live under a government, even in this world. If a man is thought-free, fancy-free, imagination-free, that which *is not* never for a long time appearing *to be* to him, unwise rulers or reformers cannot fatally interrupt him.

I know that most men think differently from myself; but those whose lives are by profession devoted to the study of these or kindred subjects content me as little as any. Statesmen and legislators, standing so completely within the institution, never distinctly and nakedly behold it. They speak of moving society, but have no resting-place without it. They may be men of a certain experience and discrimination, and have no doubt invented ingenious and even useful systems, for which we sincerely thank them; but all their wit and usefulness lie within certain not very wide limits. They are wont to forget that the world is not governed by policy and expediency. Webster never goes behind government, and so cannot speak with authority about it. His words are wisdom to those legislators who contemplate no essential reform in the existing government; but for thinkers, and those who legislate for all time, he never once glances at the subject. I know of those whose serene and wise speculations on this theme would soon reveal the limits of his mind's range and hospitality. Yet, compared with the cheap professions of most reformers, and the still cheaper wisdom and eloquence of politicians in general, his are almost the only sensible and valuable words, and we thank Heaven for him. Comparatively, he is always strong, original, and, above all, practical. Still, his quality is not wisdom, but prudence. The lawyer's truth is not Truth, but consistency or a consistent expediency. Truth is always in harmony with herself, and is not concerned chiefly to reveal the justice that may consist with wrong-doing. He well deserves to be called, as he has been called, the Defender of the Constitution. There are really no blows to be given by him but defensive ones. He is not a leader, but a follower. His leaders are the men of '87. "I have never made an effort," he says, "and never propose to make an effort; I have never countenanced an effort, and never mean to countenance an effort, to disturb the arrangement as originally made, by which the various States came into the Union." Still thinking of the sanction which the Constitution gives to slavery, he says, "Because it was a part of the original compact,—let it stand." Notwithstanding his special acuteness and ability, he is unable to take a fact out of its merely political relations, and behold it as it lies absolutely to be disposed of by the intellect,—what, for instance, it behooves a man to do here in America to-day with regard to slavery,—but ventures, or is driven, to make some such desperate answer as the following, while professing to speak absolutely, and as a private man,—from which what new and singular code of social duties might be inferred? "The manner," says he, "in which the governments of those States where slavery exists are to regulate it is for their own consideration, under their responsibility to their constituents, to the general laws of propriety, humanity, and justice, and to God. Associations formed elsewhere, springing from a feeling of humanity, or other cause, have nothing whatever to do with it. They have never received any encouragement from me, and they never will."[1]

They who know of no purer sources of truth, who have traced up its stream no higher, stand, and wisely stand, by the Bible and the Constitution, and drink at it there with reverence and humility; but they who behold where it comes trickling into this lake or that pool, gird up their loins once more, and continue their pilgrimage toward its fountain-head.

No man with a genius for legislation has appeared in America. They are rare in the history of the world. There are orators, politicians, and eloquent men, by the thousand; but the speaker has not yet opened his mouth to speak who is capable of settling the much-vexed questions of the day. We love eloquence for its own sake, and not for any truth which it may utter, or any heroism it may inspire. Our legislators have not yet learned the comparative value of free trade and of freedom, of union, and of rectitude, to a nation. They have no genius or talent for comparatively humble questions of taxation and finance, commerce and

---

1 These extracts have been inserted since the lecture was read.

manufactures and agriculture. If we were left solely to the wordy wit of legislators in Congress for our guidance, uncorrected by the seasonable experience and the effectual complaints of the people, America would not long retain her rank among the nations. For eighteen hundred years, though perchance I have no right to say it, the New Testament has been written; yet where is the legislator who has wisdom and practical talent enough to avail himself of the light which it sheds on the science of legislation?

The authority of government, even such as I am willing to submit to,—for I will cheerfully obey those who know and can do better than I, and in many things even those who neither know nor can do so well,—is still an impure one: to be strictly just, it must have the sanction and consent of the governed. It can have no pure right over my person and property but what I concede to it. The progress from an absolute to a limited monarchy, from a limited monarchy to a democracy, is a progress toward a true respect for the individual. Even the Chinese philosopher was wise enough to regard the individual as the basis of the empire. Is a democracy, such as we know it, the last improvement possible in government? It is not possible to take a step further towards recognizing and organizing the rights of man? There will never be a really free and enlightened State until the State comes to recognize the individual as a higher and independent power, from which all its own power and authority are derived, and treats him accordingly. I please myself with imagining a State at last which can afford to be just to all men, and to treat the individual with respect as a neighbor; which even would not think it inconsistent with its own repose if a few were to live aloof from it, not meddling with it, nor embraced by it, who fulfilled all the duties of neighbors and fellow-men. A State which bore this kind of fruit, and suffered it to drop off as fast as it ripened, would prepare the way for a still more perfect and glorious State, which also I have imagined, but not yet anywhere seen.

DR. MARTIN LUTHER KING JR.

1929-1968

LETTER FROM BIRMINGHAM JAIL[1]

1963

In April and May of 1963, Dr. King led demonstrations by thousands of African Americans against racial segregation, especially as it was practiced in Birmingham. The first demonstrations were broken up by police using high-pressure fire hoses and police dogs. Photographs of this outraged national public opinion against the Alabama authorities. King continued the demonstrations even after a court order banned them, and he was arrested. A group of leading white clergymen asked him to stop the demonstrations. His letter was a response to them and became the spark that set off demonstrations across the South.

Source: "Letter from Birmingham Jail," Frequently Requested Documents. *http://www.stanford,edu/group/king/frequentlydocs/birmingham.pdf*

---

1 Reprinted by arrangement with the Estate of Martin Luther King, Jr., c/o Writers House as agent for the proprietor New York, NY. *Copyright 1963 Martin Luther King, Jr., copyright renewed 1991 Coretta Scott King.*

LETTER FROM BIRMINGHAM JAIL

April 16, 1963

My Dear Fellow Clergymen:

While confined here in the Birmingham city jail, I came across your recent statement calling my present activities "unwise and untimely." Seldom do I pause to answer criticism of my work and ideas. If I sought to answer all the criticisms that cross my desk, my secretaries would have little time for anything other than such correspondence in the course of the day, and I would have no time for constructive work. But since I feel that you are men of genuine good will and that your criticisms are sincerely set forth, I want to try to answer your statements in what I hope will be patient and reasonable terms.

I think I should indicate why I am here in Birmingham, since you have been influenced by the view which argues against "outsiders coming in." I have the honor of serving as president of the Southern Christian Leadership Conference, an organization operating in every southern state, with headquarters in Atlanta, Georgia. We have some eighty-five affiliated organizations across the South, and one of them is the Alabama Christian Movement for Human Rights. Frequently we share staff, educational and financial resources with our affiliates. Several months ago the affiliate here in Birmingham asked us to be on call to engage in a nonviolent direct-action program if such were deemed necessary. We readily consented, and when the hour came we lived up to our promise. So I, along with several members of my staff, am here because I was invited here I am here because I have organizational ties here.

But more basically, I am in Birmingham because injustice is here. Just as the prophets of the eighth century B.C. left their villages and carried their "thus saith the Lord" far beyond the boundaries of their home towns, and just as the Apostle Paul left his village of Tarsus and carried the gospel of Jesus Christ to the far corners of the Greco-Roman world, so am I compelled to carry the gospel of freedom beyond my own home town. Like Paul, I must constantly respond to the Macedonian call for aid.

Moreover, I am cognizant of the interrelatedness of all communities and states. I cannot sit idly by in Atlanta and not be concerned about what happens in Birmingham. Injustice anywhere is a threat to justice everywhere. We are caught in an inescapable network of mutuality, tied in a single garment of destiny. Whatever affects one directly, affects all indirectly. Never again can we afford to live with the narrow, provincial "outside agitator" idea. Anyone who lives inside the United States can never be considered an outsider anywhere within its bounds.

You deplore the demonstrations taking place in Birmingham. But your statement, I am sorry to say, fails to express a similar concern for the conditions that brought about the demonstrations. I am sure that none of you would want to rest content with the superficial kind of social analysis that deals merely with effects and does not grapple with underlying causes. It is unfortunate that demonstrations are taking place in Birmingham, but it is even more unfortunate that the city's white power structure left the Negro community with no alternative.

In any nonviolent campaign there are four basic steps: collection of the facts to determine whether injustices exist; negotiation; self-purification; and direct action. We have gone through all these steps in Birmingham. There can be no gainsaying the fact that racial injustice engulfs this community. Birmingham is probably the most thoroughly segregated city in the United States. Its ugly record of brutality is widely known. Negroes have experienced grossly unjust treatment in the courts. There have been more unsolved bombings of Negro homes and churches in

Birmingham than in any other city in the nation. These are the hard, brutal facts of the case. On the basis of these conditions, Negro leaders sought to negotiate with the city fathers. But the latter consistently refused to engage in good-faith negotiation.

Then, last September, came the opportunity to talk with leaders of Birmingham's economic community. In the course of the negotiations, certain promises were made by the merchants—for example, to remove the store's humiliating racial signs. On the basis of these promises, the Reverend Fred Shuttlesworth and the leaders of the Alabama Christian Movement for Human Rights agreed to a moratorium on all demonstrations. As the weeks and months went by, we realized that we were the victims of a broken promise. A few signs, briefly removed, returned; the others remained.

As in so many past experiences, our hopes had been blasted, and the shadow of deep disappointment settled upon us. We had no alternative except to prepare for direct action, whereby we would present our very bodies as a means of laying our case before the conscience of the local and the national community. Mindful of the difficulties involved, we decided to undertake a process of self-purification. We began a series of workshops on nonviolence, and we repeatedly asked ourselves: "Are you able to accept blows without retaliating" "Are you able to endure the ordeal of jail?" We decided to schedule our direct-action program for the Easter season, realizing that except for Christmas, this is the main shopping period of the year. Knowing that a strong economic withdrawal program would be the by-product of direct action, we felt that this would be the best time to bring pressure to bear on the merchants for the needed change.

Then it occurred to us that Birmingham's mayoralty election was coming up in March, and we speedily decided to postpone action until after election day. When we discovered that the Commissioner of Public Safety, Eugene "Bull" Connor, had piled up enough votes to be in the run-off, we decided again to postpone action until the day after the run-off so that the demonstrations could not be used to cloud the issues. Like many others, we waited to see Mr. Connor defeated, and to this end we endured postponement after postponement. Having aided in this community need, we felt that our direct-action program could be delayed no longer.

You may well ask: "Why direct action? Why sit-ins, marches and so forth? Isn't negotiation a better path?" You are quite right in calling for negotiation. Indeed, this is the very purpose of direct action. Nonviolent direct action seeks to create such a crisis and foster such a tension that a community which has constantly refused to negotiate is forced to confront the issue. It seeks so to dramatize the issue that it can no longer be ignored. My citing the creation of tension as part of the work of the nonviolent-resister may sound rather shocking. But I must confess that I am not afraid of the word "tension." I have earnestly opposed violent tension, but there is a type of constructive, nonviolent tension which is necessary for growth. Just as Socrates felt that it was necessary to create a tension in the mind so that individuals could rise from the bondage of myths and half-truths to the unfettered realm of creative analysis and objective appraisal, so must we see the need for nonviolent gadflies to create the kind of tension in society that will help men rise from the dark depths of prejudice and racism to the majestic heights of understanding and brotherhood.

The purpose of our direct-action program is to create a situation so crisis-packed that it will inevitably open the door to negotiation. I therefore concur with you in your call for negotiation. Too long has our beloved Southland been bogged down in a tragic effort to live in monologue rather than dialogue.

One of the basic points in your statement is that the action that I and my associates have taken in Birmingham is untimely. Some have asked: "Why didn't you give the new city administration time to act?" The only answer that I can give to this query is that the new Birmingham administration must be prodded about as much as the outgoing one, before it will act. We are sadly mistaken if we feel that the election of Albert Boutwell as mayor will bring the millennium to Birmingham. While Mr. Boutwell is a much more gentle person than Mr. Connor, they are both segregationists, dedicated to maintenance of the status quo. I have hope that Mr. Boutwell will be reasonable enough to see the futility of massive resistance to desegregation. But he will not see this without pressure from devotees of civil rights. My friends, I must say to you that we have not made a single gain in civil rights without determined legal and nonviolent pressure. Lamentably, it is an historical fact that privileged groups seldom give up their privileges voluntarily. Individuals may see the moral light and voluntarily give up their unjust posture; but, as Reinhold Niebuhr has reminded us, groups tend to be more immoral than individuals.

We know through painful experience that freedom is never voluntarily given by the oppressor; it must be demanded by the oppressed. Frankly, I have yet to engage in a direct-action campaign that was "well timed" in the view of those who have not suffered unduly from the disease of segregation. For years now I have heard the word "Wait!"It rings in the ear of every Negro with piercing familiarity. This "Wait" has almost always meant "Never." We must come to see, with one of our distinguished jurists, that "justice too long delayed is justice denied."

We have waited for more than 340 years for our constitutional and God-given rights. The nations of Asia and Africa are moving with jetlike speed toward gaining political independence but we still creep at horse-and-buggy pace toward gaining a cup of coffee at a lunch counter. Perhaps it is easy for those who have never felt the stinging darts of segregation to say, "Wait." But when you have seen vicious mobs lynch your mothers and fathers at will and drown your sisters and brothers at whim; when you have seen hate-filled policemen curse, kick and even kill your black brothers and sisters; when you see the vast majority of your twenty million Negro brothers smothering in an airtight cage of poverty in the midst of an affluent society; when you suddenly find your tongue twisted and your speech stammering as you seek to explain to your six-year-old daughter why she can't go to the public amusement park that has just been advertised on television, and see tears welling up in her eyes when she is told that Funtown is closed to colored children, and see ominous clouds of inferiority beginning to form in her little mental sky, and see her beginning to distort her personality by developing an unconscious bitterness toward white people; when you have to concoct an answer for a five-year-old son who is asking: "Daddy, why do white people treat colored people so mean?"; when you take a cross-country drive and find it necessary to sleep night after night in the uncomfortable corners of your automobile because no motel will accept you; when you are humiliated day in and day out by nagging signs reading "white" and "colored"; when your first name becomes "nigger," your middle name becomes "boy" (however old you are) and your last name becomes "John," and your wife and mother are never given the respected title "Mrs."; when you are harried by day and haunted by night by the fact that you are a Negro, living constantly at tiptoe stance, never quite knowing what to expect next, and are plagued with inner fears and outer resentments; when you are forever fighting a degenerating sense of "nobodiness"—then you will understand why we find it difficult to wait. There comes a time when the cup of endurance runs over, and men are no longer willing to be plunged into the abyss of despair. I hope, sirs, you can understand our legitimate and unavoidable impatience.

You express a great deal of anxiety over our willingness to break laws. This is certainly a legitimate concern. Since we so diligently urge people to obey the Supreme Court's decision of 1954 outlawing segregation in the public schools, at first glance it may seem rather paradoxical for us consciously to break laws. One may well ask: "How can you advocate breaking some laws and obeying others?" The answer lies in the fact that there are two types of laws: just and unjust. I would be the first to advocate obeying just laws. One has not only a legal but a moral responsibility to obey just laws. Conversely, one has a moral responsibility to disobey unjust laws. I would agree with St. Augustine that "an unjust law is no law at all."

Now, what is the difference between the two? How does one determine whether a law is just or unjust? A just law is a man-made code that squares with the moral law or the law of God. An unjust law is a code that is out of harmony with the moral law. To put it in the terms of St. Thomas Aquinas: An unjust law is a human law that is not rooted in eternal law and natural law. Any law that uplifts human personality is just. Any law that degrades human personality is unjust. All segregation statutes are unjust because segregation distorts the soul and damages the personality. It gives the segregator a false sense of superiority and the segregated a false sense of inferiority. Segregation, to use the terminology of the Jewish philosopher Martin Buber, substitutes an "I-it" relationship for an "I-thou" relationship and ends up relegating persons to the status of things. Hence segregation is not only politically, economically and sociologically unsound, it is morally wrong and sinful. Paul Tillich has said that sin is separation. Is not segregation an existential expression of man's tragic separation, his awful estrangement, his terrible sinfulness? Thus it is that I can urge men to obey the 1954 decision of the Supreme Court, for it is morally right; and I can urge them to disobey segregation ordinances, for they are morally wrong.

Let us consider a more concrete example of just and unjust laws. An unjust law is a code that a numerical or power majority group compels a minority group to obey but does not make binding on itself. This is *difference* made legal. By the same token, a just law is a code that a majority compels a minority to follow and that it is willing to follow itself. This is *sameness* made legal.

Let me give another explanation. A law is unjust if it is inflicted on a minority that, as a result of being denied the right to vote, had no part in enacting or devising the law. Who can say that the legislature of Alabama which set up that state's segregation laws was democratically elected? Throughout Alabama all sorts of devious methods are used to prevent Negroes from becoming registered voters, and there are some counties in which, even though Negroes constitute a majority of the population, not a single Negro is registered. Can any law enacted under such circumstances be considered democratically structured?

Sometimes a law is just on its face and unjust in its application. For instance, I have been arrested on a charge of parading without a permit. Now, there is nothing wrong in having an ordinance which requires a permit for a parade. But such an ordinance becomes unjust when it is used to maintain segregation and to deny citizens the First-Amendment privilege of peaceful assembly and protest.

I hope you are able to see the distinction I am trying to point out. In no sense do I advocate evading or defying the law, as would the rabid segregationist. That would lead to anarchy, one who breaks an unjust law must do so openly, lovingly, and with a willingness to accept the penalty. I submit that an individual who breaks a law that conscience tells him is unjust, and who willingly accepts the penalty of imprisonment in order to arouse the conscience of the community over its injustice, is in reality expressing the highest respect for law.

Of course, there is nothing new about this kind of civil disobedience. It was evidenced sublimely in the refusal of Shadrach, Meshach and Abednego to obey the laws of Nebuchadnezzar, on the ground that a higher moral law was at stake. It was practiced superbly by the early Christians, who were willing to face hungry lions and the excruciating pain of chopping blocks rather than submit to certain unjust laws of the Roman Empire. To a degree, academic freedom is reality today because Socrates practiced civil disobedience. In our own nation, the Boston Tea Party represented a massive act of civil disobedience.

We should never forget that everything Adolf Hitler did in Germany was "legal" and everything the Hungarian freedom fighters did in Hungary was "illegal." It was "illegal" to aid and comfort a Jew in Hitler's Germany. Even so, I am sure that had I lived in Germany at the time, I would have aided and comforted my Jewish brothers. If today I lived in a Communist country where certain principles dear to the Christian faith are suppressed, I would openly advocate disobeying that country's antireligious laws.

I must make two honest confessions to you, my Christian and Jewish brothers. First, I must confess that over the past few years I have been gravely disappointed with the white moderate. I have almost reached the regrettable conclusion that the Negro's great stumbling block in his stride toward freedom is not the White Citizen's Counciler or the Ku Klux Klanner, but the white moderate, who is more devoted to "order" than to justicc; who prefers a negative peace which is the absence of tension to a positive peace which is the presence of justice; who constantly says: "I agree with you in the goal you seek, but I cannot agree with your methods of direct action"; who paternalistically believes he can set the timetable for another man's freedom; who lives by a mythical concept of time and who constantly advises the Negro to wait for a "more convenient season." Shallow understanding from people of good will is more frustrating than absolute misunderstanding from people of ill will. Lukewarm acceptance is much more bewildering than outright rejection.

I had hoped that the white moderate would understand that law and order exist for the purpose of establishing justice and that when they fail in this purpose they become the dangerously structured dams that block the flow of social progress. I had hoped that the white moderate would understand that the present tension in the South is a necessary phase of the transition from an obnoxious negative peace, in which the Negro passively accepted his unjust plight, to a substantive and positive peace, in which all men will respect the dignity and worth of human personality. Actually, we who engage in nonviolent direct action are not the creators of tension. We merely bring to the surface the hidden tension that is already alive. We bring it out in the open, where it can be seen and dealt with. Like a boil that can never be cured so long as it is covered up but must be opened with all its ugliness to the natural medicines of air and light, injustice must be exposed, with all the tension its exposure creates, to the light of human conscience and the air of national opinion before it can be cured.

In your statement you assert that our actions, even though peaceful, must be condemned because they precipitate violence. But is this a logical assertion? Isn't this like condemning a robbed man because his possession of money precipitated the evil act of robbery? Isn't this like condemning Socrates because his unswerving commitment to truth and his philosophical inquiries precipitated the act by the misguided populace in which they made him drink hemlock. Isn't this like condemning Jesus because his unique God-consciousness and never-ceasing devotion to God's will precipitated the evil act of crucifixion? We must come to see that, as the federal courts have consistently affirmed, it is wrong to urge an individual to cease his efforts to gain his basic constitutional rights because the quest may precipitate violence. Society must protect the robbed and punish the robber.

I had also hoped that the white moderate would reject the myth concerning time in relation to the struggle for freedom. I have just received a letter from a white brother in Texas. He writes: "All Christians know that the colored people will receive equal rights eventually, but it is possible that you are in too great a religious hurry. It has taken Christianity almost two thousand years to accomplish what it has. The teachings of Christ take time to come to earth." Such an attitude stems from a tragic misconception of time, from the strangely irrational notion that there is something in the very flow of time that will inevitably cure all ills. Actually, time itself is neutral; it can be used either destructively or constructively. More and more I feel that the people of ill will have used time much more effectively than have the people of good will. We will have to repent in this generation not merely for the hateful words and actions of the bad people but for the appalling silence of the good people. Human progress never rolls in on wheels of inevitability; it comes through the tireless efforts of men willing to be co-workers with God, and without this hard work, time itself becomes an ally of the forces of social stagnation. We must use time creatively, in the knowledge that the time is always ripe to do right. Now is the time to make real the promise of democracy and transform our pending national elegy into a creative psalm of brotherhood. Now is the time to lift our national policy from the quicksand of racial injustice to the solid rock of human dignity.

You speak of our activity in Birmingham as extreme. At first I was rather disappointed that fellow clergymen would see my nonviolent efforts as those of an extremist. I began thinking about the fact that I stand in the middle of two opposing forces in the Negro community. One is a force of complacency, made up in part of Negroes who, as a result of long years of oppression, are so drained of self-respect and a sense of "somebodiness" that they have adjusted to segregation; and in part of a few middle-class Negroes who, because of a degree of academic and economic security and because in some ways they profit by segregation, have become insensitive to the problems of the masses. The other force is one of bitterness and hatred, and it comes perilously close to advocating violence. It is expressed in the various black nationalist groups that are springing up across the nation, the largest and best-known being Elijah Muhammad's Muslim movement. Nourished by the Negro's frustration over the continued existence of racial discrimination, this movement is made up of people who have lost faith in America, who have absolutely repudiated Christianity, and who have concluded that the white man is an incorrigible "devil."

I have tried to stand between these two forces, saying that we need emulate neither the "do-nothingism" of the complacent nor the hatred and despair of the black nationalist. For there is the more excellent way of love and nonviolent protest. I am grateful to God that, through the influence of the Negro church, the way of nonviolence became an integral part of our struggle.

If this philosophy had not emerged, by now many streets of the South would, I am convinced, be flowing with blood. And I am further convinced that if our white brothers dismiss as "rabble-rousers" and "outside agitators" those of us who employ nonviolent direct action, and if they refuse to support our nonviolent efforts, millions of Negroes will, out of frustration and despair, seek solace and security in black-nationalist ideologies—a development that would inevitably lead to a frightening racial nightmare.

Oppressed people cannot remain oppressed forever. The yearning for freedom eventually manifests itself, and that is what has happened to the American Negro. Something within has reminded him of his birthright of freedom, and something without has reminded him that it can be gained. Consciously or unconsciously, he has been caught up by the *Zeitgeist,* and with his black brothers of Africa and his brown and yellow brothers of Asia, South America and the Caribbean, the United States Negro is moving with a sense of great urgency toward the promised land of racial justice. If one recognizes this vital urge that has engulfed the Negro community, one should readily understand why public demonstrations are taking place. The Negro has many pent-up resentments and latent frustrations, and he must release them. So let him march; let him make prayer pilgrimages to the city hall; let him go on freedom rides—and try to understand why he must do so. If his repressed emotions are not released in nonviolent ways, they will seek expression through violence; this is not a threat but a fact of history. So I have not said to my people: "Get rid of your discontent." Rather, I have tried to say that this normal and healthy discontent can be channeled into the creative outlet of nonviolent direct action. And now this approach is being termed extremist.

But though I was initially disappointed at being categorized as an extremist, as I continued to think about the matter I gradually gained a measure of satisfaction from the label. Was not Jesus an extremist for love: "Love your enemies, bless them that curse you, do good to them that hate you, and pray for them which despitefully use you, and persecute you." Was not Amos an extremist for justice: "Let justice roll down like waters and righteousness like an ever-flowing stream." Was not Paul an extremist for the Christian gospel: "I bear in my body the marks of the Lord Jesus." Was not Martin Luther an extremist: "Here I stand; I cannot do otherwise, so help me God." And John Bunyan: "I will stay in jail to the end of my days before I make a butchery of my conscience." And Abraham Lincoln: "This nation cannot survive half slave and half free." And Thomas Jefferson: "We hold these truths to be self-evident, that all men are created equal . . ." So the question is not whether we will be extremists, but what kind of extremists we will be. Will we be extremists for hate or for love? Will we be extremists for the preservation of injustice or for the extension of justice? In that dramatic scene on Calvary's hill three men were crucified. We must never forget that all three were crucified for the same crime—the crime of extremism. Two were extremists for immorality, and thus fell below their environment. The other, Jesus Christ, was an extremist for love, truth and goodness, and thereby rose above his environment. Perhaps the South, the nation and the world are in dire need of creative extremists.

I had hoped that the white moderate would see this need. Perhaps I was too optimistic; perhaps I expected too much. I suppose I should have realized that few members of the oppressor race can understand the deep groans and passionate yearnings of the oppressed race, and still fewer have the vision to see that injustice must be rooted out by strong, persistent and determined action. I am thankful, however, that some of our white brothers in the South have grasped the meaning of this social revolution and committed themselves to it. They are still too few in quantity, but they are big in quality. Some—such as Ralph McGill, Lillian Smith, Harry Golden, James McBride Dabbs, Ann Braden and Sarah Patton Boyle—have written about our struggle in eloquent and prophetic terms. Others have marched with us down nameless streets of the South. They have languished in filthy, roach-infested jails, suffering the abuse and brutality of policemen who view them as "dirty nigger-lovers." Unlike so many of their moderate brothers and sisters, they have recognized the urgency of the moment and sensed the need for powerful "action" antidotes to combat the disease of segregation.

Let me take note of my other major disappointment. I have been so greatly disappointed with the white church and its leadership. Of course, there are some notable exceptions. I am not unmindful of the fact that each of you has taken some significant stands on this issue. I commend you, Reverend Stallings, for your Christian stand on this past Sunday, in welcoming Negroes to your worship service on a nonsegregated basis. I commend the Catholic leaders of this state for integrating Spring Hill College several years ago.

But despite these notable exceptions, I must honestly reiterate that I have been disappointed with the church. I do not say this as one of those negative critics who can always find something wrong with the church. I say this as a minister of the gospel, who loves the church; who was nurtured in its bosom; who has been sustained by its spiritual blessings and who will remain true to it as long as the cord of life shall lengthen.

When I was suddenly catapulted into the leadership of the bus protest in Montgomery, Alabama, a few years ago, I felt we would be supported by the white church. I felt that the white ministers, priests and rabbis of the South would be among our strongest allies. Instead, some have been outright opponents, refusing to understand the freedom movement and misrepresenting its leaders; all too many others have been more cautious than courageous and have remained silent behind the anesthetizing security of stained-glass windows.

In spite of my shattered dreams, I came to Birmingham with the hope that the white religious leadership of this community would see the justice of our cause and, with deep moral concern, would serve as the channel through which our just grievances could reach the power structure. I had hoped that each of you would understand. But again I have been disappointed.

I have heard numerous southern religious leaders admonish their worshipers to comply with a desegregation decision because it is the law, but I have longed to hear white ministers declare: "Follow this decree because integration is morally right and because the Negro is your brother." In the midst of blatant injustices inflicted upon the Negro, I have watched white churchmen stand on the sideline and mouth pious irrelevancies and sanctimonious trivialities. In the midst of a mighty struggle to rid our nation of racial and economic injustice, I have heard many ministers say: "Those are social issues, with which the gospel has no real concern." And I have watched many churches commit themselves to a completely other-worldly religion which makes a strange, un-Biblical distinction between body and soul, between the sacred and the secular.

I have traveled the length and breadth of Alabama, Mississippi and all the other southern states. On sweltering summer days and crisp autumn mornings I have looked at the South's beautiful churches with their lofty spires pointing heavenward. I have beheld the impressive outlines of her massive religious-education buildings. Over and over I have found myself asking: "What kind of people worship here? Who is their God? Where were their voices when the lips of Governor Barnett dripped with words of interposition and nullification? Where were they when Governor Wallace gave a clarion call for defiance and hatred? Where were their voices of support when bruised and weary Negro men and women decided to rise from the dark dungeons of complacency to the bright hills of creative protest?"

Yes, these questions are still in my mind. In deep disappointment I have wept over the laxity of the church. But be assured that my tears have been tears of love. There can be no deep disappointment where there is not deep love. Yes, I love the church. How could I do otherwise? I am in the rather unique position of being the son, the grandson and the great-grandson of preachers. Yes, I see the church as the body of Christ. But, oh! How we have blemished and scarred that body through social neglect and through fear of being nonconformists.

There was a time when the church was very powerful—in the time when the early Christians rejoiced at being deemed worthy to suffer for what they believed. In those days the church was not merely a thermometer that recorded the ideas and principles of popular opinion; it was a thermostat that transformed the mores of society. Whenever the early Christians entered a town, the people in power became disturbed and immediately sought to convict the

Christians for being "disturbers of the peace" and "outside agitators." But the Christians pressed on, in the conviction that they were "a colony of heaven," called to obey God rather than man. Small in number, they were big in commitment. They were too God-intoxicated to be "astronomically intimidated." By their effort and example they brought an end to such ancient evils as infanticide and gladiatorial contests.

Things are different now. So often the contemporary church is a weak, ineffectual voice with an uncertain sound. So often it is an archdefender of the status quo. Far from being disturbed by the presence of the church, the power structure of the average community is consoled by the church's silent—and often even vocal—sanction of things as they are.

But the judgment of God is upon the church as never before. If today's church does not recapture the sacrificial spirit of the early church, it will lose its authenticity, forfeit the loyalty of millions, and be dismissed as an irrelevant social club with no meaning for the twentieth century. Every day I meet young people whose disappointment with the church has turned into outright disgust.

Perhaps I have once again been too optimistic. Is organized religion too inextricably bound to the status quo to save our nation and the world? Perhaps I must turn my faith to the inner spiritual church, the church within the church, as the true *ekklesia* and the hope of the world. But again I am thankful to God that some noble souls from the ranks of organized religion have broken loose from the paralyzing chains of conformity and joined us as active partners in the struggle for freedom. They have left their secure congregations and walked the streets of Albany, Georgia, with us. They have gone down the highways of the South on tortuous rides for freedom. Yes, they have gone to jail with us. Some have been dismissed from their churches, have lost the support of their bishops and fellow ministers.

But they have acted in the faith that right defeated is stronger than evil triumphant. Their witness has been the spiritual salt that has preserved the true meaning of the gospel in these troubled times. They have carved a tunnel of hope through the dark mountain of disappointment.

I hope the church as a whole will meet the challenge of this decisive hour. But even if the church does not come to the aid of justice, I have no despair about the future. I have no fear about the outcome of our struggle in Birmingham, even if our motives are at present misunderstood. We will reach the goal of freedom in Birmingham and all over the nation, because the goal of America is freedom. Abused and scorned though we may be, our destiny is tied up with America's destiny. Before the pilgrims landed at Plymouth, we were here. Before the pen of Jefferson etched the majestic words of the Declaration of Independence across the pages of history, we were here. For more than two centuries our forebears labored in this country without wages; they made cotton king; they built the homes of their masters while suffering gross injustice and shameful humiliation—and yet out of a bottomless vitality they continued to thrive and develop. If the inexpressible cruelties of slavery could not stop us, the opposition we now face will surely fail. We will win our freedom because the sacred heritage of our nation and the eternal will of God are embodied in our echoing demands.

Before closing I feel impelled to mention one other point in your statement that has troubled me profoundly. You warmly commended the Birmingham police force for keeping "order" and "preventing violence." I doubt that you would have so warmly commended the police force if you had seen its dogs sinking their teeth into unarmed, nonviolent Negroes. I doubt that you would so quickly commend the policemen if you were to observe their ugly and inhumane treatment of Negroes here in the city jail; if you were to watch them push and curse old Negro women and young Negro girls; if you were to see them slap and kick old Negro men and young boys; if you were to observe them, as they did on two occasions, refuse to give us food because we wanted to sing our grace together. I cannot join you in your praise of the Birmingham police department.

It is true that the police have exercised a degree of discipline in handling the demonstrators. In this sense they have conducted themselves rather "nonviolently" in public. But for what purpose? To preserve the evil system of segregation. Over the past few years I have consistently preached that nonviolence demands that the means we use must be as pure as the ends we seek. I have tried to make clear that it is wrong to use immoral means to attain moral ends. But now I must affirm that it is just as wrong, or perhaps even more so, to use moral means to preserve immoral ends. Perhaps Mr. Connor and his policemen have been rather nonviolent in public, as was Chief Pritchett in Albany, Georgia, but they have used the moral means of nonviolence to maintain the immoral end of racial injustice. As T. S. Eliot has said: "The last temptation is the greatest treason: To do the right deed for the wrong reason."

I wish you had commended the Negro sit-inners and demonstrators of Birmingham for their sublime courage, their willingness to suffer and their amazing discipline in the midst of great provocation. One day the South will recognize its real heroes. They will be the James Merediths, with the noble sense of purpose that enables them to face jeering and hostile mobs, and with the agonizing loneliness that characterizes the life of the pioneer. They will be old, oppressed, battered Negro women, symbolized in a seventy-two-year-old woman in Montgomery, Alabama, who rose up with a sense of dignity and with her people decided not to ride segregated buses, and who responded with ungrammatical profundity to one who inquired about her weariness: "My feets is tired, but my soul is at rest." They will be the young high school and college students, the young ministers of the gospel and a host of their elders, courageously and nonviolently sitting in at lunch counters and willingly going to jail for conscience's sake. One day the South will know that when these disinherited children of God sat down at lunch counters, they were in reality standing up for what is best in the American dream and for the most sacred values in our Judaeo-Christian heritage, thereby bringing our nation back to thou great wells of democracy which were dug deep by the founding fathers in their formulation of the Constitution and the Declaration of Independence.

Never before have I written so long a letter. I'm afraid it is much too long to take your precious time. I can assure you that it would have been much shorter if I had been writing from a comfortable desk, but what else can one do when he is alone in a narrow jail cell, other than write long letters, think long thoughts and pray long prayers?

If I have said anything in this letter that overstates the truth and indicates an unreasonable impatience, I beg you to forgive me. If I have said anything that understates the truth and indicates my having a patience that allows me to settle for anything less than brotherhood, I beg God to forgive me.

I hope this letter finds you strong in the faith. I also hope that circumstances will soon make it possible for me to meet each of you, not as an integrationist or a civil rights leader but as a fellow clergyman and a Christian brother. Let us all hope that the dark clouds of racial prejudice will soon pass away and the deep fog of misunderstanding will be lifted from our fear-drenched communities, and in some not too distant tomorrow the radiant stars of love and brotherhood will shine over our great nation with all their scintillating beauty.

Yours for the cause of Peace and Brotherhood,

Martin Luther King, Jr.

Following is a verbatim copy of the public statement directed to Martin Luther, King, Jr., by eight Alabama clergymen, which occasioned the above response.

April 12, 1963

We the undersigned clergymen are among those who, in January, issued "An Appeal for Law and Order and Common Sense," in dealing with racial problems in Alabama. We expressed understanding that honest convictions in racial matters could properly be pursued in the courts, but urged that decisions of those courts should in the meantime be peacefully obeyed.

Since that time there had been some evidence of increased forbearance and a willingness to face facts. Responsible citizens have undertaken to work on various problems which cause racial friction and unrest. In Birmingham, recent public events have given indication that we all have opportunity for a new constructive and realistic approach to racial problems.

However, we are now confronted by a series of demonstrations by some of our Negro citizens, directed and led in part by outsiders. We recognize the natural impatience of people who feel that their hopes are slow in being realized. But we are convinced that these demonstrations are unwise and untimely.

We agree rather with certain local Negro leadership which has called for honest and open negotiation of racial issues in our area. And we believe this kind of facing of issues can best be accomplished by citizens of our own metropolitan area, white and Negro, meeting with their knowledge and experience of the local situation. All of us need to face that responsibility and find proper channels for its accomplishment.

Just as we formerly pointed our that "hatred and violence

have no sanction in our religious and political traditions," we also point out that such actions as incite to hatred and violence, however technically peaceful those actions may be, have not contributed to the resolution of our local problems. We do not believe that these days of new hope are days when extreme measures are justified in Birmingham.

We commend the community as a whole, and the local news media and law enforcement officials in particular, on the calm manner in which those demonstrations have been handled. We urge the public to continue to show restraint should the demonstrations continue, and the law enforcement officials to remain calm and continue to protect our city from violence.

We further strongly urge our own Negro community to withdraw support from these demonstrations, and to unite locally in working peacefully for a better Birmingham. When rights are consistently denied, a cause should be pressed in the courts and in negotiations among local leaders, and not in the streets. We appeal to both our white and Negro citizenry to observe the principles of law and order and common sense.

Signed by:

C.C.J CARPENTER, D.D., LL.D.
Bishop of Alabama

JOSEPH A. DURICK, D.D.,
Auxiliary Bishop, Diocese of Mobile-Birmingham

Rabbi MILTON L. GRAFMAN,
Temple Emanu-El, Birmingham, Alabama

Bishop PAUL HARDIN,
Bishop of the Alabama-West Florida Conference of the Methodist Church

Bishop NOLAN B. HARMON,
Bishop of the North Alabama Conference of the Methodist Church

GEORGE M. MURRAY, D.D., LL.D.,
Bishop Coadjutor, Episcopal Diocese of Alabama

EDWARD V. RAMAGE,
Moderator, Synod of the Alabama Presbyterian Church in the United States

EARL STALLINGS,
Pastor, First Baptist Church, Birmingham, Alabama

VACLAV HAVEL

1936-

POWER OF THE POWERLESS[1]

1978

Havel was born into a wealthy and influential family in Prague, Czechoslovakia. At the conclusion of World War II, the Red Army drove out the Nazis, occupied Czechoslovakia, and imposed a rigid Stalinist regime on the country. Because of his class background, the Marxist-Leninist regime restricted his access to secondary and higher education. He pursued education anyway, going to night school, then managing to attend the Czech Technical University for two years. He pursued a career in drama, wrote plays, and became more deeply involved in politics in the aftermath of the "Prague Spring" of 1968, when a reformist regime was crushed by the Red Army. He was jailed repeatedly as he became more outspoken. The essay excerpted here appeared as a *samizdat*[2] publication in 1979. He was a leader

---

1 From OPEN LETTERS: SELECTED WRITINGS 1965-1990 by Vaclav Havel, translated by Paul Wilson, copyright 1991 by A.G. Brain. Preface/translation copyright 1985, 1988, 1991 by Paul Wilson. Used by permission of Alfred A. Knopf, a division of Random House, Inc.

2 underground press

100

LYNCHBURG COLLEGE

1903-2003

VERNON G. MILES, Ph.D.

Dean of the College

Professor of English

OFFICE OF THE DEAN

1501 LAKESIDE DRIVE

LYNCHBURG, VIRGINIA 24501-3199

434/544-8232

FAX: 434/544-8658

miles@lynchburg.edu

in the Charter 77 movement, a group of Czechoslovaks who sought to embarrass the regime into adhering to the human rights guarantees of the Helsinki agreements of 1975 which the regime had signed. Havel then became part of the umbrella organization Civic Forum and came to prominence in Czechoslovakia's Velvet Revolution of 1989, which ejected the Communist government without bloodshed. Havel became the first President of the newly democratic country.

Selections from: Havel, Vaclav. 1978. "Power of the Powerless." *Open Letters: Selected Writings 1965-1990.* Ed. Paul Wilson. New York: Alfred A. Knopf, 1991.

[Sections] I-IX (127-154)
[Section] XI (158-163)
[Sections] XX-XXII (205-214)

I

A SPECTER is haunting Eastern Europe: the specter of what in the West is called "dissent." This specter has not appeared out of thin air. It is a natural and inevitable consequence of the present historical phase of the system it is haunting. It was born at a time when this system, for a thousand reasons, can no longer base itself on the unadulterated brutal, and arbitrary application of power, eliminating all expressions of nonconformity. What is more, the system has become so ossified politically that there is practically no way for such nonconformity to be implemented within its official structures.

Who are these so-called dissidents? Where does their point of view come from, and what importance does it have? What is the significance of the "independent initiatives" in which "dissidents" collaborate, and what real chances do such initiatives have of success? Is it appropriate to refer to "dissidents" as an opposition? If so, what exactly is such an opposition within the framework of this system? What does it do? What role does it play in society? What are its hopes and on what are they based? Is it within the power of the "dissidents"—as a category of subcitizen outside the power establishment—to have any influence at all on society and the social system? Can they actually change anything?

I think that an examination of these questions—an examination of the potential of the "powerless"—can only begin with an examination of the nature of power in the circumstances in which these powerless people operate.

II

OUR SYSTEM is most frequently characterized as a dictatorship or, more precisely, as the dictatorship of a political bureaucracy over a society which has undergone economic and social leveling. I am afraid that the term "dictatorship," regardless of how intelligible it may otherwise be, tends to obscure rather than clarify the real nature of power in this system. We usually associate the term with the notion of a small group of people who take over the government of a given country by force; their power is wielded openly, using the direct instruments of power at their disposal, and they are easily distinguished socially from the majority over whom they rule. One of the essential aspects of this traditional or classical notion of dictatorship is the assumption that it is temporary, ephemeral, lacking historical roots. Its existence seems to be bound up with the lives of those who established it. It is usually local in extent and significance, and regardless of the ideology it utilizes to grant itself legitimacy, its power derives ultimately from the numbers and the armed might of its soldiers and police. The principal threat to its existence is felt to be the possibility that someone better equipped in this sense might appear and overthrow it.

Even this very superficial overview should make it clear that the system in which we live has very little in common with a classical dictatorship. In the first place, our system is not limited in a local, geographical sense; rather, it holds sway over a huge power bloc controlled by one of the two superpowers. And although it quite naturally exhibits a number of local and historical variations, the range of these variations is fundamentally circumscribed by a single, unifying framework throughout the power bloc. Not only is the dictatorship everywhere based on the same principles and structured in the same way (that is, in the way evolved by the ruling superpower), but each country has been completely penetrated by a network of manipulatory instruments controlled by the superpower center and totally subordinated to its interests. In the stalemated world of nuclear parity, of course, that circumstance endows the system with an unprecedented degree of external stability compared with classical dictatorships. Many local crises which, in an isolated state, would lead to a change in the system, can be resolved through direct intervention by the armed forces of the rest of the bloc.

In the second place, if a feature of classical dictatorships is their lack of historical roots (frequently they appear to be no more than historical freaks, the fortuitous consequence of fortuitous social processes or of human and mob tendencies), the same cannot be said so facilely about our system. For even though our dictatorship has long since alienated itself completely from the social movements that give birth to it, the authenticity of these movements (and I am thinking of the proletarian and socialist movements of the nineteenth century) gives it undeniable historicity. These origins provided a solid foundation of sorts on which it could build until it became the utterly new social and political reality it is today, which has become so inextricably a part of the structure of the modern world. A feature of those historical origins was the "correct" understanding of social conflicts in the period from which those original movements emerged. The fact that at the very core of this "correct" understanding there was a genetic disposition toward the monstrous alienation characteristic of its subsequent development is not essential here. And in any case, this element also grew organically from the climate of that time and therefore can be said to have its origin there as well.

One legacy of that original "correct" understanding is a third peculiarity that makes our systems different from other modern dictatorships: it commands an incomparably more precise, logically structured, generally comprehensible and, in essence, extremely flexible ideology that, in its elaborateness and completeness, is almost a secularized religion. It offers a ready answer to any question whatsoever; it can scarcely be accepted only in part, and accepting it has profound implications for human life. In an era when metaphysical and existential certainties are in a state of crisis, when people are being uprooted and alienated and are losing their sense of what this world means, this ideology inevitably has a certain hypnotic charm. To wandering humankind it offers an immediately available home: all one has to do is accept it, and suddenly everything becomes clear once more, life takes on new meaning, and all mysteries, unanswered questions, anxiety, and loneliness vanish. Of course, one pays dearly for this low-rent home: the price is abdication of one's own reason, conscience, and responsibility, for an essential aspect of this ideology is the consignment of reason and conscience to a higher authority. The principle involved here is that the center of power is identical with the center of truth. (In our case, the connection with Byzantine theocracy is direct: the highest secular authority is identical with the highest spiritual authority.) It is true of course that, all this aside, ideology no longer has any great influence on people, at least within our bloc (with the possible exception of Russia, where the serf mentality, with its blind, fatalistic respect for rulers and its automatic acceptance of all their claims, is still dominant and combined with a superpower patriotism which traditionally places the interests of empire higher than the interests of humanity). But this is not important, because ideology plays its role in our system very well (an issue to which I will return) precisely because it is what it is.

Fourth, the technique of exercising power in traditional dictatorships contains a necessary element of improvisation. The mechanisms for wielding power are for the most part established firmly, and there is considerable room for accident and for the arbitrary and unregulated application of power. Socially, psychologically, and physically, conditions still exist for the expression of some form of opposition. In short, there are many seams on the surface which can split apart before the entire power structure has managed to stabilize. Our system, on the other hand, has been developing in the Soviet Union for over sixty years, and for approximately thirty years in Eastern Europe; moreover, several of its long-established structural features are derived from Czarist absolutism. In terms of the physical aspects of power, this has led to the creation of such intricate and well-developed mechanisms for the direct and indirect manipulation of the entire population that, as a physical power base, it represents something radically new. At the same time, let us not forget that the system is made significantly more effective by state ownership and central direction of all the means of production. This gives the power structure an unprecedented and uncontrollable capacity to invest in itself (in the areas of the bureaucracy and the police, for example) and makes it easier for that structure, as the sole employer, to manipulate the day-to-day existence of all citizens.

Finally, if an atmosphere of revolutionary excitement, heroism, dedication, and boisterous violence on all sides characterizes classical dictatorships, then the last traces of such an atmosphere have vanished from the Soviet bloc. For some time now this bloc has ceased to be a kind of enclave, isolated from the rest of the developed world and immune to processes occurring in it. To the contrary, the Soviet bloc is an integral part of that larger world, and it shares and shapes the world's destiny. This means in concrete terms that the hierarchy of values existing in the developed countries of the West has, in essence, appeared in our society (the long period of co-existence with the West has only hastened this process). In other words, what we have here is simply another form of the consumer and industrial society, with all its concomitant social, intellectual, and psychological consequences. It is impossible to understand the nature of power in our system properly without taking this into account.

The profound difference between our system—in terms of the nature of power—and what we traditionally understand by dictatorship, a difference I hope is clear even from this quite superficial comparison, has caused me to search for some term appropriate for our system, purely for the purposes of this essay. If I refer to it henceforth as a "post-totalitarian" system, I am fully aware that this is perhaps not the most precise term, but I am unable to think of a better one. I do not wish to imply by the prefix "post-" that the system is no longer totalitarian; on the contrary, I mean that it is totalitarian in a way fundamentally different from classical dictatorships, different from totalitarianism as we usually understand it.

The circumstances I have mentioned, however, form only a circle of conditional factors and a kind of phenomenal framework for the actual composition of power in the post-totalitarian system, several aspects of which I shall now attempt to identify.

III

THE MANAGER of a fruit-and-vegetable shop places in his window, among the onions and carrots, the slogan: "Workers of the world, unite!" Why does he do it? What is he trying to communicate to the world? Is he genuinely enthusiastic about the idea of unity among the workers of the world? Is his enthusiasm so great that he feels an irrepressible impulse to acquaint the public with his ideals? Has he really given more than a moment's thought to how such a unification might occur and what it would mean?

I think it can safely be assumed that the overwhelming majority of shopkeepers never think about the slogans they put in their windows, nor do they use them to express their real opinions. That poster was delivered to our greengrocer from the enterprise headquarters along with the onions and carrots. He put them all into the window simply because it has been done that way for years, because everyone does it, and because that is the way it has to be. If he were to refuse, there could be trouble. He could be reproached for not having the proper decoration in his window; someone might even accuse him of disloyalty. He does it because these things must be done if one is to get along in life. It is one of the thousands of details that guarantee him a relatively tranquil life "in harmony with society," as they say.

Obviously the greengrocer is indifferent to the semantic content of the slogan on exhibit; he does not put the slogan in his window from any personal desire to acquaint the public with the ideal it expresses. This, of course, does not mean that his action has no motive or significance at all, or that the slogan communicates nothing to anyone. The slogan is really a sign, and as such it contains a subliminal but very definite message. Verbally, it might be expressed this way: "I, the greengrocer XY, live here and I know what I must do. I behave in the manner expected of me. I can be depended upon and am beyond reproach. I am obedient and therefore I have the right to be left in peace." This message, of course, has an addressee: it is directed above, to the greengrocer's superior, and at the same time it is a shield that protects the greengrocer from potential informers. The slogan's real meaning, therefore, is rooted firmly in the greengrocer's existence. It reflects his vital interests. But what are those vital interests?

Let us take note: if the greengrocer had been instructed to display the slogan "I am afraid and therefore unquestioningly obedient," he would not be nearly as indifferent to its semantics, even though the statement would reflect the truth. The greengrocer would be embarrassed and ashamed to put such an unequivocal statement of his own degradation in the shop window, and quite naturally so, for he is a human being and thus has a sense of his own dignity. To overcome this complication, his expression of loyalty must take the form of a sign which, at least on its textual surface, indicates a level of disinterested conviction. It must allow the greengrocer to say, "What's wrong with the workers of the world uniting?" Thus the sign helps the greengrocer to conceal from himself the low foundations of his obedience, at the same time concealing the low foundations of power. It hides them behind the facade of something high. And that something is ideology.

Ideology is a specious way of relating to the world. It offers human beings the illusion of an identity, of dignity, and of morality while making it easier for them to part with them. As the repository of something suprapersonal and objective, it enables people to deceive their conscience and conceal their true position and their inglorious *modus vivendi* both from the world and from themselves. It is a very pragmatic but, at the same time, an apparently dignified way of legitimizing what is above, below, and on either side. It is directed toward people and toward God. It is a veil behind which human beings can hide their own fallen existence, their trivialization, and their adaptation to the status quo. It is an excuse that everyone can use, from the greengrocer, who conceals his fear of losing his job behind an alleged interest in the unification of the workers of the world, to the highest functionary, whose interest in staying in power can be cloaked in phrases about service to the working class. The primary excusatory function of ideology, therefore, is to provide people, both as victims and pillars of the post-totalitarian system, with the illusion that the system is in harmony with the human order and the order of the universe.

The smaller a dictatorship and the less stratified by modernization the society under it, the more directly the will of the dictator can be exercised. In other words, the dictator can employ more or less naked discipline, avoiding the complex processes of relating to the world and of self-justification which ideology involves. But the more complex the mechanisms of power become, the larger and more stratified the society they embrace, and the longer they have operated historically, the more individuals must be connected to them from outside, and the greater the importance attached to the ideological excuse. It acts as a kind of bridge between the regime and the people, across which the regime approaches the people and the people approach the regime. This explains why ideology plays such an important role in the post-totalitarian system: that complex machinery of units, hierarchies, transmission belts, and indirect instruments of manipulation which ensure in countless ways the integrity of the regime, leaving nothing to chance, would be quite simply unthinkable without ideology acting as its all-embracing excuse and as the excuse for each of its parts.

IV

Between the aims of the post-totalitarian system and the aims of life there is a yawning abyss: while life, in its essence, moves toward plurality, diversity, independent self-constitution, and self-organization, in short, toward the fulfillment of its own freedom, the post-totalitarian system demands conformity, uniformity, and discipline. While life ever strives to create new and improbable structures, the post-totalitarian system contrives to force life into its most probable states. The aims of the system reveal its most essential characteristic to be introversion, a movement toward being ever more completely and unreservedly itself, which means that the radius of its influence is continually widening as well. This system serves people only to the extent necessary to ensure that people will serve it. Anything beyond this, that is to say, anything which leads people to overstep their predetermined roles is regarded by the system as an attack upon itself. And in this respect it is correct: every instance of such transgression is a genuine denial of the system. It can be said, therefore, that the inner aim of the post-totalitarian system is not mere preservation of power in the hands of a ruling clique, as appears to be the case at first sight. Rather, the social phenomenon of self-preservation is subordinated to something higher, to a kind of blind automatism which drives the system. No matter what position individuals hold in the hierarchy of power, they are not considered by the system to be worth anything in themselves, but only as things intended to fuel and serve this automatism. For this reason, an individual's desire for power is admissible only in so far as its direction coincides with the direction of the automatism of the system.

Ideology, in creating a bridge of excuses between the system and the individual, spans the abyss between the aims of the system and the aims of life. It pretends that the requirements of the system derive from the requirements of life. It is a world of appearances trying to pass for reality.

The post-totalitarian system touches people at every step, but it does so with its ideological gloves on. This is why life in the system is so thoroughly permeated with hypocrisy and lies: government by bureaucracy is called popular government; the working class is enslaved in the name of the working class; the complete degradation of the individual is presented as his ultimate liberation; depriving people of information is called making it available; the use of power to manipulate is called the public control of power, and the arbitrary abuse of power is called observing the legal code;

the repression of culture is called its development; the expansion of imperial influence is presented as support for the oppressed; the lack of free expression becomes the highest form of freedom; farcical elections become the highest form of democracy; banning independent thought becomes the most scientific of world views; military occupation becomes fraternal assistance. Because the regime is captive to its own lies, it must falsify everything. It falsifies the past. It falsifies the present, and it falsifies the future. It falsifies statistics. It pretends not to possess an omnipotent and unprincipled police apparatus. It pretends to respect human rights. It pretends to persecute no one. It pretends to fear nothing. It pretends to pretend nothing.

Individuals need not believe all these mystifications, but they must behave as though they did, or they must at least tolerate them in silence, or get along well with those who work with them. For this reason, however, they must live within a lie. They need not accept the lie. It is enough for them to have accepted their life with it and in it. For by this very fact, individuals confirm the system, fulfill the system, make the system, *are* the system.

V

We have seen that the real meaning of the greengrocer's slogan has nothing to do with what the text of the slogan actually says. Even so, this real meaning is quite clear and generally comprehensible because the code is so familiar: the greengrocer declares his loyalty (and he can do no other if his declaration is to be accepted) in the only way the regime is capable of hearing; that is, by accepting the prescribed ritual, by accepting appearances as reality, by accepting the given rules of the game. In doing so, however, he has himself become a player in the game, thus making it possible for the game to go on, for it to exist in the first place.

If ideology was originally a bridge between the system and the individual as an individual, then the moment he steps on to this bridge it becomes at the same time a bridge between the system and the individual as a component of the system. That is, if ideology originally facilitated (by acting outwardly) the constitution of power by serving as a psychological excuse, then from the moment that excuse is accepted, it constitutes power inwardly, becoming an active component of that power. It begins to function as the principal instrument of ritual communication *within* the system of power.

The whole power structure (and we have already discussed its physical articulation) could not exist at all if there were not a certain metaphysical order binding all its components together, interconnecting them and subordinating them to a uniform method of accountability, supplying the combined operation of all these components with rules of the game, that is, with certain regulations, limitations, and legalities. This metaphysical order is fundamental to, and standard throughout, the entire power structure; it integrates its communication system and makes possible the internal exchange and transfer of information and instructions. It is rather like a collection of traffic signals and directional signs, giving the process shape and structure. This metaphysical order guarantees the inner coherence of the totalitarian power structure. It is the glue holding it together, its binding principle, the instrument of its discipline. Without this glue the structure as a totalitarian structure would vanish; it would disintegrate into individual atoms chaotically colliding with one another in their unregulated particular interests and inclinations. The entire pyramid of totalitarian power, deprived of the element that binds it together, would collapse in upon itself, as it were, in a kind of material implosion.

As the interpretation of reality by the power structure, ideology is always subordinated ultimately to the interests of the structure. Therefore, it has a natural tendency to disengage itself from reality, to create a world of appearances, to become ritual. In societies where there is public competition for power and therefore public control of that power, there also exists quite naturally public control of the way that power legitimates itself ideologically. Consequently, in such conditions there are always certain correctives that effectively prevent ideology from abandoning reality altogether. Under totalitarianism, however, these correctives disappear, and thus there is nothing to prevent ideology from becoming more and more removed from reality, gradually turning into what it has already become in the post-totalitarian system: a world of appearances, a mere ritual, a formalized language deprived of semantic contact with reality and transformed into a system of ritual signs that replace reality with pseudo-reality.

Yet, as we have seen, ideology becomes at the same time an increasingly important component of power, a pillar providing it with both excusatory legitimacy and an inner coherence. As this aspect grows in importance, and as it gradually loses touch with reality, it acquires a peculiar but very real strength. It becomes reality itself, albeit a reality altogether self-contained, one that on certain levels (chiefly inside the power structure) may have even greater weight than reality as such. Increasingly, the virtuosity of the ritual becomes more important than the reality hidden behind it. The significance of phenomena no longer derives from the phenomena themselves, but from their locus as concepts in the ideological context. Reality does not shape theory, but rather the reverse. Thus power gradually draws closer to ideology than it does to reality; it draws its strength from theory and becomes entirely dependent on it. This inevitably leads, of course, to a paradoxical result: rather than theory, or rather ideology, serving power, power begins to serve ideology. It is as though ideology had appropriated power from power, as though it had become dictator itself. It then appears that theory itself, ritual itself, ideology itself, makes decisions that affect people, and not the other way around.

If ideology is the principal guarantee of the inner consistency of power, it becomes at the same time an increasingly important guarantee of its continuity. Whereas succession to power in classical dictatorship is always a rather complicated affair (the pretenders having nothing to give their claims reasonable legitimacy, thereby forcing them always to resort to confrontations of naked power), in the post-totalitarian system power is passed on from person to person, from clique to clique, and from generation to generation in an essentially more regular fashion. In the selection of pretenders, a new "king-maker" takes part: it is ritual legitimation, the ability to rely on ritual, to fulfill it and use it, to allow oneself, as it were, to be borne aloft by it. Naturally, power struggles exist in the post-totalitarian system as well, and most of them are far more brutal than in an open society, for the struggle is not open, regulated by democratic rules, and subject to public control but hidden behind the scenes. (It is difficult to recall a single instance in which the First Secretary of a ruling Communist Party has been replaced without the various military and security forces being placed at least on alert.) This struggle, however, can never (as it can in classical dictatorships) threaten the very essence of the system and its continuity. At most it will shake up the power structure, which will recover quickly precisely because the binding substance—ideology—remains undisturbed. No matter who is replaced by whom, succession is only possible against the backdrop and within the framework of a common ritual. It can never take place by denying that ritual.

Because of this dictatorship of the ritual, however, power becomes clearly anonymous. Individuals are almost dissolved in the ritual. They allow themselves to be swept along by it and frequently it seems as though ritual alone carries people from obscurity into the light of power. Is it not characteristic of the post-totalitarian system that, on all levels of the power hierarchy, individuals are increasingly being pushed aside by faceless people, puppets, those uniformed flunkeys of the rituals and routines of power?

The automatic operation of a power structure thus dehumanized and made anonymous is a feature of the fundamental automatism of this system. It would seem that it is precisely the *diktats* of this automatism which select people lacking individual will for the power structure, that it is precisely the *diktat* of the empty phrase which summons to power people who use empty phrases as the best guarantee that the automatism of the post-totalitarian system will continue.

Western Sovietologists often exaggerate the role of individuals in the post-totalitarian system and overlook the fact that the ruling figures despite the immense power they possess through the centralized structure of power, are often no more than blind executors of the system's own internal laws—laws they themselves never can, and never do, reflect upon. In any case, experience has taught us again and again that this automatism is far more powerful than the will of an individual; and should someone possess a more independent will, he must conceal it behind a ritually anonymous mask in order to have an opportunity to enter the power hierarchy at all. And when the individual finally gains a place there and tries to make his will felt within it, that automatism, with its enormous inertia, will triumph sooner or later, and either the individual will be ejected by the power structure like a foreign organism, or he will be compelled to resign his individuality gradually, once again blending with the automatism and becoming its servant, almost indistinguishable from those who preceded him and those who will follow. (Let us recall, for instance, the development of Husák or Gomulka.) The necessity of continually hiding behind and relating to ritual means that even the more enlightened members of the power structure are often obsessed with ideology. They are never able to plunge straight to the bottom of naked reality, and they always confuse it, in the final analysis, with ideological pseudo-reality. (In my opinion, one of the reasons the Dubèek leadership lost control of the situation in 1968 was precisely because, in extreme situations and in final questions, its members were never capable of extricating themselves completely from the world of appearances.)

It can be said, therefore, that ideology, as that instrument of internal communication which assures the power structure of inner cohesion is, in the post-totalitarian system, something that transcends the physical aspects of power, something that dominates it to a considerable degree and, therefore, tends to assure its continuity as well. It is one of the pillars of the system's external stability. This pillar, however, is built on a very unstable foundation. It is built on lies. It works only as long as people are willing to live within the lie.

VI

WHY IN FACT did our greengrocer have to put his loyalty on display in the shop window? Had he not already displayed it sufficiently in various internal or semipublic ways? At trade union meetings, after all, he had always voted as he should. He had always taken part in various competitions. He voted in elections like a good citizen. He had even signed the "anti-Charter." Why, on top of all that, should he have to declare his loyalty publicly? After all, the people who walk past his window will certainly not stop to read that, in the greengrocer's opinion, the workers of the world ought to unite. The fact of the matter is, they don't read the slogan at all, and it can be fairly assumed they don't even see it. If you were to ask a woman who had stopped in front of his shop what she saw in the window, she could certainly tell whether or not they had tomatoes today, but it is highly unlikely that she noticed the slogan at all, let alone what it said.

It seems senseless to require the greengrocer to declare his loyalty publicly. But it makes sense nevertheless. People ignore his slogan, but they do so because such slogans are also found in other shop windows, on lampposts, bulletin boards, in apartment windows, and on buildings; they are everywhere, in fact. They form part of the panorama of everyday life. Of course, while they ignore the details, people are very aware of that panorama as a whole. And what else is the greengrocer's slogan but a small component in that huge backdrop to daily life?

The greengrocer had to put the slogan in his window, therefore, not in the hope that someone might read it or be persuaded by it, but to contribute, along with thousands of other slogans, to the panorama that everyone is very much aware of. This panorama, of course, has a subliminal meaning as well: it reminds people where they are living and what is expected of them. It tells them what everyone else is doing, and indicates to them what they must do as well, if they don't want to be excluded, to fall into isolation, alienate themselves from society, break the rules of the game, and risk the loss of their peace and tranquility and security.

The woman who ignored the greengrocer's slogan may well have hung a similar slogan just an hour before in a corridor of the office where she works. She did it more or less without thinking, just as our greengrocer did, and she could do so precisely because she was doing it against the background of the general panorama and with some awareness of it, that is, against the background of the panorama of which the green grocer's shop window forms a part. When the greengrocer visits her office, he will not notice her slogan either, just as she failed to notice his. Nevertheless, their slogans are mutually dependent: both were displayed with some awareness of the general panorama and, we might say, under its *diktat*. Both, however, assist in the creation of that panorama, and therefore they assist in the creation of that *diktat* as well. The greengrocer and the office worker have both adapted to the conditions in which they live, but in doing so, they help to create those conditions. They do what is done, what is to be done, what must be done, but at the same time—by that very token—they confirm that it must be done in fact. They conform to a particular requirement and in so doing they themselves perpetuate that requirement. Metaphysically speaking, without the greengrocer's slogan the office worker's slogan could not exist, and vice versa. Each proposes to the other that something be repeated and each accepts the other's proposal. Their mutual indifference to each other's slogans is only an illusion: in reality, by exhibiting their slogans, each compels the other to accept the rules of the game and to confirm thereby the power that requires the slogans in the first place. Quite simply, each helps the other to be obedient. Both are objects in a system of control, but at the same time they are its subjects as well. They are both victims of the system and its instruments.

If an entire district town is plastered with slogans that no one reads, it is on the one hand a message from the district secretary to the regional secretary, but it is also something more: a small example of the principle of social auto-totality at work. Part of the essence of the post-totalitarian system is that it draws everyone into its sphere of power, not so they may realize themselves as human beings, but so they may surrender their human identity in favor of the identity of the system, that is, so they may become agents of the system's general automatism and servants of its self-determined goals, so they may participate in the common responsibility for it, so they may be pulled into and ensnared by it, like Faust by Mephistopheles. More than this: so they may create through their involvement a general norm and, thus, bring pressure to bear on their fellow citizens. And further: so they may learn to be comfortable with their involvement, to identify with it as though it were something natural and inevitable and, ultimately, so they may—with no external urging—come to treat any non-involvement as an abnormality, as arrogance, as an attack on themselves, as a form of dropping out of society. By pulling everyone into its power structure, the post-totalitarian system makes everyone an instrument of a mutual totality, the auto-totality of society.

Everyone, however, is in fact involved and enslaved, not only the greengrocers but also the prime ministers. Differing positions in the hierarchy merely establish differing degrees of involvement: the greengrocer is involved only to a minor extent, but he also has very little power. The prime minister, naturally, has greater power, but in return he is far more deeply involved. Both, however, are unfree, each merely in a somewhat different way. The real accomplice in this involvement, therefore, is not another person, but the system itself. Position in the power hierarchy determines the degree of responsibility and guilt, but it gives no one unlimited responsibility and guilt, nor does it completely absolve anyone. Thus the conflict between the aims of life and the aims of the system is not a conflict between two socially defined and separate communities; and only a very generalized view (and even that only approximative) permits us to divide society into the rulers and the ruled. Here, by the way, is one of the most important differences between the post-totalitarian system and classical dictatorships, in which this line of conflict can still be drawn according to social class. In the post-totalitarian system, this line runs *defacto* through each person, for everyone in his own way is both a victim and a supporter of the system. What we understand by the system is not, therefore, a social order imposed by one group upon another, but rather something which permeates the entire society and is a factor in shaping it, something which may seem impossible to grasp or define (for it is in the nature of a mere principle), but which is expressed by the entire society as an important feature of its life.

The fact that human beings have created, and daily create, this self-directed system through which they divest themselves of their innermost identity is not therefore the result of some incomprehensible misunderstanding of history, nor is it history somehow gone off its rails. Neither is it the product of some diabolical higher will which has decided, for reasons unknown, to torment a portion of humanity in this way. It can happen and did happen only because there is obviously in modern humanity a certain tendency toward the creation, or at least the toleration, of such a system. There is obviously something in human beings which responds to this system, something they reflect and accommodate, something within them which paralyzes every effort of their better selves to revolt. Human beings are compelled to live within a lie, but they can be compelled to do so only because they are in fact capable of living in this way. Therefore not only does the system alienate humanity, but at the same time alienated humanity supports this system as its own involuntary master-plan, as a degenerate image of its own degeneration, as a record of people's own failure as individuals.

The essential aims of life are present naturally in every person. In everyone there is some longing for humanity's rightful dignity, for moral integrity, for free expression of being and a sense of transcendence over the world of existence. Yet, at the same time, each person is capable, to a greater or lesser degree, of coming to terms with living within the lie. Each person somehow succumbs to a profane trivialization of his inherent humanity, and to utilitarianism. In everyone there is some willingness to merge with the anonymous crowd and to flow comfortably along with it down the river of pseudo-life. This is much more than a simple conflict between two identities. It is something far worse: it is a challenge to the very notion of identity itself.

In highly simplified terms, it could be said that the post-totalitarian system has been built on foundations laid by the historical encounter between dictatorship and the consumer society. Is it not true that the far-reaching adaptability to living a lie and the effortless spread of social auto-totality have some connection with the general unwillingness of consumption-oriented people to sacrifice some material certainties for the sake of their own spiritual and moral integrity? With their willingness to surrender higher values when faced with the trivializing temptations of modern civilization? With their vulnerability to the attractions of mass indifference? And in the end, is not the grayness and the emptiness of life in the post-totalitarian system only an inflated caricature of modern life in general? And do we not in fact stand (although in the external measures of civilization, we are far behind) as a kind of warning to the West, revealing to its own latent tendencies?

VII

Let us now imagine that one day something in our greengrocer snaps and he stops putting up the slogans merely to ingratiate himself. He stops voting in elections he knows are a farce. He begins to say what he really thinks at political meetings. And he even finds the strength in himself to express solidarity with those whom his conscience commands him to support. In this revolt the greengrocer steps out of living within the lie. He rejects the ritual and breaks the rules of the game. He discovers once more his suppressed identity and dignity. He gives his freedom a concrete significance. His revolt is an attempt to live within the truth.

The bill is not long in coming. He will be relieved of his post as manager of the shop and transferred to the warehouse. His pay will be reduced. His hopes for a holiday in Bulgaria will evaporate. His children's access to higher education will be threatened. His superiors will harass him and his fellow workers will wonder about him. Most of those who apply these sanctions, however, will not do so from any authentic inner conviction but simply under pressure from conditions, the same conditions that once pressured the greengrocer to display the official slogans. They will persecute the greengrocer either because it is expected of them, or to demonstrate their loyalty, or simply as part of the general panorama, to which belongs an awareness that this is how situations of this sort are dealt with, that this, in fact, is how things are always done, particularly if one is not to become suspect oneself. The executors, therefore, behave essentially like everyone else, to a greater or lesser degree: as components of the post-totalitarian system, as agents of its automatism, as petty instruments of the social auto-totality.

Thus the power structure, through the agency of those who carry out the sanctions, those anonymous components of the system, will spew the greengrocer from its mouth. The system, through its alienating presence in people, will punish him for his rebellion. It must do so because the logic of its automatism and self-defense dictate it. The greengrocer has not committed a simple, individual offense, isolated in its own uniqueness, but something incomparably more serious. By breaking the rules of the game, he has disrupted the game as such. He has exposed it as a mere game. He has shattered the world of appearances, the fundamental pillar of the system. He has upset the power structure by tearing apart what holds it together. He has demonstrated that living a lie is living a lie. He has broken through the exalted facade of the system and exposed the real, base foundations of power. He has said that the emperor is naked. And because the emperor is in fact naked something extremely dangerous has happened: by his action, the greengrocer has addressed the world. He has enabled everyone to peer behind the curtain. He has shown everyone that it *is* possible to live within the truth. Living within the lie can constitute the system only if it is universal. The principle must embrace and permeate everything. There are no terms whatsoever on which it can co-exist with living within the truth, and therefore everyone who steps out of line denies it in principle and threatens it in its entirety.

This is understandable: as long as appearance is not confronted with reality, it does not seem to be appearance.

As long as living a lie is not confronted with living the truth, the perspective needed to expose its mendacity is lacking. As soon as the alternative appears, however, it threatens the very existence of appearance and living a lie in terms of what they are, both their essence and their all-inclusiveness. And at the same time, it is utterly unimportant how large a space this alternative occupies: its power does not consist in its physical attributes but in the light it casts on those pillars of the system and on its unstable foundations. After all, the greengrocer was a threat to the system not because of any physical or actual power he had, but because his action went beyond it—self, because it illuminated its surroundings and, of course, because of the incalculable consequences of that illumination. In the post-totalitarian system, therefore, living within the truth has more than a mere existential dimension (returning humanity to its inherent nature), or a noetic dimension (revealing reality as it is), or a moral dimension (setting an example for others). It also has an unambiguous political dimension. If the main pillar of the system is living a lie, then it is not surprising that the fundamental threat to it is living the truth. This is why it must be suppressed more severely than anything else.

In the post-totalitarian system, truth in the widest sense of the word has a very special import, one unknown in other contexts. In this system, truth plays a far greater (and, above all, a far different) role as a factor of power, or as an outright political force. How does the power of truth operate? How does truth as a factor of power work? How can its power—as power—be realized?

VIII

Individuals can be alienated from themselves only because there is something in them to alienate. The terrain of this violation is their authentic existence. Living the truth is thus woven directly into the texture of living a lie. It is the repressed alternative, the authentic aim to which living a lie is an inauthentic response. Only against this background does living a lie make any sense: it exists *because* of that background, in its excusatory, chimerical rootedness in the human order, it is a response to nothing other than the human predisposition to truth. Under the orderly surface of the life of lies, therefore, there slumbers the hidden sphere of life in its real aims, of its hidden openness to truth.

The singular, explosive, incalculable political power of living within the truth resides in the fact that living openly within the truth has an ally, invisible to be sure, but omnipresent: this hidden sphere. It is from this sphere that life lived open in the truth grows; it is to this sphere that it speaks, and in it that it finds understanding. This is where the potential for communication exists. But this place is hidden and therefore, from the perspective of power, very dangerous. The complex ferment that takes place within it goes on in semidarkness, and by the time it finally surfaces into the light of day as an assortment of shocking surprises to the system, it is usually too late to cover them up in the usual fashion. Thus they create a situation in which the regime is confounded, invariably causing panic and driving it to react in inappropriate ways.

It seems that the primary breeding ground for what might, in the widest possible sense of the word, be understood as an opposition in the post-totalitarian system is living within the truth. The confrontation between these opposition forces and the powers that be, of course, will obviously take a form essentially different from that typical of an open society or a classical dictatorship. Initially, this confrontation does not take place on the level of real, institutionalized, quantifiable power which relies on the various instruments of power, but on a different level altogether: the level of human consciousness and conscience, the existential level. The effective range of this special power cannot be measured in terms of disciples, voters, or soldiers, because it lies spread out in the fifth column of social consciousness, in the hidden aims of life, in human beings' repressed longing for dignity and fundamental rights, for the realization of their real social and political interests. Its power, therefore, does not reside in the strength of definable political or social groups, but chiefly in the strength of a potential, which is hidden throughout the whole of society, including the official power structures of that society. Therefore this power does not rely on soldiers of its own, but on the soldiers of the enemy as it were—that is to say, on everyone who is living within the lie and who may be struck at any moment (in theory, at least) by the force of truth (or who, out of an instinctive desire to protect their position, may at least adapt to that force). It is a bacteriological weapon, so to speak, utilized when conditions are ripe by a single civilian to disarm an entire division. This power does not participate in any direct struggle for power; rather, it makes its influence felt in the obscure arena of being itself. The hidden movements it gives rise to there, however, can issue forth (when, where, under what circumstances, and to what extent are difficult to predict) in something visible: a real political act or event, a social movement, a sudden explosion of civil unrest, a sharp conflict inside an apparently monolithic power structure, or simply an irrepressible transformation in the social and intellectual climate. And since all genuine problems and matters of critical importance are hidden beneath a thick crust of lies, it is never quite clear when the proverbial last straw will fall, or what that straw will be. This, too, is why the regime prosecutes, almost as a reflex action preventively, even the most modest attempts to live within the truth.

Why was Solzhenitsyn driven out of his own country? Certainly not because he represented a unit of real power, that is, not because any of the regime's representatives felt he might unseat them and take their place in government. Solzhenitsyn's expulsion was something else: a desperate attempt to plug up the dreadful wellspring of truth, a truth which might cause incalculable transformations in social consciousness, which in turn might one day produce political debacles unpredictable in their consequences. And so the post-totalitarian system behaved in a characteristic way: it defended the integrity of the world of appearances in order to defend itself. For the crust presented by the life of lies is made of strange stuff. As long as it seals off hermetically the entire society, it appears to be made of stone. But the moment someone breaks through in one place, when one person cries out, "The emperor is naked!"—when a single person breaks the rules of the game, thus exposing it as a game—everything suddenly appears in another light and the whole crust seems then to be made of a tissue on the point of tearing and disintegrating uncontrollably.

When I speak of living within the truth, I naturally do not have in mind only products of conceptual thought, such as a protest or a letter written by a group of intellectuals. It can be any means by which a person or a group revolts against manipulation: anything from a letter by intellectuals to a workers' strike, from a rock concert to a student demonstration, from refusing to vote in the farcical elections to making an open speech at some official congress, or even a hunger strike, for instance. If the suppression of the aims of life is a complex process, and if it is based on the multifaceted manipulation of all expressions of life, then, by the same token, every free expression of life indirectly threatens the post-totalitarian system politically, including forms of expression to which, in other social systems, no one would attribute any potential political significance, not to mention explosive power.

The Prague Spring is usually understood as a clash between two groups on the level of real power: those who wanted to maintain the system as it was and those who wanted to reform it. It is frequently forgotten, however, that this encounter was merely the final act and the inevitable consequence of a long drama originally played out chiefly in the theatre of the spirit and the conscience of society.

And that somewhere at the beginning of this drama, there were individuals who were willing to live within the truth, even when things were at their worst. These people had no access to real power, nor did they aspire to it. The sphere in which they were living the truth was not necessarily even that of political thought. They could equally have been poets, painters, musicians, or simply ordinary citizens who were able to maintain their human dignity. Today it is naturally difficult to pinpoint when and through which hidden, winding channel a certain action or attitude influenced a given milieu, and to trace the virus of truth as it slowly spread through the tissue of the life of lies, gradually causing it to disintegrate. One thing, however, seems clear: the attempt at political reform was not the cause of society's reawakening, but rather the final outcome of that reawakening.

I think the present also can be better understood in the light of this experience. The confrontation between a thousand Chartists and the post-totalitarian system would appear to be politically hopeless. This is true, of course, if we look at it through the traditional lens of the open political system, in which, quite naturally, every political force is measured chiefly in terms of the positions it holds on the level of real power. Given that perspective, a mini-party like the Charter would certainly not stand a chance. If, however, this confrontation is seen against the background of what we know about power in the post-totalitarian system, it appears in a fundamentally different light. For the time being, it is impossible to say with any precision what impact the appearance of Charter 77, its existence, and its work has had in the hidden sphere, and how the Charter's attempt to rekindle civic self-awareness and confidence is regarded there. Whether, when, and how this investment will eventually produce dividends in the form of specific political changes is even less possible to predict. But that, of course, is all part of living within the truth. As an existential solution, it takes individuals back to the solid ground of their own identity; as politics, it throws them into a game of chance where the stakes are all or nothing. For this reason it is undertaken only by those for whom the former is worth risking the latter, or who have come to the conclusion that there is no other way to conduct real politics in Czechoslovakia today. Which, by the way, is the same thing: this conclusion can be reached only by someone who is unwilling to sacrifice his own human identity to politics, or rather, who does not believe in a politics that requires such a sacrifice.

The more thoroughly the post-totalitarian system frustrates any rival alternative on the level of real power, as well as any form of politics independent of the laws of its own automatism, the more definitively the center of gravity of any potential political threat shifts to the area of the existential and the pre-political: usually without any conscious effort, living within the truth becomes the one natural point of departure for all activities that work against the automatism of the system. And even if such activities ultimately grow beyond the area of living within the truth (which means they are transformed into various parallel structures, movements, institutions, they begin to be regarded as political activity, they bring real pressure to bear on the official structures and begin in fact to have a certain influence on the level of real power), they always carry with them the specific hallmark of their origins. Therefore it seems to me that not even the so-called dissident movements can be properly understood without constantly bearing in mind this special background from which they emerge.

IX

THE PROFOUND crisis of human identity brought on by living within a lie, a crisis which in turn makes such a life possible, certainly possesses a moral dimension as well; it appears, a deep moral crisis in society. A person who has been seduced by the consumer value system, whose identity is dissolved in an amalgam of the accouterments of mass civilization, and who has no roots in the order of being, no sense of responsibility for anything higher than his own personal survival, is a demoralized person. The system depends on this demoralization, deepens it, is in fact a projection of it into society.

Living within the truth, as humanity's revolt against an enforced position, is, on the contrary, an attempt to regain control over one's own sense of responsibility. In other words, it is clearly a moral act, not only because one must pay so dearly for it, but principally because it is not self-serving: the risk may bring rewards in the form of a general amelioration in the situation, or it may not. In this regard, as I stated previously, it is an all-or-nothing gamble, and it is difficult to imagine a reasonable person embarking on such a course merely because he reckons that sacrifice today will bring rewards tomorrow, be it only in the form of general gratitude. (By the way, the representatives of power invariably come to terms with those who live within the truth by persistently ascribing utilitarian motivations to them—a lust for power or fame or wealth—and thus they try, at least, to implicate them in their own world, the world of general demoralization.)

If living within the truth in the post-totalitarian system becomes the chief breeding ground for independent, alternative political ideas, then all considerations about the nature and future prospects of these ideas must necessarily reflect this moral dimension as a political phenomenon. (And if the revolutionary Marxist belief about morality as a product of the "superstructure" inhibits any of our friends from realizing the full significance of this dimension and, in one way or another, from including it in their view of the world, it is to their own detriment: an anxious fidelity to the postulates of that world view prevents them from properly understanding the mechanisms of their own political influence, thus paradoxically making them precisely what they, as Marxists, so often suspect others of being—victims of "false consciousness.") The very special political significance of morality in the post-totalitarian system is a phenomenon that is at the very least unusual in modern political history, a phenomenon that might well have—as I shall soon attempt to show—far-reaching consequences.

XI

In societies under the post-totalitarian system, all political life in the traditional sense has been eliminated. People have no opportunity to express themselves politically in public, let alone to organize politically. The gap that results is filled by ideological ritual. In such a situation, people's interest in political matters naturally dwindles and independent political thought., insofar as it exists at all, is seen by the majority as unrealistic, farfetched, a kind of self-indulgent game, hopelessly distant from their everyday concerns; something admirable, perhaps, but quite pointless, because it is on the one hand entirely utopian and on the other hand extraordinarily dangerous, in view of the unusual vigor with which any move in that direction is persecuted by the regime.

Yet even in such societies, individuals and groups of people exist who do not abandon politics as a vocation and who, in one way or another, strive to think independently, to express themselves and in some cases even to organize politically, because that is a part of their attempt to live within the truth.

The fact that these people exist and work is in itself immensely important and worthwhile. Even in the worst of times, they maintain the continuity of political thought. If some genuine political impulse emerges from this or that "pre-political" confrontation and is properly articulated early enough, thus increasing its chances of relative success, then this is frequently due to these isolated generals without an army who, because they have maintained the continuity of political thought in the face of enormous difficulties, can at the right moment enrich the new impulse with the fruits of their own political thinking. Once again, there is ample evidence for this process in Czechoslovakia. Almost all those who were political prisoners in the early 1970s, who had apparently been made to suffer in vain because of their quixotic efforts to work politically among an utterly apathetic and demoralized society, belong today—inevitably—among the most active Chartists. In Charter 77, the moral legacy of their earlier sacrifices is valued, and they have enriched this movement with their experience and that element of political thinking.

And yet it seems to me that the thought and activity of those friends who have never given up direct political work and who are always ready to assume direct political responsibility very often suffer from one chronic fault: an insufficient understanding of the historical uniqueness of the post-totalitarian system as a social and political reality. They have little understanding of the specific nature of power that is typical for this system and therefore they overestimate the importance of direct political work in the traditional sense. Moreover, they fail to appreciate the political significance of those "pre-political" events and processes that provide the living humus from which genuine political change usually springs. As political actors—or, rather, as people with political ambitions—they frequently try to pick up where natural political life left off. They maintain models of behavior that may have been appropriate in more normal political circumstances and thus, without really being aware of it, they bring an outmoded way of thinking, old habits, conceptions, categories, and notions to bear on circumstances that are quite new and radically different, without first giving adequate thought to the meaning and substance of such things in the new circumstances, to what politics as such means now, to what sort of thing can have political impact and potential, and in what way. Because such people have been excluded from the structures of power and are no longer able to influence those structures directly (and because they remain faithful to traditional notions of politics established in more or less democratic societies or in classical dictatorships) they frequently, in a sense, lose touch with reality. Why make compromises with reality, they say, when none of our proposals will ever be accepted anyway? Thus they find themselves in a world of genuinely utopian thinking.

As I have already tried to indicate, however, genuinely far-reaching political events do not emerge from the same sources and in the same way in the post-totalitarian system as they do in a democracy. And if a large portion of the public is indifferent to, even skeptical of, alternative political models and programs and the private establishment of opposition political parties, this is not merely because there is a general feeling of apathy toward public affairs and a loss of that sense of higher responsibility; in other words, it is not just a consequence of the general demoralization. There is also a bit of healthy social instinct at work in this attitude. It is as if people sensed intuitively that "nothing is what it seems any longer," as the saying goes, and that from now on, therefore, things must be done entirely differently as well.

If some of the most important political impulses in Soviet bloc countries in recent years have come initially—that is, before being felt on the level of actual power—from mathematicians, philosophers, physicians, writers, historians, ordinary workers, and so on, more frequently than from politicians, and if the driving force behind the various dissident movements comes from so many people in nonpolitical professions, this is not because these people are more clever than those who see themselves primarily as politicians. It is because those who are not politicians are also not so bound by traditional political thinking and political habits and therefore, paradoxically, they are more aware of genuine political reality and more sensitive to what can and should be done under the circumstances.

There is no way around it: no matter how beautiful an alternative political model can be, it can no longer speak to the "hidden sphere," inspire people and society, call for real political ferment. The real sphere of potential politics in the post-totalitarian system is elsewhere: in the continuing and cruel tension between the complex demands of that system and the aims of life, that is, the elementary need of human beings to live, to a certain extent at least, in harmony with themselves, that is, to live in a bearable way, not to be humiliated by their superiors and officials, not to be continually watched by the police, to be able to express themselves freely, to find an outlet for their creativity, to enjoy legal security, and so on. Anything that touches this field concretely, anything that relates to this fundamental, omnipresent, and living tension, will inevitably speak to people. Abstract projects for an ideal political or economic order do not interest them to anything like the same extent—and rightly so—not only because everyone knows how little chance they have of succeeding, but also because today people feel that the less political policies are derived from a concrete and human here and now and the more they fix their sights on an abstract "someday," the more easily they can degenerate into new forms of human enslavement. People who live in the post-totalitarian system know only too well that the question of whether one or several political parties are in power, and how these parties define and label themselves, is of far less importance than the question of whether or not it is possible to live like a human being.

To shed the burden of traditional political categories and habits and open oneself up fully to the world of human existence and then to draw political conclusions only after having analyzed it: this is not only politically more realistic but at the same time, from the point of view of an "ideal state of affairs," politically more promising as well. A genuine, profound, and lasting change for the better—as I shall attempt to show—can no longer result from the victory (were such a victory possible) of any particular traditional political conception, which can ultimately be only external, that is, a structural or systemic conception. More than ever before, such a change will have to derive from human existence, from the fundamental reconstitution of the position of people in the world, their relationships to themselves and to each other, and to the universe. If a better economic and political model is to be created, then perhaps more than ever before it must derive from profound existential and moral changes in society. This is not something that can be designed and introduced like a new car. If it is to be more than just a new variation of the old degeneration, it must above all be an expression of life in the process of transforming itself. A better system will not automatically ensure a better life. In fact, the opposite is true: only by creating a better life can a better system be developed.

Once more I repeat that I am not underestimating the importance of political thought and conceptual political work. On the contrary, I think that genuine political thought and genuinely political work is precisely what we continually fail to achieve. If I say "genuine," however, I have in mind the kind of thought and conceptual work that has freed itself of all the traditional political schemata that have been imported into our circumstances from a world that will never return (and whose return, even were it possible, would provide no permanent solution to the most important problems).

The Second and Fourth Internationals, like many other political powers and organizations, may naturally provide significant political support for various efforts of ours, but neither of them can solve our problems for us. They operate in a different world and are a product of different circumstances. Their theoretical concepts can be interesting and instructive to us, but one thing is certain: we cannot

Index

A

B

C

G

K

L

M

P

Q

R

S

T

Y

Z